Time and Poverty in Western Welfare States
United Germany in Perspective

Time and Poverty in Western Welfare States is the English-language adaptation of one of the most important contributions to the sociology and economics of the welfare state published in recent years. Professors Leisering and Leibfried explore the relationship between welfare policies and individual life trajectories by way of a time-based (dynamic) analysis of poverty, combining quantitative and qualitative methods, and suggest the need for a radical rethinking of conventional theoretical and policy approaches. The core of this study is the empirical analysis of the life courses of claimants of 'Social Assistance' in West and East Germany, although the conclusions are put into a wider context of socio-economic, socio-political and historical analysis and comparative observations are made with other countries, notably the USA.

Time and Poverty in Western Welfare States will be of interest to upper-level students, researchers and policy-makers in a wide range of social science disciplines, including sociology, economics, social policy, psychology and European studies.

Lutz Leisering is Professor of Social Policy at the department of sociology, Bielefeld University. With Stephan Leibfried he co-directed the Bremen Long-Term Study of Social Assistance at the Research Centre on Life Course Studies, which was established in 1988. He has widely written on poverty (most recently with Robert Walker, eds., *The Dynamics of Modern Society: Policy, Poverty and Welfare*, 1998), on the historical and cultural foundations of the welfare state and on intergenerational relations. He is also active as a policy consultant at German federal and local levels.

Stephan Leibfried is Professor of Social Policy and Social Administration at Bremen University. He co-directs two well-known research centers at Bremen University, the Centre for Social Policy Research and the Research Centre on Life Course Studies, co-directing the Bremen Long-Term Study of Social Assistance, which he initiated. He has also written on the effects of European integration on national welfare states (with Paul Pierson, eds., *European Social Policy*, 1995) and on welfare state limits to globalisation (with Elmar Rieger, in *Politics and Society*, 1998).

Time and Poverty in Western Welfare States

United Germany in Perspective

LUTZ LEISERING

and

STEPHAN LEIBFRIED

with contributions by Petra Buhr, Monika Ludwig and others
Translation by
John Veit-Wilson
with Lutz Leisering

CAMBRIDGE
UNIVERSITY PRESS

PUBLISHED BY THE PRESS SYNDICATE OF THE UNIVERSITY OF CAMBRIDGE
The Pitt Building, Trumpington Street, Cambridge CB2 1RP, United Kingdom

CAMBRIDGE UNIVERSITY PRESS
The Edinburgh Building, Cambridge CB2 2RU, UK   http://www.cup.cam.ac.uk
40 West 20th Street, New York, NY 10011–4211, USA   http://www.cup.org
10 Stamford Road, Oakleigh, Melbourne 3166, Australia

Originally published in German as *Zeit der Armut: Lebensläufe im Sozialstaat*
by Suhrkamp Verlag 1995
and © Suhrkamp Verlag
First published in English by Cambridge University Press 1999 as *Time and Poverty in Western Welfare States: United Germany in Perspective*

English translation © Cambridge University Press 1999

Printed in the United Kingdom at the University Press, Cambridge

A catalogue record for this book is available from the British Library

Typeset in Monotype Times New Roman 10/12.5pt, in QuarkXPress™ [SE]

ISBN 0 521 59013 2 hardback

Contents

List of figures	*page* vii
List of tables	viii
Foreword by Ralf Dahrendorf	ix
Plan of the book	xiii
Acknowledgements	xv

I The welfare state and the life course: passages through poverty 1

1 Poverty in the welfare state: the life-course approach 3

2 Life course as politics 23

II Poverty in the life course: the dynamics of social decline and ascent 55

3 Objective time: how long do people claim Social Assistance? 59

4 Subjective time: how Social Assistance is perceived and evaluated 89

5 Living time: poverty careers between exclusion and integration 109

6 Institutional time: does Social Assistance create dependency? 144

III Poverty and social change: debates and policies 169

7 Between denial and dramatisation: images of poverty in post-war Germany 175

8 Disruption and continuity in life courses: poverty in unified Germany 200

9 Increasingly dynamic? The impact of social change on Social Assistance dynamics 224

IV Poverty and society: towards a new welfare state? 237

10 Time and poverty: towards a new picture of poverty and social exclusion 239

11 Paths out of poverty: perspectives on active policy   257
12 Social inequality in transition   279
13 Individual lives and the welfare state: recasting the German   293
   welfare regime

References   323
Subject index   359
Index of names   374

Figures

2.1 The institutionalisation of the life course by the welfare state *page* 25
3.1 The overall duration of Social Assistance claims in the city of
    Bremen   63
3.2 Three measures of duration of claiming Social Assistance   65
3.3 Social Assistance claimants in the applicant cohort 1989 by
    ethnicity and residential status   68
3.4 The chief reasons for claiming Social Assistance   71
3.5 Reasons for terminating Social Assistance claims   73
3.6 Duration of Social Assistance by reasons for claiming   75
3.7 Duration of Social Assistance claims for particular
    configurations of reasons for claiming   77
3.8 Short and long Social Assistance claims by the unemployed   78
3.9 Chief reasons for short Social Assistance claims   80
3.10 Duration of Social Assistance among 'waiting' and 'not-
    waiting' claimants   81
3.11 Short and long Social Assistance claims among different
    social groups   84
4.1 Subjective time on Social Assistance – a typology   91
5.1 Life courses of Social Assistance claimants   115
5.2 Living with Social Assistance – a typology   125
9.1 Immigration in Germany, 1980–1996   229
10.1 The '70-20-10 society': income poverty in West Germany,
    1984–1994   253

Tables

2.1 Life-course policies under different welfare-state regimes   *page* 49

3.1 The distribution of short- and long-term Social Assistance
claims by different duration measures   66

5.1 A typology of poverty careers   133

5.2 Poverty careers between exclusion and inclusion   138

7.1 Changing images of poverty in the Federal Republic of
Germany, 1949–1999   194

8.1 Poverty in the GDR   211

8.2 Social Welfare recipients in the GDR   214

8.3 Poverty in Germany, 1990–1996   216

8.4 Claiming Social Assistance in Germany, 1990–1997   219

Foreword

Ralf Dahrendorf

Arguably the most exciting dimension of social analysis is time. Yet it has long been neglected by mainstream sociology. Much of the study of social stratification, even of mobility, is static, based on snapshots which ignore the place of such moments in people's life histories. The book by Lutz Leisering and Stephan Leibfried is part of a recent tendency designed to remedy this deficiency with respect to poverty. It presents what the authors themselves call, a dynamic approach.

The findings are, as a result, striking. They suggest rethinking conventional views of poverty as well as methods to remedy a condition which is the original target of the welfare state.

Such re-orientation is not easy, even in terms of language. One of the key concepts of this book is that of 'life course'. We all know what a *curriculum vitae* is, but translating it into the course which lives take, into social biographies is unfamiliar. It will not be that for long. Just as Habermas's 'life world' has caught on, 'life course' will. This is helped by the fact that the translator, John Veit-Wilson, along with one of the authors, Lutz Leisering, has done a truly outstanding job in rendering a complex study into an eminently readable text.

The core of this study is the empirical analysis of the life course of recipients of 'Social Assistance' in the German city of Bremen through a period of change – alleged or real – since the 1970s. A comparative study of more recent data from the East German city of Halle is added. Poverty, operationally defined as entitlement to Social Assistance, is however put in a wider context of socio-economic and socio-political analysis, including some highly perceptive comparative observations notably about the United States. Mary Jo Bane and David Ellwood, students of poverty in the US but also advisers of President Clinton, have clearly left their imprint on the authors.

If there is any one central finding it is that 'poverty has many faces'. More significantly, there are 'poverty careers'. We are, in other words, not just talking about one group of those permanently condemned to poverty. Many individuals experience poverty for a period. They cope in different ways. Some actually do not cope. Most however find a way out, or at any rate manage to use their condition strategically. Social cleavages and inequalities have certainly not disappeared, but they are overlaid by risks which affect many at certain points of their life course, notably as children, after divorce, in case of unemployment, or when ruptures of an unexpected kind occur.

The approach leads to some splendid counter-intuitive findings. It appears that the East German condition is not worse than that of West Germany, though it is different on account of the collective 'rupture' of unification. It also emerges that the seeming deterioration of poverty in a decade of growing unemployment and little growth is in fact largely due to the influx of immigrants and asylum-seekers entitled to Social Assistance. The poverty experience of indigenous Germans has not changed much.

But I must not betray all the exciting results of the study, nor anticipate the debate about its framework and its policy conclusions. It is perhaps a pity that the authors were not able to digest fully Mr Frank Field's Green Paper. It has been described as the 'menu' from which future policies will be chosen; in other words, it sets out the framework of a new welfare policy. This takes Mr Field – and who knows? perhaps the Government in which he was a minister – to conclusions which are not dissimilar from those suggested in this book. There is a notable similarity with regard to 'enabling' rather than remedial welfare policies.

The policy debate has shifted from inequality and poverty to social exclusion. Leisering and Leibfried can show that poverty and exclusion are not the same phenomenon. Many are poor but not excluded; some, notably among immigrants, may be excluded without being poor. In any age, 'social exclusion and rigid social cleavages coexist with a remarkable fluidity in life situations and lifestyles'. Exclusion too requires a fresh approach.

At one point in the last quarter of the book, Leisering and Leibfried stop the flow of their argument to ask the question: 'Are we sounding the "all clear" signal to the current state of society?' This, it appears, is not done in social-science circles. The authors therefore proceed to list the problems of the risk society. Yet one difference between 'static' and 'dynamic' – class and life-course – approaches to poverty and related problems is that the former tend to be gloomy whereas the latter sound a note of hope and opportunity. It is no accident that the authors quote Anthony Giddens and Ulrich Beck. Re-defining problems can lead to the discovery of unexpected solutions. 'Flexible risk management and regulatory control of non-state welfare provision' may not sound like the clarion call for a revolution of social policy. Readers of this splendid book will however find that it takes them a long way not just to better understanding but to better prospects for the future.

London, 1998

Una traccia mostraci di giustizia.
La tua legge qual è?

Show us one trace of justice.
What is your law?

(Giuseppe Ungaretti, La pietà)

For Leonie Carla Martine
and Philipp Laurids Martin

Plan of the book

The book is divided into four sections: the theoretical and comparative foundations of 'the welfare state and the life course'; our empirical findings concerning 'poverty in the life course'; an analysis of social change in post-war Germany with reference to institutions, social policies and poverty discourses; and a stock-taking conclusion with policy perspectives.

In the first, theoretical, section, we begin by delineating the life-course approach to the study of poverty (chapter 1). Chapter 2 then elaborates the more general relationship between the activities of the welfare state and individual life courses. 'The life course as politics' is introduced as a concept to describe policies that form and secure the life course against social risks through education, social security and old-age pensions. The chapter starts by locating poverty as a risk arising in the German welfare regime. This model is then compared with those of the USA and Sweden, as well as with the former East German model of 1949–1990.

The second, empirical, section (chapters 3–6) expounds the quantitative and qualitative analyses of poverty which form the core of the Bremen dynamic study. Chapter 3 gives basic information about the course and duration of Social Assistance claims which was not available before the 1990s. Chapter 4 addresses the question of how this objectively measurable time dimension is subjectively perceived and evaluated by the subjects of our research. Chapter 5 locates the subjects' 'careers' of claiming Social Assistance in their overall life courses, and asks what other kinds of Social Assistance 'careers' are to be found besides the notorious downward type. Throughout this study, the research subjects are understood as active agents involved in forming their own lives in many different ways. Chapter 6 concludes with an attempt to answer the important social-policy question of whether long-term state support, in this instance through Social Assistance, cultivates 'dependency' and terminates in an irreversibly descending spiral.

In the third section (chapters 7–9) we review the historical and societal context of poverty in Germany. It is important to trace the 'images of poverty' that have shaped the German socio-political discourse from the post-war years to the present day (chapter 7), as these images continue to influence the way in which society deals with the problem of poverty. Chapter 8 summarises the state of this problem in reunified Germany, examining both life-course patterns and the risks of poverty in East and West Germany before and after reunification in 1990. In particular, we ask how the welfare state's institutions have adapted to the transformation in the East. Chapter 9 reverts to the quantitative analysis of individual Social Assistance careers in order to investigate whether the temporal patterns of such careers (individual time) have changed over historical time. To do this we compare the careers analysed in part 2 with careers of West German claimants six years earlier. Using data from our longitudinal survey in the city of Halle, we also look at Social Assistance careers in the East German transformation.

In the fourth and final section (chapters 10–13) we draw conclusions and place the new findings in the wider context of current changes and challenges in society. First, the empirical analyses of poverty conditions and the study of social-policy discourses and institutions are brought together to outline perspectives on a new image of poverty (chapter 10) as well as new social policies to combat poverty (chapter 11). We hope that these proposals will point beyond worn-out political positions. In chapter 12 we attempt to use the findings to shed new light on the current social stratification and structures of inequality. In chapter 13 we look into the future of the welfare state's life-course regime: to outline the challenges policy-makers and citizens face at a time when life courses and social structures are in the midst of radical change.

Acknowledgements

Above all we are indebted to David Ellwood, Harvard, for his path-breaking analysis of welfare dynamics and welfare reform in the USA. After meeting him in the late 1980s, we brought his ideas to Germany. This volume has emerged from the research project 'Social Assistance Careers' headed by the authors at the Special Research Programme 186 (*Sonderforschungsbereich 186*) of the German Research Council (*Deutsche Forschungsgemeinschaft*) and the Centre for Social Policy Research (*CeS*) at the University of Bremen in Northern Germany. Since the project was launched in 1988, its research team has included Petra Buhr, Monika Ludwig, Andreas Weber, Michael Zwick and Wolfgang Voges, who formerly co-directed the project. The partner project at the University of Halle-Wittenberg in East Germany is directed by Thomas Olk, assisted by the research associates Eva Mädje, Johanna Mierendorff and Doris Rentzsch. We thank all of them for their commitment and devotion to the task of elaborating a new perspective for poverty research.

We thank Johann Behrens, Wolfgang Glatzer and Werner Hübinger, Frankfurt, and Tom Priester, Bern, for conceptual and empirical insights during the project's preparatory phase in 1987. We also thank Greg Duncan, Evanston, IL, and Michael Wiseman, Washington, D.C., for stimulating communication at different points in the history of the project. We are indebted to Götz Rohwer for creating the programme SHD for the analysis of time data in Social Assistance and to Wolfgang Voges for assisting in the quantitative analysis. Wolfgang Ludwig-Mayerhofer's incisive quantitative analysis was a boon to the project. Peter Krause readily supplied recent calculations on the basis of the German Socio-Economic Household Panel. Uwe Schwarze analysed the interviews with staff members of the Social Assistance administration. Norman Ginsburg, Werner Hübinger, Peter Klein, Jon Eivind Kolberg, Klaus Kortmann, Weyma Lübbe, Elmar Rieger and Peter Taylor-Gooby made important comments on the manuscript. We have also much profited from discussions

xvi   **Acknowledgements**

with Robert Walker. Gitta Klein and Gisela Hegemann-Mahltig made useful suggestions. We also thank our many critics in the political and scholarly debate who challenged us to clarify and sharpen our arguments and put them into context. Of course, responsibility for all remaining short-comings rests with the authors.

We also thank our secretarial staff, above all Gitta Klein, Karin Müller, Dörte Simon and Lisa Zimmermann-Bäuml, and our student assistants, especially Susanne Borchers-Tempel, Olaf Jürgens and Silvia Rosenberger, for their unceasing and reliable support. Paul B. Baltes, Florian Tennstedt, Karen Schniedewind and the librarians of the Institute for Advanced Study, Berlin, helped us in finding appropriate illustrations.

As regards funding and administrative support, we owe thanks to the German Research Council (*Deutsche Forschungsgemeinschaft*), to the University of Bremen and its CeS (making the translation possible) and to officials of various municipal authorities in Bremen and Halle, especially to Hans-Christoph Hoppensack, Gertrud Janzer-Bertzbach, Wolf Klatt, Gerd Wenzel, Jochen Eckertz, Hans-Günther Schneller, Dagmar Szabados and the staff of the Bremen and the Halle Social Assistance Administrations.

The original idea of this book was to translate and update our German book *Zeit der Armut* (Suhrkamp Publishers, Frankfurt/Main 1995). In the process we carried out extensive revisions, rewrote almost all key sections and added new chapters while dropping others so that a whole new book has emerged.

We thank John Veit-Wilson, Newcastle, for translating the book, in cooperation with the first author, with a degree of commitment that went beyond what we could normally have expected. Through his incisive comments he also forced us to rethink and rephrase various critical arguments. Benjamin Veghte's extensive comments on difficulties in the translation were also very valuable. And we are grateful to Cambridge University Press for nursing this publication over several years.

Last but not least we are indebted to our research subjects, the claimants of Social Assistance, who were prepared to give their time for long interviews about their personal life histories. We have learnt a lot from them.

Lutz Leisering and Stephan Leibfried

Part I
The welfare state and the life course: passages through poverty

Plate 1 'The Ages of Man', Abraham Bach (†1680). Augsburg c. 1680. Original title of the woodcut is '*Das Zehen Jährige Alter*'. (*Städtische Kunstsammlungen in Augsburg*)

1 Poverty in the welfare state: the life-course approach

In the last two decades of the twentieth century, poverty has again been troubling Western societies. Unemployment, declining wages, lone parenthood, ethnic cleavages, immigration pressures as well as growing inequality and insecurity are seen as corroding the idea of citizenship, not only for the lower social strata. The social contract is at stake. Domestic fiscal constraints, pervasive ideological shifts to deregulation, 'global' economic challenges as well as problems of European integration have re-ignited debates on the direction in which European societies are drifting. These reflections are accompanied by worries about the waning capacity of nation-states to channel such developments constructively.

In today's world capitalism seems to be the only surviving model of society. But capitalist nations differ radically with respect to the socio-economic and political institutions that shape the lives of their citizens (Kitschelt et al. 1999). There is more than one world of capitalism. This applies even to the sphere of the market: David Soskice (e.g., 1990) has contrasted Germany and the UK as 'coordinated' and 'non-coordinated economies' – or as 'trust' and 'distrust' societies (Allmendinger and Hinz 1998). And this diversity is particularly apparent when we look at the institutionalisation of state welfare. Instead of 'ending history' we begin to refocus on different models in the West itself, or in the OECD, and thus also on differences in social insecurity and poverty (Andreß 1998, McFate et al. 1995).

This study addresses poverty in one major European welfare state, unified Germany, and also places what many see as the 'Bismarckian model' into a comparative perspective (see chapters 2, 6 and 11).[1] Germany is nowadays considered by many to be the laggard in the move towards more competitiveness in a globalising economy, not least because of its systems of social protection which are seen as oversized and overregulated

---

[1] For analyses of the German welfare state in a comparative and historical perspective see Schmidt (1998), Kaufmann (1997), Lampert (1998), van Kersbergen (1995), Ritter (1991), Alber (1986a, b; 1989; 1998) and Neumann and Schaper (1998).

(see, e.g., OECD 1997). A trade-off between equality and employment seems to unfold, as Gøsta Esping-Andersen (1996, p. 25) put it when looking at the development of the three 'worlds of welfare capitalism' he had identified. In his terminology Germany is a 'conservative' welfare-state regime, in contrast to the 'liberal' regimes found in the UK and the USA, and the 'social-democratic' regimes of the Scandinavian countries, especially in Sweden (Esping-Andersen 1990).[2] Rather than convergence towards the liberal model, Esping-Andersen traces different national responses,[3] different ways of dealing with unemployment and inequality, and the trade-off between the two. In the 1990s, the Swedish welfare state has been reconstructed, not simply 'deregulated', and the Blair government has been heading for a new start in Britain, while Germany has been slow to move. Esping-Andersen emphasises the problems of inequality, poverty and social dislocation that arise in employment-oriented economies like the USA and Britain. High unemployment was accepted for many years in Germany while poverty is generally less tolerated than in the employment-oriented countries (see Amartya Sen 1997, p. 160). Could it be that Germany is now heading towards the worst of both worlds, that is high unemployment *and* rising poverty?

With poverty also spreading to societies hitherto less affected by it, the national systems of social assistance have become important elements in the economic performance and political control of advanced societies (see the first comprehensive comparative study of social assistance in OECD countries by Tony Eardley *et al.* 1996, and the comparative study by John Ditch *et al.* 1996). Our empirical and theoretical study focuses on poverty as politically addressed by Social Assistance (*Sozialhilfe*). The latter is a basic component of the German welfare state, the social safety net of last resort for any person in need. A close examination of its functioning reveals much about the fabric of German society and of the welfare state at large. While the German welfare state may appear like a dinosaur to some observers, this strong tradition of state welfare can still offer ample stimulation for the international debate on restructuring welfare states. Bill Clinton's original health-insurance plan, for example, was influenced by the German model. The pillars of the German welfare state are the systems of Social Insurance with their complex legal and administrative fabric, above all Old-Age Pensions and Health Insurance, supplemented by a social assistance scheme that offers comprehensive entitlements to need-oriented benefits.

---

[2] For an empirical and theoretical reappraisal of the concept of 'welfare-state regimes' besides Esping-Andersen's own volume (1996) see Leibfried (1993) and the volume by Lessenich and Ostner (1998).

[3] For a different critique of 'globalisation' as a new version of convergence theory see Paul Pierson (1996).

Social Assistance caters for fewer people than the British equivalent because of the strong insurance schemes that form the higher tiers of social security. How has this welfare state fared in the 1990s in the face of growing unemployment and, unique to Germany, constrained by the incorporation of the economically run-down Eastern part and the influx of more immigrants than in any other European country? Has it coped with the attendant problems of poverty? Does the two-tier system – Social Insurance combined with Social Assistance – still work? Why do Germans care about things other than their partners in the Western world, e.g., why do 'welfare mothers' not figure in the social policy debate, in contrast to the US-American and British debates?

Poverty is a good social indicator of the state of the social contract in any country. The malaise it reveals is connected with more general social fault lines. Here we find the whole panoply of social risks concentrated, be they economic, health-related or psychological in nature. The German sociologist Georg Simmel noted in 1908:

Especially in modern society, the class of the poor is the common destination of a great variety of fates. People from the whole range of social backgrounds end up here. No change, development, crisis or decline in social life takes place without leaving its residue in the class of the poor, as if in a settling tank.[4] (Translated from Simmel 1908, p. 373)

In writing about poverty, Simmel referred to recipients of poor relief as the truly poor because public support, not deprivation as such, establishes poverty as a social phenomenon of exclusion. For present-day analysis, data on Social Assistance, the primary public programme in the German struggle against poverty, are good social indicators of the reliability and effectiveness of the German welfare state as a whole. Comprehensive German Social Assistance acts as a 'welfare state in reserve' (Leibfried and Tennstedt 1985b, p. 24). The demand for Social Assistance reflects the total or partial failure of labour markets and employment policies, as well as of the prior social security systems, to make adequate provision, and it reveals the shortcomings of social support for families. In federal welfare states, especially in Germany, national politicians of every persuasion are eager to pass on the increasing social strains to local government institutions, even to the extent of increasing the local burden by restricting the principal national social security budgets. Social Assistance is thus actively used as a 'safety valve'. Such 'downzoning' and 'destandardisation' may, in the short

---

[4] 'Die Klasse der Armen, insbesondere innerhalb der modernen Gesellschaft, ist der gemeinsame Endpunkt von Schicksalen der verschiedensten Art, von dem ganzen Umfang der gesellschaftlichen Unterschiedenheiten her münden Personen in ihr, keine Wandlung, Entwicklung, Zuspitzung oder Senkung des gesellschaftlichen Lebens geht vorüber, ohne ein Residuum in der Schicht der Armen wie in einem Sammelbecken abzulagern.'

run, contribute to making poverty less visible in national politics. But in contrast to the USA, Germany has a federal polity which presupposes substantial homogeneity, and centripetalism where differences persist (or where they suddenly emerge as in reunification). In this political climate, such buck-passing is stopped sooner rather than later.

When Esping-Andersen refers to 'welfare regimes' rather than 'welfare states', he implies that different institutional structures of state welfare entail different 'employment regimes' as well as 'stratification regimes' (see Allmendinger and Hinz 1998). Considering how massively European welfare states impact on individual lives, welfare states can also be said to contribute to distinct 'life-course regimes': they produce and sustain specific temporal structures of life by institutional definitions of events, phases, episodes and transitions that are linked to individual expectations and 'life plans'. Different welfare regimes give rise to different life-course regimes.

The *life-course* perspective on poverty adopted in this study builds on the 'dynamic' approach to poverty and 'welfare' (social assistance) developed in the USA in the 1970s and 1980s (see Bane and Ellwood 1994, Duncan *et al.* 1995, Leisering and Walker 1998a). The dynamic approach is, first of all, a method of empirical enquiry. Longitudinal data tell us more – and different things – about people's lives than cross-sectional data ever can: we want movies, not stills. But the life-course approach is more than a method. It also represents and encompasses the real dynamics of social life. Reference to the 'life course', then, means analysing poverty in a dynamic perspective framed by both institutional arrangements and individual biographical horizons. These two levels interact to produce the temporal structure of the entire life span.

The life-course approach, therefore, goes beyond the older dynamic approach employed in the US research. It focuses on how the institutions of the welfare state – which are part and parcel of a more general German moral economy of standardising life trajectories – shape individual lives. Our research strategy combines quantitative investigations of poverty careers with qualitative biographical analyses of Social Assistance claimants. As the American tradition of state welfare is much less developed than in Europe, involving little formal life-course 'regimentation', American writers on poverty dynamics have not been able to embed their analyses in an overall view of the life course and its regulation by the welfare state.

The notion of a dynamism of individual lives, of a 'life course', is essential to modern society and to the concept of the modern individual (Giddens 1991, Leisering and Walker 1998b). Social mobility is a central tenet of a free society, rooted in the freedom of the market. However, the notion of the individual and his or her life course is also linked to the concept of the modern state. John W. Meyer (1986) has described the 'self' as a cultural project of modernity, the idea of personal development over the life span, furthered by education and human development agencies, psychologists and social professionals. In Meyer's view, this notion is a key tenet of American civilisation. Morris Janowitz (1976, pp. 23ff.) argues similarly: according to him, the welfare state – and not merely market individualism – implements the idea of human self-perfection expounded in the Enlightenment. Martin Kohli (1986a) has shown that changes in the medical sciences, culture and social institutions have created 'the life course' as a new horizon for the orientation of individual action. The expectation – and challenge – of a secure life span opens up new horizons for individuals but also imposes new strains on them.

A major force in establishing such a 'life course' is the welfare state. Security, not only – in many countries not even primarily – equality, is the key goal of social policy. Since its foundation, the German welfare state has set the pace of individual lives: a comprehensive system of public *education* supports entries into work society, lays down career tracks and provides opportunities; a developed *old-age pension* system offers a secure life span for those individuals who lead a 'normal' adult life in regular employment or marriage, thus indicating a model of normality; and finally, for those 'less forseeable' risks not attended to otherwise, special institutions of *risk management* have been established like health and unemployment insurance, social assistance and social work – to secure the continuity of biographies.

At the turn of the millenium a major question in continental Europe and elsewhere emerges: Is the welfare state still capable of securing individual life courses? Is this one of the welfare state's tasks? If so, how? Which institutional reforms are required in the current situation?

National welfare traditions differ with regard to life-course policy: they pursue different normative models of the life course, they intervene to different degrees in people's lives, and they emphasise different fields of life-course policy. The USA, for example, puts more emphasis on education at the beginning than on management of acute risks later on. In 1996, a pivotal year, major changes in social assistance and welfare systems were enacted. In Britain Job Seekers Allowance replaced Unemployment Benefit and Income Support for the unemployed. Later changes in Income Support under the Blair government affected among others lone mothers. Whereas the Clinton Act seems to mark a historic break, truly putting an end to 'welfare as we know it' by introducing time limits and suspending welfare as a right, the German reforms merely consolidated the country's far more comprehensive and costly Social Assistance regime, with only slight cuts and even some enhancements.

Discourses on poverty

When people talk about poverty, they generally have in mind some particular group such as the homeless, 'welfare mothers', the unemployed or pensioners, or they think of deprived areas or even a whole 'underclass' in
society. What poverty is taken to mean, then, is a condition in which individuals and groups find themselves, a situation in life which is more or less
consciously assumed to be relatively long lasting. This view is based on a
static way of looking at things. Ideas such as that poverty conditions
change over time, and that there is something like a poverty 'career', are
commonly heard, but they refer to the process of descent into poverty as
well as to reinforcements of the conditions of poverty: in other words, to
relatively long-lasting experiences of poverty situations and to fixed groups
of poor. 'Dynamic' assumptions do play a role here, but only in the negative sense of something unavoidable. The guiding assumption, both in the
public sphere and in academic circles, is that most poor people are sunk in
a vicious circle of hopeless poverty for very long periods.

In the Western European debates on the 'new poverty' (Room 1990) and
'social exclusion' (Kronauer 1998, Leviathan 1997, Vranken, Geldof and
van Menxel 1997, Leisering 1997c, Jordan 1996, Paugam 1998, Room
1995) during the last two decades, these well-worn images of poverty have
been given sharper profiles. Political circles and also some scholars in
Germany, France, Britain and other countries see the growth in long-term
unemployment, social polarisation and urban cleavages as the key problems for social policy in our time.[5] In Germany the terms 'new poverty' and
'the two-thirds society' were coined in 1984 (Glotz 1984). In the same year,
Ralf Dahrendorf (1984, chapter 7) opened the debate on a new 'underclass', followed up in later works (1988[1992]). The concept of 'social exclusion' became increasingly important in France (Paugam 1996) and in the
poverty action research programmes initiated by the European
Community, now the European Union (Huster 1997, Alcock 1997, pp.
56–61). The European Commission also funded research on exclusion
within its 'Targeted Socio-Economic Research' programme (TSER,
1994–1998). By the mid-1990s 'exclusion' had virtually superseded
'poverty' as the key term. It has come to denote problems of deprivation
and inequality among all kinds of groups – the unemployed, ethnic minor-
ities, the elderly, the homeless and even women. The fall of communism in
Eastern Europe heightened public concern about these issues, both in terms

---

[5] Among German scholars see, e.g., Dangschat (1995) and Becker and Hauser (1997, p. 11).
For a world-wide view of the increasing concentration of affluence and poverty see
Massey's (1996) presidential address at the annual meeting of the Population Association
of America.

of these countries' domestic problems and resulting migration to Western Europe.

The welfare state appears as both object and agent in these debates. On the one hand, the new poverty puts pressure on the established social security systems. In Germany, for example, Unemployment Insurance and Social Assistance are said to have degenerated into pension-like provisions for long-term cases instead of fulfilling their original aim of bridging situations of crisis. This diagnosis is based on the assumption of persistent poverty. On the other hand, welfare-state institutions are criticised for creating, or at least reinforcing, social problems by undermining people's ability and inclination to help themselves. The welfare state is seen as a cause of poverty rather than a response to it. This view is again closely linked to assumptions about long-term processes, in this instance the notion that people become 'dependent' on state aid or are 'trapped' in poverty. Both cases lead to demands for a thorough-going reform of state welfare.

This book aims to endow this debate with an empirical foundation, and to delineate new theoretical perspectives on the basis of original sociological research findings. It is the first comprehensive presentation of the 'dynamic' or 'life-course' approach to poverty in Europe, using the German case.[6] This approach has revealed that poverty conditions are far more transient than has hitherto been believed; poverty is often no more than an episode in the course of life and is actively overcome by most of those afflicted by it. Furthermore, the experience of poverty as a temporary situation and a latent risk extends well into the middle classes, and it is not confined (if in fact it ever was) to traditional marginal groups or to an excluded bottom third of society. The thesis of this book is, in short, that *poverty is time-related ('temporalisation') and that it transcends social boundaries ('transcendence')*. In this sense, it is *'individualised'*.[7]

Poverty has many faces. The typical images of poverty convey only a limited picture of the many forms in which poverty appears. The key to understanding the new approach lies in moving from the static to a dynamic perspective. Poverty is not just a characteristic of groups of individuals, but is in effect an event or phase in the individual life course. Experiences of poverty have a beginning, a specified duration, a certain course, and often a conclusion. Escape from poverty is feasible. Being poor at some point in time does not necessarily entail becoming a permanent member of a poor group.

---

[6] A dynamic account of poverty with a much narrower empirical and theoretical scope was presented for Britain by Robert Walker (1994).

[7] For a general explication of the concept of individualisation see below and chapter 2. For its application to poverty see Berger (1994) and Andreß and Schulte (1998) who put the thesis of an individualisation of poverty to an empirical test.

To say that poverty lasts shorter than previously thought, and that poor people are more capable than suggested by the passive stereotype of the excluded needy, almost sounds like an 'all clear' signal. It is true that this study calls into question stereotyped negative assumptions about inevitable spirals of decline. However, the fact that vulnerable life courses are far more complex than suggested by undifferentiated images of the problems of 'the unemployed', 'the old' or 'single mothers on welfare'; the fact that poverty as a temporary condition affects a great many more people than the usual statistics reveal; the fact that even the middle classes experience poverty – all this shows that poverty – far from waning – has become more complex, more tangled and more menacing. The new approaches have not made poverty policy easier and less pressing but, on the contrary, have made it more difficult and urgent.

The dynamic approach to poverty cannot be classified under outworn labels, whether 'right' or 'left', 'critical' or 'ameliorative'. Rather, what comes into view are the outlines of a new, complex landscape of poverty, challenging the established political classes and social movements of both right and left to a new relationship to this growing structural problem facing society today.

In most countries the debates about poverty tend to reveal strongly held beliefs and deep-seated convictions, and it is hard to find non-partisan views. One common way of dealing with the problem of poverty has been to deny its existence altogether, or at least to refuse to accept poverty as a structural problem requiring social reform, and to instead blame poverty on the poor themselves. Poverty in the German Federal Republic has long been concealed or underestimated, or declared to have already been abolished. This was facilitated by the successful reconstruction in the 1950s, the so-called 'economic miracle', and by the fact that in Germany there were fewer obvious divisions within the labour market and among ethnic groups than in other countries.[8] The common conclusion that poverty was concealed or denied is only one side of the coin. There has always been an opposing tendency in political circles, particularly since the 1970s, which emphatically rebuked the tendency toward complacency in welfare society. The political history of poverty in the Federal Republic is inadequately described as a history of denial, since it was at the same time a history of dramatisation – of the attempts by critical social scientists, journalists and representatives of the social welfare professions to present the public with a convincing picture of the unmet needs of those who had been left behind in the wake of economic progress.

---

[8] For the reasons why poverty remained underestimated in Germany see Leibfried and Voges (1992b, pp. 12–15).

These two 'cultures' of social policy stood in direct opposition to each other over a broad front and continue to ignore each other to the present day. While some see poverty as a self-evident burning problem which has increased in severity in recent years, others view it as a 'non-subject', a topic which does not appear on the list of currently salient political issues, or if it does, only because it costs the state money. Today, unemployment is recognised as an issue of the highest priority by all political groups – but this recognition still does not apply to poverty even though the 'new poverty' was proclaimed years ago. The boundary between the two cultures over this topic does not invariably fall on the line that divides 'left' and 'right'. In addition, there is an intervening position of 'normal' unperturbed awareness of poverty, but it remains rare.

Those who deny the problematic status of poverty justify themselves by history. Over a century ago poverty in Germany was declared to be a marginal problem, in that 'the social question' was defined as a question of labour and not of poverty. Differently than in the USA or Britain, 'the poor' were defined as a residual category in social policy. The general deprivation of the early years after the Second World War formed the background for the take-off of 'the people's path from poverty to new wealth', as Ludwig Erhard, the long-time Minister of Economic Affairs and 'father of the economic miracle', expressed it. From this perspective, in 'normal' times the developed industrial societies are societies without 'real' poverty. Poverty is perceived as simply relative; as temporary, as it is currently held to be in the New Federal Territories of Eastern Germany; as a necessary counterpart to excessive levels of consumption under the pressure of global competition (as seen from Germany); or, when it refers back to older moralistic notions, as the culpable consequence of workshyness and irresponsibility. In rebuttal, dramatisers and critics insist that relative poverty in developed societies is no less offensive to human dignity than is absolute poverty in developing societies. They point to the increase in poverty since the 1980s and the growth in old and new forms of impoverishment such as unemployment, homelessness and overindebtedness.

A negative dramatisation also exists, connected with the strategy of denial and used by market liberals and neo-conservative politicians, especially in times of economic crisis. This focuses less on the social needs of the poor than on the assumed threat to German economic competitiveness, with slogans such as workshyness, dependency culture and excessive social security benefits.

The time would therefore seem ripe to shatter the outdated and unquestioned assumptions of both sides, and to halt the blind incomprehension of society's dealings with poverty. The fact is that both sides exclude the poor: the deniers define poverty as a marginal problem of 'the asocial', while the dramatisers relegate it to being a problem of the victims of social conditions condemned to passive suffering. Both perspectives have outlived their time. Poverty today is predominantly a problem of and for 'normal' people, neither asocial nor hopelessly marginalised, and for whom there are rational political solutions. From the outset, this rationality has been furthered by the dynamic approach to poverty. Two leading representatives of dynamic research in the USA, Mary Jo Bane and David Ellwood (Bane and Ellwood 1994), served as Assistant Secretaries in the US Department of Health and Human Services in order to conceive a reform of the American welfare system for the Clinton administration (1993–1995; see the vivid account by DeParle 1996), before welfare 'reform' turned into the radical bill signed by Clinton in August 1996.

Poverty has – once again – become a structural problem in our societies. In Germany it is no longer a neglected or cut-off peripheral zone, but a central field of social policy, precisely at this time when the 'old' West German, the new East German and the ethnically coloured poverties come together (Hauser 1997a). A book about poverty, therefore, cannot aim only to meet the expectations of those who already know that poverty is a pressing social problem. Work of this kind must also be able to address those who until now have taken a rather reserved stance towards the dramatised presentation of real need in today's society. A new, differentiated and less ideological image of poverty is required which suggests avenues to a new approach to poverty and to an effective reform of society.

The sociological treatment of poverty reflects both of these two cultures as well as the neutral middle ground. The sociological approach to poverty in Germany can be divided into three tendencies. First is the traditional research into *social inequalities*, which is concerned with classes and strata and which stems directly from the origins of sociology in the eighteenth and nineteenth centuries. Second is the research into *marginalised groups* which flourished in the 1970s, building on older American traditions, and which has led to a great many studies of the homeless and 'street people', juvenile delinquents and the like. The third tendency is a broad and somewhat undefined tradition which is more *empirically descriptive* and oriented towards social policy rather than theory, based on statistics of unemployment, Social Assistance claims and income data, and influenced by the two other tendencies according to context. The two former traditions closely resemble, respectively, the denying and the dramatising approaches to poverty.

One might have expected the inequality approach to make a contribution to the subject of poverty, but in Germany research into inequality and into poverty have largely ignored each other. Studies of inequality have chiefly focused on the earning 'core population' and have thus ignored the non-earning population (children and young people, housewives and the old) or relegated them to dependent positions (Kreckel 1992, p. 43, Berger and Hradil 1990b, p. 5). But these are precisely the groups which are most at risk of impoverishment. In addition, a further limitation arises:

A silent premise of current inequality research is the exclusion of certain categories of socially disadvantaged people, the so-called 'marginal groups', from its domain. Traditional inequality research is concerned only with 'normal' inequalities and not with the 'deviant' ones. (Translated from Kreckel 1992, p. 43)

The lowest zone in the structure of inequality becomes an undefined residual category, something which is left over when the mass of the population has been allocated to the conventional classes or strata.[9] This academic approach to inequality reflects the dominant public denial of poverty, but it also reflects the reality of life in West German society after the war, when gainful employment and family membership ensured participation in increasing affluence for most people.

The research into marginalised groups was more responsive when confronted with the intricate realities of poverty, but precisely for this reason it was more inclined to concentrate on the hopeless cases and to play down the situation of those poor whose suffering was not as obvious or extreme. Here we find the prevailing origins of the dramatising approach to poverty.

The descriptive social-policy tradition, by contrast, was more open, but its theoretical horizons and its links to recognised fields of sociology were limited. German poverty research was for a long time peripheral to the development of sociology (Hauser and Neumann 1992, Leibfried and Voges 1992b) – by comparison with the Anglo-Saxon world in which poverty is always perceived as part of the sociological analysis of inequality. In the British tradition in particular, from the early nineteenth century onward poverty constituted a central theme of the conflicts between economics, philosophy, political science and the field of social administration (Pinker 1992).

The shortcomings of German research were especially notable in the 1980s, in that it omitted to pay appropriate attention to the dynamic aspects of poverty. It is true that analysis of marginal groups took account of time, but only in the context of predetermined downwardly mobile careers. If life courses have become more unstable and risky for members of the middle classes, the social sciences must react to these developments and deal with the dynamics of poverty in a more realistic manner. That is what the dynamic approach aims to do. It contributes to the 'sociologising' of German poverty research and at the same time takes up relevant ideas from

---

[9] See for example Karl Martin Bolte's summary of West German post-war sociology's stratification models (1990).

each of the three modes of research mentioned above and pursues them further.

The dynamic approach

The new approach was developed in the USA.[10] Since the end of the 1980s it has been taken up in Germany and Britain and in some other countries, to analyse the dynamics of income poverty and of social assistance receipt, also in the context of municipal social reporting.[11] The approach was introduced into Germany in the long-term study of Social Assistance claimants in Bremen (Leibfried 1987, Leibfried, Leisering *et al.* 1995), which is the subject of this book. This research project has carried out longitudinal studies since 1989, which have been facilitated by the availability of longitudinal data and influenced by theoretical and methodological developments in sociology, especially life-course research (Kohli 1986a, Mayer 1986, Heinz 1991a). Comparative studies of social assistance dynamics in Western societies are also emerging (Duncan and Voges 1994, Duncan *et al.* 1995, Gustafsson and Voges 1998, Leisering and Walker 1998d, Buhr 1998).[12]

Since 1990, the new branch of poverty research has also been furthered by the dynamic methods of socio-structural analysis which have been developed using the Socio-Economic Panel (SOEP, internationally available as GSOEP), a panel of several thousand private households throughout Germany (Rendtel and Wagner 1991, DFG 1994). Following the

[10] See especially Rydell *et al.* (1974), Duncan (1984) and Bane and Ellwood (1986); see also Rainwater, Rein and Schwartz (1986). An overview of US publications is provided by Buhr (1991).

[11] The German and British pioneers include Leibfried (1987), Buhr *et al.* (1989), Leisering and Zwick (1990), Headey, Habich and Krause (1990), Bonß and Plum (1990), Berger (1990), Ashworth *et al.* (1992), Ashworth and Walker (1992), Walker (1994) and Leisering, Leibfried *et al.* (1995). For Sweden see Salonen (1993), for Norway Nervik (1997) and Hvinden (1994), for the Nordic countries in general Fridberg (1993); for Hungary see Andorka and Spéder (1996), for Austria Stelzer-Orthofer (1997) and for Switzerland Salzgeber and Suter (1997). Further British studies include Jarvis and Jenkins (1997, 1998), Walker (1998), Walker and Shaw (1998), Noble *et al.* (1998), Shaw *et al.* (1996) and ongoing research by the Centre for Analysis of Social Exclusion (CASE), London School of Economics, directed by John Hills. For further German publications see p. 57. The volume by Leisering and Walker (1998a) gives a comprehensive account of the new approach, with contributions on theory, methods and policy conclusions and longitudinal case studies by authors from various countries.

[12] Two research projects are currently working on a cross-national study of social assistance dynamics: our own Bremen project and Chiara Saraceno's research network, The Evaluation of Social Policies Against Social Exclusion at the Local Urban Level *(ESOP0)*. Adequate administrative data are still rare in Europe, with the German data used in this book ranking among the best in Europe. Household panel data on social assistance dynamics (see e.g. the analyses by Ashworth *et al.* 1995 for Britain and by Voges and Rohwer 1992 for Germany) are less satisfactory than administrative data.

example of the Michigan Panel Study of Income Dynamics (PSID; see Hill 1992) in the USA, household panel studies have been established in many European countries in the 1980s and 1990s. Panel studies have normally been confined to quantitative analyses of income trajectories, without systematic theoretical references to institutions, policies and political discourses related to the structure of life courses (as exceptions see Headey, Habich and Krause 1990, Berger 1990 and Bonß and Plum 1990) and without qualitative analyses of people's biographical orientations of action. In this sense, the panel studies express a dynamic approach, but fall short of a full life-course approach.

The founding father of what nowadays is known as the dynamic or life-course approach to poverty was Benjamin Seebohm Rowntree (1871–1954), a pioneer of empirical research into poverty. In his epoch-making study of poverty in York, a city in the North of England, he discovered a century ago that workers typically were not poor throughout their whole lives but only during certain stages: when they had dependent families or their earning power was limited, for instance by ageing. Rowntree wrote:

The life of a labourer is marked by five alternating periods of want and comparative plenty. . . . A labourer is thus in poverty and therefore underfed –
(a) In childhood – when his constitution is being built up.
(b) In early middle life – when he should be in his prime.
(c) In old age.
The accompanying diagram may serve to illustrate this:-

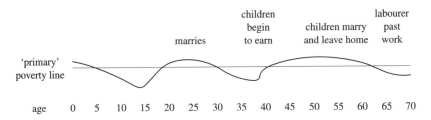

It should be noted that the women are in poverty during the greater part of the period that they are bearing children.

We thus see that the 7230 persons shown by this enquiry to be in a state of 'primary' poverty, *represent merely that section who happened to be in one of those poverty periods at the time the enquiry was made.* Many of these will, in course of time, pass on into a period of comparative prosperity; this will take place as soon as the children, now dependent, begin to earn. But their places below the poverty line will be taken by others who are at present living in that prosperous period previous to, or shortly after, marriage. Again, many now classed as above the poverty line were below it until the children began to earn. The proportion of the community who at one period or another of their lives suffer from poverty to the point of physical privation is therefore much greater, and the injurious effects of such a condition are much more widespread than would appear from a consideration of the number who can be shown to be below the poverty line at any given moment. (Rowntree 1901, pp. 169–172)

This passage depicts how Rowntree explained the life-cycle perspective on poverty. He stated explicitly why he found the static perspective misleading: only the longitudinal perspective allows one to see how poverty tends to arise only at certain points in the life cycle. Poverty cannot be equated with belonging to any specific group. To be a member of the manual working class is not synonymous with being poor – in contradiction to the equation of 'the working classes' with 'the poor', a notion that prevailed up to the nineteenth century. As far as the poor population as a whole is concerned, Rowntree established that a count confined to the number on a single day (or in a single year) – as is still the practice in most countries – underestimates those affected, since it conceals those who experienced poverty at an earlier stage of their lives or may do so in the future.

Current poverty research based on life-course theory generalises Rowntree's approach.[13] This does not confine the periods of poverty to those of increased family needs and reduced earning power previously found by Rowntree, but it inquires more generally into any periods of poverty during the life course, since they may have widely differing causes and may occur at very disparate points during life. The demand that poverty should be studied in the light of temporal considerations was made in German poverty research many years ago, for instance in the initial studies of marginal groups (see the foreword to Otto Blume's study (1960), or Wolfgang Glatzer and Hans-Jürgen Krupp 1975, p. 222). However, for a long time there were neither the longitudinal data sources nor the theoretical sociological tools of life-course research required to meet this demand.[14]

Today it is becoming increasingly apparent that it is not only poverty but social inequality as a whole which must be seen in a temporal perspective. Ulrich Beck pointed out, in his book *Risk Society* (1992, German 1986), that current inequalities divide less and less predetermined classes and strata, but generally take the form of temporary 'periods of inequality' in people's individual biographies (see also Berger 1990, Kohli 1990). The

---

[13] Rowntree himself carried out further studies of poverty in York in 1936 and 1950. His 1950 survey data were re-analysed by Anthony B. Atkinson (1989, chapter 4). On Rowntree's relevance in general see John Veit-Wilson (1986).

[14] In Britain, Pete Alcock (1997) included sections on poverty dynamics in his comprehensive textbook on poverty.

instability of people's social status is not just one of sociology's discoveries: rather, it is a precondition and legitimating model for the freedom of our social order. It is only the openness of access to social positions, in theory giving every individual opportunities for advancement in economic, political and other fields of activity, which makes the structural inequality of positions in society at all acceptable to the mass of the population. But at the margins of society, among the lower-income groups and the 'socially vulnerable' and 'underclass', the model of equal opportunity is feeble. The suggestion that socially excluded people should re-establish themselves in the normal realms of social life is usually no more than a vapid abstraction, since it has no realistic chance of success.

Although the conventional viewpoint underestimates the dynamic aspects of poverty, it does contain some elements of the perspective which can be taken up and generalised. We have distinguished three significant strands of research which have been important in analysing poverty: macro-sociological research into inequalities (the analysis of classes and strata); micro-sociological research into marginalised groups; and the descriptive social-policy-oriented study of poverty. All three strands offer contributions to a dynamic approach.

Research into inequality has been based on static conditions and nowadays often still is (Rohwer 1992, pp. 367ff.). The unequal distribution of the population, for instance by their occupational positions on a single sample day, is presented as more or less permanent and understood as the class structure, illustrated in the form of the familiar stratified pyramid. The assertion that Germany is a two-thirds society, or well on the way towards one, is a simplified and politically overstated version of this approach. But even in this research tradition one finds the instability of life being taken into account. Research into social mobility[15] investigates the processes of ascent and descent, particularly in occupational careers, though it usually excludes the marginalised sections of the population. In such studies they are considered only as members of the undifferentiated category of 'unskilled workers'. If one examines the educational and occupational status of their fathers, one can to that extent empirically fathom the depth of the roots of underprivilege over the generations.

In the *descriptive social-policy approach* to poverty research, the dynamic element is found most clearly in the life-cycle theory of poverty, as proposed by Rowntree. However, the 'problem groups' (such as the old, the unemployed, single parents and large families) in which this approach typically locates poverty are more or less statically defined, even though one

---

[15] See the comprehensive study by Erikson and Goldthorpe (1992), who conclude by calling for what amounts to life-course analysis (p. 397).

could say that they correspond to particular stages in working and family life. Some writers in this research tradition have therefore concluded that poverty arises only or especially at certain stages of life (e.g., Krause 1993, pp. 25ff., Salonen 1993, pp. 107ff., Room 1990, chapter 7).

Research into marginalised groups is based on sociological action-oriented approaches, particularly labelling theory. This research tradition is fundamentally dynamic. The dynamics of marginalisation are identified in three ways, in the first place through institutionally induced downward careers and exclusionary processes. It shows that social institutions – the 'forces of social control' such as the police, social work and psychiatry – have a lasting effect on the dynamic evolution of individuals' problems such as criminality, homelessness and mental disorder (for an early summary see Karstedt 1975). The relationship here between the welfare state and the life course is painted in sombre colours. Furthermore, students of marginalisation also investigate the cumulative processes of psycho-social collapse which follow from prolonged deprivations, even if social institutions did not contribute to the effects (the momentum of social deprivation). The best-known example of this kind of study is the analysis conducted by Marie Jahoda *et al.* (1975, German 1933) of the impact of long-term unemployment upon individuals. Finally, transmitted deprivation from one generation to another is an important poverty dynamic commonly considered in studies of marginalised groups. The 'culture-of-poverty' version actually assumes that the poor live in some enclosed world of their own which facilitates the 'transmission' of poverty within the affected family. The intergenerational approach thus makes most use of the time dimension – possibly too much, since the few longitudinal studies carried out in this field tend instead to qualify the associations claimed (Rutter and Madge 1976, Atkinson 1989, chapter 5, see also Buhr 1991, p. 428).

References to dynamic aspects found in the existing research outlined here are limited and biased. The assertion that, as a rule, poverty lasts a long time and becomes entrenched in the course of time, is still dominant. How can this belief have arisen? The reasons are to be found in the data, the methods and the theories used.

The first reason is that the groups of poor which were the subject of this research were unrepresentative of the poor as a whole. Marginalised groups such as the homeless and street people are no more than segments of the poor population among which long durations of poverty are more commonplace, but they do not reflect the experience of the majority whose poverty is generally less visible.

The descriptive social-policy approach to poverty research covered a wider spectrum of poverty, as in studies of representative samples of all Social Assistance claimants in a city (e.g., Strang 1970) or all inhabitants of the Federal Republic with incomes below 50 per cent of mean or median household incomes (e.g., Hauser *et al.* 1981), but the data collected contained scarcely any information on the course and duration of poverty. The same was true of official data such as the Federal statistics on Social Assistance. Apart from two special surveys from 1972 and 1981,[16] information on the duration of claims has only been available since 1994, following the revision of the Social Assistance statistics (Beck and Seewald 1994). In Germany and most other European countries, e.g., Britain, the simple questions of how long poverty lasted, and how many short-term and long-term claimants there were, could not be answered until 1990, and they were generally not even asked. Most restricted themselves, for no good reason, to the poverty of the long-term and socially excluded, as did even the high profile empirical research into the 'new poverty' by Lompe *et al.* (1987).

Second, the limited perspective of existing research has its methodological roots. One of the usual aims of biographical studies, such as of the residents of hostels for the homeless, was to determine the history of their earlier lives – how it came about that they arrived on the margins of society – but they were almost never asked about what happened afterwards, about the further history of their poverty. The respondents were generally interviewed during and not after a spell of poverty. Thus the dominant conclusion reached was that poverty and deprivation were fundamentally long lasting, and that poverty lasting for an extended period inevitably led to marginalisation and the loss of the respondent's capacity to act. In the 1980s and 1990s it was generally assumed that there was an increase in the number of long-term Social Assistance claimants, which was blamed on rising unemployment. By contrast, the dynamic approach to poverty research took into its ambit not only the paths into poverty and the deprived conditions but also the escape routes from poverty.

Finally, we must also highlight the theoretical problems of older research traditions, principally the assumption that 'careers' in the field of poverty were cumulatively reinforcing and could only lead in a downward direction (as in Hess and Mechler 1973). When one treats social exclusion as the consequence of social labelling processes, those affected are casually transformed into the passive victims of external social influences (by officials and social workers, and the stigmatisation of neighbours), which makes active opposition and escape from poverty seem hopeless.[17] Poor people are frequently not taken seriously as capable of autonomous action, as active

---

[16] Statistisches Bundesamt (1974a, 1974b, 1983b, 1983c). For time data on claimants of Social Welfare (*Fürsorge*) before the Social Assistance Reform Act of 1962 see Statistisches Bundesamt (1962).

[17] For an examination of the varieties of the labelling approach and the different gradations of 'victimisation' of the poor see Rains (1975).

subjects who can take part in shaping their own life courses. Even in social policy studies other than research into marginalised groups, the assumption is widespread that social problems become fundamentally reinforced with the passage of time (as in Hauser and Hübinger 1993, pp. 70ff.). This belief is itself so deeply rooted that even the study of Social Assistance in Bremen originally assumed the general validity of such processes (Leibfried 1987, pp. 835–837).

The dynamic perspective arose out of earlier work in this field. Three sources may be distinguished, growing out of each of the three traditions of poverty research described above: the theory of 'individualisation of social inequality', critical research into Social Assistance, and the social indicator movement.

In the 1980s Ulrich Beck had already criticised the outdated macrosociological research into inequality. The crude social groupings of class, strata and culture no longer reflected the realities of contemporary society. Even poverty had become *'individualised'* and 'temporalised' (Beck 1986). If inequality were to be understood, biographies would have to be analysed in their rich variety. According to Beck, collective forces such as traditional morals, religion or family have lost their power to give order to life, while 'secondary institutions' such as the labour market, the welfare state and the mass media have acquired significance as the engines of individualised life courses. 'Individualisation' in Beck's and our usage does not, therefore, imply an a-structural concept of the individual as an agent free to choose and be held responsible for his or her situation (see chapter 2). Rather, 'individualisation' means the rise of 'secondary' institutions which control individual behaviour less directly than did the older, collectivist institutions (Leisering 1997a). 'Individualisation' in this sense offers individuals chances to pursue their goals, but at the same time puts more pressure on them to take personal control over their lives under the given circumstances. Beck was the first in Germany to offer a theoretical formulation of the dynamic approach to poverty research (1992 [German edition, 1986, pp. 143–151]).[18]

Besides individualisation theory, the second source of the dynamic perspective was *critical research into Social Assistance*. This was the starting point of the Bremen study of Social Assistance: like the research into marginalised groups, we aimed to study processes of social exclusion. This was connected to theoretical aspects of the recent sociological research into the life course (Leibfried 1987). The life-course approach (see chapter 2) combines micro- and macro-sociological perspectives, taking account of the activities and life projects of the subjects as much as of the directive

---

[18] This section is not included in the English translation (Beck 1992).

interventions of the welfare state and other institutions. What also helped was a specially commissioned data set giving details of the course and duration of Social Assistance claims from the official files, the first of its kind in Germany. All this made it possible to carry over the older forms of dynamic analysis into a more open approach, one which did not presuppose downward careers but instead treated them as one type among others.

Third, dynamic longitudinal analyses also developed from the descriptive social policy approach to poverty research. As long ago as the 1970s, poverty was a theme of the *social-indicator movement* which aimed to monitor society on an on-going basis by means of statistical indicators of important dimensions of life. As longitudinal data started to become available from the annual Socio-Economic Panel Study from the end of the 1980s, it became possible to analyse the dynamics of poverty. The forerunner was a study carried out by the Social Science Research Center Berlin (*Wissenschaftszentrum Berlin für Sozialforschung, WZB*) (Headey, Habich and Krause 1990), the authors of which were recognised as the first to question the widespread belief in a 'two-thirds society' on the basis of empirical findings.

As regards our approach of seeing the poor as active agents and not simply as passive victims, we received a crucial methodological stimulus from an analysis of processes outside the poverty research field: namely from the study of 'patient careers' carried out in London and other cities by the German sociologist Uta Gerhardt. Her research approach systematically treats the subjects as active agents, and thus aims to illustrate the variety of ways in which they cope with or overcome problem situations. Chapter 5 in this book is modelled on this approach. More generally, Gerhardt's Weberian methodology provides a way of linking action and structure, biography and society, in the study of social inequality (see chapter 12, pp. 283f; see also pp. 112–114).

Previous poverty research also included studies which revealed that the ways of coping with poverty vary among individuals. Some authors emphasised the individual's experience of poverty in its social context (such as Münke 1956, Strang 1985 and Lompe 1987), while others also took into account the connections between total life history and the life stage spent in poverty (such as Tobias and Boettner 1992, Hübinger 1989, 1991). However, none of these authors took the further step of systematically looking at routes out of poverty. At a theoretical level, the ability of poor people to act as agents has been highlighted by Amartya Sen's concept of capability (1983, 1992), and by the related concept of *Lebenslage* (life situation) proposed in the German literature for example by Glatzer and Hübinger (1990) and by Hartmann (1992).

To sum up: if the findings reported in this book call some well-worn assumptions about poverty into question, it is chiefly because they are based on three methodological approaches which are novel or rarely used in combination in European poverty research. These approaches can be summarised as follows:

(1) By taking a longitudinal view of each individual's life we bring the whole of their poverty history into the picture – including the pre-history, any changes which took place during the periods of poverty and, depending on the individual case, the escape routes from poverty – instead of examining solely the acute condition of poverty. Longitudinal surveys of social assistance careers were not available in Europe before the 1990s.

(2) A representative sample in one city of all those who made Social Assistance claims in the course of one particular year makes it possible to include a broad range of all the different problem situations which arise. It is little known that representative surveys have rarely been carried out in German poverty research (exceptions include Strang 1970, Kopnarski 1990, Jacobs and Ringbeck 1994). Instead, the usual method has been to study selected groups of poor people who are homeless, unemployed or long-term Social Assistance claimants.[19]

(3) In addition to the statistical analyses, the research subjects have themselves been given a distinct voice through intensive biographical interviews. Instead of assuming from the outset that they were passive victims of external forces, the research has taken them as seriously as anybody else in society, as active subjects who deal with their situations in various ways.

There are several reasons why the problem of poverty should be studied through the experiences of current and former Social Assistance claimants. The Social Assistance threshold is a politically established boundary of considerable social significance. To claim Social Assistance is a sign of social descent. By studying Social Assistance claimants we can see how welfare-state institutions deal with poverty situations, and it allows us to test in particular the effectiveness of Social Assistance itself. Since we are examining Social Assistance claimants' entire life courses, we can also shed light on poverty situations which fall beyond the restricted perspective of the official poverty administration.

---

[19] The Federal Statistical Office's Income and Expenditure Sample Survey (EVS), which has been used for poverty analyses in the course of social-indicator research (e.g. by Hauser and Semrau 1990, Becker 1997, Hauser 1997a) and other nationwide data sets such as the Welfare Survey, are in fact representative (though with exceptions) of the whole Federal territory, but have generally been used only to collate information about some of the cruder aspects of poverty, such as the socio-demographic composition of the poor population. Most of the numerous poverty reports from the German local authorities (see Habich and Noll 1993) supply data which are already available.

2   Life course as politics

From a common sense perspective, the life course appears shaped by occupation and family. Most people grow up in their parents' homes, start a career and marry, may become unemployed or divorced, and have children. And finally they finish raising their children and working, and retire. The state influences this development most directly through the school system and pensions. What people are generally less aware of is that, in a wide-ranging sense, the state gives a structure to the life course, something which is also easily overlooked in the doctrines of market individualism. Sociological research into life courses has, too, only gradually acknowledged the welfare state's formative role in creating and shaping modern life courses.[1] The life course is political; and, conversely, politics is significantly concerned with life-course policy. Individual paths through life are politically predetermined, and state policies are largely directed towards influencing life courses.

In searching for the avenues which historically have linked the life course and the state one encounters the category of 'the individual'. The modern individual and the modern state did not emerge in mutual contradistinction to each other, but reciprocally enabled each other to emerge. Rights of participation extended and implemented by the state first created the individual as an autonomous subject. This is the origin of the notion of the welfare state, understood as the institutionalised responsibility of the state for the social participation of all its citizens. The welfare state is the third stage in the social foundation of citizen rights, according to the evolutionary model of Western societies developed by T. H. Marshall (1950) on the basis of the British example. Roughly speaking, legal rights for all citizens were established in the eighteenth century, political rights in the nineteenth and finally social rights in the twentieth century. Welfare-state measures are

[1] Mayer and Müller (1986), Mayer and Schöpflin (1989), Leisering (1992), Allmendinger (1994); for a cross-national perspective see Mayer (1996); for related analyses by economists of the impact of welfare policies on the life cycle see Falkingham and Hills (1995).

geared to individuals. The objective is not to increase global indicators such as GDP or export statistics, but to give individual claims the assurance of law.

In this lies the connection with the structure of the life course, since the modern individual is defined in terms of both time and biography. It is constituted as a 'Self' directed towards developing itself (J.W. Meyer 1986). According to this conception, the idea of Self is a cultural project which is pursued by educationalists, psychologists and other professionals and administrators, and it extends even to developing countries. John W. Meyer conceived of the 'life course' as the institutionalisation of the stages of development and career through childhood, working age and retirement according to legal rules. Martin Kohli (1986a) pointed out that in the nineteenth and twentieth centuries individuals have become unavoidably aware of the whole life span: people can and must prepare for longer lives, they can make life plans facilitated by the welfare state's temporal structurations, and they are affected by cultural images of individual development. All of this transforms the 'life course' into an institution which frames the development of a person's individuality during his or her life.

Social policy as life-course policy: a model

Almost every political action has some effect on human lives. The thesis that (social) policy is the politics of the life course goes further to assert a formative engagement with the temporal organisation of life. The first important social policy measures in Europe in the nineteenth century were of this kind: the prohibition of child labour, complemented by the introduction of compulsory education, and the introduction of pension insurance. They contributed to the creation of childhood and old age as genuine social phases of life. Age groups, or groups defined by their stage in the life course, were historically the first 'welfare classes' (Lepsius 1990, pp. 128–131, Alber 1984, Leisering 1992, p. 22). The three core components of the welfare state's rule over the life course are *education, security in old age*, and what we term *social risk management*. These are the ways in which politics temporally orders citizens' lives. The educational system paves the way to future opportunities; provision for old age secures individuals' expectations of a safe life span; and the systems for managing social risks, such as sickness, injury and unemployment insurance, social assistance and social work, bridge crisis periods in life.

Historically, risk management was the origin of the state's involvement in welfare. The statutory poor relief of the sixteenth to the eighteenth centuries was an early welfare state in miniature (Sachße and Tennstedt 1980). Education and security in old age were introduced in the nineteenth century

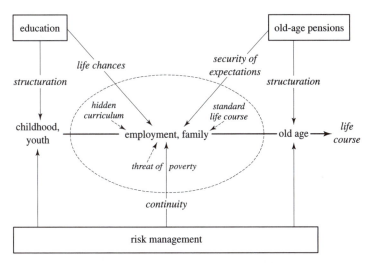

Figure 2.1 *The institutionalisation of the life course by the welfare state*

and were greatly extended in the second half of the twentieth century – in Germany the catchphrases 'the great pension reform of 1957' and 'the educational expansion' since the late 1960s refer to these developments. After a long period of expansion, the welfare state's life-course regime has become disjointed in the last two decades of this century. The emphasis on the life course is highly accentuated in the *'social* state', the German welfare-state variant anchored in the country's constitution and entrenched in detailed social codes. Yet all three components have become precarious, not because of accidental, temporary or external disturbances, but because of structural problems afflicting the politics of the welfare state: the inherent contradictions of welfare-state order.

Cutting across these three main fields of life-course policy we can distinguish three analytical dimensions, as shown in figure 2.1. These three dimensions can be envisaged as the layers or 'onion skins' of the welfare state's institutionalisation of the life course. First, the welfare state imposes a definition of stages in life such as 'childhood' or 'old age'. We can term this action *structuration* or *differentiation* of the life course. This is the outer skin of the diagram. Second, the welfare state influences the connections between the three main stages of life. Thus it contributes to the *integration* of the life course and lays down cross-references over the life span. In the diagram this is the middle skin: life chances, security of expectations and continuity. Third, the welfare state affects the deepest foundations of the development of people's lives, the patterns of social, economic and gender-related inequalities and differences. This can be described as the *formation* of the life course (the innermost skin shown by the dotted line: hidden curriculum, standard life course and threat of poverty). Some of these forms and effects of life-course policies are explicit, while others tend to be more latent or 'tacit', especially the third, innermost skin. All of these policies follow normative models of the life course.

Welfare states differ in the importance and pattern of each of the three fields of life-course policy (education, provision for old age and risk management), and equally in respect of the three layers or skins. In what follows, we analyse each of the three fields in terms of the first two skins, followed by a joint analysis of the innermost skin for all fields. While we refer primarily to the German welfare state, the chapter concludes by comparing the German with other models.

Life-course policy I: education[2]

Educational policies affect the life course in at least three different ways. Of the three major stages, childhood and youth, occupational and family life, and finally retirement, educational institutions are most directly influential in the first stage, in that they structure life courses. Education as vocational training and qualification is a (pre)determinant of occupational careers and therefore of central life chances in today's work society. That this is a matter of creating opportunities and not of determining outcomes is a fundamental aspect of a free society (Dahrendorf 1979). By contrast, in the German Democratic Republic (GDR) the connection between the educational and occupational systems was completely short circuited, since the flow of people within and between these systems was directly controlled. The educational opportunities which the state decreed for the children of workers and peasants were, however, a significant method of legitimating the system of 'real socialism'. For the post-war 'reconstruction' generation, the experience of upward mobility through education was a reality – the goal of equality of opportunity was closer than in the Federal Republic – but this did not apply to succeeding generations (Mayer and Solga 1994). The obstruction of opportunities for those born around 1960 was one of the reasons for the collapse of the GDR.

Through socialisation and teaching, the educational system additionally provides social competences and cultural orientations which are no less

---

[2] In Germany educational provision is not generally considered to be a social service or as a function of the welfare state, and is therefore not included in the government's social expenditure budget. But in the systems of governmental social policy which affect the life course it plays a central role, so that in this respect we adopt the Anglo-Saxon concept of social policy which includes education (Allmendinger 1999). In analysing welfare states both social insurance and educational provision must be taken into account, as shown by Heidenheimer (1981) in a comparison of Germany and the USA.

behaviourally relevant than immediately usable occupational qualifications. This has particularly influenced the relationship between women's educational status and childbearing plans (Klein 1989). The fact that the German educational system influences life courses so forcibly is regularly noted in international debates, both positively and negatively. The system is remarkable for the dual school–workplace training system, the extended duration of secondary and tertiary level study, as well as the stratification of occupational structure through educational certification and similar qualification ladders. The labour market has long been able to rely on this preselection (Allmendinger 1989b).

To the extent that educational certificates can no longer guarantee professional advancement, the impact of education on life chances diminishes. The risk of unemployment also affects the highly qualified. Certificates lose value: apprentices now have their high-school certificates and taxi drivers have their doctorates (Schlegelmilch 1987). Because of accelerating changes in the demand for qualifications, part of the occupationally relevant training is transferred to the workplace. As the earning phase in life is pared down at both ends, so the phase in which occupational qualifications can have any direct influence itself eventually shrinks. Even education seen as socialisation runs up against boundaries: calls for the reintroduction of the teaching of discipline and values in schools are remarkably ineffective in the face of increasingly blatant behaviour such as violence, right-wing radicalism and drug addiction. The loosening of the relationship between education and occupation is, as often noted, a paradoxical consequence of the expansion of education itself. The wider distribution of higher educational qualifications reduces their worth. Similarly, the remaining possessors of lower-value certificates, especially in secondary education, are pushed to outsider positions.

Life-course policy II: provision for old age

Like education, the statutory pension insurance founded by Bismarck in 1889 (with major reforms in 1911, 1957, 1972, 1992 and the suspended reform of 1997/1999) also affects life courses in more than one respect. It directly defines and moulds the third major stage of modern life, the 'evening' of life (Göckenjan 1999; Conrad 1994). It also offers younger people a horizon of expected security throughout their life spans. In addition, the German system places a premium on a regular working life: the model is the 'typical' pensioner (*Eckrentner*) with 45 years of insurance contributions and average wages. This constitutes a normative model of a 'normal biography', requiring and rewarding an unbroken working career or a marriage which lasts until retirement. The German pension system is internationally unique in making benefits depend almost entirely on contributions from work, unlike benefits based on citizenship rights (as in the Swedish model) or income-tested payments oriented to meeting need (as in the Australian welfare state).[3] This focus on work is the core of the German social insurance state. The target formula of security – the guarantee of an income status, once achieved, beyond working life – as against the competing target formula of equality is especially pronounced in the German welfare state. In this model, redistribution takes place less between higher and lower earners than over the life span between times of paying contributions and times of receiving benefit – what Fritz W. Scharpf described as 'socialism within one class' (1987, p. 336).

This kind of construct has its dangers, especially in an age of unstable labour markets and discontinuous family life. To the extent that it becomes harder to live a 'normal biography', the foundations of this system become shaky. A cleavage is growing between the legally required and the realistically achievable 'normality' of individual biographies. This is precisely what will affect the pensioners of the future, those who are earning their pension claims under current conditions (Allmendinger 1994, pp. 239–241). Other changes in life-course patterns are creating additional problems. The unexpected unceasing growth in life expectancy destabilises old-age insurance and, less obviously, the public sector pension systems for civil servants and farmers. This happens at the same time as the contributor base is narrowing as a result of the declining birth rate. The balance between these two 'life-course groups' defined by the welfare state, those of middle working age and the old, is becoming seriously upset. The inclusion of the population from the new East German *Länder* has not significantly altered the demographic prospects. Further immigration would bring only temporary relief as well as additional poverty.

Any system so linked to the structure and current pattern of the life course as is the old-age pension, remains vulnerable to radical changes in these structures. But even here the situation is paradoxical: it was social policy itself which created these structures and dependencies, inasfar as it made these life-course groups its primary targets and its financial contributors. It has even directly influenced some demographic processes, such as increased population ageing (Kaufmann 1990, Leisering 1992): the state old-age provisions have contributed to the secular decline in the birth rate in the twentieth century, and life expectancy has increased significantly as a result of public health policies.

---

[3] However, supplementary pension schemes that top up basic pensions are earnings related in many countries, as in the case of the State Earnings-Related Pension Scheme (SERPS) in Britain.

Life-course policy III: social risk management

The institutions of the third field of welfare-state policies for the life course, the management of social risks, come into play when the idealised assumptions of the model fail to materialise in individual cases: the assumptions of effective socialisation and of 'normal' biographies as embodied in the educational and old-age security systems. They are safety nets for 'deviant' life courses. Education and retirement define lengthy standardised periods of life and represent continuity. By contrast, the agencies of risk management react mainly to short-term circumstances and episodes which may affect individual lives at various points in the lifetime; they represent discontinuity.[4] In the case of Unemployment and Health Insurance the point of exposure to risk is not predetermined, nor, furthermore, can Health Insurance foresee the kind of risk management individuals need. In Social Assistance and social work both the type of service and the time of delivery depend on the individual case. Services for education and old age provide for the normal flow of life, while the risk-management systems deal with damage to it.

Until recently, social scientists studying the life course have almost totally overlooked the welfare state's management of risks, even though it is a major force in modern life courses. In any case, its relevance for the life course has not been so easy to grasp as in the case of educational or pensions systems. Thus the middle stages of the life course have been seen as merely periods of working and family life, even though it is precisely during this stage that state interventions to manage social risk are most important. The repercussions of the state's risk management on life situations are generally neglected because the conventional variables and categories used in the analysis of social structure and mobility – education, occupation, family status, social class and socio-economic group – are too crude to encompass the discontinuities in the life course which are relevant in this context. This also applies to some of the empirical studies by Karl Ulrich Mayer and his associates.[5] Discontinuity is nevertheless an element of normal life. It is a matter of a precarious balancing act: the institutionally guaranteed continuities in fact permit some degree of divergence, but if it becomes too severe, the whole life course may dither.[6]

---

[4] The Special Research Programme 186 at the University of Bremen (Heinz 1991b) in which this study originated in fact focuses on such discontinuities as 'status passages' and 'risk situations'. They are critical junctures in the life course which are more suitable than comprehensive biographical accounts for studies of how life courses are shaped by the interaction of institutional control and individual behaviour.

[5] See the reflection by Mayer and Müller (1986, p. 42).

[6] An elaborate concept of the life course in which both continuities and discontinuities are systematically considered can be found in the too-seldom cited, path-breaking work of René Levy (1977; 1996), as well as in Uwe Schimank's outline of a systems theory of biography (1988).

It is therefore not surprising that social scientists who do qualitative bio-graphical research focus their attention on deviant life courses. However, these scientists, especially in Germany, have tended to adopt a one-sided perspective in which such life courses are seen in a process of decline con-nected with increasing stigmatisation and marginalisation.[7] Preferred fields of investigation in this tradition of poverty research are, for example, slums, the homeless and the long-term unemployed. The total institution, the asylum, exemplifies the extreme of social administrative direction of life courses, hence the totally state-controlled life course in the psychiatric ward or the sheltered workshop. We aim to overcome the limitations of both conventional approaches, mobility studies and biographical research. Our thesis is that the management of risk by the welfare state is just as much a form of general life-course policy. It can open options for the individual life course which go beyond mere rectification of downward careers.

Germany's final social safety net, i.e., its lowest level of risk management, Social Assistance, is often criticised as 'bad basic security' (Vobruba 1990b, p. 62), even though it compares well internationally. It has a particularly lasting influence on life courses. Since the Federal Administrative Court ruling of 1954, individuals have had a justifiable right to claim social assis-tance. This departure from the traditional principle of the poor law is not found universally in other countries. Two further peculiarities of German Social Assistance are the almost exhaustive range of exposed needs which it can meet from Basic Income Support (*Hilfe zum Lebensunterhalt*) to the manifold forms of Special Needs Support (*Hilfe in besonderen Lebenslagen*) and the widely drawn circle of those entitled to claim – potentially every-one living in Germany (comprehensive approach). (Since 1993, asylum seekers have been assigned to a different benefit scheme with a reduced level of benefits.) In other countries, by contrast, the pattern is generally one of distinct systems for different target groups (categorical approach). Thus in the UK, for instance, programmes for the poor distinguish between those who work and those who do not (Spicker 1992), while in the USA the focus is on single mothers (Danziger *et al.* 1994, Piven and Cloward 1993, Piven 1998). Compared to other countries' systems, then, the German Social Assistance system is a more comprehensive seismograph of the changing risks in society.[8]

---

[7] The most significant exceptions are the analyses of 'patient careers' by Uta Gerhardt (see pp. 112f.). Besides studies of deviant behaviour and social problem conditions, Monika Wohlrab-Sahr (1993) showed – using the example of female temporary workers – that indi-viduals are capable of making purposive sense of their life trajectory even in the face of chance events and biographical insecurities.

[8] Significant numbers of those entitled to Social Assistance, however, do not implement their rights (see pp. 268, 276f.). This group of 'latent poor' is distributed right across the entire social spectrum. The omission of this section of the poor – due to the lack of

The current problems confronting the welfare state's risk management are familiar: Unemployment Insurance and Social Assistance are overwhelmed by claimants, straining social security institutions which were intended only as emergency systems. The proportion of claimants of Social Assistance (Basic Income Support) in the population has grown fourfold since the beginning of the 1970s, from 1.2 per cent to more than 5 per cent.[9] It is, however, an open question if this rise has reached administratively or politically critical threshold values. German society has become accustomed to a persistently high level of unemployment in the 1980s, a level which previously would not have been considered politically tolerable. In other countries such as the UK, the number of claimants in certain groups, such as the elderly, has long been much higher than in Germany. The reform of the Federal Social Assistance Law in 1961 was accompanied by the expectation that 'atypical life courses' (at that time this meant chiefly the diverse fates of the wartime generation, above all elderly widows) would diminish as economic affluence increased, and therefore decreasing numbers would fall through the meshes of the social security net into Social Assistance. The problems of the labour market, together with the changes in family life styles which can be seen in the increase in single motherhood, have negated this expectation.

Besides these above types of discontinuous or otherwise irregular biographies which are not unique to Germany, the German welfare state confronts two special varieties of precarious biography in the 1990s. First, Social Assistance claims by foreigners have risen sharply and disproportionately since the 1980s (from 3 per cent of all foreigners in 1980 to 7.7 per cent in 1986, to 17.9 per cent in 1992; foreigners thus constituted 33.1 per cent of all claimants in 1992). After the exclusion of refugees from Social Assistance in 1993 only 8.9 per cent of all foreigners received Assistance on 31 December 1997; foreigners thus accounted for 23 per cent of all claimants.[10] The number of claimants of Basic Income Support increased at the end of the 1980s and beginning of the 1990s in West Germany mainly because of immigration (see pp. 226–230). Foreigners – resident foreigners or even their descendants as well as new immigrants – may well remain a problem group in the future, mainly because they possess lower educational

specific data in this as in virtually all other studies – is scientifically defensible, even though it remains unsatisfactory. Moreover, Bremen seems to be a region of high take-up (Hartmann 1981).

[9] Basis of calculation: claimants not resident in institutions, whole-year figures (the number of claimants from January to December in any year as opposed to the head count on 31 December). For 1994 and later years, whole-year figures are no longer available and can only be estimated (see p. 219). People receiving Special Needs Support are not included.

[10] Claimants of Basic Income Support not resident in institutions (cf. note 9); calculated from Statistisches Bundesamt (1997b; 1998c).

qualifications (Alba *et al.* 1994) and therefore have poorer chances in the labour market.

The second factor in the increased demand for social security in Germany since 1990 are the ruptures and discontinuities in the lives of the former citizens of the GDR. As far as the elderly in East Germany are concerned, the principles of the Statutory Insurance Pension – earnings-related benefits at a level comparable to earned income – have allowed working careers in the GDR to translate into differentiated pension entitlements at a considerable level of benefits. Because the pension system has been financed on a pay-as-you-go basis since 1957, the new pensions were immediately payable from contributory revenue, even though the compulsory contributions made during the GDR period had never entered Western pension funds and were now no longer accessible. Had the pension system been run on a funded basis, the inclusion of the pensioners from East Germany would have been far more difficult. Nevertheless, the old-age pensions reveal the problems for the social security system which have followed from German reunification. From 1990 to 1996 a top-up supplement for low pensions was provided in East Germany, aiming to guarantee a minimum pension and prevent the elderly from slipping into Social Assistance, which was still being set up in the East in the early 1990s. This limited concession shows that the principle of contributory (and thereby biography-based) pensions, which excludes minimum benefits according to the ingrained social-policy doctrine in Germany, could not be politically maintained. It is also notable that in the very beginning, lacking every form of administrative infrastructure, the legal right to Social Assistance in East Germany was made dependent on the administrative capacity of the local authorities (Hanesch 1991).

During the 1990s, two further significant political breaches in the Social Assistance system can be seen: the expulsion of asylum seekers into a segregated system with reduced benefits (Asylum Seekers Benefit Law (*Asylbewerberleistungsgesetz*) of 30 June 1993 which went into force on 1 November of that year); and the introduction of Care Insurance (*Pflegeversicherung*; the Law for Social Insurance for the Risk of Care Needs of 28 May 1994) whose benefits commenced on 1 April 1995 (see Rothgang 1994). The Care Insurance, designed for people in need of long-term care, can be seen positively from a social-policy perspective. Being dependent on contributions, however, it is financially vulnerable when the insured become unable to make contributions during unemployment.

There are signs that the problems of risk management described in this section, too, are in part caused by the welfare state itself. Some of the increase in the clientele of Social Assistance is due to repeated cuts in Unemployment Insurance benefits. Meanwhile, the Federal government has often tried to limit entitlement to means-tested Unemployment Assistance to one year to push the long-term unemployed on to Social Assistance, which is financed by the municipalities and the states. This is part of a massive Federal operation to redistribute social costs between central and local government. The fiscal problems of Unemployment Insurance have political causes of a different kind, since the costs of reunification, especially with regard to employment schemes and early retirement for East Germans, were simply transferred to the body of insurance contributors instead of being borne by the wider community of all citizens as taxpayers.

Tacit life-course policies

Education, provision for old age and social risk management are the three pillars on which the welfare state's control over the life course rests. But this picture is incomplete. In politics there is usually a 'hidden agenda', that is, objectives and strategies which are less overt but no less consequential than the officially pursued policies. Life-course policies are no exception in this regard. We would describe these alternative life-course policies as 'tacit' social policy, as implicit life-course policies, in order to distinguish them from the 'explicit' policies[11] discussed hitherto which expressly target the life course. Even tacit life-course policies give the life course a political form. They have an indirect or soft influence on life patterns, implying common models of the life course as unexpressed goals. A strategy of this kind can be very effective, perhaps or precisely because it is not overtly pursued. Jutta Allmendinger commented (1994, p. 262) on the consequences of old-age pensions for the life course: 'their effect on the life-course regime is rather an indirect one . . . This "ecological" effect . . .' is as hidden as it is telling. Moreover, it is very hard to prove such effects. In as far as tacit life-course policies touch on sensitive social questions like gender inequalities and socio-economic divisions (such as the 'two-thirds society'), it is tempting to take plausible effects as already proven. We see examples of tacit policy in each of the three core components of the state's involvement in life-course formation (as shown in the ellipse in figure 2.1 on p. 25).

In the field of provision for old age (though with effects on the entire life

[11] The concept of 'explicit life-course policy' draws on Franz-Xaver Kaufmann (1982) who defines social policy by its explicitly declared objectives. The connection of social policy with the life course is not, as Karl Ulrich Mayer assumes (1991a, p. 177), simply an analytical matter. From an analytical point of view all political measures would be life-course policies. By 'tacit life-course policies' we mean those political strategies in which the connection with the life course is neither explicit nor simply analytical. This is similar to Lee Rainwater's and others' concept of 'tacit social policy' (1986, pp. 22f.).

course), tacit social policy is clearly apparent in the divided institutionalisation of the life course[12] via the German statutory pension scheme (Allmendinger 1994).[13] In formal terms the scheme treats men and women equally: whoever makes contributions is entitled to the corresponding pension benefits. Both sexes are entitled to survivors' pensions and to credits for child-rearing years; the latter were augmented in the suspended 1997/1999 reform. Under current social conditions, however, both these entitlements operate as rewards for wives and mothers who fulfill traditional roles. The employment of women and thus women's own pension claims are actually increasing, but many of these pensions do not reach levels adequate for subsistence in old age. It is precisely the adjustments of pension law to suit women, motivated by family policy, which damage the course of women's lives (Allmendinger 1994, p. 264). Women's competitiveness in the labour market is reduced after years of childbearing and childrearing, and the corresponding acquired pension rights do not compensate for this. This is a problem of gender inequality. Taken as a whole, the insurance pension endorses and supports the 'normal biography' which prescribes lasting full-time employment for men and directs women to 'female' roles.

A second type of tacit policy is encountered in the field of social risk management, embodied in the graduation of transfer payments. The downward ladder – contributory Unemployment Insurance, means-tested Unemployment Assistance, then Social Assistance – is forged by law and used, if not explicitly advocated, as an incentive to work through fear. Wolf Wagner (1982) described German social insurance as a 'reverse safety net' which drives individuals toward the edge when they fail to meet the work norms of productive society. Wagner therefore writes of 'useful poverty', which permanently intimidates citizens into leading a 'normal' life.[14] Insofar as social policy always carries the threat of poverty with it, it is not only policy against but also policy with poverty.

A third model of tacit social policy is found in the education component, in the form of the hidden curriculum, the unspoken teaching plan in schools. Besides transmitting knowledge and basic skills, schools also embed fine but consequential differences – differences in the characteristics and behaviour of the sexes, differences in cultural patterns of activity among the social classes,

[12] The contribution by Jutta Allmendinger is critically distinct from the work of Martin Kohli, whose conceptualisation of the institutionalisation of the life course is centred on working life and thus on the model of the male life course. Some time ago René Levy developed a concept of the life course which aimed to take account of the structural inequalities between men's and women's life courses (1977).

[13] See also Allmendinger, Brückner and Brückner's (1993) and Scheiwe's (1994) concept of 'gendered times' in German Old-Age Pension Insurance.

[14] Herbert J. Gans offered a stimulating analysis of the 'positive functions of poverty' for the USA (1972) (see chapter 12, pp. 286f.).

and differences in the career aspirations of various groups. These shape the decisions individuals make about their lives, often unaware of the pathways to which they have been directed by the hidden curriculum. Does the segregation of children in the German tripartite secondary-school system (and in a milder form in the comprehensive schools) not act as a directive to 'know their place in society'? Does this separation not operate as a warning sign on the ladder of upward social mobility, just as the threat of descent into poverty and Social Assistance warns against downward mobility?

Finally, there is a type of tacit social policy which cannot be unequivocally allocated to any of the three components but which is the outcome of a variety of economic and social policy measures. This is the general trend towards deregulation and privatisation of social provisions which implies notions of more open, more responsive, more insecure life courses, and thus calls into question the German model of the welfare state as a secure framework for the life course.

The individual as a 'life-course runner': individualisation and agency

To describe the life course as 'political' does not mean that the state determines individual life courses completely. The welfare state is not a mechanical 'contrivance of happiness' which imposes well-being on people irrespective of their participation, as imagined by late-Enlightenment philosophers such as Jeremy Bentham. The orientation which the welfare state gives to life courses is indirect and mediated, in that it creates rights and chances for participation. Education, occupation and housing are not centrally awarded or allocated, as to a large extent they were in the GDR. Intellectuals such as Ivan Illich (1976) have branded the relationship between the state and the individual as a one-sided culture of subordination, disempowerment and dependency.

It is correct that the welfare state impinges on the sphere of the individual, targeting each body and soul, not general social structures or global indicators of welfare. But this action is not directive; rather, it focuses on the general preconditions for individual behaviour required for achieving individual projects. Cash benefits make generalised resources available to people to use as they themselves wish. Social service provision such as counselling and medical care create individual competences. Workers' protection and tenants' protection provide individual rights, while arrangements in the social infrastructure of the local environment in which people live offer opportunities.[15] The effect is to enhance people's ability to act.

---

[15] The distinction between these four dimensions of life conditions and opportunities which can be influenced by social policy is drawn from Franz-Xaver Kaufmann (1988).

Total tutelage is found only in some special educational or medical fields. Even modern social work generally aims to enhance the participation of its clients, not encourage their infantilism and dependency. This reflects the ever-present deep structure of the welfare state's power over the life course, even if it is rarely acknowledged: it is not just a matter of life stages, of transitions or of risk situations during the life course, but the general capacity of each individual to cope with everyday life is partly an outcome of state action.

The welfare state's modern life-course regime both produces and pre-supposes the individual as active subject – it enables and requires individual action. The expression 'the life course is politics' therefore also means that the life course is 'individual politics' – it is the outcome of individual action in an institutionalised context. Political control is only feasible in a complex society if space has been allowed for individual action. No central system would be able to control the multiplicity of individual actions. Even the thoroughgoing direction of social processes in the GDR depended on openings for individual and informal activities (Huinink *et al.* 1995). 'The life course' thus has a double meaning. One is the model of regulated paths which lives should follow pre-formed by the state and other institutions and organised by controllers implementing cultural norms. The other is the sub-jective encounter with one's own life history and with individual tracks within the predetermined institutional pathways, and sometimes beyond them. The subjective track is 'biography' in the narrow sense, as distinct from the standardised institutional programme of the 'life course' (Kohli 1986a). 'Biographisation', meaning the '"institutionalised" of permanent reflexivity with regard to experiences relevant to life history', is character-istic of modern life (Brose and Hildenbrand 1988b, p. 18; see also Giddens 1991). A society's institutionally defined life-course programme realises itself only in individuals' everyday biographical reflections. At the same time, these reflections always contain the embryo of rebellion against the proffered life patterns.

In view of the social situation in Germany and Europe, of mass unemployment and the abrupt transposition of new structures on to the peoples of the East European countries, the question arises whether con-cepts such as individualisation and biographisation are not just intellectual toys of the 1980s whose use seems cynical at times of overwhelming social upheaval. Is it not rather more true that large segments of the population are subject to forced action, than that they are free to act of their own will and forge their own life plans? Is not the very idea of an individual 'biog-raphy' more than ever a noble illusion (Bourdieu 1986)? Or, more generally speaking, do the hard realities of modern life leave any room at all for indi-vidual biographical projects, or should the life course be understood, in

Karl Ulrich Mayer's phrase, as an 'endogenous causal nexus' (1987, p. 60)? Such a causal relationship holds, as far as can be empirically ascertained, in that a person's educational status and achieved occupational position are still as closely correlated as before with his or her father's education and occupation (Mayer and Blossfeld 1990). Do not the dominant institutional frameworks of our society – family, educational system, labour market and welfare state – still determine most people's life courses?

These questions can only be answered if the meaning of 'individualisation' is explained more precisely. This term is part of a German discourse of the 1990s triggered by Ulrich Beck (1983, 1992[1986], Beck and Beck-Gernsheim 1994)[16] not to be confounded with Thatcherite or Reaganite political notions of free agents to be held responsible for their fortunes and misfortunes. Not infrequently one hears powerful heroic undertones associated with these concepts. The individual, understood as an autonomous subject who is not rigidly constrained by the circumstances of society, became a figure in the history of ideas in the bourgeois world around 1800 (Brose and Hildenbrand 1988b, p. 13). In sociology, Talcott Parsons had already resolved the fallacy of solipsistic individuality in his discussion of 'institutionalised individualism'. In this vein, even against the background of American society, John W. Meyer (1986) has expounded the position that individualism is a social construct with tremendous pressure towards conformity, namely the constant demand that one should behave in an 'individual' manner. What is today described as the biographisation of experience and action is already a restricted version of the idea of the unity of an autonomous person, as it still appeared feasible in the bourgeois notions of 'identity' and 'individual':

Individual identity, whose development has been hampered by the weakening of identity-enhancing environments and milieus . . . and the lack of actual serviceable identity models worthy of emulation, is supplanted by self-descriptions and self-portrayals, self-evaluations and self-certainties related to relevant events in the life history. These 'biographisation processes' supersede the search for individual identity. (Brose and Hildenbrand 1988b, p. 18; see also Giddens 1991, pp. 33ff.)

Individuality is thus not the unique gesture, the creative life project, but the tapestry of more and less important decisions and everyday activities. The meaning of individualisation is, quite modestly, that in modern society in which religion, morals, family and class have lost much of their binding power as collective arrangements, each person can and must increasingly decide and act on their own initiative (Beck 1992[1986]). This includes individualised forms of morality, religion and family life that supersede

[16] For an empirical reappraisal of the theory of 'individualisation' see Berger (1996), Beck and Sopp (1997) and Friedrichs (1998b).

traditional collective forms.[17] The concept of individualisation is akin to Anthony Giddens's concept of the modern 'reflexive self' (Giddens 1991; see also Beck, Giddens and Lash 1995). Individualisation in this sense means not only the opportunity to shape one's own life but also the imperative that one must. And this imperative is conveyed by institutions. An 'individualistic fallacy' (Beck and Beck-Gernsheim 1993, pp. 18f.) is found in parts of the debate on this topic, treating the individual as an unconstrained subject. Older institutional bonds have indeed become weaker or assumed an individualised mould, but newer, 'secondary institutions' (Beck 1992 [1986, p. 211], Leisering 1997a) such as the labour market, the media and to a considerable extent the welfare state, emerged in their place. They require increased capacities for individual self-direction. 'Individualisation' means social conditions 'in which, within the framework of the welfare state, people have to produce, stage and craft their own patterns of life and social relationships' (Beck and Beck-Gernsheim 1993, p. 178; see also Zapf *et al.* 1987). While 'individual', 'individualism' and 'self' are long-standing projects of modernity central to the sociological classics, Beck's concept of 'individualisation' is specifically geared to the conditions of post-Second World War Germany with its economic growth, mass consumerism and expansive welfare state. The modern individualised life course is the product of the interplay between the welfare state and the individual. By individualisation we therefore mean neither pure market individualism nor a conception of humans in society which assigns all responsibility for social action to the individual level.

Carried to its logical conclusion, this means that the individual person cannot even be considered as 'free of the state' any longer. If the welfare state acquires new powers and capacities in important aspects of life, people's life orientations change. In this context, Karl Ulrich Mayer and Walter Müller (1986) have taken up Karl Mannheim's apposite distinction between 'substantive' and 'functional' rationality. The welfare state elicits a functional rationality whose goals do not lie in itself but are directed towards gaining social service benefits. People take up subsidies for building owner-occupied houses for the sake of financial benefits, irrespective of their actual financial need. Scholarships tend to prevent studies being terminated before the end of the entitlement period. 'Whenever the state establishes rules, provides services, or offers monetary incentives, it is functionally rational for individuals to make use of such opportunities' (Mayer and Müller 1986, p. 237).

However, Mayer and Müller's conclusion that '[this] may lead to deci-

---

[17] See Beck's discussion of Parsons' analysis of a new, individualistic form of religion and love (Beck, Giddens and Lash 1995 [1996, p. 21]).

sions concerning the individual organization of the life course which might be discrepant from actual individual needs or initial individual orientations' (1986, p. 237) must be put into perspective. The connections are tangled. The welfare state's services do promote behaviour based on the existence of the services. But to the extent that they strengthen individuals' general capacity to act, they also create the conditions in which actual individual needs or initial individual orientations can be pursued more effectively in other areas of life.

None of this seems to apply to marginal or endangered life courses. Dominant structures seem to allow the socially disadvantaged no free space in which to form their own life plans. Our thesis is that even *poor and marginalised people are basically competent actors* who may change their conditions or at least may actively cope with them. How far this applies and under what conditions, and which groups have particular opportunities to make something of their individual lives, naturally varies from case to case. Our empirical studies have led us to distinguish between different types. The thesis that the institutions of the welfare state do not merely passively 'process' threatened life courses but (according to circumstances) actively shape them, can be complemented by the related thesis that socially vulnerable people are not just the victims of state and social institutions but can themselves take part in influencing the course of their lives. That 'the life course is political' in this double sense thus applies to the poor as well.

This viewpoint cuts right across the predominant public and academic images. Countless studies of marginalised groups have more or less straightforwardly portrayed them as the lifelong victims of disadvantageous circumstances in their parental homes and in their neighbourhoods, and the objects of the 'social control services'. Similarly, in the debate about individualisation some scholars have assumed that this concept could not be applied to the lower social classes, such as black single mothers in American cities, because structural forces gave no scope for individual action. Individuality was said to be restricted to privileged social groups (Burkart 1993, pp. 172ff.). Among the political 'left' the capacity for action of the poor seems to have been played down, among other reasons because this notion often leads people to hold the poor responsible for their own situation, that is to 'blame the victims'.

Such views have not escaped criticism. It can be shown that welfare benefits could provide even black single mothers with a basis on which to make strategic decisions (Rainwater *et al.* 1986, p. 223, Rank 1994). When structures undergo change, such as when the emigration of men from the ghettos reduces choices in the marriage market (Wilson 1987), the women affected are even more strongly pushed towards taking control over their own lives, and this may include making use of welfare payments.[18] Even the severely ill do not simply 'endure'; they also 'act', though they cope in disparate ways with their situation as studies of patient careers have shown (Uta Gerhardt 1986a).[19] Naturally one must distinguish here between the various types of people affected, and one must also do so historically. Individuality as a way of life only developed gradually among the male middle classes, the *bourgeois*, but as the welfare state flourished so the idea broadened its appeal to the male working classes, and in the last few decades increasingly to women as well (Kohli 1988a, pp. 38f.).

Even the 'official poor', the recipients of social assistance, are not simply passive objects of society's manifestations of help, devoid of rights, as Georg Simmel portrayed them as long ago as 1908. Their legal status has been improved through the extension of the right to vote and the establishment of an individually justiciable right to support. In addition, a change in social attitudes has taken place in recent years, in which the younger generation finds it easier to go and apply for Social Assistance than older generations did. Even the material conditions and life experiences of most of the poor are not so constrained in every sense that they are not capable of making decisions about how to cope with their situation.

A similar point has been made by Anthony Giddens in the context of a theory of modernity. Under the conditions created by modern institutions, even the most underprivileged are forced to construct their self-identity and lives reflexively (1991, pp. 85ff.). Giddens also criticises Foucault who views modern institutions such as hospitals and prisons simply as forms of repression and exclusion justified in the name of reason. Giddens diagnoses a more fundamental process of an ambivalent kind: social institutions imply a 'sequestration of experience', a 'social incorporation' of aspects of human existence hitherto considered extrinsic to society, such as madness, poverty and illness. In this way, 'existential questions become institutionally repressed at the same time as new fields of opportunity are created for social activity and for personal development' (Giddens 1991, pp. 164ff.; see also pp. 156–158).

Changes in life-course policies and poverty risks

Now that we have identified its separate elements, we can see the contours of the total welfare state's patterning of the life course. It is revealed as a life course structured and secured by the state. Figure 2.1 (p. 25) showed the three core components as education, provision for old age and risk

---

[18] For the connection between poverty and individualisation see Berger (1994).
[19] See the critique of Fritz Schütze (1981) by Uta Gerhardt (1986a) and by Martin Kohli (1981).

management, and their effects on the life course's three layers or 'skins'. The tacit or hidden social policies were represented in the hatched ellipse.

The life course is political: since its introduction in the nineteenth century, state social policy has made a considerable contribution to shaping the modern life course. Fundamental to this influence have been education and old-age pensions, as well as the institutions of social risk management which are often overlooked in this context. The norms and institutions of the welfare state give life a structure of standardised stages; at the same time, they define events and episodes in individual lives (the temporal structuration or differentiation of the life course, outer skin). Additionally, the welfare state secures the connections between the three major life stages (integration, middle skin): the educational system steers the life course by offering occupational qualifications and cultural skills, thereby opening up life chances. Pension Insurance and the systems of risk management provide for security of expectations and continuity over the life span and thereby integrate the life course as a whole. Finally, tacit policies reinforce patterns of social inequalities (formation of life course).

Sociological research has hitherto dealt with the various types of influence only in isolation from one another. Education's directive function relative to the occupational system is emphasised to demonstrate that the life course is an 'endogenous causal nexus' (Karl Ulrich Mayer). The cultural and socialising functions of the educational system are highlighted in John W. Meyer's conception of 'the Self' and 'the Life Course' as cultural projects of modernity. The security-giving function of old-age insurance in modern society helps underpin the temporal horizon of the whole life course, which in Martin Kohli's view is fundamental to the institutionalisation of the life course. The various forms of the welfare state's risk management are particularly pertinent in biographical studies of marginal groups, where the focus is on social work and social control services.

The life course formed by the state – its structure and its vulnerabilities – is only comprehensible if perceived as the outcome of the interaction of all three elements of state life-course policies. Education and pensions obviously have structuring effects: the stages of education or old age define relatively stable status positions and *welfare classes*, that is, schoolchildren, apprentices, students and pensioners. By contrast, the welfare state's risk management is directed towards risk *situations*, which are generally shorter and do not necessarily settle into a new status or class. If the risk situations are prolonged – as for instance with long-term unemployment – or if the risks become entrenched as *careers* (such as drug addiction, homelessness or a 'social assistance' career [see chapter 5]), then problems arise for those affected as well as for policy makers. In extreme cases risk episodes and careers may drive individuals into a dependent class, for instance when illness or accident leads to permanent disability and a corresponding pension, or when unemployment assistance becomes a lasting source of income. From this perspective the life course is a network of welfare classes, risk situations and problematic careers induced by the welfare state.[20]

To be precise: social welfare law defines certain risks as episodes of limited duration. The state deals with situations of need only if and as far as they conform to the legal definitions of illness, unemployment, poverty and so on.[21] Thus in Germany Sickness Benefit is in principle unlimited, but paid in each instance of illness for only 78 weeks within a period of three years. Thereafter the case is examined to see if there is an irreversible permanent disability, or if rehabilitation measures would promise success. Unemployment Benefit is similarly payable for only a limited period, for instance up to a year for an employee aged under 42. Unemployment is thus perceived as a merely temporary risk. Unemployment Assistance, which is paid indefinitely after termination of Unemployment Benefit, is lower and subject to a means test: this marks it as a benefit for exceptional cases.

These political assumptions about the limited duration of risk situations may match social realities in times of frictional or cyclical unemployment, but difficulties arise when the legal definition and assumptions are overtaken by the development of social reality. The welfare state's management of the life course is challenged. Basic principles of the social security system nowadays seem increasingly out of step with the way that actual life courses develop. In many respects, social policy no longer manages to achieve much of its intended influence on the life course, as we have seen in the example of educational policy. Conversely, clients' life courses no longer correspond to the assumptions of normality which underlie the unemployment and pensions insurance systems, thus causing functional problems. As a result, social risks in the life course have been increasing since the 1970s. The well-adjusted interplay of the educational system, old-age insurance and state risk management becomes unsettled. The 'new poverty' of the 1980s and 1990s as a settling tank of various economic and social risks reflects the erosion of the life-course regime.

This is the point at which social policy discussions often end. But it seems to us that, beyond the rhetoric of crisis, one should examine rather more closely if and how social risks have in fact changed and what is problematic if they have.

Poverty was historically more than a risk. Originally, in early modern times, 'the poor' were a socio-economic class, the class of wage labourers

---

[20] The welfare state has substantially influenced the structure of inequality in modern society. See Gøsta Esping-Andersen (1990, 1993, 1996) for an institutional theory of stratification in post-industrial society which takes systematic account of these issues.

[21] For legal definitions of the duration of various risk situations see Buhr (1995, pp. 33–35).

which was then emerging. In the nineteenth century the term came to be confined to the recipients of public relief, thus denoting a dependent class. In Germany, soon after the Second World War poverty came to be seen as a merely individual risk. At the time when the Federal Social Assistance Law was passed in 1961 it was assumed that individual spells of poverty would be increasingly transitory, though the possibility of long-term dependence was acknowledged (see chapter 7). Social Assistance continues to embody this unresolved dualism to the present day, exemplified in the lack of a temporal cap on benefit receipt. In this respect Social Assistance differs from most other systems of social risk management (see chapter 3).[22] Since the 1980s the assumption of increasingly transitory poverty has been called into question. Has poverty once again become a long-lasting condition of life affecting a larger segment of the population?

A change in social risks, especially poverty risks, becomes particularly problematic for the welfare state when the frequency of their occurrence increases, when the duration of individual risk occurrences grows, and when they cluster at particular points in the life course (life-course concentration). The last may be a sign that the institutionalised management of the life course is not working as well as it was intended to. Finally, a further form of change among risks is the emergence of new risks or the worsening of old risks. These four indicators point to problem areas. However, not every increase or change in risks is problematic. The extent to which more common, longer lasting and more concentrated poverty in fact represents a problem is a matter for clarification by empirical analysis. In what follows, the current developments are outlined in the light of these four indicators.

(1) An increase in the *frequency* (or incidence) of poverty – the first indicator – should be treated as less problematic when it is recognisably associated with defined historical events which suggest that a transition is taking place. This was the case in the foundation years of the Federal Republic after 1949. Politicians like to interpret the situation in East Germany in the same way. The fact that in West Germany Social Assistance receipt has been generally on the rise since 1970 and that in United Germany unemployment shows no sign of decreasing in the foreseeable future, suggests that this is a new historical phase which can hardly be interpreted as transitional.[23] It is

---

[22] In our conceptualisation Old-Age Pension does not count as part of the social risk management system. The exceptional case of Unemployment Assistance is discussed above.

[23] The assertion that poverty has increased in recent decades is commonplace in the poverty debate. However, the Socio-Economic Panel data show that income poverty declined slightly during the period 1984–1992 (Krause 1993, p. 21, table 15). The increase in the number of Social Assistance claimants during part of this period was mainly due to immigration (see chapter 9, pp. 226–230).

notable that after 1993, following the economic boom of reunification, the number of Unemployment Insurance and Social Assistance recipients rose again sharply. However, the growth of unemployment and poverty has not led to political unrest – unlike in France where the unemployed revolted in early 1998, and it is open to question where limits of public tolerance of this growth lie.

(2) The increased occurrence of poverty in the Federal Republic is connected to changes in its individual *duration* – the second indicator. The social policy debate is guided by the presumption that long-term dependency is growing. What must be explained is whether for certain groups Social Assistance really has become a long-term benefit similar to pensions, as is widely asserted (pp. 63–68, 227f., 230, 233). Even if the proportion of long-term cases among the poor and unemployed has not increased, their number has. To what extent does this threaten the cohesion of society and the functioning of its institutions? The answers to these questions depend to a significant degree on the consequences of long-lasting poverty on those affected, on how far inevitable processes of psychological decline and social marginalisation set in. This, too, is a matter for empirical elucidation in the ensuing chapters.

(3) Social risk situations may occur at any stage of life from birth to death. By contrast with the standardised benefit systems, the risk management programmes are directed towards intervening flexibly at any point in the life course. Difficulties arise, however, when risks are *concentrated* at a particular point or stage in life – the third indicator of a potentially problematic change in risks. During the 1960s, poverty disproportionately afflicted the elderly in Germany, particularly widows, but since then the relationship between age and poverty has been reversed. Today children are the age group most severely affected – 7.2 per cent of under 15 year olds received Social Assistance as of 31 December 1997. This led to claims of an 'infantilisation' of poverty (Hauser and Semrau 1990). Poverty among children is an especially serious problem because it can have consequences for the rest of their lives.

For a long time the transition phases between the three stages of life have also been problematic. When risks are concentrated in these periods (youth unemployment in the transition to the working stage, and invalidity and unemployment in the transition from work to old age), conventional risk management policies reach their limits. For this reason, 'extensions' have had to be added to the core schemes of social security in recent years. Thus disability pensions composed more than half of all new entrants to old-age insurance pensions until well into the later 1980s (Leisering 1992, p. 120, figure 9), in effect constituting premature old-age pensions, and hereby overloading the pension system. Attempts to relieve the latter were made in the 1980s, such as restricting women's entitlements to disability pensions after periods of absence from the labour market. Yet the overdue reform of disability pensions has been deferred to the present day. Benefit levels were cut in the suspended 1997 Pension Reform Act, but no new concept was introduced.

At the other end, at the entry to the working stage of life, the ever-extended duration of education functions as a 'queue' for adulthood. Academic study still lasts far longer in Germany than in Anglo-Saxon countries. The welfare state's shortening of the working stage of life at both ends was doubtless a not unsuccessful attempt to deal with increasing risk conditions (Rhein-Kress 1993). The risks in East Germany were also largely dealt with in this manner (Wolf 1991, Rosenow 1992). Soon, however, associated problems have become apparent. Those starting work are too old and pensioners are too young. To counter this, the Pension Reform Act of 1989 (effective from 1992, reinforced by the 1997 Act) has deferred the pension-entitlement age in stages over the coming years. Early retirement will be penalised by reduced benefits, which itself increases poverty risks. But the introduction of partial pensions in 1992 has made the entry to old age more flexible.

(4) The fourth indicator of a change in risks is the appearance of *new risks* or the exacerbation of old ones. The ambit of large-scale risks covered by social insurance has changed only at historically long intervals: Health and Accident Insurance were introduced in 1883 and 1884; Unemployment Insurance in 1927; and Care Insurance in 1994.[24] But there are many other kinds of risk, whether new or changed, which from a social-policy perspective are no less pressing.

Not every social problem is politically perceived and dealt with as a risk. 'New' risks are the outcome of struggles to have a problem situation recognised by society as a risk and to institutionalise a collective response. Few problem conditions successfully pass through this strainer, even though the welfare state has set the stage for the identification of an increasing number of risks. Under modern political conditions, almost every social need seems 'politicisable' to give rise to redistributive policy measures (Luhmann 1990). The three new kinds of risk mentioned above (the socio-economic problems of foreigners, problem situations in East Germany and the need for care in old age) have in varying degrees been politically recognised and

---

[24] The Invalidity and Old-Age Pension introduced in 1889/1891 lies at the border between social risk management and old-age pensions in the sense discussed here.

confronted. The need for care has been given the status of a 'standard' risk by establishing a special new branch of social insurance. The problems in the East are being addressed by large subventions and new but impermanent institutions (see chapter 8). The foreigners' problems of occupational and social integration are still generally unaddressed. As a result of political pressure a separate discriminatory benefit system replaced Social Assistance for asylum seekers in 1993, with lower benefit. A further new problematic condition is overindebtedness among private households. A new law on bankruptcy provision for private households is effective from 1999 (see chapter 13, pp. 299f.).

The explosive nature of the new risks mentioned so far arises from the fact that none of them are confined to traditional 'marginal' groups. On the contrary, they extend into previously protected segments of society. Case-oriented services such as Social Assistance and social work are over-stretched. The new risks expose the functional problems of core societal institutions such as the housing market, the domestic consumption market and the finance market. The new risks are politically problematic because they require a bundle of different measures to deal with them. Universal panaceas like a general basic income scheme are insufficient. To guarantee a minimum living standard requires the arrangement and coordination of minimum security provisions in many areas of life (Leibfried 1990; see chapters 11 and 13).

Risks associated with the family are particularly salient among the 'new' risks. The problems of divorced and single parents have only been peripherally addressed by social policy, for instance by the Advance Alimony Fund (*Unterhaltsvorschußkasse*). One may interpret the discussion of family policy in the 1990s in part as an argument about whether children should be seen as a social risk which obliges the state to offer a more effective redistribution of the burdens. In that social policy has to a large extent nationalised the care of the elderly but, conversely, generally privatised the care of the young (Kaufmann 1997, p. 79, Leisering 1992, p. 138), it contributes to turning the birth of a child into a family poverty risk. A higher level of child benefit, perhaps even matching real needs, would diminish both poverty and entitlement to Social Assistance. Further, it would render the issue of Social Assistance levels exceeding low wages – 'less eligibility' – less acute, as the problem arises only for a few large families. In 1996, the Federal Constitutional Court obliged legislators in Germany to exempt incomes at or below a minimum standard (represented by Social Assistance levels) from direct taxation. Apart from this, the court urged the removal of tax disadvantages the state currently places on families (see pp. 190 f., 271f.). Here, too, the problem of poverty touches on basic questions of social order throughout society, not just on lives at the margins of society. But at least in Germany no one questions the use of Social Assistance to support single mothers in caring for their children without compelling them into employment, unlike in the USA and Britain.

The German life-course regime in comparative perspective

A view beyond national borders can help to expose the structure and problems of the German life-course regime more clearly. This section examines differences in poverty risks in various countries and goes on to show how the findings relate to differences between the national welfare-state regimes themselves.

For more than a decade now the 'new poverty' has been a topic of discussion throughout Europe. In different countries, however, this general phenomenon has assumed quite different contours. As far as poverty's prevalence among OECD countries is concerned, the USA has the highest rate and Norway and Sweden have low (though rising) rates. The German Federal Republic lies in between,[25] closer to Sweden, while the UK rate tends towards that of the USA (Huster 1997, Kohl 1994, pp. 408ff., Duncan *et al.* 1995). In addition, poverty is perceived and evaluated differently in different national contexts. The persistently high poverty rates in the USA and in Britain are more generally accepted than in Germany. This shows that the political threshold to be surmounted before the poverty rate seems intolerable can be very high.

Detailed findings about the duration of individual poverty spells in other countries are available chiefly from the USA and Britain. In Britain, people in most social groups receive social assistance for much longer periods of time than in Germany (Leisering and Walker 1998d; data for 1995). Since British old-age pensioners have to resort to social assistance much more often, average total duration is even higher in Britain. Although dynamic research into poverty started in the USA, and revealed that many more US citizens were only temporarily poor than had previously been supposed, the duration of welfare benefit claims is significantly longer than in Germany. This is because the clientele of the corresponding system, AFDC (Aid to Families with Dependent Children; now TANF, Temporary Assistance for Needy Families), are mainly single mothers, many of them black. But poverty tends to last for a long time, sometimes lifelong, also for the working poor – that is, those whose earnings are inadequate for a minimally decent life. Since the 1980s, US social policy has targeted this group for support, chiefly through tax reform (Myles and Pierson 1997), while at the same time the rest of the poor were severely disadvantaged, for instance by

---

[25] It is harder to be precise about poverty in the GDR; see chapter 8, especially pp. 210–213.

the cuts in welfare benefits enforced under Presidents Reagan and Bush (Handler and Hasenfeld 1991, Seeleib-Kaiser 1993, Pierson 1994) and eventually by Clinton's 'welfare reform' of 1996. To this extent poverty in the USA should rather be seen as a deliberately normalised social condition than as a particular 'risk'.

In Germany, poverty among full-time workers is rare because of higher wages. This is apparent, for example, in that the proportion of the working poor who top up their earnings with Social Assistance has remained at a low level, and these cases are often only the result of inadequate family benefits. Finally, in the GDR poverty in the sense of biographical collapse seems to have been inconsiderable and confined to deviant lives (see chapter 8). It coexisted with the general collective poverty which was taken for granted politically, being created by the inefficiencies of the system itself, and which (in the form of a shortage of resources) was the permanent experience of the majority of the population.

Under different welfare-state regimes (Esping-Andersen 1990; see also Ferrera 1998 on Southern Europe) social policy has varying consequences for the life course.[26] In order to make sense of the variety of poverty risks we therefore have to examine the national types of welfare state and the life-course regimes associated with them.[27] What is the specific temperament of the German life-course regime, what opportunities does it offer citizens and which risks does it expect them to carry? In what follows we shall also outline the welfare-state regimes of the USA, Sweden, the German Federal Republic and the GDR (table 2.1).[28] This order reflects the increasing influence of these countries' social policies on the life course.

In the residual welfare-state model, which the USA most closely resembles, any connection between an individual's life course and the welfare

---

[26] As examples of the growing comparative literature on the institutional determinants of different life-course patterns see Mayer (1996), DiPrete et al. (1997) and Allmendinger and Hinz (1998).

[27] Eardley et al. (1996) construct a useful typology of welfare states in view of the role played by social assistance. Germany, Britain, Ireland and Canada rank among the 'welfare states with integrated safety nets', characterised by a high degree of centralisation of social assistance and a low degree of discretion in the provision of benefits. (It is debatable if Germany and Britain should be assigned to the same type since British social assistance covers a much broader section of the population, 23 per cent as compared to 2.8 per cent in Germany in 1994.) The USA constitute a type of their own, the 'public assistance state', with a strong emphasis on means-testing, work incentives and stigma and a low level of benefits. The Nordic states are characterised by 'residual social assistance' because social assistance plays a marginal role due to full employment policies and extensive higher-tier benefit schemes. However, in the 1990s, the clientele of social assistance has increased to make the term 'residual' obsolete (Buhr 1999). We do not use this typology here because we are interested in more general welfare state structures and related life-course regimes.

[28] Parts of table 2.1 are based on suggestions by Allmendinger (1994, chapters 1 and 7) and by Allmendinger and Leibfried (1991).

Table 2.1 *Life-course policies under different welfare-state regimes*

	Model life course	Effect on life course	Form of life course	Poverty risk
Residual welfare state (US model)	work-centred biography (punitive workfare)	minimal security/ insecurity	fluid life-course structure; good opportunities; high risks	high; passed on to society
Citizenship provision (Swedish model)	work-centred biography (obligation to work encouraged by labour and family policy)	formative influence	standardised; good opportunities; low risks	low/rising; taken by the state
Social insurance state (German model)	gendered normal biography (rewarded by social insurance)	formative influence	standardised; good opportunities (unequally distributed); low risks	limited; taken by the state
Authoritarian welfare state (East German model 1949–90)	work-centred biography	direct control	highly standardised; poor opportunities; minimal risks	minimal/high collective poverty

state is generally loose or non-existent on both sides: the benefits systems place little weight on previous contributions and similarly contribute little towards the formation of biographies. People in need may count on help even when no prior contributions have been made, although such help offers no more and often less than minimal support (see Danziger *et al.* 1994; Heclo 1994). The social security systems do not shape individual life courses, but at best they offer life belts to individuals whose life courses are caught in risky trajectories for which they are often held responsible. The national social security pension system, however, does shape life courses to a degree.

From a different perspective, the American system has lasting effects on life courses, but in a 'negative' manner. The minimum benefits for welfare recipients are so designed as to give them a powerful incentive to return to work quickly, even at very low wages, or even illicitly. This is a workfare state (Jessop 1994). The risk of poverty in the American system is high and poverty is an 'immediate' experience: trends in the economy directly affect individual lives, compared with Germany, where the welfare state cushions the shock of economic fluctuations.

In the original *Swedish* model, which has been moderately restructured during the 1990s, only one side of the linkage between welfare state and life course has been disconnected. Following the idea of equal provision for all citizens, the normal record of individual contributions is hardly relevant since one has only to be a citizen of the country in order to have rights. However, as far as services are concerned, the Swedish welfare state lastingly affects the whole life course: it makes a deep impression on the life courses of all male and female citizens. In particular, active labour-market policy including the provision of service jobs for women in the public sector, and extensive measures for the integration of paid work with motherhood, ensure that a working career is the norm in the lives of both sexes. This, too, is a 'workfare state', but in a very different way, in the sense of a worker's state: it is distinguished from the punitive American version through the integration of the positive aspects of work in return for welfare in the widest sense. Swedish employment policy is universalistic and directed towards the whole population in order to facilitate an appropriate occupation for everyone. Under this regime, the consequent risk of falling into poverty or social assistance is low though rising in the 1980s and 1990s.

In the *German* model – from 1949 to 1990 only in West Germany – the life course is very closely bound up with social policy, and in both directions. Major benefits depend on individual contributions made during working life, with normal biographies being positively rewarded by Social Insurance. More than in many other welfare states, the ways in which this is done are differentiated, as is described above, according to gender. The

German welfare state has a complex network of measures which actively configure the life course and make it amenable to individual configuration. The disadvantages are clearly marked and structure the life course more emphatically than for instance in the USA or Sweden where the thresholds and transitions are more fluid and diffuse. The strength of the structuration and the scope of security measures (where else is there Social Assistance with a right to medical rehabilitation and vocational retraining?) limit risks and alleviate poverty situations. But because the life course in Germany is so subject to state influence, the insurance against risks has become a risk in itself: in as far as it arises at all, poverty is largely conditioned or intensified by the state (Hauser and Neumann 1992, pp. 250, 262, Leisering and Voges 1997), for instance when unemployment is followed by a series of cuts in Unemployment Benefits.

The German welfare state's life-course model does offer the citizen something: good opportunities and limited risks in life. But all good things have their price.[29] The opportunities are unequally distributed, access to rewarding trajectories being graded according to sex, class and ethnicity, rendering this access less open than in the American model. The allocative process starts at school: the streamed school system offers graded school leaving qualifications which open career prospects for the restricted group of those who hold higher certificates but close these avenues for others. This continues in occupational training, through which the state and employers organise flows into the labour market. Conversely, in the USA a much larger proportion of young people have graduated from high school on a formally equal basis, and 'training on the job' is more important than having a certificate. Hence the selection function shifts from the educational system to the employers' side. Beyond the formal gradation of school leaving qualifications in Germany, the parallel class-based 'hidden curriculum' has its influence in the segregation of social backgrounds in the streamed school system, which is then carried over into socio-cultural differences and distances between the classes and the sexes in working life. In terms of the three core components of life-course policy discussed above, we can say that the US model places an overriding emphasis on education, less emphasis on social security and little emphasis on risk management, mainly Welfare, although Welfare acquires more relative importance in the face of weak higher tier social security systems (see p. 147). By contrast, the German model balances these three components in its life-course policy more equally.

In the *GDR model* the life course and social policy were even more closely linked than in West Germany. Life courses were pre-planned and actively

---

[29] On the following, see Allmendinger (1989a, 1989b), Allmendinger and Hinz (1998).

controlled. The norm for both sexes was a full-employment biography. There was no discussion of life chances in terms of choices, only of careers imposed by the state. These policies managed to destroy the bourgeois 'hidden curriculum' and even (although only in the 1950s) to offer higher occupational qualifications to the working classes. Social insurance benefits, especially old-age pensions, were set at low levels and therefore depended less on previous contributions in life than in the West German model. Poverty and 'impoverishment' were collective and permanent. The ruling elites, however, enjoyed special benefit supplements and other privileges. Within this framework, life bore few risks, even if there were significant income inequalities and individual poverty (see chapter 8). The state did not, however, treat these issues as poverty problems.

The GDR's life-course regime has collapsed. To what extent is the Federal Republic's welfare-state regime, which supplanted it, itself in crisis? Has the model had its day, partly due to the problems it created itself? Were the 1960s and 1970s the high point of the welfare state's formation of life courses, which has since been on the wane (Mayer and Müller 1986, p. 43)? Has the era of welfare-state expansion given way to an era of wholesale retrenchment (Pierson 1996)? What potential for development does the current socio-political order have, and what reforms are possible or necessary in a changing global environment? These might be the more optimistic questions and that is how we aim to proceed. A more pointed question might be to ask if we need a different welfare state, a transformation of the system to resemble something like the Swedish model (so far as it can still be found in its country of origin). Or should it move more in the American direction as suggested in Germany since 1993 by certain voices in the debate over 'the German condition', and by European Union White Papers as well as by the OECD (Kappeler 1994)? Seen through this type of lens the German welfare state may appear as an authoritarian provider state in a negative sense, inescapably escorting people from the cradle to the grave.

What this will involve is nothing less than the attempt to redefine the modern individual without the statist backing. Should the welfare state give way to other social orders which direct individuals rather more towards market control over their lives? Should we count on a 'de-institutionalisation' of the life course, meaning the removal of hitherto life-long guarantees, or rather on a de-standardisation, meaning new and more flexible institutions as a basis for a new order (Kohli 1986a)? Besides market-liberal images of the life course free of state intervention, other models of society figure in the public debate that call into question the combination of individualism and universalism which is typical for the German welfare state. Are we facing a new more closed social order based on traditional forms of family and community, of religion or ethnicity,[30] or are we even 'on the threshold of the authoritarian century' (Dahrendorf 1997)?

Which of the above visions and ideas becomes realised depends, among other things, on the interests which are bound up with them. Have the positive functions which the welfare state has fulfilled for the economy and for the qualification and social pacification of labour become superfluous? Historically, the welfare state was so successful precisely because its management of the life course was so beneficial to diverse social interests (Kaufmann 1997, chapter 4). Through the socio-political structuration of the life course, in particular,

it was possible simultaneously to induce greater discipline in the labour force and to exclude less productive groups of the population from the labour market. This sharp dividing-line [between the active and inactive age groups – L.L./S.L.] is an advantage both for employers whose concern is to have the most productive labour available, and for employees who can keep the supply of labour within fairly strict limits. (Kaufmann and Leisering 1984, p. 390)

In the historical competition among nation states it was precisely the German welfare state's leading position which was seen as a comparative advantage in the race against Britain (Hennock 1987). Is this implicit social contract, which has provided both economic and social foundations for the last hundred years, no longer valid? The proponents of the debate on the German condition maintain that it is precisely in such areas as poverty and Social Assistance that state-provided continuity in the life course runs increasingly counter to the higher public interest in a free labour market. Or does adaptation to more life-course dynamics require an even more refined welfare-state framework in continental Europe (see Rieger and Leibfried 1997 [1998])?

---

[30] See René Levy's (1996) reference to the decline of religious and military influences on the life course.

Part II
Poverty in the life course: the dynamics of social decline and ascent

Plate 2 'The Wheel of Fortune' Georg Pencz (c. 1500 Nuremberg–†11 October 1550 Leipzig). C. 1534. Titled *'Das waltzend Glück, Das Glücksrad'* the woodcut first illustrated a poem of Hans Sachs of the same title and date. (*Universitätsbibliothek Erlangen*)

The dynamics of social decline and revival are illustrated in the medieval picture of the wheel of fortune. The wheel turns irrespective of social circumstances; it points to an uncontrolled power in the life course.

An individual might pass through the cycle of gain and loss repeatedly. The man at the bottom may soon be on top. The man enjoying success should ready himself for a plunge. (Sears 1986, p 144)

The findings of the Bremen Longitudinal Study of Social Assistance (LSA) are set out in the following four chapters. They are based on an analysis of a representative 10 per cent sample of Social Assistance claim files (Basic Income Support, *Hilfe zum Lebensunterhalt*) in the city of Bremen in North Germany, and on open qualitative interviews with former and current claimants. The results presented in this section draw on the analysis of a cohort of those who first made Social Assistance claims during 1989 ('applicant cohort') and whose subsequent lives or 'careers' were then followed up to 1994. In chapter 9 this cohort is compared with an earlier one, those who first made claims during 1983 and were followed up to 1989. The comparison also embraces the findings of a twin study from East Germany, carried out in the city of Halle/Saale. Longitudinal analyses are necessarily 'dated'. The 1999 applicant cohort, for example, would have to be observed until at least 2004 to obtain meaningful results.

In the 1983 cohort (586 files), the households covered by the applicant files contained a total of 1570 persons, but only 935 of these actually received Social Assistance. The files, therefore, represent claiming units, not necessarily entire households. The comparable figures for the 1989 cohort (922 files) are 2063 and 1420 persons.

The intensive qualitative interviews were carried out in the early 1990s to review the claimants' experiences retrospectively. We conducted problem-centred focused interviews with narrative passages which were completely transcribed and subjected to a complex procedure of case analysis and case comparison (for details see Ludwig 1996, chapter 3). The interview sample was drawn from members of the 1983 cohort supplemented by some from the 1984 cohort and respondents contacted through snowball sampling. The group of respondents interviewed closely matched the representative quantitative sample in terms of basic socio-demographic characteristics such as age, gender and household type. The interviews also included persons with special problems, such as the homeless and women living in

56

Women's Refuges. The analysis was based on 74 of the total of 89 qualitative interviews carried out. The remaining 15 interviews could not be properly analysed because of, for instance, mental disturbance of the respondent or language difficulties with foreigners. In one case the respondent withdrew permission to evaluate the interview.

The results of the analyses can be taken to be indicative of the structure of Social Assistance and poverty throughout Germany. Three similar studies in other German cities and towns modelled on the Bremen example found that the duration and dynamics of Social Assistance claiming there were very similar or virtually identical (Samson 1992, Andreß 1994, Hagen and Hock 1996a, b, Hilkert 1998). Similarly, analyses of income and poverty based on the findings of the German household panel study (Socio-Economic Panel, SOEP) match our findings.[1] The dynamic analysis of unemployment careers has also led to comparable results (for Germany see Mutz et al. 1995, Ludwig-Mayerhofer 1990, 1992, Landua 1990). Unemployment, like poverty and claiming Social Assistance, is more volatile and shorter than commonly assumed. The findings of our qualitative analysis were also corroborated by similar studies, for instance among lone mothers in the city of Berlin by Mädje and Neusüß (1996).

Time is the focus of dynamic research. 'Time' means first of all *objective* time, as measured by the day, the week, the month or the calendar year. This is the subject of chapter 3. For how long do people claim Social Assistance and which temporal patterns of claiming histories can be identified? Is it true that Social Assistance claiming tends to be long-term? But there is also a *subjective* dimension to time. In chapter 4, therefore, we look at how people themselves perceive their time on Assistance and how they evaluate it within the context of their biographies. This allows us to examine the widespread assumption that long periods of poverty or of Social Assistance claiming necessarily entail processes of psycho-social decay and a loss of autonomy. Chapter 5 deals with the most encompassing dimension of time, *living time*, that is the life history of claimants before, during and after claiming Assistance. Which 'careers' of claimants can be identified, which career types can be distinguished? Finally, time also means *institutional time*, that is periods during which people are dependent on public institutions even though such dependence is less oppressive than it is, for instance, in the case of institutionalised clients of mental hospitals. On the basis of our findings on objective and subjective time we test the

[1] Hauser (1997a, p. 540). Panel-based analyses include Headey, Habich and Krause (1990), Berger (1990), Bonß and Plum (1990), Hauser and Berntsen (1991), Rendtel and Wagner (1991), Voges and Rohwer (1991), Krause (1993, 1994a, b, 1998, 1999), Hanesch et al. (1994), Habich and Krause (1994, 1997). For longitudinal analyses of income poverty and social assistance in other countries see chapter 1, pp. 14f.

notion that Social Assistance makes people dependent ('welfarisation'; chapter 6).

The following chapters have a double focus: On the one hand claiming Social Assistance is treated as a form of poverty, with similar questions to be posed as about income poverty, for instance as defined by having an income below half of the average.[2] In this respect data on claiming histories gained from administrative files give a more precise and reliable picture of poverty careers than data on income poverty from general household panel surveys. On the other hand we consider the impact and effects of welfare state institutions on their clients. In this way we can evaluate the effectiveness of Social Assistance as the basic scheme of income maintenance. Indeed, both aspects are closely related. Social Assistance legislation is explicitly or implicitly based on assumptions about the duration and the temporal patterns of poverty (see chapter 3, pp. 59–63). When these assumptions erode due to social change, legislation no longer reflects the new realities and may become ineffective. Hence, the analysis of Social Assistance aims at contributing both to poverty research and to the institutional analysis of the welfare state.

---

[2] We are not saying that escaping Social Assistance necessarily implies overcoming poverty as defined in some other way, e.g., by a certain level of income or material deprivation (see the critical discussion of this issue in a review of our study by Mary Daly 1997, pp. 437f.). In fact, in chapter 5 we provide a theoretical and empirical analysis of the paths people take after claiming Assistance. We distinguish different forms of 'normalisation' off benefit, including cases in which normalisation fails.

3   Objective time: how long do people claim Social Assistance?

The suggestion that the problem of poverty consists chiefly of long-term poverty came mainly from research into marginalised groups (see chapter 1). In the 1980s it gained new support when it became clear that mass unemployment was not a transitory phenomenon and that the number of long-term unemployed was rising. This development presented a challenge to the social security system, since the welfare state's methods of 'risk management' (as we have called it in chapter 2, referring to such provisions as Unemployment Benefit) are intended primarily for temporary contingencies. How do matters stand with Social Assistance? It has an exceptional position in that it is the final safety net for those who fail to be caught by the prior social security provisions. Is Social Assistance also directed chiefly towards covering transitory situations? Or have long-term benefit claims come to dominate?

The treatment of 'time' in Social Assistance

The Federal Social Assistance Act (*Bundessozialhilfegesetz*, BSHG, here referred to as 'the Act') was passed in 1961 and came into force in 1962. From a purely legal point of view, the Act does not restrict the duration of benefit, as is the case with Unemployment Benefit and, subject to conditions, also with Sickness Benefit (paid by employers for the first six weeks of absence from work and by the contributory funds thereafter). Social Assistance resembles Unemployment Assistance in that it is paid without time limit as long as the need continues. This reflects its purpose, to guarantee a civilised minimum income to all citizens. In sharp contrast to the Clinton reform of welfare in the USA in 1996, time limits were not even considered in the German debates leading to the reform of Social Assistance enacted in the same year.

Co-authors: Petra Buhr, Andreas Weber.

59

In spite of this, entitlement to Social Assistance is still assumed to be short-term: even if nothing in the Act explicitly requires it, a number of regulations imply that claim spells should be as brief as possible. It is this unresolved dualism, this ambivalence about the duration of benefits offered by the statute, which creates stress for the institution of Social Assistance and makes it vulnerable to criticism.

Three principles in the Act incorporate the contradictory approach to time which the clients and administrators of this system themselves have to confront: *Residuality* (meaning that all other services and benefits must first have been exhausted); *Individuality* (meaning that each application must be individually assessed to determine what cash or other benefits the claimant is entitled to in that specific situation); and *Help towards Self-help*.

One may not use Social Assistance during one's life simply when it is objectively needed; instead, it must follow the *residuality* principle (section 2 of the Act). It may not be claimed until all other potential sources of support have been exhausted, including not only other social transfer payments but also earnings, personal savings and support by close relations, chiefly by parents, children and partners. Regulations set out in detail the conditions under which these sources of support may exceptionally be disregarded. The duration of benefit is shortened by delaying the commencement of payments as long as possible.

The principle of *individuality* (section 3 of the Act) also contains temporal implications for claimants. Examination of the intentions of the Act at the time when it was being debated (1961) show that it was originally intended to provide 'transitional emergency assistance'. When the Act was passed, people assumed that the mass material deprivation which had required long-lasting economic support would diminish because of the growth of economic well-being and the development of the social security system, and that this would at last allow Social Assistance to play its rightful role in providing individualised support for special needs.[1] Compared with the preceding public welfare system (the last major reform had taken place in 1924), these new provisions involved changes both in the clientele and in the time horizons of Social Assistance. There was a presumption that the group composed of people with unremittingly low incomes would gradually 'die out'. In particular it was assumed that the number of those with inadequate pensions ('welfare pensioners') would fall as a result of the major pension reform of 1957, so that Social Assistance would finally be available to meet individual needs of a generally transitory kind not primarily defined in material terms.

The third principle is that of *'help towards self-help'*. 'Assistance should

---

[1] See the Justification for the Bill in 1960 (Federal Parliamentary Papers 3/1799, p. 31).

as far as possible equip [the claimant] to live without it, and he [sic] must cooperate with this aim as far as is in his power' (section 1.II.2). One may conclude from this that Social Assistance should be 'only a temporary state support, in accordance with its aims' and should not be 'a long-lasting attractive alternative to material self-sufficiency' (Schulte and Trenk-Hinterberger 1986, p. 107). Rather, the claimant should 'stand on his own feet as soon as possible' (Schellhorn *et al.* 1993, p. 34). The Act does not directly limit the duration of benefit but instead uses an imprecise and open-ended notion of time – by contrast with the Employment Promotion Act or the public welfare systems in some countries. Other parts of the Federal Social Assistance Act refer to 'a short period' without defining this concept more precisely.[2] Legal interpretations of this paragraph have generally taken it to mean up to six months. As an ideal, the self-help principle inherently implies that support must be temporary; benefit unlimited in time could only be feasible if self-help failed or were unachievable.

The Act itself ignores the short-term perspective to the extent that from the outset certain groups are excluded from the self-help principle – groups such as children, old people, those who are ill or disabled, and those who have responsibility for the care of children or other family members. In accordance with prevailing values about such questions as the employment of mothers, they are not required to work (full time). The legislators did not see long-term or even permanent Social Assistance benefits to these groups as desirable, but they nevertheless assented to it. For mothers with young children in Germany, such approval lasts only until the children no longer need care, unlike in the UK or even more strongly in the USA where 'welfare mothers' have been the target of criticism and attack by politicians. Some politicians were aware of the unresolved ambivalence of the Act (targeting benefits on short spells but permitting long ones); thus when the Act was passed, a Christian-Democratic Member of the *Bundestag* remarked: 'Of course we know that in spite of the preventive benefits a certain proportion of needy people will be long-term claimants. I'm thinking particularly of certain groups of the elderly who cannot be made independent of Social Assistance by means of pensions or social services' (Mrs Niggemeyer, Federal Parliament, Proceedings 1960, p. 6257). The Act thus legitimates certain groups to have long-term benefits, and thereby limits the self-help principle and its objective of only short-term benefits.

Long-term Social Assistance claims are seen as problems when individuals' rights to benefit are questioned, for instance when a fit person appears work shy. If necessary, a claimant can be compelled to return to work by

---

[2] Section 15b of the Act, introduced 1 January 1982, states that 'if it appears that periodic cash payments towards living costs are likely to be made for only a short period, they may be made in the form of repayable loans'.

reducing benefits (section 25), but the agency must offer employment opportunities (section 19, section 20). Claimants who are not actively looking for work but who ought to be doing so are in effect getting long-term benefits which have not been legitimated by society.

The Federal Social Assistance Act thus does not formally delimit the duration of benefits, in contrast with Unemployment Insurance (insurance pensions are of course terminated at death). Social Assistance is universally available for all contingencies of need and all social groups (though not for political asylum seekers since 1993), and is payable as long as the need continues. But the underlying principles of Social Assistance (residuality, self-help and the maintenance of incentives to work, such as less-eligibility by comparison with the lowest wages) nevertheless act as generalised norms which influence the duration of Social Assistance during the life course – Assistance should only meet needs when other possibilities of self-help have failed (as late as possible), and then only temporarily (as briefly as possible). The promise of benefits which are needs-driven and unlimited in duration stands in a tense relationship with the time-constrained standards but leads to the formula that Social Assistance should be paid 'as briefly as possible but as long as necessary'. Long-term Assistance claiming is always a possibility.

In the mid 1960s, the Commission of Enquiry into Social Policy saw Social Assistance in its early years as being well on the way to achieving its self-appointed goals: 'Recent examples have shown that support for special needs is continuing to develop strongly, while the provision of income support for everyday needs, the chief task of the previous public welfare system, continues to diminish' (Sozialenquête 1966, p. 339). Ten years later a leading expert reiterated this view (Gerhard Brück 1976, p. 283). But since the middle of the 1970s it has become increasingly clear that Social Assistance's expected development as support for individuals' special needs has not been fulfilled. The number of claimants of Basic Income Support rose and the question was raised – and continues to be raised – whether Social Assistance was in practice working according to its own rules. It had, in particular, become a long-lasting basic benefit for the old, single parents and the unemployed:

Adjusting Social Assistance to *individualised contingencies of need* corresponds to the situation in which it is typically geared to providing *only temporary* support. It presupposes that need contingencies arise incidentally, following singly from the adversities of fate. But it is increasingly obvious that this adjustment is structurally unsound. Because of the way their situations are structured and because they have only limited opportunities to alter them, single parents, the unemployed or pensioners are often forced to rely on Social Assistance *permanently* or for many years, therefore in effect relying on a *basic social security benefit*. (Wenzel and Leibfried 1986, p. 35; emphasis in original)

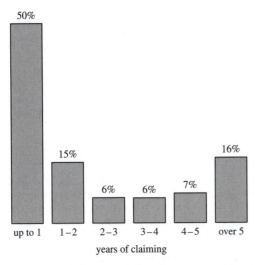

Figure 3.1 *The overall duration of Social Assistance claims in the city of Bremen*
Note: Life table estimates. 10 per cent sample (922 records) of all new Social Assistance
claims made in the city of Bremen in 1989 (see page 56).

Nowadays, critics of Social Assistance from all political parties take it
for granted that it has become a permanent pension-like benefit for certain
groups, so that calls are increasingly heard for the introduction of an independent basic security benefit into the German social services system.

How long do Social Assistance claims last? The question needs an
answer, not only to test the current assumptions about the dynamics of
poverty empirically, but also to examine the effectiveness of poverty policies. Do the course and duration of Social Assistance claims correspond to
the temporal assumptions of the Act? How many short- and long-term
claimants are there? Are disproportionate numbers of long-term claimants
found in some social groups? How can differences in the duration of benefit
be explained? To answer these questions, this chapter examines the 'objective' aspects of time; that is, the precise periods over which Social
Assistance was paid to claimants.

The duration of benefit claims

Against all expectations, we found that most claimants in the Bremen
study received Social Assistance for only brief periods. This is true even if
we take into account that some claimants have several spells of Social
Assistance, interrupted by periods without benefit payments. Figure 3.1
shows the overall or gross duration from the start of the first claim to the

end of the last or current claim, including the interruptions. The data given here and elsewhere in this section derive from the cohort of successful new claims for Social Assistance (Basic Income Support, *Hilfe zum Lebensunterhalt*) made in 1989 in the City of Bremen, followed up to September 1994 (for details see p. 56).[3] If instead we take into account only the net duration (excluding the interruptions in benefit) we find that 58 per cent of claimants were claiming Social Assistance benefits for one year or less, and only 12 per cent were claimants for five or more years. The large proportion of short claims is not an exceptional case found only during these years and in this city (see p. 57).

Beside the unexpected findings about duration, the findings about *continuity*, the second dimension of 'objective' time, are also surprising. Some 31 per cent of the claimants in Bremen had at least two spells of claiming; that is, there was an interruption. Only 6 per cent of the claimants had an unbroken spell of Social Assistance for more than five years.

The situation of poverty thus presents a complex picture of periods of deprivation, intermissions and repeated poverty, and sometimes of final escape. Stereotypical assumptions about irreversible downward careers are misleading. We do not yet know enough about what really changes in the lives of persons whose incomes periodically or finally exceed the poverty line. Findings on income dynamics suggest that leaving poverty often implies a substantial rise in income, although the new income tends to remain below the average.[4] In the case of Social Assistance claimants, finishing a spell of claiming has a special social significance because of the stigma attached to this kind of benefit, irrespective of the new income level. In any case, those who have once become poor are more likely to experience further poverty than the never-poor are to become poor. Since the analysis is based on an observation period lasting about six years from the date of the first claim, the statement in the first column of figure 3.1 that the total years of claiming were 'up to 1 year' means that these claimants made no further benefit claims during the subsequent years. A renewed claim later on is possible but not very likely.

To the extent that these claimants permanently managed to overcome their need to claim Social Assistance within a relatively short time, this benefit seems to have met its objective of being a temporary 'help to self-help' for many of them. These findings show that the proportion of Social

[3] Some people were still claiming benefit at the end of the observation period ('right censored cases') and we therefore used statistical methods to estimate the probable further duration of these instances (Kaplan-Meier). Long-term duration would be underestimated if all periods were assumed to end on that date.
[4] Krause (1998); for the OECD countries see Duncan *et al.* (1995). Berntsen and Rendtel (1991, pp. 484ff.) distinguish between short- and long-term income fluctuations.

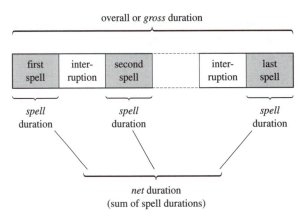

overall or *gross* duration

| first spell | inter- ruption | second spell | | inter- ruption | last spell |

spell duration   *spell* duration   *spell* duration

net duration
(sum of spell durations)

Figure 3.2 *Three measures of duration of claiming Social Assistance*

Assistance claimants who received it as a permanent basic social security benefit was appreciably smaller than that of short-term claimants.

How is duration measured?

The measurement of the duration of spells of deprivation or benefit is a political construct and not just a technical matter for the social science experts. For instance, the German statistics of 'long-term' unemployment regularly quoted in the media are based on the current convention that long-term means a duration of over one year. If unemployment were not defined as long-term until it had lasted for two (or more) years, the number of chronically unemployed people would fall considerably. Conversely, it would rise if previous spells of unemployment were included in the measure (as, for example, in the OECD statistics). Thus analysis of the duration of Social Assistance demands clarity about how it is measured. The answers to the questions 'what is the duration of spells of Social Assistance?' and 'what is the number of short- and long-term claimants?' will vary widely depending on which concept of duration is used and how 'short' and 'long' are defined. We can distinguish three separate concepts of duration (see figure 3.2).

The concept of *spell duration* is used only to measure each separate spell of Social Assistance benefit, whether the first or subsequent ones, irrespective of whether there have been other spells before or after. The concept of *net duration* refers to the combined length of all spells of benefit of one claimant within the observation period. *Gross duration* means the total period of time from the start of the first claim to the end of the last claim (if completed), including periods of interruption of benefit. The net and

Table 3.1 *The distribution of short- and long-term Social Assistance claims by different duration measures* (percentages of claimants)

	Measure of duration		
Duration	gross	net	single spell*
short (1 year or less)	50	58	72
medium (1 to 3 years)	21	24	18
long (3 to 5 years)	13	6	4
very long (over 5 years)	16	12	6

Note: *percentage of spells.
Source: Ten per cent sample of all new Social Assistance claims in the city of Bremen in 1989 (see page 56) (922 records; 1402 benefit spells).

gross concepts reflect the overall significance of Social Assistance in the life of the claimant, the gross concept expressing the fact that interruptions of claims are often only aspects of lives in continuing deprivation.

Since there are often several spells in a period of claiming, the sole use of the concept of spell duration for measurement exaggerates the incidence of short benefit claims, underrepresents prolonged dependency, and thus does not seem well suited to assessing the effectiveness of the Social Assistance Act. Regrettably, this concept of measurement was adopted in the revision of the German Social Assistance statistics in 1994.[5] By contrast, both gross and net duration, used as measures of the overall span of Social Assistance claiming, are relatively good indicators of how effective the Social Assistance Agencies are in enabling people to become independent of this type of state aid. These measures facilitate the study of questions about social stratification, such as the existence of an 'underclass'. Both measures allow for the fact that a person may have many spells on benefit, and that his or her financial situation between spells may have improved only temporarily.

Irrespective of which measure of duration is used, the short-term claimant is by far the most common type. Depending on which measure of duration is used, between half and three-quarters of all claims last for less than a year, and only between one in twenty and one in six last for more than five years (table 3.1; for a comparison with US data, see Duncan and

---

[5] In this respect the official statistics play down the extent of long-term claims. However, since claimants are sampled on a single day (31 December) the statistics at the same time tend to overestimate long-term claims (see pp. 67f.). These two effects may compensate each other. In actual fact, half of all claimants in the whole of Germany turn out to be short termers (Statistisches Bundesamt 1997b). This matches our findings for Bremen.

Hoffman 1988, p. 243). In what follows, we shall generally use the overall (gross) measure of duration. If we were to use the net measure, which also gives a meaningful picture of duration, or even the length of individual spells, it would reduce even further the number of long-term claimants and increase the short-term, thus reinforcing our message.

The statements in this chapter are based on a 'cohort' of people who first claimed Social Assistance in a specific year (1989) and whose claiming records were studied for almost six further years. Conventional cross-sectional surveys, by contrast, which count all the claimants on a chosen date, show a much higher proportion of long-term claimants. The reason is purely statistical: as long-termers are there longer, they have a higher probability of being 'caught' on the day the sample is taken.

Cross-sectional measures therefore do not give a representative picture of the lives of all those who ever experience poverty or claim Social Assistance. For example, a study in the USA showed that 65 per cent of all claimants on a single sample day had been receiving benefit for eight years or more. By contrast, only 30 per cent of all persons who had ever claimed within a specified period had received benefits for so long a time (see Buhr 1995, p. 46; table 1).[6]

A similar impression can be gained in a hospital. Visiting on a single day one would meet many long-stay patients (with, for example, cancer) while missing the large numbers of short-stay patients (e.g. for appendicectomies) who left the day before only to be replaced by other short-stay patients during the next few days. Only the medical staff who see all the patients realise how many short-stay cases pass through the wards over time. From the patient's point of view, the most typical length of a hospital stay is quite short, too. The cross-sectional measure is instead a method best suited to accounting: the finance department of the hospital (or the Social Agency) is concerned with the costs incurred every day, and from a cost point of view each long-term claimant in total outweighs many short-term claimants.

By contrast, the proportion of short-term claimants in an 'entry cohort' mirrors the average chance of terminating benefit claims. Unlike cross-sectional approaches, the longitudinal cohort approach thus measures individual life chances. It is therefore well suited to the analysis of processes of social mobility and exclusion. A similar approach has been adopted, for instance, in the study of divorce: the individual chances of having a stable marital relationship are best analysed and explained by examining marriage

---

[6] Cf. Bane and Ellwood's (1986) crucial distinction between an *ever begun* sample and a *point in time* sample. An 'ever begun' sample reflects the prevalence of poverty whereas a 'point in time' sample reflects incidence (see Walker and Leisering 1998, who give a survey of the tools of dynamic analysis). The cohort approach employed in the study reported here is a third option lying somewhere in between.

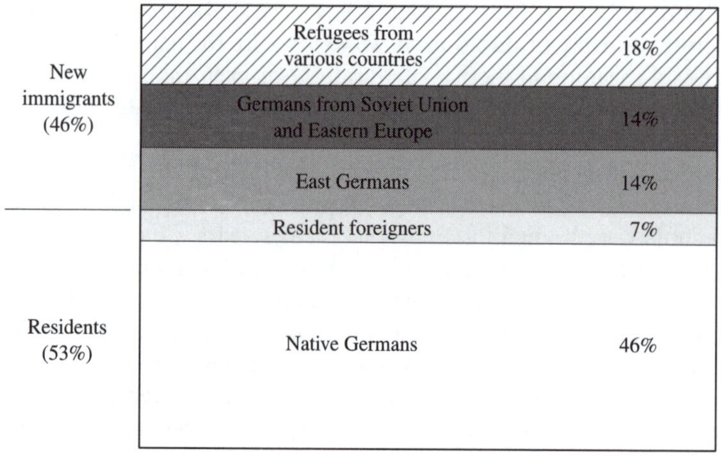

New immigrants (46%)	Refugees from various countries	18%
	Germans from Soviet Union and Eastern Europe	14%
	East Germans	14%
Residents (53%)	Resident foreigners	7%
	Native Germans	46%

Figure 3.3 *Social Assistance claimants in the applicant cohort 1989 by ethnicity and residential status*
Note: 10 per cent sample (922 records) of all new Social Assistance claims made in the city of Bremen in 1989 (see page 56).

cohorts rather than the number of divorces compared with the number of married couples in a given year. Cross-sectional measures obscure and confuse the complexity of heterogeneous factors.

Immigration and ethnicity

Almost half of those who made their first applications for Social Assistance in 1989 were people who entered Germany in that year. In previous years new immigrants accounted for only a small proportion of Social Assistance claimants, but immigration began to rise sharply from 1988 onwards. The social composition of the 1989 cohort is shown in figure 3.3 (on pp. 225–230 we compare this cohort with the new claimants of 1983, together with an outline of the underlying social changes). Note that in this section we are dealing with people who immigrated in 1989, not with 'foreigners' who may have lived in Germany for a long time or even been born in this country. In addition, many of the new immigrants are not foreigners but ethnic Germans (see below).

Slightly over half of the new claimants had been resident in Germany; that is, they were native Germans or foreigners normally resident in Germany. These foreigners, mostly Turkish, are migrant labourers who came to Germany in the three decades after 1960, or their descendants. Although they have been assimilated to some extent, social integration affecting the second and third generations is a problem for policy makers. Incidence of both income poverty and Social Assistance receipt is almost three times as high as among the German population (Habich and Krause 1997, p. 523, Hauser 1997a, pp. 538f.).

The new wave of immigrants in 1989 included three heterogeneous groups (figure 3.3). In the first were refugees from all over the world who came to Germany to apply for *political asylum*. This individual right is guaranteed by Article 16 of the Federal Republic of Germany's Constitution which, however, was amended in 1993 to contain the influx of asylum seekers. Most applications fail because the authorities or the courts deny that the person seeking asylum suffers political persecution in his or her home country. In this study the term 'refugees' refers to people who are in the process of applying for asylum, and to the large number of people whose application has been rejected but who are 'tolerated', i.e. are not facing deportation.

The second immigrant group consists of people recognised as *ethnically German* coming from the Communist countries of Eastern Europe, chiefly from Poland, and from the (then) Soviet Union. A Federal Law permits members of German communities, whose ancestors had left Germany often as long as two hundred years ago, to settle freely in Germany subject to certain regulations and annual limits. Following the changes in the Soviet Union associated with Gorbachev, the influx from these countries began to increase sharply in 1988.

The third group were *citizens of the then German Democratic Republic*, i.e., the communist eastern part of Germany. They streamed into West Germany after the Berlin Wall was opened on 9 November 1989, though small numbers had entered before that date. Until Unification Day on 3 October 1990, they had the status of immigrants. In this respect, our sample year is untypical.

We thus have a situation in which the category 'immigrants' includes large numbers of people from German ethnic or national backgrounds. Those who come from the Soviet Union, its successor states or Eastern Europe, often have occupational qualifications below German standards, and some do not even speak German. Although a considerable amount of public funding has gone to these 'foreign Germans' they do not figure as a separate group in Social Assistance statistics, not even following the statistical revisions of 1994. The statistics refer only to 'Germans', meaning Germans previously resident as well as immigrant. Our study revealed for the first time that German immigrants composed a large number of Social Assistance claimants.[7] Since this form of immigration was a hotly contested

---

[7] Hauser and Kinstler (1995) were the first to hint at immigrants among the clientele of Social Assistance though based on a selective sample.

issue in German politics in 1996, these findings made a considerable impact on the public debate. The official statistics did not distinguish between resident foreigners and recent refugee entrants either (from November 1993, though, refugees are covered by a separate benefit scheme and thus are counted separately).

These two groups of claimants – resident and immigrant – clearly differ in their life situations. Ideally, immigrants go through a period of transition. Many of them depend on Social Assistance while waiting for other benefits, and because of this their claims are often shorter than those of residents. A key conclusion of this study is that modern life gives rise to disjunctures, contingencies and crises which may lead people into temporary poverty or Social Assistance. Migration is one of these conditions. Short-term claiming is more common among immigrants than residents: 41 per cent of all resident applicants claim for a year or less, compared to 60 per cent of immigrants. By contrast, only 9 per cent of immigrants made benefit claims for over five years compared with 22 per cent of residents. Thus, Social Assistance largely acts as a means of integrating immigrants into German society.[8]

The reasons for claiming and leaving Social Assistance

Social Assistance is often criticised for requiring applicants to disclose more details about their private lives than the other social services do. But because it is designed for individual cases of need, residually after all other channels have been exhausted, a detailed enquiry into the eligibility of each individual claimant is inevitable. What the claimant experiences as a form of bureaucratic intrusion offers the social scientist a wide-ranging source of information.[9]

Until now these records have not been systematically evaluated as a source of representative data. The official statistics of reasons for claiming Social Assistance in Germany have serious shortcomings. In extracting information from the case papers we distinguished 45 distinct individual grounds for claiming, and up to three reasons per file. By comparison with other studies and with the official Social Assistance statistics, we are offering a more accurate analysis of reasons for claiming by reporting multiple reasons. Furthermore, this is the first systematic study of whether

---

[8] Büchel *et al.* (1997) arrive at the same conclusion using data from the German Socio-Economic Panel. For the USA Borjas and Hilton (1996), by contrast, report longer welfare spells for immigrant households as compared to native households.

[9] For a description of the sampling procedure and data see Buhr (1995). The sociological standard variables, education and occupation, together with health and social integration, were not always recorded in the case papers.

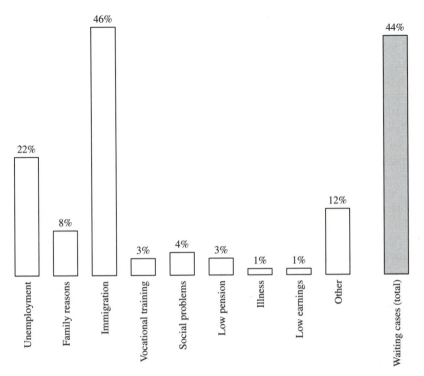

Figure 3.4 *The chief reasons for claiming Social Assistance* (at the time of the
original claim)
Note: 10 per cent sample (922 records) of all new Social Assistance claims made in the city
of Bremen in 1989 (see page 56). 'Waiting' is cutting across the other categories.

and how these reasons change during one or more of the spells of claiming
(Buhr and Voges 1991) and what the reasons are which led to the cessation
of Social Assistance claims. In addition, we were able to examine new kinds
of reasons which cut across the conventional categories.

Before we turn to reasons such as immigration, unemployment or
marital disruption, we have to emphasise a factor not normally mentioned
as a major cause of claims: in almost half of the cases studied, Social
Assistance was paid pending a decision on entitlement to or payment of a
prior benefit (see figure 3.4). This waiting for prior benefits to be paid could
be the single reason (as in 8 per cent of the cases) or it could occur in
association with others (35 per cent) such as family reasons or social problems. The reason 'waiting' shows that poverty can be caused by the welfare
state: the omissions of other state institutions are automatically passed to
Social Assistance to deal with. Unemployment Benefit due may not yet

have been paid, or the first pension payment has been held up. The path for people in straitened circumstances then soon leads to the Social Assistance Agency. But at any rate most of these 'waiting' payments of Social Assistance are of short duration.

The largest single reason for claiming Social Assistance was *immigration* (46 per cent, figure 3.4).[10] Since most applicants for political asylum lack work permits, they were hardly in a position to become independent of Social Assistance (from 1991 asylum seekers could obtain work permits). Immigrants of German ethnic origin from the Soviet Union or Eastern Europe were also forced to claim Social Assistance, since they had to pass through certain integration procedures such as first being assigned to a Transit Camp, having to attend full-time language training, or waiting for Unemployment Benefits or Old-Age Pensions to be paid. As a result, more than 90 per cent of such immigrant claimants were 'waiting'. Since they were in Germany by political invitation, their poverty could also be considered as state induced.

Unemployment was the next largest single reason, after immigration, for claiming Social Assistance (figure 3.4). One half of the claimants for whom unemployment was the chief reason were not entitled to Unemployment Benefit or Unemployment Assistance, or these benefits were too low; the other half were still 'waiting'. This, too, is clear evidence of the gaps in the prior systems of social security, for which Social Assistance is obviously filling an essential safety net function. Unemployment was also a contributory factor in many cases where the chief reason involved family problems.

Family reasons, especially following separation or divorce when the alimony or maintenance payments from the previous partner or father of the children were too low, were the chief reason for claiming in 8 per cent of the cases. 'Social problems' – meaning addictions, discharge from prison or homelessness – were the reason for claiming Social Assistance in 4 per cent of cases. These were often combined with other reasons, particularly unemployment and waiting for prior benefits. In 3 per cent of cases, Social Assistance was to enable the claimant or a member of the household to further their education or training. Here, too, there was a distinction between waiting cases and those for whom the cash benefits for occupational retraining or for further education were too low.

Inadequate pensions, sickness and low pay played only minor roles as reasons for claiming. It must be kept in mind that the sample was drawn from the cohort of new entrants to Social Assistance in 1989 and not of all

---

[10] Figure 3.4 on p. 71 refers to the 'chief reasons' for claiming, which we inferred from the (up to) three reasons recorded for every claimant (and each spell) following certain rules. If the three reasons included immigration, then this was always taken as the chief reason. Other reasons, singly or in combination, are analysed below.

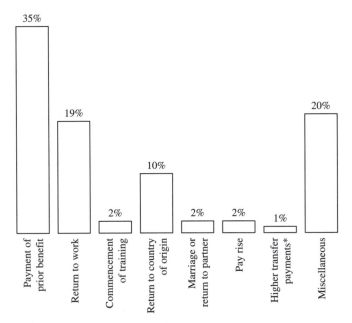

Figure 3.5 *Reasons for terminating Social Assistance claims*
Note* Fewer than 20 instances. 10 per cent sample of all new Social Assistance claims in the
city of Bremen in 1989; *n* = 1402 benefit spells (out of 922 records) (see page 56).

those who applied in earlier years and whose claims were still running in
1989. The need to supplement inadequate pensions for the elderly had been
declining since the 1970s, and the new claims of 1989 reflected that fact
more clearly than a study of all running claims would have done. It is not
yet fully recognised by the public that the elderly, often presumed to be a
group at risk of poverty, have over the past quarter century in Germany
become the least likely to be poor or claim Social Assistance. The claimants
whose low pay is being supplemented by Social Assistance – workers on
low-paid jobs, the 'working poor' – have historically composed a large proportion of the poor in the UK and the USA but in Germany they have
never been so numerous – a non-existent minimum wage notwith-
standing – and therefore appear less frequently among Social Assistance
claimants.

We now turn to the reasons for leaving Social Assistance (figure 3.5).[11]
Until 1993 the official statistics did not report these reasons.

---

[11] Figure 3.5 shows the reasons for the termination of all claiming spells and not only the last
one which could be treated as the final exit from Social Assistance. In total there were 1402
spells of claiming, of which 9 per cent were not completed.

The numerically most important reason for terminating Social Assistance claims is the payment of a prior benefit, corresponding to the 'waiting' reason for claiming. But fewer spells were concluded by the payment of prior benefits than were caused by waiting for them. This is a reflection of the fact that the reasons may change during the course of a spell; for instance, when Unemployment Benefit finally comes through it may be inadequate and require supplementation. Conversely, a spell which was not caused by waiting may be ended by payment of a prior benefit. Return to work or the commencement of training are also significant reasons for ending spells. The return to work is counted as a reason only if it was immediate; if Unemployment Assistance was paid in between, it is recorded as 'payment of prior benefit'. One in five of those returning to work did so under the special employment scheme for Social Assistance claimants (*Hilfe zur Arbeit*) which enables workers to build up entitlements to ordinary Unemployment Benefits. But in general a return to work is much less significant than might be expected from the way in which the political debate commonly blames Social Assistance exclusively on unemployment. That debate also overlooks the way in which marriage and the return to a partner can be reasons for stopping claiming (although this occurs less frequently than in the USA). The third most important reason for leaving Social Assistance is the return of immigrants to their country of origin, or removal to a different Federal *Land*.

The duration of Social Assistance in relation to the reasons for claiming

What are the connections between the reasons for claiming Social Assistance and the duration of the claims? We shall first consider the chief reasons, and then look at various combinations of reasons. Considerable differences are apparent depending on which combination of reasons caused the first claim. The shortest claims follow immigration and waiting for prior benefits, six and eight months respectively (figure 3.6).[12] Surprisingly, unemployment, too, causes only a relatively short median duration (13 months). Single claim spells caused by unemployment even last as little as three months (not shown in the figure). Where the reason was waiting for prior benefits, the median duration of Social Assistance was fully two months.

As might be expected, sickness and family reasons caused long claims. This is consistent with the findings of other studies. The comparatively short duration of claims caused by unemployment (even for claimants other than those simply waiting for benefits from the Unemployment Agency) seems to run against the assumption that unemployment has been

---

[12] This refers to the conventional statistical measure of median rather than arithmetic mean (average). In the case of the duration of claims, 'median' means that half the cases lasted longer and half lasted for a shorter period.

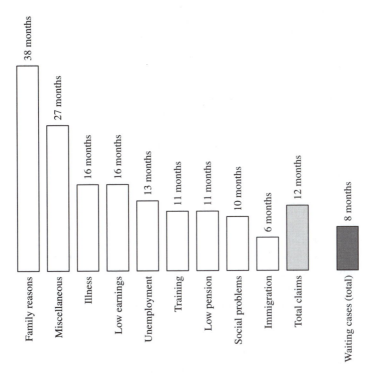

Figure 3.6 *Duration of Social Assistance by reasons for claiming*
Note: For the size of the individual groups by reason see figure 3.4 (chief reasons) on p. 71.
10 per cent sample (922 records) of all new Social Assistance claims in the city of Bremen in
1989 (see page 56).

a cause of the increase in long-term Social Assistance claims: 'As long-term
unemployment grew after 1982, the proportion of the unemployed who
subsequently had to claim Social Assistance long term has tended to
increase rather than decrease' (Schneider 1989, p. 271, similarly Scharpf
1993, p. 436). In fact the reverse seems to be true: in the Bremen entry
cohort of 1983 (see p. 227) the median duration of claiming among the
unemployed was far lower than the median duration for the whole cohort.
It follows that (other things being equal) an increase in unemployment
leads to shorter durations. In the 1989 cohort, the median duration among
the unemployed was slightly above the overall average because the large
number of short-term claims by immigrants lowered the average.

Regrettably, we do not have the information to test this hypothesis
throughout the Federal Republic. However, we know that in the north
German medium-sized city of Bielefeld the proportion of short-term
Social Assistance claimants grew throughout the 1980s. We also know that

between 1984 and 1988 when long-term unemployment reached its peak (before the labour market became tighter again in the mid 1990s), over two-thirds of the unemployed were out of work for less than a year (Klems and Schmid 1992, p. 449; in 1997 it was 66 per cent).[13] It is therefore plausible to assume that mass unemployment, at least during the 1980s and the early 1990s, has increased the proportion of short-term Social Assistance claims. This can be explained as a result of the economic crisis: labour market problems have also affected people with higher qualifications who previously would not have been vulnerable to unemployment or Social Assistance and who have a better chance of escaping from the need to claim (Andreß 1994, p. 102). By comparison with the 1960s, it is likely that average duration fell simply because the unemployed took over from the old as the largest group of claimants.

We move now from the chief reasons for claiming to a consideration of combinations of reasons. About 60 per cent of claims were occasioned by a combination of factors, in some cases very diverse and complex. Such combinations may include reasons from very different aspects of people's lives. This was almost always the case for immigrants, since their reasons for claiming included waiting for prior benefits, often associated with unemployment. We therefore look first at multiple causality among residents (figure 3.7). On average, the duration of Social Assistance rose with the number of problems a claimant had, and the more complex the combination the longer the duration. Figure 3.7 uses the number of reasons for claiming as an indicator of problems: claims lasted on average for 20 months for those with many reasons as opposed to 16 months for those with only one reason. This association also applied more weakly to those who were waiting for other benefits; as soon as an additional cause applied, the duration of the claim rose on average from nine to 16 months. Thus the shortest waiting claims were those which were ended by the payment of the relevant benefit, while the claims which ended for other reasons tended to be longer. These findings are in line with the commonsense view that the most difficult situations are those where deprivations or crises in several different areas of a person's life come together.

How far were the combinations of causes related to different types of duration of claims? The analysis in figure 3.8 on p. 78 takes unemployment as one of the causes, combined with others, and it applies to the whole

---

[13] Since 1985 spells of unemployment have been treated as new spells after each interruption, whereas up to 1984 interruptions of 13 weeks and less were disregarded (Klems and Schmid 1992, p. 449). The proportion of people unemployed long term have therefore been under-estimated since 1985. In a different respect they have been overestimated, since the data are based on cross-sectional surveys of all the unemployed in one month (September), which leads to longer durations being overrepresented. It is difficult to determine which of these two biases is the greater.

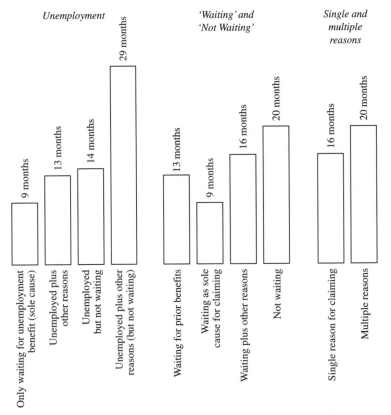

Figure 3.7 *Duration of Social Assistance claims for particular configurations of reasons for claiming* (resident claimants only)

Note: 10 per cent sample (922 records) of all new Social Assistance claims made in the city of Bremen in 1989 (see page 56).

sample, both resident and immigrant. Four types of duration are distinguished: short duration (one year or less), medium duration (one to three years), long duration (three to five years) and very long (over five years).[14]

As the analysis of average duration and chief reasons for claiming Social Assistance has already shown, unemployment is not inevitably the same as

---

[14] There are no definitive criteria of what is 'short' or 'long' duration. In defining 'short' as being 'up to one year' we are referring to the German convention that unemployment of over one year is defined as long term. In addition to these simple classifications of overall claim duration, there are also typologies of claiming careers which take account of the degree of continuity of claiming as well as the overall duration. These include 'commuters' with several long claiming spells, and 'multiple bridgers' with many shorter spells (Leisering and Zwick 1990, p. 737, similarly Salonen 1993, p. 147 for Sweden, and Bane and Ellwood 1994, pp. 40ff. for the USA, as well as Ashworth *et al.* 1992 and Walker 1994 for the UK).

78   **Poverty in the life course**

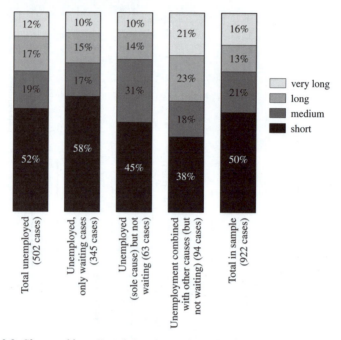

Figure 3.8 *Short and long Social Assistance claims by the unemployed*
Note: Short duration: one year or less; medium duration: one to three years; long duration: three to five years; and very long: over five years. 10 per cent sample (922 records) of all new Social Assistance claims in the city of Bremen in 1989 (see page 56).

long-term receipt of Social Assistance, even if the public discussion of the New Poverty often assumes it to be. Even if we take all claimants with unemployment as their chief or subsidiary reason for claiming (which includes most of the ethnic German immigrants from the Soviet Union and Eastern Europe) we find that 12 per cent had long durations but 52 per cent had short ones. As before, these figures apply to the gross duration of claims, including any interruptions between spells of claiming. If we take net duration alone (the sum of spells, not including the duration of interruptions), then the proportion of short-term claims is even greater (see table 3.1 on p. 66).

As expected, the proportion of short durations among unemployed people waiting for prior benefits is higher than among those who were not waiting. But even among the unemployed who were not waiting the proportion of short periods was 45 per cent. Only one in ten remained claimants for more than five years. The difference depends on whether unemployment was the sole reason for claiming in the first place or if there were further reasons, such as social problems or changes in family relationships. Claimants with a complex set of reasons had longer durations. The findings suggest that unemployment has provided Social Assistance with a class of potentially short-term clients. However, figure 3.8 suggests that unemployed people fall into a variety of groups.

Family reasons (not shown in figure 3.8), such as (lone) parenthood or inadequate maintenance after separation or divorce, were stronger reasons for 'long' or 'very long' durations of claiming than was unemployment (18 per cent and 36 per cent respectively of all cases with family reasons) and more rarely for 'short' periods (24 per cent). Nevertheless, the high proportion of short durations even among the claimants with family reasons shows that the inadequacy of social security after separation or divorce as well as for lone parents does not inevitably lead to long-term claiming.

Short durations and waiting

Are short durations of Social Assistance matters of interest to social policy or sociology? Should we describe temporary cash shortages as 'poverty' at all? Or does the 'discovery' of short periods of poverty and short Social Assistance claims divert attention away from the 'real' problem of chronic impoverishment, as dynamic poverty research has been accused of doing (Busch-Geertsema and Ruhstrat 1992)?

Since the waiting cases are very numerous in our sample, one might almost assume that most of the people whom we have categorised as short-duration claimants are 'merely' waiting cases. In fact by no means were all short-duration claimants waiting; only half of them were. While the proportion of waiting cases was 44 per cent of the total, it was 50 per cent of the short-duration claims, of which 9 per cent were only waiting and 41 per cent had a further reason for claiming. Although one would expect waiting cases to be overrepresented among the short-duration claimants, not all waiting claimants had short durations. A high proportion of short claims remains even if we remove all instances of administrative delay. Non-waiting short termers were immigrants (45 per cent), chiefly asylum seekers, and claimants whose main reason was unemployment with little or no entitlement to Unemployment Benefit or Unemployment Assistance (19 per cent; see figure 3.9).

Taking overall or gross duration (as throughout this chapter), figure 3.10 shows that for claimants not waiting for a prior benefit, short claims accounted for 44 per cent of the total, compared with 50 per cent for the whole sample. But if net durations are considered (that is, not including interruptions in the total duration), the proportion of non-waiting claimants with short durations was over half (51 per cent). In both cases,

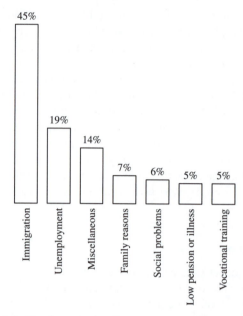

Figure 3.9 *Chief reasons for short Social Assistance claims* (one year or less; excluding waiting for prior benefits)

Note: n = 231 cases of short claims (excluding waiting cases) from 922 cases in total. 10 per cent sample (922 records) of all new Social Assistance claims in the city of Bremen in 1989 (see page 56).

therefore, short claims were just as typical for claimants who were not waiting for prior benefits.

However, since about half of all short-term claimants were waiting for other benefits, we must examine the reasons. On inspection, it emerged that what seemed a simple situation is in fact complicated. 'Waiting' may take a number of forms; it can be accompanied by other reasons for poverty; it may be the start of a long period of claiming; it could be the first link in a long chain of spells of claiming; and, finally, spells which started with waiting may not be concluded when the prior benefit arrives, or may end for other reasons. We thus found several different situations among the 401 claimants who were waiting:

(1) Claimants who were simply waiting for a prior benefit (75 people), by comparison with those whose waiting was combined with some other reason for claiming Social Assistance (326 people).
(2) Claimants with rather shorter durations (226 people waiting for 12 months or less) or with rather longer durations (175 people waiting over 12 months).

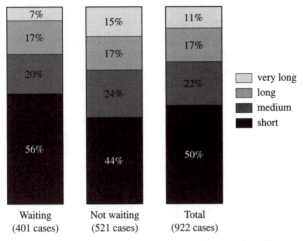

Figure 3.10 *Duration of Social Assistance among 'waiting' and 'not-waiting' claimants*

Note: Short duration: one year or less; medium duration: one to three years; long duration: three to five years; and very long: over five years. 10 per cent sample (922 records) of all new Social Assistance claims in the city of Bremen in 1989 (see page 56).

(3) Claimants whose waiting simply occasioned a single spell of claiming (261 people), compared with those who had further spells, suggesting the start of a longer claiming career (140 people).

(4) Claimants whose waiting was, as expected, terminated by the arrival of a prior benefit (235 people), as compared with those whose claims ended for other reasons (in 166 instances). In this latter group the reasons for claiming may have changed during the claim period.

The first aspect in each of these four contrasting types contains an element of the 'ideal type' of waiting. In the ideal type the four aspects would coincide: simply waiting, receiving benefit for only a single spell, which lasted for a short duration, and which was ended by payment of the prior benefit. This combination occurred in only 24 instances, representing 6 per cent of the waiting cases and barely 3 per cent in the total cohort of claimants. In such cases the initial prognosis of a short and limited duration based on the evident reason for the claim was perfectly fulfilled. The other waiting cases deviated from this ideal type to a greater or lesser degree. Most of the waiting cases concealed, behind the apparently unproblematic fact of waiting for prior benefit, more deep-seated problems which only later became apparent. These included immigration and its attendant problems of social integration or a marginal position in the labour market with insufficient entitlements to social security benefits. Waiting may be the point of departure for a longer period of dependency on Social Assistance. Even if the administrators of the prior benefits, such as the Employment Agencies, were to accelerate the delivery of their benefits, it would only have solved some of the problems of many waiting claimants. Waiting is not solely a problem of inefficient public authorities.

What, then, is poverty? Short-term claimants and those who are waiting are poor during their spells of claiming, at least to the extent that during those periods they are unable to meet their needs through their own efforts. But whoever has to rely on Social Assistance even for short periods may be thought of as poor in a wider sense: the 'asset-poor' are those who have few assets or cash reserves and who need support as soon as there is any disturbance to the normal flow of resources in their lives. 'Asset poverty' may make itself felt only at certain stages in life, for instance when people have to use Social Assistance to bridge the time until they start vocational training, although they will later achieve a secure professional position. For people in this kind of position Social Assistance can represent a sort of liquid asset, a credit which does not have to be repaid.[15] If the insecure situation lasts longer, a person has to live under the constant threat of sliding into serious poverty; one could call such situations 'structural asset poverty'. Most of those who were waiting seemed to be in this situation of poverty. What the extent of short claims and 'waiting' shows is that a great many people have very limited material resources to fall back on.

Such short periods of poverty and waiting claims are evidence of considerable social problems among the population. Since the scale of the waiting problem directly affects the volume of Social Assistance claims which is so widely debated, this form of poverty is a serious political issue. In chapter 4 we use the findings of intensive personal interviews to examine the use of Social Assistance as a means of 'bridging' periods of need.

How can the variety of durations be explained?

So far we have been treating the reasons for claiming in the narrow sense of the specific circumstances which directly caused the first claim for Social Assistance to be made. These reasons can to some extent explain why the overall duration lasted as long as it did. Certain reasons led to shorter average claiming durations than did others, but this correlation was limited and each reason gave rise to a range of both longer and shorter durations.

[15] Note that since 1982 'short' Social Assistance payments may be treated as repayable loans; 'short' being taken to mean 'up to six months' (see note 2, p.61). This applies only if it is clear at the outset of the spell that the duration will be short and limited. By contrast, Social Assistance to those 'waiting' is not reclaimed from the claimant but from the relevant administering authorities such as the Employment Agency or the Pension Insurance.

We must therefore look for better explanations of the overall duration of Social Assistance claims. In addition to the immediate causes there may be underlying factors which influence the length of claims. These may include such variables as national origin, gender, family situation, occupational qualifications or age. These background factors may offer people different chances of escaping from Social Assistance, for instance by finding a job or through access to other social services. They locate a person in the social system and are the characteristics which social scientists use to illustrate the divisions of social class and inequality. Politicians also use these crude categories when they want to describe some 'problem group' for which special measures must be designed, such as older workers, lone mothers or immigrant youth. As these background factors are widely assumed to be important to both social policy and social science, we must find out if they help to explain the duration of Social Assistance claiming.[16]

As might be anticipated, our findings are that people had to claim Social Assistance longer if they were weaker in the labour market, had limited rights to social security benefits, were older, had fewer qualifications, or were burdened by family responsibilities. Women, lone parents, people without occupational qualifications, people with children and large families were all likely to claim Social Assistance longer on average than any other comparable group. If we look at the age factor, we find a U-shape: both old people and the young had relatively longer durations of Social Assistance claims, while the middle-aged groups managed to leave Social Assistance more quickly. This probably reflects the problems older workers experience in the labour market, the inadequacy of pension entitlements in some groups, and the difficulties young people encounter in finding jobs after leaving school.

By contrast, nationality as such did not help to explain differences in the duration of claiming. Instead, the differentiating characteristic seemed to have been migration, that is residential status: whether or not people had recently entered the country or had acquired residence rights. Foreigners resident in Germany for a long time had a similar – in fact slightly shorter – duration of claiming than resident Germans (15 months on average against 18 months). But immigrants of German ethnic origin from the Soviet Union and Eastern Europe (and the immigrants from East Germany) had a significantly shorter average duration of only six months, while the refugees from Europe and other parts of the world had an average duration of eight months.

Do these background social characteristics also help to differentiate the

---

[16] The following section examines the effects of each social variable taken on its own. The effect of combinations of variables is examined in Buhr (1995, pp. 149–159) (see also chapter 6, pp. 151f.).

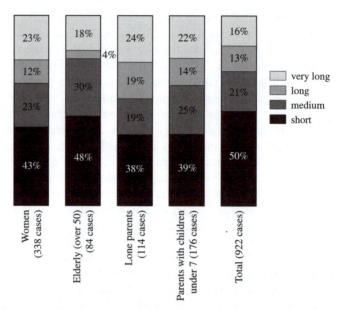

Figure 3.11 *Short and long Social Assistance claims among different social groups*
Note: Short duration: one year or less; medium duration: one to three years; long duration: three to five years; and very long: over five years. 10 per cent sample (922 records) of all new Social Assistance claims in the city of Bremen in 1989 (see page 56).

types of duration – short, medium, long and very long? Is there any correlation between the duration types and conventional 'social problem' groups? Figure 3.11 shows how the claims of some typical social groups fell into different types of duration. What was apparent from the examination of social groups' average duration is confirmed by the types of duration: women and lone parents with young children were disproportionately represented among longer-term claimants. People without occupational qualifications were also more likely to have medium or longer periods of claiming.

Social characteristics do therefore correlate with the duration of claiming, but in each social group we found some people with both longer or shorter claiming periods. Thus these demographic categories can offer only a qualified explanation why some people managed to become independent of Social Assistance quickly and made no further claims during the period of almost six years which we observed, while others did not. What this means for social policy is that conventional social characteristics are only of very limited use in identifying 'social problem groups'. Within any of these 'problem' groups, whether 'the unemployed' or 'women', the need to claim Social Assistance can vary greatly, possibly indicating what a variety of situations people find themselves in. An unemployed person who claims Social Assistance briefly and soon finds another job needs different kinds of support than a person unemployed for a long time. On the time dimension, being poor is a very heterogeneous condition (Leisering and Zwick 1990).

If time is then a meaningful dimension of poverty, we ought to not only examine the duration profiles of the 'social problem groups' but also, the other way round, the social profiles of the different types of duration. In the light of our findings we should expect the duration types to be equally heterogeneous. In what follows, we have therefore differentiated the claimants not only by the overall duration but also by the continuity of their claims. People with only one spell count as continuous claimants, those with more than one spell as discontinuous.

Our database allows us to detect distinct differences between short-term claimants and continuous claimants with very long durations. Women, the old, lone parents and parents with young children were particularly strongly represented among continuous long duration claimants. At the same time, an unexpected finding was that continuous short duration claimants (that is, with one spell lasting a year or less) and claimants who had a discontinuous record (with several spells, including claimants with very long durations) had similar social characteristics. It follows that the comparison of short- and long-term claiming as such may not get us far. Continuous long duration claimants seem to correspond most closely to the conventional stereotype of the typical long-term claimant,[17] while the people who also make long duration claims, but do so with interruptions, live in a variety of other social situations. It was also obvious that short duration claimants should not be dismissed as 'not really poor', since in terms of their social characteristics they could not easily be distinguished from long duration discontinuous claimants.

Until now different durations of claiming could only be explained to a limited extent. Neither the immediate reasons for claiming nor the under-lying social characteristics wholly account for the duration of claims. However, a totally different approach may explain duration: it is possible that the Social Assistance system itself contributes to some people's longer dependency on it. This question is examined further in chapter 6.

Conclusion

The analysis has shown that poverty situations are more unstable and there-fore harder to pin down precisely than has hitherto been assumed.

---

[17] The qualitative analysis in chapters 4 and 5 yields a further differentiation among long-term claimants, showing that only a sub-group of them comes close to the stereotype.

Assumptions that poverty is solely long term or that a large section of the population is permanently excluded are called into question. Both poverty and claiming Social Assistance are often only temporary situations, and whichever way one measures duration this generally remains the case. Long-term claimants form only a minority, albeit a not inconsiderable one. Many long-term claimants manage to leave Social Assistance periodically; some manage to make themselves independent even after long and seemingly inescapable dependency. Only one claimant in every 16 in our sample (6 per cent) had claimed Social Assistance for an unbroken period of more than five years.

Such are the findings if one takes a 'cohort' of one year's new claimants of Social Assistance and follows their records for several years, as we have done – in other words, carries out a longitudinal study. Analysis of all the current claimants on a single sample day – a cross-sectional study – would show a larger proportion of long-term claimants. But for the reasons explained above, we have not used this conventional method.

How far the exit from Social Assistance marked the end of a period of poverty was a question we could not determine using the quantitative methods reported in this chapter, but it seems to have been common (it is for instance likely when paid employment starts). Our qualitative findings point in this direction (see pp. 115, 138).The quantitative study allowed us to check that short-term claimants had not returned to Social Assistance for at least five years. Other studies based on the Socio-Economic Panel (GSOEP) confirm that this is not just a matter of income fluctuations barely above the poverty line. They suggest that income poverty in all poverty measures – Social Assistance benefit levels and above – is generally brief.

Poverty policies in Germany can thus be given a clean report in an important respect: as far as the duration of typical claims is concerned, Social Assistance in general performs its intended function of providing support in temporary situations of need. Social Assistance seen as a whole has not become a permanent pension-like benefit. On the contrary, the proportion (not the number) of long-term claimants has fallen considerably since the 1960s. That does not mean that Social Assistance has no problems, but long-term dependency is not one of them.

The problem of the increase in the number (but not the proportion) of long-term claimants remains. It is true that, contrary to its original aims, Social Assistance has increasingly been unable to confine itself to 'atypical' conditions of need; instead, it has dealt with our society's typical problems: unemployment, lone parenthood, asylum-seeking, ethnic immigration and the need for personal care in cases of disability and old age (an aspect of

Social Assistance not covered by this study). But the German political system has reacted only to the need for personal care, through the introduction of the Care Insurance scheme in 1994. It has found a 'negative solution' for asylum seekers: from 1993 the same public authorities have operated an independent support scheme, Asylum Seekers Benefit, which is similar to Social Assistance but offers lower levels of benefit. Old people who do not need personal care services are a further example of typical Social Assistance claimants (even if not as affected by poverty as before) whose inadequate incomes could better be dealt with by means of the prior social security system. This finding points to the wider question of how far poverty policies could be better integrated into social policy as a whole (see chapter 11, pp. 266–273). Finally, the inadequacies of the level of Social Assistance cash benefits and the discriminatory service administration by the Social Agencies remain critical issues which repeatedly came up in the interviews with respondents. In recent years, administrative practices have not kept pace with the changing expectations of client-centred modern social services.

What, then, are the reasons for short-term claims? Short claims are most commonly found where people are waiting for prior benefits to be paid. If we exclude these waiting cases, then immigration and unemployment are the two main factors. Our findings show that, contrary to prevailing opinion, unemployment is more likely to be connected with the risk of short- than long-term poverty. Interruptions in working careers and other discontinuities in the course of life are reflected in brief claims for Social Assistance. Short periods of claiming also result from family changes such as the birth of a child, or from intervals before taking up education or training. In all of these instances, Social Assistance takes on an important bridging function, and may provide a person with several bridging spells.

Short-term claims are also sometimes caused administratively: external institutional factors affect the Social Assistance system and contribute to short transitory periods of poverty in people's lives. The reason 'waiting' which one would assume would lead to a quick conclusion of the claim, can also mark the first step of entering a long Social Assistance career with changing reasons and many spells of claiming.

The example of unemployment shows that long-term claims cannot be blamed on any single group. It is much more common to find both short- and long-term claimants in every one of the social groups whose problems are highlighted in the debate over poverty. The usual differentiation of 'social problem' groups by their demographic characteristics (such as elderly women, young unemployed men or lone parents) conceals the fact that there are major differences within each of these groups in respect of their poverty and their duration of claiming Social Assistance. The dimension of time reveals the diversity of the problem situations within each group. The differences in the length of claims can only be explained inadequately in terms of the classic sociological variables such as age, gender and occupational status.

4 Subjective time: how Social Assistance is perceived and evaluated

The effects of Social Assistance on people's lives cannot be simply read off from how long they were dependent. What is decisive is their individual interpretations and the biographical context. We therefore have to ask how the respondents themselves saw Social Assistance, and how they evaluated claiming Social Assistance within the broader picture of their lives. While the last chapter described the receipt of Social Assistance in terms of quantitative data, in this chapter we are concerned about how the picture looked 'from the inside', as revealed by intensive open interviews which lasted sometimes several hours.

The existing literature usually assumes that claiming Social Assistance has lasting negative effects on a person's life, especially if it continues for long (e.g., Day 1992). From this perspective, the status of claimant becomes a master status[1] which obscures other aspects of individual status such as education, occupation and gender. Georg Simmel assumed that the receipt of welfare benefits totally affects the individual:

The dreadful thing about this poverty [receiving poor relief – L.L./S.L.], as opposed to merely being poor, something which everyone has to cope with on their own and which only colours one's individual situation, is that there are people whose entire social status is defined by their poverty and nothing else. (Simmel 1908, pp. 373f.)

As against this view, we aim to find out if the life histories of Social Assistance claimants are really no more than simply 'Social Assistance biographies'.

We start with the question of the claimants' subjective conceptions of time. How did they perceive time on Social Assistance? Were there subjective assumptions about the duration of claiming? Can one distinguish types of the subjective perception of time?[2] And how far do the objective

Co-author: Petra Buhr.
[1] This concept was used by Howard Becker (1963, pp. 32f.) following Everett C. Hughes.
[2] On the concept of subjective poverty in general see Hagenaars (1986).

duration and the subjective perceptions of time correspond with one another? Did the short-term claimants see their claims as merely transitional episodes, while the long-term claimants see them as a situation without end? Did the long-term claimants see themselves as caught in a vicious circle without any chance of altering their situation? Are conventional categories of short- and long-term poverty based on 'real' time at all meaningful? Subjective perspectives can help us to gain a better understanding of the meaning of time in considering poverty and Social Assistance.

The analysis of subjective time can also help to clarify the issue of the effectiveness of the Social Assistance system. The Federal Social Assistance Act is based on the assumption that ideally spells are short, and it uses precautionary measures to prevent the development of 'welfare dependency' attitudes. Do the claimants themselves make every effort not to become dependent on state benefits and to cease claiming as quickly as possible? Do they see claiming Assistance from the outset as a temporary stage in life? Or are there claimants who deliberately plan to live on Social Assistance because it is 'comfortable', thus giving new support to the debate about abuse?

Our analysis aimed to determine if there were different subjective conceptions of time among the claimants. The typology is based on the respondents' own evaluations of their spells of claiming, both those who were no longer claiming Social Assistance at the time of interview as well as those who were. The latter were also asked about their hopes and plans for getting off Social Assistance. The analysis of this qualitative material has thrown up three subjective conceptions of time which we typify as: *subjective bridgers, unsuccessful bridgers* and *subjective long-term claimants*. Figure 4.1 summarises these types and the sub-groups which compose them. The analysis was based on 62 retrospective interviews, most of which were conducted some seven to eight years after the first application for Social Assistance. Most of the respondents had thus completed their spells of claiming at some time long before the date of the interview.[3]

---

[3] Note that only 62 of the total of 74 interviews we analysed have been taken into account in this chapter. These were drawn from the earlier cohort (first application in 1983/4) supplemented by some more recent applicants. Of the 12 discarded respondents, seven gave no clear response on the subject of time; three denied they had claimed Social Assistance ('subjective non-claimants') and a further two had applied but apparently not received benefits as a result. Details of the sample can be found on page 56f. As there were few quantitative differences between the members of the 1983/4 and 1989 cohorts (see pp. 225–230), we may assume that the qualitative analysis of the more recent cohort might produce similar results. However, we can say little about immigrants since they hardly appeared in the earlier cohort. Interviews with a third cohort of new claimants interviewed in 1995 only months and not years after their first application, were being analysed and extended by a second wave of interviews at the time of writing.

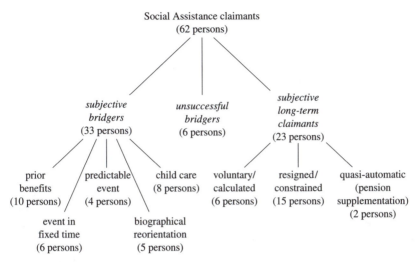

Figure 4.1 *Subjective time on Social Assistance – a typology*
Source: Social Assistance claimants in the city of Bremen, first application in 1983/84
interviewed in 1990/91 (see note 3, *n* = 62).

Subjective bridgers

'Subjective bridgers' are people who see receiving Social Assistance as a
temporary and restricted phase in their life. They composed 33 of the 62
respondents. Respondents who were no longer claiming benefits and retrospectively interpreted claiming as a bridging activity, had in general already
taken this view when they first applied. Subjective bridgers were also found
among claimants who were continuing to receive Social Assistance, who
included the few more recent claimants in the sample and those who had
been doing so for many years. In other words, it is not a matter of individual claimants retrospectively rationalising their claiming as always
intended to be of limited duration. Claimants with several spells often saw
a single spell of claiming, perhaps the current one, as a bridging episode.
Long-term claimants tend to develop a 'bridging' view or an 'escape' perspective during the period of claiming itself.

What is the relationship between the objective duration of claiming and the
subjective time perspective? Almost all those whose spells were objectively
short were also subjective bridgers. But some of the long-term claimants,
both those who had ceased claiming and those who were still doing so, nevertheless saw the spell as a temporary condition.[4] Such *subjective long-term*

[4] This type of objectively long-term 'subjective bridger' claimant has also been identified in
an American study (see Rainwater *et al.* 1986, p. 224).

bridgers as a rule expect their spell to last a long time but to have a predict-able end. These include many single parents, who expect to return to employ-ment once their children are older. Long spells of claiming can thus be subjectively viewed as 'bridging',[5] as for example by a 30-year-old single mother who had already been claiming Social Assistance for eight years when she was interviewed:

It's only temporary, even if it lasts eight or 12 years for me (respondent 27).[6]

For these 'subjective long-term bridgers' there was harmony between the intended and the objective duration of claims, by contrast with the 'unsuccessful bridgers' to be discussed below.

What is being bridged and when? Five patterns can be distinguished, which can be seen as functions of Social Assistance, both subjectively and objectively.

Bridging function 1: support while waiting for a prior benefit to be paid (ten cases)

These claimants are waiting for Unemployment Benefits or Old-Age Pensions to start, or for Unemployment Benefits to be reinstated after a period of disqualification. In the quantitative analysis these cases are described as 'waiting' cases. The reason for ending the claiming spell is already known; it is only the precise date which is uncertain. One claimant may have several such bridging spells, since the administration of such ser-vices is often very slow.

The bridging, well, it was just tiding me over until the Unemployment Benefit came. (respondent 71)

There are two typical patterns by which bridgers come to apply for Social Assistance. One group is advised by outsiders to make a claim; one might call it a passive, externally initiated, entry. These respondents might never have applied for Social Assistance if it had not been suggested by, for example, friends, relations or other authorities:

---

[5] We did not find that respondents 'cleaned up' their actual claiming careers by suggesting for instance that they had been claimants for only a year instead of the actual five. Instead, objectively longer spells were subjectively treated as 'welfare transitions' rather than 'welfare traps'.

[6] The quotations from recorded interviews with respondents in this chapter and in chapter 5 are translated from the German vernacular transcripts. The translation into comparable English expressions instead of into 'correct' English is a necessary fiction to reflect the respondents' own views and feelings as well as reporting the factual content. The authors and translator realise that this may raise ethical issues, but no judgement about the respon-dents' mode of expression is intended.

So then I was unemployed and had to wait ages for the Unemployment Benefit to come through, and so they sent me from the Employment Agency to the Social Assistance Agency. (respondent 50)

The other group had tried every possible alternative to bridge the period without help from the state until they got the service they were waiting for. These people apply for Social Assistance only when the service is delayed even longer and they find that they cannot cope any more because their savings have run out and their credit with banks and friends has been exhausted:

No, we went up with only the vaguest idea of what we might get, because we were up to the eyes in it. We only had my DM1000 a month. The rent took DM700 of that. We still haven't got Housing Benefit. You don't get Housing Benefit if you're an apprentice. We just honestly didn't know what to do. (respondent 71)

This might be called a case of delayed entry. The pattern of delayed entry was found not only among the 'waiting' cases but also in a respondent who was also a subjective bridger (for the third time) and who kept delaying claiming Social Assistance after a back operation:

All the time I hoped I'd be able to manage without that agency, I mean the Social Assistance Agency. That just didn't work out, so then I had to apply for Social Assistance. I just kept putting it off because I didn't want to [claim]. (respondent 5)

Bridging function 2: support until an event in fixed time occurs (six cases)

These are the cases where the duration and termination of the spell are fixed in advance, for example when one has to use Social Assistance to bridge the gap until higher education or training starts or continues:

Well, that was only for, well, we knew then it would only be for the five months. (respondent 26)

The claiming spells of the 'waiting' cases were terminated by institutional factors over which the claimants had no influence themselves. Against this, the claimants who were waiting for studies to start or some other fixed event to occur were using Social Assistance strategically in the knowledge that it would only be for a limited bridging period. Many used the benefit as a kind of temporary credit, insofar as Social Assistance benefits paid for periods of less than six months may be treated as repayable loans. These claimants often have no chance of getting a job in the meantime, and sometimes do not want to get one:

Anyway, the way I saw it then, was that I'd rather live off 'the Social' than do some shitty job. (respondent 26)

Bridging function 3: support until a predictable but not precisely fixed event occurs (four cases)

These people have fallen into a situation of having to claim Social Assistance unwillingly and without planning, for instance because of a separation or an increasing disability. At the start of such spells it is uncertain when the claimants will stop claiming. At the same time, they have a bridging perspective: they are claiming Social Assistance until an employment tribunal has reached a decision, or until they are fit after another operation.

I knew that it was only a temporary problem. Anyway, what I thought was that I'd be well enough again, and then I'd be able to work again. (respondent 1)

Bridging function 4: support during a period of biographical reorientation (five cases)

Here one finds people who want to change their careers, for professional development or retraining, such as a young woman whose education was interrupted, or a younger man who wants to be retrained because security and stability have become increasingly important to him. During retraining he would be able to continue to claim Social Assistance. In both examples demand for Social Assistance is calculated up to a point but seen as limited in time:

Somehow I thought . . . well, my goodness, why not take a year off, it's not the end of the world, so I may as well claim my rights for once. And then I can take my time, try to find out what I really want to do. And that's how it worked out OK. (respondent 8)

Those single parents who want to make a new start and be independent after separation or divorce also belong among the 'biographical changers' aiming at reorientation. The children then help to set the timeframe for finishing claiming Social Assistance. Hence at first sight these cases could be included among the 'bridgers during the years of child care' (the fifth bridging function). But by contrast with these bridgers, the career changers do not have the upbringing or the desire to provide child care themselves as their primary goal. These women aim to take up employment and earn their own money or pursue their careers:

Because I always need time to work out what I want to do, and other people have been claiming for years, that's how I always justify it . . . and now I realise I want to work again, I don't want to be dependent any more. (respondent 6)

Anyway, I've always had the idea that I'd do something else when the children were old enough. I mean, that was always my aim. And anyway I think it's pretty important to be able to feel that way about it. I think if I'd known then that it was going to take as long as it's turned out, I think I'd have done something else. (respondent 7)

Bridging function 5: support during the child care years (eight cases)

This group consists of women, chiefly single parents, who claim Social Assistance because they want to care for their children themselves. The reason for this may simply be that they cannot see any other way of ensuring adequate care for their children:

Well, I can't just leave them alone. That's impossible! Who's going to be responsible for the lass? My mother is ill. She can't do it. So I've got to see to it until she [the child] is old enough to be given the key and get in and out by herself and get herself something to eat. (respondent 27)

I can only work half-time. Because I've got no one to look after B. and I don't want to work full-time. I think he's far too young yet for going to a child-minder all day, that's what I think. (respondent 2)

Other women tried to get back to employment but had to give it up because of the adverse effects on the children:

I've already tried to get out to work, like a couple of hours cleaning in the morning, and I had a carer for J. but it didn't work. The kid changed for the worse, somehow, she was very weepy, and so I thought, no, this won't do. (respondent 49)

Some women were determined to put their children's welfare first by bringing them up themselves. These women have deliberately chosen Social Assistance instead of employment or occupational training:

At that point in fact I'd decided to live very simply, just for the sake of the child. And that's what I've done. It's simply the right thing to do. I didn't study for nothing and I know all about the development stages small children go through, and I'm not going to risk that for anything. (respondent 14)

Yes, that's when it started, I decided to stay at home, and because you can get it in this country I lived off Social Assistance, so I wasn't working any longer. . . . that was what I chose to do, because I was a single parent, and anyway I could manage OK to begin with . . . (respondent 3)

And I just took it for granted that what I'm here for is to look after my children and don't have to go out to earn my living myself. (respondent 4)

The time perspective of these 'bridgers for child care' refers to the future: they want to escape from Social Assistance and think it may be possible when the children are older. These women want to return to their careers or continue with their education or training. Some women preferred a partial escape from Social Assistance, by working part time to begin with and only working full time later on. We have called them 'subjective long-term bridgers' because they are taking a long duration of claiming into account.

Because I'd already said that when the children were in the kindergarten I'd go back to work. I don't want to live on Social Assistance all my life. (respondent 36)

You only get Social Assistance until the child is 12 and then it's finished. Then I won't get it any longer. And I don't want to. I want to do something for myself again. (respondent 27)

Women who claim Social Assistance until the child has reached a specific age, such as for entering kindergarten, could in principle also be included under the second bridging function, seeking support until an event in fixed time occurs. But by contrast with the cases in which it is already clear how and when the spell of claiming will end, these women cannot be sure that when the time comes they will find suitable employment. Other women left open the question of precisely when they might want to return to work, even if they used a fixed point in time as a guide, such as the child's entry to kindergarten or school. They defined this point in relation to the development of the child:

I've assumed that it would go on like this until the second school year, I mean, from the third school year at the earliest, that is, in three or four years, I'd be able to get back to some job. (respondent 3)

These cases could also be allocated to bridging function 3: 'support until a predictable but not precisely fixed event occurs', in this case the independence of the child. The common feature is the women's emphasis on upbringing and child care, which is why they have been treated as forming a single specialised sub-group.

One can summarise the situation of subjective bridgers by emphasising that at least they did not display any of the dangerous consequences of long-term dependence on Social Assistance. On the contrary, they used Social Assistance as the Federal Social Assistance Act intended, as a form of transitional help. These claimants were perfectly aware that Social Assistance was or would be no more than a temporary stage in their lives, even if it was a long stage especially for single parents. The respondents were not counting on life-long dependence on Social Assistance.

The case of a particular group of claimants, especially women, who deliberately chose Social Assistance to make full use of their statutory freedom not to work while bringing up a family, shows that the availability of Social Assistance can influence life choices. These claimants were found right across the five sub-groups and should be described as calculated bridgers, by contrast with the 'calculated long-term claimants' to be described below.

Unsuccessful bridgers

At the outset, the 'unsuccessful bridgers' (six out of 62 respondents) were using Social Assistance as no more than a temporary expedient. But whatever their initial time perspectives when claiming started, they ended up with a continuous (or occasionally discontinuous) long claiming career. The respondents had to claim Social Assistance following a separation or divorce, or because of unemployment related to illness. All of them, however, thought that they would only have to use Social Assistance temporarily until they were able to stand on their own feet again or find a foothold in the job market:

Maybe I thought I'd be able to start over again with it. I mean, get a new flat and Social Assistance for a start, that's what I thought. But not that I'd stay stuck in it so long. (respondent 72)

At that time I was still thinking I'd get Social Assistance to tide me over. Because no one else wanted to help any longer. (respondent 85)

The respondents tried to terminate their claiming spells by applying for jobs or retraining opportunities, but they still did not manage to become permanently independent of Social Assistance:

Every time it got a bit better, when I earned some money as a cashier, it soon got worse again . . . (respondent 85)

The repeated trip to the Social Assistance Agency could then seem very hard:

Well, I mean, I'd lost my job again. I thought, oh bugger it, now you've got to go down to the Social Assistance Agency again. (respondent 46)

When it became clear that their escape from Social Assistance could not be accomplished as fast as they had anticipated, the respondents felt they were caught in a vicious circle. The longer duration of claiming Social Assistance among the unsuccessful bridgers cannot be traced back to institutional factors in the sense that the respondents were deprived of incentives to work. One exception was the woman who was prevented from taking up a job offer by the authorities because her child was too young:

Now, to tell the truth, I hadn't thought it would work out like that. It was only meant to help me over, like. I mean, I said to myself, you'll go and get a job then, night cleaning or anything. And then the Social Work Department put its foot down and said, no, the kiddy is too young, you mustn't go out to work. (respondent 59)

Nevertheless, most of the unsuccessful bridgers managed to break away from Social Assistance after many years and many unsuccessful attempts. Some of them managed to escape not through their own efforts at earning a living but by help of some external event, such as reconciliation with their former husband or because a new partner found work. The actual duration of claiming was not always 'very long' judged by objective criteria, but the point was that subjectively it had lasted far longer than originally expected. The respondents saw the discrepancy between their original subjective perspective and the actual duration as oppressive. Nor would they have been happy to start with the expectation that the spell of claiming was likely to be a long one, as in the case of the subjective long-term bridgers above. Social Assistance was simply not a satisfactory solution in the eyes of the unsuccessful bridgers; rather, it was a bad solution with which they did not feel comfortable:

I didn't want to! And to be honest I'd rather have gone back 'on the game' again [prostitution] than back to the [Social Assistance] Agency. (respondent 46)

Subjective long-term claimants

'Subjective long-term claimants' (23 out of 62 cases) were the respondents who, in the absence of any alternatives or for reasons of convenience, accepted living for a long time on Social Assistance, or who could imagine doing so and said so explicitly. Three sub-groups can be distinguished.

Sub-group 1: voluntary or calculated long-term claimants (six cases)

While some of the subjective bridgers also deliberately decided to depend on Social Assistance for a while, the subjective long-term claimants did not see Social Assistance merely as a bridging device to use, for instance, until a specific event took place, or a stage of child rearing or career development was completed. Instead, much more commonly they had not rejected the possibility of claiming repeatedly or for life, because claiming seemed to them to be a viable solution or an easy way out. Even people who have only just started claiming Social Assistance may be calculating to depend on it for a long time. These respondents could see life as a claimant as among the acceptable options available to them in making their life choices.

Among the voluntary long-term claimants were not only those who had been claiming for a single long spell, often for years, but also those who claimed for many separate spells, some of them quite short, spread over a very long period. Seen as individual spells they appear to reflect subjective bridging, but seen as a whole they instead suggest voluntary long-term claiming. The claimants 'keep going back' to Social Assistance. A subjective long-term perspective does not necessarily lead to claiming for a single continuous spell. In these instances Social Assistance supports an irregular employment career interspersed with periods of voluntary unemployment. Social Assistance then provides a way of repeatedly bridging the gap until Unemployment Benefit becomes payable after the disqualification period, or until a new job turns up or a new retraining scheme is started:

And if that safety net hadn't been hanging there, I probably wouldn't have pranced about in that foolhardy way, or I would've felt less like doing something new, and perhaps I might even have looked after my money better. (respondent 54)

Some of these instances seem to reflect the common public stereotypes of claimants. The respondents fully realised that this was the case:

The way they talk about it is, I'm deliberately scrounging on the welfare. Yeah, yeah, I know, I know! (respondent 18)

In other instances Social Assistance was not used 'yet again' but as a permanent alternative to (full-time) work or to being kept in a marriage (four cases):

I mean, he's a good chap, we get on OK, but no, I'm not going to move in with him or join up with him somehow, just for money or whatever, no, I won't do that. No, then I'd rather go on living like this, you know? (respondent 76)

This woman was working part time because she thought it important not to be fully dependent on Social Assistance:

Because, then you can always say, well, I'm working aren't I? That's always better than saying I'm living off the state. (respondent 76)

Another respondent found herself in a 'poverty trap'. Her job was still open to her, but she would have earned so little from it that it would not have improved her situation compared with life on Social Assistance. It was thus rational for her to continue to claim Social Assistance for the time being. We could have classified her in the next sub-group (resigned or constrained long-term claimants) because she found it hard to get jobs because of her age and health, but because she continued to seek out openings in the labour market and weighed up the available alternatives we placed her among the voluntary long-term claimants.

A calculated intention to adopt a long-term perspective may change in the course of time. Institutional factors such as conflicts with officials may play some role in this, as in the case of a woman who quarrelled with Agency staff over removal costs and decided to escape from Social Assistance instead.

Sub-group 2: resigned or constrained long-term claimants (15 cases)

These respondents no longer saw any escape routes from dependency and/or had been compelled to accommodate themselves to life as a claimant. This did not necessarily mean that the respondents had a resigned or despondent outlook on every aspect of life, although it may be the case. They were not 'living off the state' because it was comfortable or because it seemed the best alternative for their situation. Rather, they had become claimants against their wills and continued to remain so because there seemed to be no alternative. In general they reckoned they had little chance of ever escaping from Social Assistance:

I've asked again and again for them to sign me off the sick and fit for work, but they won't . . . because the doctors won't take the responsibility, because there are always bumps, like, and then I start to bleed again. Well, now . . . I've got to get a disability pension, at 37. (respondent 92)

In some instances it seemed as if the respondents had given up expecting anything from life:

Nowadays, I'm not counting on anything in life, anyway, not any longer, since everything has gone wrong. I've got nothing, what can I hope for? No job, no cash, no girlfriend or wife, I just hang around with nothing to do. (respondent 9)

In such instances the reasons why Social Assistance was claimed for many years may have had their roots in the family situation, for example, when a mother had to provide permanent care for a child with disabilities:

They told me that she'd never be able to talk, never walk, never sit up or be able to do anything at all. Well, that's how it was, so then I couldn't do anything else, I had to be there to look after her all the time, didn't I? (respondent 25)

In other cases the reasons why claimants depended on Social Assistance for so long lay in the limited openings which the labour market offered them, because of their age, illness or disabilities, or limited skills (illiteracy in one case). These conditions make sustained employment difficult and can lead to complete unemployability. In some instances addictions, debts or a criminal record added to the problems. It was striking how often respondents who fell into this group reported growing up in families suffering many problems, violence or removal of the children into care. The causes of later problems often seemed rooted early in life:

And so I was labelled a casual labourer, just like that, and that was that. (respondent 62)

This group contained not only those with many years of unbroken claiming (six cases) but rather more for whom claiming was often an extremely spasmodic event (nine cases). These discontinuous claimants often tried repeatedly but in vain to overcome the need to claim:

And I tried being retrained. I tried absolutely everything. And in spite of all that I'm still sitting here, I'm still out of work. (respondent 62)

In many ways the resigned claimants resembled the popular view of 'the (long-term) poor'. The difference was that in four instances resigned or constrained claimants actually managed to break their dependence on Social Assistance. Each of these respondents had only the faintest idea at the start of their claiming period that their situation might ever improve. They felt that they were caught in a vicious circle, as respondent 64 said, or thought that they would have to claim Social Assistance until they were pensioned (respondent 53), or they were simply labelled as a hopeless case by the Social Assistance Agency officials (respondent 61). As they nevertheless managed to stop claiming after a long period, we could call this averted dependency.

Sub-group 3: quasi-automatic long-term claiming through pension supplementation (two cases)

These are people who claimed Social Assistance continuously for years (or with only minor breaks) simply because their pension for either age or disability was too low. In this sub-group it was clear from the outset that claimants were unlikely ever to escape from Social Assistance, not at any rate by their own efforts. Nevertheless, claimants might become ineligible for Social Assistance if the pension levels were raised – or if the Social Assistance benefit rates were frozen, as has happened several times since the 1970s.

I got my pension and then they added this on. Then it all goes on by itself, doesn't it, even now. (respondent 40)

Objective and subjective time

Conclusions can now be drawn from this evidence about the subjective perspectives on time held by Social Assistance claimants. Analysis shows that most of the claimants consciously plan in terms of time. Very few – only seven out of 74 claimants – expressed no clear perspectives on time. However, the objective duration of claiming and the subjective perception of time did not always coincide. Even those who were objectively long-term claimants could at the same time be 'subjective bridgers'. They depended on Social Assistance for long periods but were always conscious that the time would be delimited. 'Subjective time' thus relativises objective duration. Social Assistance performs an important function for longer-term subjective bridgers in that it covers a critical period in their lives. We have distinguished five of these bridging functions which correspond to the different kinds of critical periods. The point is that 'bridging' is not just a theoretical way of seeing short spells of claiming, but reflects an idea which claimants themselves associate with Social Assistance.

This analysis of people's own perspectives on time, and especially the discovery that people can have the intention of bridging and escape even when claiming for long periods, leads to the conclusion that long-term claimants by no means necessarily fit the stereotype of marginalised and apathetic Social Assistance dependents. Even among those we classified as subjective long-term claimants (those who assume an indefinite duration of claiming) are some for whom psycho-social deterioration is unlikely: calculated long-term claimants count on claiming for very long periods or life-long because it seems a passable solution in the context of their restricted options and limitations. Both they and the subjective long-term bridgers have an active approach to Social Assistance.

The real 'problem cases' are found elsewhere. Resigned or constrained claimants, and to some extent the unsuccessful bridgers (those for whom a temporary claim grew longer than envisaged), stand out as the categories closest to those most commonly pictured in other studies of poverty. What stands out here is progressive decline and the claimants' sense of being inescapably excluded from society. Their self-esteem has been damaged to some degree, and they feel they are in a constant state of psychological crisis.

What does this mean for an evaluation of the effectiveness of Social Assistance? First, long-term claiming is the exceptional case, and Social Assistance mainly provides temporary emergency help as intended (see chapter 3). Second, even long-term claims, which the Federal Social Assistance Act had foreseen at least as a possibility, do not inevitably lead into the vicious circles of popular imagination. In reality, what Social Assistance does is to carry out various useful functions which enable people to get on with their lives, which they see as quite helpful or positively supportive. Only in rare cases can the life histories of people who claim Social Assistance for a shorter or longer period be seen as 'Social Assistance biographies', in the sense of a life of passive suffering ruled by Social Assistance. The common situation is that in the broad context of people's whole lives, Social Assistance means nothing more than temporary support, even if sometimes for an objectively long time.

Making sense of Social Assistance – biographical evaluations by claimants

We have seen that one cannot understand what poverty means to claimants simply by measuring by the calendar how long their claims lasted. It is necessary to know how claiming fitted into the whole plan of their lives, to find, for instance, that a long spell was just a way of bridging a gap. So far, when we have referred to the biographical context we have chiefly focused on the temporal structure of life. We have already touched upon evaluative aspects, such as claimants' life projects and assessments of what was important or unimportant in their lives, what was worth striving for and what was not. Thus some women valued Social Assistance positively because it enabled them to devote themselves to their children's upbringing. In what follows, we examine more closely the place respondents gave to Social Assistance in making sense of their lives.

The effects of relying on Social Assistance on the attitudes and capacities of the respondents must be interpreted through such *biographical evaluations*. We insist that the effects of claiming Social Assistance have to be understood in the context of each individual life history; one cannot assume a standardised effect based on the discriminating characteristics of Social Assistance in general, or on common social variables such as age, gender, occupational status or the duration of benefit.

Poverty research until now has assumed that the effects of poverty grow increasingly severe and deep-seated over time. Against this, some studies suggest that economic deprivation can have different meanings for the individuals affected, depending on social conditions. But it is more than that: depending on the circumstances, claiming Social Assistance can be part of a person's deliberate attempt to take active control over his or her life, and in that way it can acquire significance for their life history. By contrast with almost all previous studies which have tried to interpret the life histories of disadvantaged people, the biographical approach adopted here does not confine itself to the antecedents of the problem but includes the parallel and subsequent life history. And by antecedents we do not mean just the cumulative process of the descent into Social Assistance, but equally the biographical background against which Social Assistance can instead stand out as a positive feature.

Many of the respondents criticised the Social Assistance Agency in one way or another, and referred to negative aspects of claiming. In these respects our findings fully coincide with those of previous studies such as Lompe (1987) or Jacobs and Ringbeck (1994), and for this reason we are not analysing these direct outcomes of claiming in greater detail here (for details see Buhr 1995, pp. 203–207). But the direct, oppressive concomitants of claiming do not necessarily result in a negative evaluation of Social Assistance as a whole. That can only be determined in the context of the whole life history.

The analysis of the interviews suggests four patterns of evaluating Social Assistance claiming. We call them patterns rather than types because some respondents made use of more than one pattern at a time.

1 *Neutral evaluation (simultaneous):* a qualified view of Social Assistance by comparison with simultaneous experiences in other parts of their lives which were experienced as being even more stressful;
2 *Neutral evaluation (retrospective):* a qualified view of Social Assistance against the background of earlier less-satisfying experiences;
3 *Positive evaluation:* a balanced biographical view which accepts the negative aspects of claiming because Social Assistance simultaneously

supports the pursuit of other more highly valued goals in life (a positive function of Social Assistance);

4 *Negative evaluation:* an overall negative view of Social Assistance where the results of claiming could not be positively balanced, neither in comparative terms nor against any positive function of Social Assistance.

Pattern 1: Neutral evaluation (simultaneous): A qualified view of Social Assistance because of the eclipsing effect of other even more stressful experiences

In these instances Social Assistance was given limited emphasis because it was outweighed by other experiences. It was seen as less significant than events which were felt to be considerably more burdensome. It was relegated to a secondary position in people's struggles, outweighed by more pressing concerns. These included the after-effects of illness (two cases) and divorce (two cases[7]), or other events such as an impending criminal prosecution, but unemployment was the chief example, in five instances.

God, this business of going to the Social Agency, that wasn't so bad, that was just a side-effect. When you get divorced, well, I mean, it wasn't a real divorce but a separation and you're ill like I was, that was all a lot worse. (respondent 1)

All I can say is, being unemployed is the worst thing that can happen to you. It's the last straw. It's like being in jail, just about. You don't have to have done anything wrong but it soon feels just like it. (respondent 30)

Many of the limitations in the quality of their lives about which the respondents complained, such as isolation, were thus not the direct results of claiming Social Assistance but were apparent before, perhaps because of unemployment or other circumstances like illness. The social decline often began much earlier for the respondents:

Well, yes, I mean, what hit me hardest in all those years was that I had to drop out of high school and go to the disabled workshop, that was. That was the breaking point. That's this social decline, isn't it? That hit me very hard. But you can cope with it. (respondent 53)

I had a job in the shipyard, just before it closed, then I was on the dole again. Yes, that's when everything started to go down for me, and for the family. That started with the Unemployment Benefit, it only ran for a year. Then it went down to Unemployment Assistance, with the Social Assistance supplement. (respondent 62)

---

[7] In both of these cases it was the stress of the prior separation which diminished the significance of the claim for Social Assistance which had resulted from the split-up. In another instance (respondent 42) the separation, which was extremely painful, took place years after the initial claim for Social Assistance, but this later experience made the Social Assistance claim seem less weighty in retrospect.

Pattern 2: Neutral evaluation (retrospective): a qualified view of Social Assistance against the background of earlier experiences.

Poverty is relative. The concept of 'relative deprivation' (Runciman 1966) means that the experience of deprivation arises from making comparisons with other groups (reference groups) or with one's own future goals or one's position earlier in life. For several of the respondents in our study the antecedents to their claims were important in explaining how far they perceived the financial restrictions as burdensome. One group hardly experienced any financial loss through claiming Social Assistance:

But I can't really say that it was any worse for me at that time, because I'd never really had much money any time in my life. (respondent 44)

For some, Social Assistance actually improved the situation, for instance for a woman married to a compulsive gambler:

Well, there wasn't anything left when he'd been playing. It was a lot easier after he'd left, at least I'd got the rent and all, the electricity and all the rest. (respondent 25)

Social Assistance is a low level of material existence but it is not the lowest. At bottom, the financial limitations were not felt to be troublesome by those respondents who lived in social milieux in which it is normal not to have much money:

Well, it was probably because we were living in a student hostel and no one had any money. (respondent 10)

Pattern 3: Positive evaluation: a balanced biographical view – weighing the immediate negative aspects against the wider lifetime benefits

Social Assistance can be subjectively seen in a positive light when it has a wider utility in enabling life plans to be carried through. The possible negative effects on the quality of life may be balanced out in some way. Thus Social Assistance can actually have the positive effect of helping to prevent social decline and the loss of a person's home:

I think it's very good that Social Assistance is there; it's a kind of emergency life belt. You aren't thrown right onto the street. In my case I was terrified I'd lose my apartment because I couldn't afford to pay the rent. I was pretty depressed just then. (respondent 20; respondent 21 was similar)

In other instances Social Assistance enabled people to sort out their situations, to make a fresh start in their lives and find a new independence. This was particularly the case for women who were escaping from unbearable marriages:

That's why I must say, after all that, I thought it was absolutely great getting that Social Assistance . . . I felt somehow quite rich, anyway more secure and a lot more independent. In spite of everything. (respondent 7)

I just about became an adult for the first time, six years ago, yes, it was like I grew up at last. (respondent 11)

Finally, Social Assistance also enables people to achieve their goals in life, especially (in five instances) to bring up their children:[8]

At that point in fact I'd decided to live very simply, just for the sake of the child. (respondent 14)

And then I looked on it as some kind of a present. Now I could get some sleep, now I could look after my children, I could be at home for them, I could help them and all that, and then we were able to have a real family life. (respondent 25)

What is important in all these cases is the biographical perspective: the perception of Social Assistance is framed against a background of other earlier experiences (the pattern of a qualified view) or the opportunities in life which it opens up (the pattern of a balanced biographical view). There is fluidity between the two patterns. Recounting the negative accompanying aspects of claiming Social Assistance does not necessarily imply attaching a negative meaning to it as a whole. The possible negative consequences are not experienced as burdensome because there are wider implications of Social Assistance claiming which are more important to the claimants. Social Assistance can therefore be a reasonably attractive option.

These findings correspond with those of the (few) similar research studies. A study of single parent claimants in Berlin reported:

The attitude of respondents to Social Assistance in West Berlin is ambivalent. Almost all the women who completed a written questionnaire felt that claiming Social Assistance restricted their opportunities for development in one way or another . . . What is, however, notable is that the qualitative data show so clearly that significantly fewer respondents than expected expressed their perception of a loss of self-respect. They felt they had a legitimate right . . . as long as the children's age and need for care continued, or as long as they were not offered any reasonable alternative by which to combine child care with employment or retraining, or they had no chance of achieving a reasonable level of income . . . The way the women evaluated their position varied according to how they weighed up their previous

---

[8] The instances described above as 'subjective bridgers during child care years' and the respondents referred to here, who saw Social Assistance as having the positive function of enabling them to care for their children, were not precisely the same groups, because not all subjective bridgers had a clearly articulated child-care goal. Conversely, some of the groups with other subjective perspectives on time contained people who were enabled by Social Assistance to care for their children or provide them with a 'proper' family life (as in the case of one mother whose attitude was that of a 'resigned or constrained claimant').

lives, that is, which life experiences they took into account and how they felt about them. From this longer perspective, claiming Social Assistance did not always seem a deterioration. (Drauschke *et al.* 1993, pp. 304 f., similarly Mädje and Neusüß 1996)

Another study, of poverty in the rural area of the Westerwald, remarked on the position of divorced or separated women:

The benefits of Social Assistance allowed the women to rearrange their lives in ways which were both necessary and personally attractive. . . . In this way, Social Assistance functioned to give these women some autonomy for the first time. (Hübinger 1991, p. 84)

Pattern 4: Negative evaluation: an overall negative view in the light of predominantly negative consequences

Social Assistance attracts a negative subjective meaning when the burdensome aspects dominate and there is no possibility of balancing them against any wider functions. In that respect, one can see this as reflecting a type of claimant rather than a pattern of evaluation comparable with other patterns. In some instances claiming had such lasting consequences that the overall judgement was negative even if some isolated positive features of Social Assistance were seen. In these instances Social Assistance had not enabled people to pursue their personal goals. Rather, it was in clear conflict with the achievement of objectives relating to individual independence or consumption. This picture of a 'generally negative attitude' corresponds to the stereotype of the 'typical' claimant held by the public and many of the research studies. But it refers to only one attitudinal type among several, and one which was not even dominant in our sample.

Other studies have also found some evidence that people make judgements about claiming Social Assistance against the background of their total life experiences. A study by Herbert Jacobs and Anna Ringbeck (1994) asked: 'How has your life changed by claiming Social Assistance?', and thus raised the question of 'life before claiming' as a point of comparison. A total of 52 per cent of those questioned considered that living on Social Assistance had made little or no difference to their lives. In spite of this the authors of the study felt that a cautionary note was required:

Many of the current claimants who replied that it made no difference to them to live on Social Assistance nevertheless reported negative experiences which they had had as the result of claiming. Thus 35% mentioned financial restrictions; 12% thought that they were patronised and made to feel dependent; 9% said that their lives were monotonous; and 7% said that their self-respect had fallen. This supports our view that we are justified in being sceptical about the response that claiming made no difference. (Jacobs and Ringbeck 1994, p. 86)

This statement fails to do justice to the complexity of the relationship between the objective consequences of Social Assistance claiming and their subjective evaluation. It is not a matter of the objectively negative aspects simply being subjectively revalued and dismissively glossed over by respondents. Instead, our qualitative analysis shows that an overall modest or positive evaluation of Social Assistance and the experience of problematic consequences are not mutually exclusive. Claimants place the claiming experience in the context of their biographies by way of 'biographical qualification' of claiming and by drawing up 'biographical balance-sheets'.

We conclude that when people claim Social Assistance, even for a long time, it does not necessarily affect their whole lives negatively. Claiming can have a positive significance in the lives of both short- and long-term claimants. For instance, it can help people to avoid homelessness, to reorientate themselves in their occupational lives or qualifications, to gain a breathing space at a time of crisis, to start an independent life, to enable them to care for their children, or to support a period of integration into German society after immigration. All these purposes can help to outweigh the individual negative concomitants of claiming. The significance of Social Assistance to the claimants depends on how they personally make sense of it in their lives as a whole. What is decisive in this process is the individuals' subjective perception of time and their evaluation of their lives. Thus the life histories of Social Assistance claimants are seldom if ever simply 'Social Assistance biographies'.

5   Living time: poverty careers between exclusion and integration

The life courses of disadvantaged or marginalised people are often described as 'poverty careers' by social scientists and the public. Of course this is not meant in the sense of pursuing a career, as on an occupational ladder, but its opposite, i.e. cumulative social decline. We sometimes talk about 'domestic careers' or 'drug careers', and there are similar expressions like 'the vicious circle of poverty' or 'poverty traps'. While so far we have been looking at phases of claiming Social Assistance, including subjective biographical evaluations (chapters 3 and 4), we now turn to the whole *life course* of the respondents, including more of their histories before and after claiming. This calls into question the way in which the idea of a 'poverty career' has been used in poverty research focusing solely on decline. We shall develop a more complex model of careers, one which takes in the popular view but which also allows consideration of rising careers and other types of life course. This chapter therefore aims to contribute to an overarching theoretical perspective on the sociology of poverty.

'Careers' as components of the *life course* are the outcome of the interplay of *individual action* and *institutional control*. One can see this in occupational careers, where people climb the institutionally predefined rungs of a career ladder. As far as poverty careers are concerned, all three aspects are conventionally dealt with in a one-sided manner: people always refer to *problematic* life courses, such as careers in decline; to *problematic* behaviours, chiefly deviant, though also apathetic behaviour as a victim of overwhelming fate; and to *problematic* consequences of social institutions in the form of social control, stigmatisation and discrimination by the welfare state. There is a presumed causal connection between these three elements: Social developments such as unemployment and lack of housing are said to push the life courses of poor people or of Social Assistance claimants towards the margins without hope of escape. The pressure of

Co-author: Monika Ludwig.

material deprivations, it is assumed, makes subjectively meaningful action impossible; deviant behaviour may occur, but generally passive endurance prevails. Finally, the welfare state is depicted as promoting the exclusion of the poor instead of working to reintegrate them into society.

On these assumptions, poverty careers appear as processes of marginalisation and exclusion in a comprehensive sense: they embrace social decline (the loss of status), individual enduring and institutional exclusion. But the theme of this chapter is that this is not always the case. The conventional perspective does not do justice to the reality of poverty. Poverty careers may also end in social revival or at least in a normalisation of the life course, achieved through the action of the person affected and supported by welfare state institutions.

'Poverty careers': old and new concepts

The sociological concept of 'career' originated in the Chicago school of sociology and the work of other early sociologists such as Karl Mannheim (1940). It started with an emphasis on occupational careers, but later social-problems theorists, mainly symbolic interactionists such as Howard Becker (1963), applied it more explicitly to problematic or deviant careers.[1] These influences affected German sociological research into marginalised groups in the 1960s and particularly in the 1970s, focusing especially on the *Obdachlosen* (literally 'homeless': those in low-standard municipal housing and deprived of the legal rights of tenants or other residents). A full-blown 'sociology of homelessness' was developed, and in its wake other forms of poverty attracted scarcely any interest among German sociologists (Haferkamp 1977, p. 193). Drawing on cultural sociology, such as Oscar Lewis's (sub-) 'Culture of Poverty' (Lewis 1959), and the labelling approach which emphasised the stigmatisation of the poor, sociologists began to focus on long-term processes of reinforcement. German sociological research into poverty, deprivation and underprivilege thus developed an explicitly dynamic perspective, one which seems almost to have been forgotten today, but which was always directed 'downwards'.

The analyses of reinforcement processes were always focused upon specific groups among the poor and were strongly critical of society. This resulted in processes, behaviours and institutions being analysed in terms of a *deterministic career model* which assumed a pre-programmed process of social decline. This approach faded in the later 1970s and gradually gave way to greater differentiation, for example with regard to the duration of living

---

[1] For a thorough-going historical reconstruction of the concept of career in sociology see Ludwig (1996, chapter 1).

under poverty conditions (Albrecht 1973, Friedrich *et al.* 1979). What was becoming apparent in the research on the *Obdachlosen* at the end of the 1970s became fully developed in the research on the *Nichtseßhaften* (literally 'unsettled': street people, 'rough sleepers', or those sleeping in municipal and other hostels) in the 1980s: a distinctively biographical approach to poverty research (Giesbrecht 1987, Rohrmann 1987, Albrecht *et al.* 1990). Researchers discovered that some of the poor were dealing with their problems successfully and, depending on their circumstances, were even able to find ways of escaping from poverty. Thus towards the end of the 1970s, theoretical outlines were being developed of a probable but not fully determined process, a *probabilistic career model*.

German poverty research in the 1980s did not, however, pick up this development. Instead, the new dominant discussion was not about marginalised groups but about the phenomenon of mass unemployment, and poverty research formed part of the body of research on the unemployed. The debate was more macro-sociological and led to the concepts of the 'new poverty' and the 'two-thirds society' which are still in use today (see pp. 188, 194, 251–4). The 'new poverty' was conceived in terms of careers: long-term unemployment was seen to become a problem of poverty caused by institutional processes; Unemployment Insurance forced the unemployed downwards step by step and paved the way to their poverty or to the Social Assistance Agency which then confirmed their exclusion from normal society. The debate about the 'new poverty' was influenced by a deterministic career model in which (in contrast to the research on marginal groups) the behaviour of those affected was not given any particular attention. This narrowing was paradoxically connected with the concept of the *Lebenslage* (life situation; see p. 21). Originally formulated in German theoretical usage by Gerhard Weisser to emphasise scope of action, it is nowadays chiefly used as a tool in considering multiple deprivations in a range of aspects of living, and thus to determine the general restriction of life by poverty, in other words the degree of behavioural incapacity (Nahnsen 1975, Lompe 1987, Döring *et al.* 1990b).

The concept of the poverty career has been used in three distinct ways: to describe a process of downward occupational class mobility, as a process of socialisation into a deviant lifestyle, and as a process of social 'coping'.

Poverty careers conceived as *downward class mobility* are derived from the occupational careers of the research subjects and their families. The path to poverty is seen as a loss of status brought about by powerful social forces which can only be endured but not contested. This is based on a deterministic model. Unemployment, the 'new poverty', and the poverty of old age, were each treated as phenomena which could be explained by downward class mobility (such as by Lompe *et al.* 1987 and Bujard and Lange 1978).

Research into homelessness and rough sleepers expresses the assumption that poverty careers can be identified by *deviant lifestyles*. Such a concept of poverty career is also deterministic, assuming a generationally transmitted intensification of poverty. Socialisation into a sub-cultural milieu and labelling by the forces of social control mean that the affected person compulsorily develops a deviant identity and cannot escape from the marginalised position, with consequences for occupational behaviour, family formation and education.

If poverty careers are seen as social *coping*, they are also pathways through poverty.[2] Instead of assuming that poverty careers are necessarily connected with passive endurance or deviant behaviour, the representatives of this tendency seize on the 'probabilistic' career model mentioned above: the social behaviour of the affected person is directed towards conquering a crisis or a poverty condition and may be so successful that the damaged occupational or family process is once again repaired and poverty is not allowed to become entrenched. At the same time, poverty careers are seen as processes of change in status affecting several aspects of life but without suggesting that all such aspects are negatively affected to the same extent. However, the escape routes from poverty have not been systematically elaborated in the formation of this theory, and the dominant model is still the process of social decline.

The deterministic and probabilistic career models – independently of their use in poverty research – have both been thoroughly criticised by sociologists since the 1980s. David Luckenbill and Joel Best (1981) as well as Axel Groenemeyer (1990) support their case with a body of empirical studies into individual aspects of deviancy. Groenemeyer, for instance, showed that even the 'drug career' did not accord with the ruling assumptions of programmed social decline. Luckenbill and Best conceptualised career as social coping. This variant had previously been significant in the field of medical sociology and had been especially developed by Uta Gerhardt since the 1970s in her concept of the 'patient career' (Gerhardt 1979, 1986a, 1990, 1991). She suggested a *contingent career model* which leads beyond both the deterministic and the probabilistic models. In this model, the development of the career is unpredictable and therefore a variety of outcomes are possible. The social behaviour or action of the affected person (in Gerhardt's case medical patients) is to be seen as actual coping with work and family problems ('socio-economic coping') and not

---

[2] For a comprehensive descriptive study of coping with 'Life on a low income', including references to processes of downward class mobility, see Elaine Kempson (1996) on Britain.

simply as a matter of interpreting the life situation the person is in, as some studies would have it ('psychological coping'). Uta Gerhardt's approach and her related method based on the construction of 'ideal types' (after Max Weber) have become the model which this chapter follows (Gerhardt 1986b, 1994, 1996, 1998, 1999b; exemplary case studies 1986a, 1998b).

Poverty researchers, by contrast, have continued to view coping behaviours through the probabilistic, if not actually deterministic, lens. German poverty research still awaits a contingent career model that systematically considers routes out of poverty, i.e., escape careers. Isolated examples can be found in the USA and England. Frank F. Furstenberg and others (1987) studied the life trajectories of young single mothers in the USA in later life, showing the relevance of a model of this kind for social problem groups. Escape from poverty is a possibility. Among the chief UK studies were Rutter and Madge (1976) and Coffield *et al.* (1980), whose work was part of a research programme set up by the government to test its political assertion that, in spite of economic growth and the welfare state, the poor were stuck in a 'cycle of deprivation' or a 'cycle of disadvantage'. In spite of enormous research efforts no evidence for this assertion was found in the UK. That has not thwarted continued belief in the political myth. These studies drew attention to a new career type: if escape from poverty was in fact possible, then the career of a poor individual could be a rising one.

The one-sidedness of conventional research also has methodological roots: if one studies exclusively those who are currently poor one sees only social decline, because those who have successfully escaped from poverty are not found among those poor. However, if one follows a 'cohort' (a group followed over time from the common outset of their careers, as in our study of all individuals who began claiming Social Assistance in Bremen in 1983 and 1989), or if one carries out a panel study (the same people are periodically interviewed over an extended time-span), then the question of the course of a person's further career becomes an empirical one.

Three career models can thus be distinguished: a deterministic variant – the 'one-way street' model, in which movement is possible in only a single direction; a probabilistic model – the 'corridor' model, in which movement is possible in more than one direction but within narrow confines; and a contingent model – the 'cross-roads' model, in which a number of routes are possible. The deterministic and probabilistic models still predominate in research circles, but the outlines of a more comprehensive contingent model with greater explanatory power are beginning to become apparent. We therefore want to test three hypotheses in this chapter as the basis of a new contingent cross-roads model of poverty careers:

(1) *Life courses* can be as variable (that is, contingent) within the ambit of poverty as elsewhere. A wide range of patterns may be found: social

decline; reinforcement; relative stabilisation and consolidation at a low standard of living; as well as genuine upward social mobility.

(2) The *individuals* affected by poverty are active agents, not necessarily passive victims. A wide range of behaviour patterns can be found: active coping; apathy; deviant behaviour; overcoming poverty – all are empirically identified patterns. Even poor people can learn new modes of action.

(3) Social policy *institutions* do not work in an exclusively repressive and excluding manner, but can also be beneficial to their users. The balance which users draw between the costs and benefits determines the significance of Social Assistance to their lives.

The outcome of a poverty career does not have to be exclusion, downward social mobility, a deviant lifestyle or a greater or lesser adjustment to living in poverty; indeed, a potential foreseeable outcome of the contingent cross-roads model is the re-normalisation of vulnerable life courses. In this context 'normalisation' means reintegration into the myriad conventional ways in which people find security in their lives, in the labour market, in their families or in non-stigmatising systems of social security.

Three research questions follow from the above hypotheses: What are the different vulnerable life-course patterns? What individual behaviour patterns are found among the poor in their interactions with social institutions? What sorts of 'poverty careers' are there, seen as the interaction of observed life-course patterns with individual behavioural patterns? For instance, do downward courses necessarily correspond to passive behaviour and upward ones to active responses, or are there unexpected combinations of behaviours and life-course patterns? To answer these questions we turn now to the findings of a wide-ranging qualitative study of a sample of new claimants of Social Assistance in Bremen in 1983, based on intensive open interviews carried out in 1990–91 (for further details see pp. 56f.; 90, and Ludwig 1996).[3]

---

[3] The research method follows that of Uta Gerhardt, which is based on Max Weber (for references to Gerhardt's writings on methodology and exemplary studies see p. 112f.). Each case is individually analysed (with information from the administrative case files supplementing the interview data) and then compared with others. 'Ideal types' of life courses, orientations of action and careers are formulated and the real cases are then compared with the ideal types in order to delimit the range of variation of the actual cases and to 'understand' them (*Verstehen*). As this type of analysis is highly labour intensive, this chapter will report on the in-depth analysis of 31 of the 74 usable interviews (out of a total of 89 completed interviews). Comparison of the 31 cases with the full qualitative sample, as well as with the entire survey population of 586 recorded cases, showed a high degree of consistency in terms of variables such as age and gender, although longer-term claimants were overrepresented. This minor distortion may rather strengthen our assertion that permanent decline is only one type among others. Details of the lives of the respondents have been altered to prevent identification.

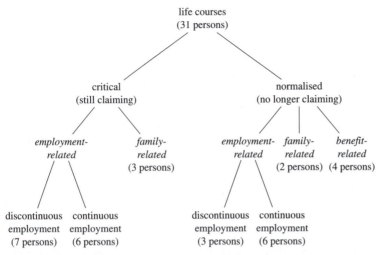

Figure 5.1 *Life courses of Social Assistance claimants*
Source: Social Assistance claimants in the city of Bremen, first applications in 1983/84, interviewed in 1990/91 (see note 3, *n* = 31).

Where do they come from, where do they go to?
Critical and normalised life courses

Two principal types of vulnerable life course can be distinguished, the critical and the normal. We have divided them into five sub-groups, two of which are critical courses and three are normalised. Two of these sub-groups can be subdivided even further (figure 5.1). How did this typology arise and what were the criteria by which these distinctions were made?

Since the poor are defined in this study as those who claim Social Assistance, the current claiming status is the first distinguishing criterion in the comparison of life courses. In this chapter we focus on people who first claimed Social Assistance in 1983 and whose claiming careers were followed in their case papers and files up to 1989. They were then interviewed two years later. We counted as normalised the life courses of those people who at the time of the interview had not claimed Social Assistance in the preceding two years, because to cease claiming was a step forward towards access to the normal sources of a secure existence, such as work, family or prior social security benefits. But if the claiming was still continuing or had ceased less than two years previously, the life course was treated as being critical. Critical life courses can be seen as careers in decline, while normalised life courses suggest careers in ascent because to claim Social Assistance implies lowering one's status while to cease claiming is the ideal to strive towards (even if the Federal Social Assistance Act allows the possibility of making permanent claims; see pp. 59–63). The distinction between decline and ascent may seem crude, but it is useful as a starting point of an ideal-typical approach which allows for further differentiation in the course of the research process.

The second criterion for distinguishing life courses was the reason for first claiming Social Assistance or – for those with normalised life courses – the reason for ceasing to claim. We do not confine our analysis to reasons related to the labour market, such as the preceding employment record (as happens in the class-mobility model of poverty careers). We call these employment-related life courses. Family events can be just as important reasons for claiming: we call these family-related life courses. Nowadays, individual life experiences in the welfare state are also significant, i.e., the various (successful) pathways people traverse through the programmes of income maintenance, these could be considered 'benefit-related' normalisation of the life course.

In the third place, life courses (and occupational careers in particular) can be distinguished by how continuous and secure they are. To consider continuous and discontinuous, interrupted careers is a further step away from the deterministic one-way model towards the contingent cross-roads career model, since it avoids simplistic causal associations: our findings suggest that a critical life course is not necessarily indicative of an insecure and interrupted occupational career, and conversely, people's life courses can become normalised even where their situation is not simply a temporary interruption of an otherwise continuous occupational career.

We turn now to the details of the five types summarised in figure 5.1.

Employment-related critical life course

This group consists of people who continue to claim Social Assistance or who have only recently ceased doing so, who first became eligible to claim because of a crisis in their occupational position. Two sub-groups can be distinguished: (a) those with a work record (employment record) which had previously been periodically interrupted, and (b) those with a previously unbroken work record.

Discontinuous employment history
before claiming Social Assistance

This group with an interrupted work record roughly corresponds to the one-dimensional picture presented in many studies of poverty careers. The occupational career breaks down at an early stage, perhaps because training is unfinished or is not matched by entry to a corresponding occupation. This is then followed by intermittent periods of work, unemployment and

Social Assistance claiming. The chances of escape are slim and the whole way of life settles down to a marginal existence. Signs of social marginalisation often appear at an early stage, becoming apparent well before the first Social Assistance claim is made. A 'pure' example can be seen when a person's life started in a poor family and remained there; in other words when membership in a low social class developed into a marginal position, or when such a position was itself transferred between generations. In many of these instances one cannot really see any downward social mobility, since the person simply moves horizontally from one low status position to another, for instance from prisoner to Social Assistance claimant.

Specific social problems are the decisive factors. The three cases which come closest to the ideal type share three salient characteristics: early experience of contact with welfare organisations (in care as children), an early failure and discouragement in employment, and, connected with this, a deviant lifestyle in the form of homelessness and minor crime, at least periodically. Working careers which are interrupted not just by unemployment but by such problems as homelessness or crime lead to permanently marginalised life courses – we did not find such examples among those with normalised life courses, that is, those who had ceased to claim Social Assistance. One may conclude that representatives of the group of 'employment-related critical life courses, discontinuous cases' do not normally have a chance to permanently escape Social Assistance.

Things look better for those whose working careers were interrupted 'only' by unemployment. There are some indications that this is a phenomenon which occurs mainly during a limited period of life and is caused by ambivalent attitudes towards working. The men in question (respondents 24 and 54) both reported changing their attitude towards work in order to give themselves greater security. And we did in fact find one respondent who showed the same tendencies in the period before claiming, but who ceased claiming and thus normalised his life course. Some people manage to escape Social Assistance if only to an interrupted working career.

The discontinuous sub-group of the employment-related critical life courses seem to reflect male poverty careers, though the sample contains one woman whose career shows many of the same characteristics, even if not so clearly (respondent 72).

Continuous employment history before claiming Social Assistance
This group contains those whose work record did not run into difficulty until later in their life course. The respondents worked for years, sometimes for decades, without interruptions in their occupations until some critical event or experience led to an abrupt break in their work and forced them to claim Social Assistance. By contrast with the discontinuous type, this group

showed signs of a 'real' change in social position: the respondent fell from a middle or even high status to a low one (a vertical status shift). In the ideal type the fall is very distinct, that is, the respondent held a high occupational status position before claiming. Such long-lasting continuous working careers were found across a range from highly qualified to unqualified occupations. Again by contrast with the discontinuous working careers, in this group the path to Social Assistance was marked by unpredictable critical events (contingencies). Even 'normal' working-class families are often vulnerable to poverty, as they have little protection against the adverse circumstances which can easily overwhelm them. Their entitlements to Social Insurance benefits or benefits from private insurances in the case of the self-employed may be inadequate to cover their needs.

Accidents and the onset of long-term sickness were two events which particularly affected the life careers of (later) Social Assistance claimants. People with discontinuous working careers also experienced events like these as handicaps in the labour market. Respondent 9 was disabled by a road accident at an early age, with consequences which completely prevented him from entering the labour market. The onset of long-term sickness later in working life can have effects no less decisive. Illness caused a massive occupational decline for respondent 85 from which his good education and long work for the same employer could not protect him. Unlike respondent 9, respondent 85 suffered badly from the negative public reactions to the visible and obvious symptoms of his illness, and these were more serious than his reduced ability to work.

The chances of escape from Social Assistance were not equally distributed among this group, especially not in terms of gender. The men, such as respondent 39 and respondent 85, had educational qualifications, had achieved correspondingly high salary levels over the years and had thus acquired rights to Social Insurance benefits that they will be able to claim when they reach pension age or become unable to work. Claiming a pension, then, will be a transition into a 'normal benefit career', that is, escape from Social Assistance through the payment of prior Social Insurance benefits. For younger men like respondent 23, return to work was an escape route from Social Assistance. But the women with continuous working careers were generally earning less because they lacked qualifications; their earnings-related pension entitlements were correspondingly lower and therefore they had no route out of Social Assistance (respondents 11 and 40).

Family-related critical life course

This group consists of people who were forced to claim Social Assistance because of crises in their family life or relations with their partners and whose claims still continued or had only recently ceased. It contained only three out of the 31 respondents; in each case the reason for claiming was a separation or divorce. The children were still young and employment was scarcely a realistic option for their mothers. The paucity of examples of this type is significant, in that there seem to be few instances in which family-related events and developments lead to long-lasting claiming. Unlike employment-related poverty, poverty careers triggered by family events may cease even after periods of six, seven or eight years of Social Assistance. Family problems seem less likely to lead to inevitable social decline than problematic employment careers do. People, often with children, who are forced by separation or divorce into claiming Social Assistance, usually manage to escape sooner or later; they then automatically fall out of this group of 'critical life courses' (defined as still claiming Social Assistance at the time of the interview or less than two years before).

The respondents can be ranked according to the extent to which social problems were apparent even before their Social Assistance claims. Some women's claims were predictable early in their lives, while for others the claim was the consequence of a comparatively unproblematic separation in an unexceptional family career. A definitive escape from Social Assistance seems a possibility in all the cases studied, for two reasons. First, they may make themselves independent of Social Assistance through the normalisation of their family career, that is to say, through a new marriage or partnership. Respondent 49 would have managed this if her new husband had not become unemployed just before their marriage. We did in fact find women with normalised family careers who became independent of Social Assistance in this way after long periods of claiming. Second, women could finally escape from Social Assistance by normalising their working careers. This is more difficult for them than for men because their lower qualifications and part-time working make it hard to achieve earnings above Social Assistance levels. In the group of 'continuous employment-related normalised' respondents there was one woman who had found this way out of Social Assistance (respondent 1), but even her experience was only made possible because she received regular maintenance payments from her former husband.

We turn now from the 'critical' to the 'normalised' life courses, that is, from those respondents who were continuing to claim Social Assistance to those who had ceased to do so at least two years before the interview (that is, six years after their first application for Assistance at the latest).

Employment-related normalised life course

This group consists of people who were able to cease claiming because they had resumed work and who had been able to remain independent of Social

Assistance for some time. Like the 'critical' group, this too can be divided into two sub-groups according to whether their employment record after ceasing to claim was continuous or interrupted.

Discontinuous employment career after claiming

There were few cases in this group. What they had in common was that their working careers had not stabilised in the two years which had elapsed between ceasing to claim and being interviewed. The respondents had not been able to find any well-paid or secure employment and a return to Social Assistance was possible at any time. Nevertheless, these people were in fact back at work after ceasing to claim, but it was in low-paid, insecure jobs not tied to Social Insurance (without opportunity to make employer-matched contributions to build up benefit entitlements) or deficient in some other way. But the instability of social recovery was not in all cases obvious at the moment of ceasing to claim. Moreover, even when the previous working career had been normal and stable, Social Assistance receipt could be terminated by discontinuous employment (as with respondent 52). The respondents who normalised their careers through discontinuous employment have such heterogeneous previous histories that no single categorisation can cover them all.

Continuous employment career after claiming

This group consists of those people who were able to escape from Social Assistance by finding work and were then able to stabilise their careers. This reflects a genuine social ascent, by contrast to the previous 'interrupted' group where good pay and security were lacking and return to Social Assistance was always a risk. For the continuous group, the history preceding Social Assistance ran along the normal lines of work and family, lacking notable events until whatever precipitated the Social Assistance claim. The only exception was respondent 7 whose family career was fraught with problems even before the Social Assistance claim.

The escape from Social Assistance generally tended in an upward direction, even if the return to work did not always follow immediately after the cessation of claiming. Social Assistance was followed by a further spell of unemployment or illness for respondents 20 and 21; further education supported by special benefits was what allowed respondents 7 and 26 to leave Social Assistance. These former claimants reached occupational positions which evinced notable stability, even if the grade of these positions differed by education.

There was no single factor marking the lives of respondents in this group (those for whom the way out of Social Assistance led to continuous employment) before they first claimed Social Assistance, but two patterns emerged. In one, the respondent had a full work record for years before first claiming, but for a variety of different employers. In the 1970s frequent job changes incurred little risk, but in the 1980s this pattern was often accompanied by short periods of unemployment between jobs and also by Social Assistance claims. The other pattern was that claiming began as a result of family crisis, but was terminated by taking up work (only women showed this pattern).

In this group the duration of the Social Assistance claim was generally of short, or at most of medium duration. The path to Social Assistance often reflected the problems of a critical period of transition in life. Respondents 20 and 21 often changed jobs and suffered short periods of unemployment in between. In as far as Social Assistance had to be claimed because prior Social Insurance benefits such as Unemployment Insurance had not been paid (the 'waiting' category; see chapter 3), the claim was predictably limited in duration. But even the unemployment itself could be seen in these cases as a transitional event in life. Not all Social Assistance spells can be explained in this way, though. For instance, the entry to Social Assistance by respondent 7 had been well signposted long before it happened, but it had then been impossible to estimate how long it would last.

Family-related normalised life course

Family events facilitated permanent exit from Social Assistance for respondents in this group. Taking up employment added to that: the respondents' own work efforts furthered the social and economic recovery of their families. But the crucial factor was the change in the family situation. There were two instances in this group, and like the 'family-related critical' group they were all women. For women, change in family status was a potential escape route from Social Assistance, but there were no cases where a man was enabled to give up claiming Social Assistance through the normalisation of his family situation.

Both women forming this group found new partners who were good earners and married them after some years; around the same time the women themselves returned to work. Permanent escape from Social Assistance signals social recovery. Both instances show that the need to claim Social Assistance can be overcome even after long periods of claiming – but this was more true of family-related claiming careers than of employment-related ones. We have seen the potential for escape even among the respondents with family-related critical careers still claiming Social Assistance. The prehistory of claiming was similar for women with both critical and normalised claiming careers; in all cases there was a critical family situation, compounded in one instance by particular social problems which at least temporarily contributed to the social decline.

Benefit-related normalised life course

Some people achieve a decisive end to their period of claiming Social Assistance even without work or family careers. These are the life courses which became normalised through a switch to the 'regular' systems of social security. The quantitative analysis in chapter 3 has already shown that transfer payments based on prior Social Insurance entitlements – chiefly Unemployment Benefit, but also pension payments – were one of the most important reasons for terminating Social Assistance receipt. 'Benefit-related normalised life courses', however, only refers to those people who transferred to dependence on Social Insurance benefits permanently.[4] It is a heterogeneous group: after all, permanent receipt of a pension is commonplace and is a normal social expectation after a given age, but the permanent receipt of unemployment benefits would be seen as a sign of marginalisation. The financial difference, too, can be great, since the replacement rate in earnings-related Unemployment Insurance is usually lower than for pensions. While claiming contributory Unemployment Benefit is felt to be 'normal' by comparison with Social Assistance, the means-tested Unemployment Assistance is already on the boundary between respectable and marginal and seen instead as a low-status programme of transfer payments.

Two respondents transferred to pensions: respondent 37 claimed a pension on age grounds, and respondent 53 claimed early retirement on sickness grounds. In both cases the pension gave them higher incomes. Respondent 53, who tops up his pension by working in a sheltered workshop, actually achieved an income level which he had never previously enjoyed. Pensions are secure and the risk of social decline is minimal. There were no significant common features in the lives of the members of this group before first claiming Social Assistance. There were irregular work records as well as regular ones.

We can now summarise our analysis of life-course patterns under Social Assistance. There are two types: the critical life course in which Social Assistance claiming persists, and the normalised one in which it has been terminated. Permanent social decline (understood as long-lasting Social Assistance still in payment at the time of interviewing) is thus only one type

---

[4] This means that the group does not include, for example, 'waiting cases' who overcame their Social Assistance claim through prior entitlements and then their unemployment as well. Such instances would have been allocated to the 'employment-related normalised life course'.

of life course (the critical kind) beside the normalised kind in which the temporary need to claim Social Assistance has been permanently over-come. This distinction with which we started the analysis, based on theo-retical assumptions and a pilot study, has turned out to yield a meaningful interpretation of the empirical data.

The key constellation which distinguishes critical from normalised life courses is an unsuccessful employment career at an early stage combined with certain social problems. This constellation was indeed found only among critical life courses. But, by contrast, it is not uncommon for respon-dents with early difficulties in their family careers to escape from Social Assistance; such problems were found in both principal types of life course. Favourable prehistories were found not only among respondents with normalised life courses but also among those with critical careers; a crisis in one's employment at a later stage is most likely to lead to continuing Social Assistance claims when it occurs in later life or when associated with chronic illness. But family crises later in life do not necessarily lead to permanent Social Assistance; at any rate, no such instances were found in our sample.

Living with poverty: endurance or coping?

From the 1960s onwards, the interest in marginalised groups in society and the sociological theory of social problems both contributed to the tendency for researchers in Germany and elsewhere to identify social work and Social Assistance as forces of social control.[5] They criticised the way in which the 'controlling' welfare system validated the existing structure of society and stigmatised deviant people. Their model of social control allowed for a structural ambiguity between the supportive and controlling functions of welfare, between the needs of the clients and the interests of the administra-tion. In their critique of society, however, these researchers tended to place more weight on the control function; they saw the supportive aspects of ser-vices as playing only a peripheral or rather ideological role. The 'costs' of Social Assistance were always emphasised without mentioning 'benefits' (for an exception, see Henkel and Pavelka 1981).

However, the relationship between Social Assistance and its claimants is influenced not simply by controlling but also by supportive orientations, and this leads to tensions. We therefore sought to examine the claimants' action orientations in all their ambivalence, to find out how the aspects of control and support interacted. Did the respondents see themselves as

---

[5] See Blum (1964), Peters (1968), Hollstein and Meinhold (1973), Peters and Cremer-Schäfer (1975) and Bellebaum *et al.* (1985).

passive victims of social control or as active users of the supportive services? The control perspective suggests that people are victimised, that they become passive objects of stigmatisation and exclusion. Conversely, the support perspective implies opportunities for autonomous action. Drawing on concepts developed by Fritz Schütze (1981) we ask: did the claimants see poverty as a matter of (passive) *endurance* or of *'action'* (active *coping*)? (see also chapter 2, pp. 35–40.)[6]

If poverty careers are conceptualised in a way which allows for support (by institutions) and active coping (by individuals), one must ask to what coping refers. With what problems do individuals try to cope? Coping strategies can considerably influence a poverty career. From a control perspective the claimants' lives seem largely determined by Social Assistance and the welfare state. Then the immediate problems associated with claiming Assistance become the focus of inquiry, such as unacceptable treatment in the Social Assistance Agency or by neighbours, feelings of shame, struggling with arbitrary behaviour by the authorities, trying to manage with inadequate benefits and so on. But poor people must not be seen as confined to their roles as claimants: they naturally experience the same biographical problems which face everyone, such as bringing up children, suffering illness, or having their plans upset by changes in their lives. Such problems may strike them as far more important.

Thus, claimants see themselves as fighting to cope on two fronts: against the problems caused by the institutions of the welfare state and against their more general biographical problems. One can understand the claimants' life chances and their ways of coping only if one looks at their overall biographical orientations and not simply at the immediate problems of claiming Social Assistance. It is these orientations and goals that give a different meaning to periods spent on Social Assistance in each life (see the analysis of biographical evaluation processes in chapter 4). There is no justification for the stereotyped assumption that biographical orientations

---

[6] Schütze's terms are *Erleiden* and *Handeln*. In this section we often use the narrower term '(active) coping' instead of 'action' (*Handeln*) because this is what we are mainly interested in. Besides 'coping', 'action' also encompasses 'strategic action'. The following typology of individual ways of dealing with Social Assistance includes both forms of action, but the focus of our analysis is on coping (for the distinction between coping with Social Assistance and strategic use of it see Leisering 1997c). Instead of 'career' Schütze uses the concept of *Verlaufskurve* (trajectory) adapted from Glaser and Strauss. Following Uta Gerhardt (1986a) we prefer the term 'career' which places a stronger emphasis on the agency of the persons involved in the sense of Max Weber's concept of meaningful action (for a critique of Schütze see Gerhardt 1986a, pp. 26–30; see also the illuminating critique by Martin Kohli 1981). In the case of 'endurance' the concept of 'career' may be disputed. But even in the most extreme type of mere endurance identified in our study – the 'victim' – behaviours could still be referred to as 'action' in the general sociological sense. Moreover, we do not suggest, as Schütze tends to, that endurance is the characteristic type of behaviour in marginality.

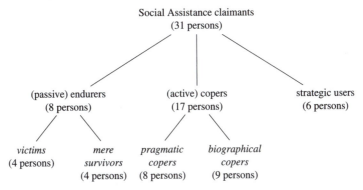

Figure 5.2 *Living with Social Assistance – a typology*
Source: Social Assistance claimants in the city of Bremen, first applications in 1983/84, interviewed in 1990/91 (see note 3 on p. 114, *n* = 31).

are virtually extinguished by the marginalised status of Social Assistance claimants. One has to examine coping strategies more broadly: living with poverty is more than simply coping with being poor. As we shall show, Social Assistance claimants vary widely in respect of their horizon of action.[7]

When asking for coping strategies we do not just mean 'psychological coping' or the maintenance of personal identity – whether claimants come to terms with their situations and can give them some meaning in their lives in the senses studied by analysts of change in identities and subjective meanings. What we are chiefly concerned with is the question of 'socio-economic coping' (Gerhardt 1986a). How did the respondents deal with their practical problems, such as how to organise their family lives, how to keep up social relationships and plan for their further education and occupation? This kind of coping can make a big difference to the way in which the poverty career proceeds. It is about changing a situation, not just about interpreting it in a different way.

We distinguish five modes of dealing with Social Assistance on the basis of our intensive analysis and systematic comparison of the interviews. They ranged all the way from a totally restricted lifestyle, ruled by the social control of the Social Assistance Agency, to an active use of Social Assistance in order to achieve broader objectives in life. The 31 respondents were distributed among the five types as follows: four victims; four mere survivors; eight pragmatic copers; nine biographical copers; and, as a special group, six strategic users (figure 5.2).

Victims see no future in their lives in any important respect. The chief

---

[7] Cf. the concept of 'biographisation' of action in chapter 2, pp. 36f.

problem for them all was long-term unemployment, whether continuous or interrupted. Respondents found it impossible to overcome unemployment as well as its consequences; they could not come to terms with having no work and having to live on Social Assistance, and could not even settle into a deviant lifestyle. They could find neither greater nor lesser solutions to their problems, yet always expected they would find work again one day. But since they could not see any way out through their own efforts, their hopes turned instead to the welfare state. That, however, created new problems for them, since the state simply confirmed their feelings that they could achieve nothing by themselves and that they were thoroughly disadvantaged. Above all, they experienced Social Assistance as offering them nothing more than bare existence, and that rather worse than better. Long-term unemployment and Social Assistance claiming became entrenched over time, and the respondents found themselves caught in a vicious circle of poverty. There was little that could have made their lives on the margins of society tolerable.

The most typical instance is respondent 62. He is in his late thirties and has claimed Social Assistance for four years spread over eight spells, generally with his family. His encounters with Social Assistance started in his early youth when he was in residential care, an experience which considerably restricted his chances later in life:

Other people were making decisions about my life without asking me and basically they mucked my life up . . . I've been fighting with the authorities more or less all my life, really fighting because there wasn't any other way. I mean, if you want to live like you want to, that's just impossible in this country, because of all those laws and paragraphs and regulations, they make your life a hell, and they tie you down so much that you can't make your own space to live at all, like you want, know what I mean? There's just simply no way you can do it.

Respondent 9 is another member of this 'victims' group. He was 20 when he first claimed Social Assistance in 1983 and continued to claim for five years, with two interruptions. Lack of money is a great problem for him in that it restricts his freedom of action. He suffers from not being able to take a holiday or even go out. He cannot find a partner and no longer has any friends, and he is isolated and bored. Unlike respondent 62, respondent 9 is not integrated in any social network and so he has difficulty filling his time. His general dissatisfaction is very apparent:

You get really depressed, and you really don't get any pleasure out of life any more, well, you know, you're always stuck in these four walls and you have to count every penny over and again, and you can't do anything. OK, yes, I'm paying the rent, got to keep a roof over my head, but there's nothing else at all.

Mere survivors keep finding limited solutions to their problems in the course of their Social Assistance careers. Long-term unemployment is the major problem in life for this group as well. By contrast with the 'victims', members of this group do confront at least some of their problems of limited resources after a while, and in ideal cases actually manage to deal with them. We have called them 'mere survivors' because the way they deal with their problems is broadly directed towards immediate material survival. Driven by necessity, they meet their regular unavoidable everyday expenditures. Even when they are able to terminate their Social Assistance claim this does not satisfy them, as they measure their success only in terms of the cash which flows into their household purse. They often lack biographical goals that go beyond financial interests, so that even getting off Social Assistance, if they could manage it, would not necessarily make them significantly more satisfied and would offer only a critical solution. Their relations with the staff of the Social Assistance Agency are not always productive, but unlike the 'victims' their relationships with the Agency have not become separate problems in themselves.

Respondent 23 is typical. He was only just 30 when he first claimed Social Assistance in 1983 and remained a claimant for six years with one interruption. He sees long-term unemployment and not Social Assistance as his principal problem in life. Claiming Social Assistance is 'really only a question of money' but 'the real problem is about work'. There are no alternatives, but Social Assistance is nevertheless a legitimate means of survival: 'I claimed it as the only way to get somewhere to live.' Of course he refers to the lack of cash and calls for improved information by the Social Assistance Agency about benefits, but he puts these poverty experiences into perspective: 'I was never desperate, I was never hungry, no, I really can't say I was.' Against this background he does not see his (incomplete) escape from Social Assistance as a complete success, as it is only a critical solution of his life-long problem of unemployment: in spite of the self-employed activity which he has taken up he is still dependent on Social Assistance to supplement his low income. The solution is not part of some greater life plan but is once again just an expedient 'problem management'. He will only feel there has been a positive change for the better 'when there's a bit more money in my wallet'.

Pragmatic copers look for more wide-ranging solutions while they claim Social Assistance. By contrast with the groups described above, these people are pursuing life goals that go beyond securing their daily material existence. What have to be overcome are problems such as separation crises, single parenthood, security in old age; unemployment is less pressing. Unlike the 'mere survivors', they tackle these problems not only in terms of economic survival. Since they are able to pursue their important, broader personal goals because of – or in spite of – Social Assistance, they can more easily put up with the restrictions of claiming. They are behaving pragmatically because they are not aiming at the maximum but are satisfied with second-best solutions. Their points of reference are not grandiose future prospects but the demands of everyday living. Pragmatists understand how to bring their interests in line with contextual constraints: they come to terms with the situation.

Respondent 1 represents this approach. She was in her mid 40s when she claimed Social Assistance following divorce, and she claimed for one and a half years. It was the Housing Agency who referred her to the Social Assistance Agency: 'They said I had to go there, so, God, I just got myself down there.' She distinguishes between her two problems of overcoming the crisis of divorce and ensuring her material existence:

> God, this business about going for Social Assistance . . . well, I knew I'd have to go, so I went straightaway, though I knew that it would only be for a while. God, this business of going to the Social Agency, that wasn't so bad, that was just a side effect. When you get divorced, well, I mean, it wasn't a real divorce but a separation and you're ill like I was, that was all a lot worse. Well, all that about going to the Social Assistance, I just thought, . . . you've got to make the money go round somehow, we've got to get by somehow, haven't we?

Respondent 1 ranked her two problems and defined the separation crisis as the most important; the arrangement of her financial affairs is secondary by comparison. Social Assistance is available to deal with the latter, something which she sees pragmatically as 'simply a certain necessity'. Thus the support offered by Social Assistance is seen in neither a particularly positive nor negative light.

Biographical copers aim for even more extensive solutions to their problems. They may include a wide range of different problems: unemployment, illness, separation crises or – in instances where the respondent has a reduced working ability or lacks employment opportunities – a life without paid work. Like the 'pragmatic copers', the 'biographical copers' define their problems in the light of both economic and biographical interests. They differ in how they deal with their problems. 'Biographical copers' pursue wide-ranging goals which they are sometimes lucky enough to achieve. They take account not only of immediate interests but also of the future, and proceed according to plan. If a change in circumstances forces them to alter direction, they still try to pursue their original interests and underlying purpose. They pursue their goals even when facing problems of cash shortage, difficulties with the authorities or the negative reactions of their social environment. They learn, change and optimise their action strategies in order to achieve and retain favourable conditions in life.

An example of such a biographical coper is respondent 14, who first claimed Social Assistance after the birth of a child when she was in her twenties. Why did she have to claim? After the maternity leave from her position as a teacher had run out, respondent 14 wanted to continue to care for her child, in spite of the fact that her husband was unemployed. The background to the situation of need is an individual reorientation during a period of social and economic insecurity:

I wanted to stay at home with her for the first three years. That's how I saw it at the beginning. I thought, if my husband still hasn't got a job, I'll go back after six months. So I took unpaid leave. But then I had the little tot there in my arms, and thought, I can't go back to work, I can't simply give her up to someone else to look after while I go back to school and teach other people's children. That didn't suit me at all. No, I'd got to stay at home with the child.

The family wanted to 'see how to get by somehow' and claimed Social Assistance for her and her daughter. Her husband, who had not been able to find employment after his graduation from university and did not want to do casual work, enrolled for a further academic qualification and claimed the relevant educational grant. The path to Social Assistance was thus not simply the calculated consequence of previous decisions, but a deliberate decision in itself. She did not feel oppressed by claiming Social Assistance because 'in fact I'd decided to live very simply, just for the sake of the child'. The termination of the claim was planned, the family calculating that it would take place 'in a year or two, because we've always been sure that when my husband's finished his second course, then he'd really be able to find a job'. Social Assistance was intended to last for a period of time, and things worked out as the couple intended: after completing his further qualification, the husband was indeed able to find a well-paid and secure position in his profession.

Respondent 7, who could also be included in this group of 'biographical copers', left her alcoholic husband soon after the birth of their second child and claimed Social Assistance although she was only a teenager. She does not see her lack of resources and of work as major problems in life. 'I didn't really think they were big problems, because I said to myself, I'll look after the kids now, and when they are old enough then I'll go and get some training.' Social Assistance is simply a means of bridging the period while the children are small, so that she can take up vocational training later on. But before respondent 7 can pursue her long-existent but latent educational aspirations she has to solve other problems in life: her separation and personality crisis. Compared with her difficult marriage, during which she lived in extreme poverty at times, Social Assistance gives her a degree of economic security and individual independence which she has not previously enjoyed:

That's why I must say, after all that, I thought it was absolutely great getting that Social Assistance for the first time. I even had to open a bank account to put the cash in. I can't think why I never had one before but I didn't. Everything went into his account. And then I had my own account and got my own money. And all those years, I never had a penny for myself. I felt somehow quite rich, anyway more secure and a lot more independent. In spite of everything.

Social Assistance helped her to achieve her goal 'to get some independence'. So in the end she was able to translate into fact what had been only a vague aspiration before: she could begin her further education and cease to claim Social Assistance. By dint of further effort in the following years, respondent 7 pursued a highly successful educational career.

Strategic users are a group in their own right. They do not fit into the sequence of the groups above, in which Social Assistance is used increasingly to pursue wider biographical goals. Unlike 'pragmatic copers', they do not see economic and biographical interests as equally important; they are much more inclined to rank securing their material existence above wider biographical interests. They want to survive, in comfort if possible, perhaps during self-chosen unemployment or after a separation (see pp. 98f.). If the situation seems to require it, Social Assistance is used as a resource along with others, whether permanently or periodically. Given their limited goals, Social Assistance is a good solution. The claim is made in a strategic manner. In their relations with the authorities, avoiding or kindling conflict can each play a role according to how things stand, and they may use fraud or other illegitimate means to achieve their ends. This pattern of managing can be recognised in the behaviour of a minority of people for limited periods at certain stages of their lives, and it often depends on the particular sub-cultural context in which those people are living. The existence of this specific type provides no justification for restrictions in Social Assistance or more general cuts in social services (see chapter 6, pp. 167f.).

A typical example is respondent 24, who had been claiming Social Assistance with shorter and longer interruptions since 1983. He finds claiming completely unproblematic. It complements well his conception of work life: 'to do casual jobs when I feel like it and when I need the cash'. What is far more important to him than work is his freedom to play football, which has been the 'number-one' activity in his life since childhood. He needs Social Assistance only in order to survive: 'I've got to live somehow'. In this way Social Assistance is taken for granted as a viable alternative to paid work and an easy solution to life's problems:

OK, let's say the Agency was always an easy way out. I'd thought a lot about other ways if I could not have claimed, I'll tell you. Well, at least to tide me over. Then I would have disciplined myself at work . . . when I didn't feel like it any more . . . maybe it's there in the back of my mind, if I'd been without a penny for three weeks, then I might have thought about it twice [giving up a job].

We can summarise the situation as follows: the spectrum of types shows that Social Assistance is not simply a matter of social control, but that it is used by claimants to varying degrees as a form of support in order to pursue biographical goals. The clients of the state are not just controlled and directed, but they are offered opportunities to develop their lives in their own ways. Life on Social Assistance does not necessarily mean passive endurance; it can also mean opportunities for action. 'Victims' and 'mere survivors' are closer to passive 'endurance', while 'pragmatic copers', 'biographical copers' and 'strategic users' are all more 'active' types. What chiefly distinguishes the five groups is the degree to which they use their time on Social Assistance to cope with broader problems in life that go beyond the immediate need of securing material survival.

'Action' and 'active coping' do not mean that the respondents were able simply to surmount the restrictions of external circumstances or the limitations of their own capacities. What it does mean is that people subject to similar conditions can find different ways of dealing with them. 'Active coping' does not mean that all problems are solved. If, for instance, an unqualified woman who has spent a long time out of the labour market has very limited objective chances of finding employment, then 'active coping' may mean only the pursuit of other interests in life in a relatively satisfying way while claiming Social Assistance on a continuing basis – by contrast with a person who does not manage to do so. In addition, people may move from one type to another during the course of their poverty careers. If 'copers' repeatedly fail, whether because of overwhelming social circumstances or their own shortcomings, they may become simply 'mere survivors' or even 'victims', in other words shift from action to endurance (cf. chapter 6, pp. 162f.).

How are life courses and individual behaviour related?
Three types of poverty career

We have distinguished two types of life course – critical, remaining in Social Assistance, and normalised, leading out of Social Assistance – and also two principal types of individual response towards Social Assistance – endurance, in the sense of restricted capacity for action, and action (active coping), in the sense of a positive and (in the best cases) successful approach to problem solving. We can then ask, what kinds of poverty career are there? A simple answer could be given using the first distinction: critical life courses can be seen as downward careers, normalised life courses as upward careers (with each of these 'ideal types' covering a broad range from narrowly limited to highly pronounced decline or ascent).

But the concept of career carries with it more than the simple idea of an externally observable pattern of progression. Careers have an action dimension: people pursue their own careers, for instance in their professions, by acting in ways which meet social expectations. By contrast, addiction or domestic careers can be seen as being produced by unfavourable socialisation conditions and by institutions of social control which direct the people affected. Both perspectives imply assumptions about individual behaviour. Upward careers are in general thought to be mobilised by the active efforts of the people in question while in downward careers it is more common to assume that, at least at some point, people become mere victims, caught in a self-intensifying downward motion. In this view, a normalised life course (escape from Social Assistance) implies action; a critical one (continuing Social Assistance) suggests endurance. The two dimensions – critical versus normalised and endurance versus action – thus seem to coincide, with other combinations (action in critical courses; normalisation coupled with endurance) being excluded. In the traditional, narrow perspective, the reality of poverty is even reduced to the combination of critical life course and endurance.

This narrow view of career is called into question by our findings. Hidden behind the appearance of similar careers may be very different individual ways of dealing with problems. The two dimensions of critical/normal and endurance/action logically give four and not two combinations, each of which can in theory represent a type of poverty career (see table 5.1). Each cell of the table corresponds to one of four principal types, each of which may have sub-divisions. One of the cells includes only two instances and is not treated as a type in itself. We are left with *three types*: entrenched poverty career, welfare-state normalised poverty career and optimised poverty management.

The pure type of social decline, the entrenched poverty career – long and continuing Social Assistance claiming accompanied by apathy and endurance – is only one type of poverty career. Another type is the permanent escape from Social Assistance through the claimants' own efforts, described as optimised poverty management. In addition to these types of decline and ascent, there is a third type in between, where the claimant remains on Assistance but copes actively with his or her situation in life. This is not a normalisation in the ordinary sense, but a kind of secondary normalisation through the welfare state, within Social Assistance itself.

What is the relationship between life-course patterns and individual behaviour? We find 'endurance' almost only among those with continuing Social Assistance claims (critical life courses) and among only very few of those with normalised life courses. But 'action' is found not only among those who have terminated claiming (optimised poverty management) but also among those who are still claiming (welfare-state normalised poverty

Table 5.1 *A typology of poverty careers*

	endurance	*action* (coping, strategic use)
critical life courses (still claiming)	'entrenched poverty career' (6 persons):	'welfare-state normalised poverty career' (11 persons):
	'victims' with discontinuous employment careers (4 persons) others (2 persons)	'copers' with continuous employment careers (5 persons) 'strategic users' with discontinuous employment careers (men; 3 persons) others (3 persons)
normalised life *courses* (no longer claiming)	(2 persons)	'optimised poverty management' (12 persons):
		'biographical copers' with escape to continuous employment careers (4 persons) persons with escape to underqualified work (5 persons) others (3 persons)

Source: Social Assistance claimants in the city of Bremen, first application in 1983/84, interviewed in 1990/91 (see note 3 on p. 114; $n = 31$).

careers). This puts into perspective the criticisms of the left and the right, who normally assume that long periods of Social Assistance discourage claimants and make them apathetic. Claimants who really only endure Social Assistance cannot cease claiming, though; they are in an entrenched poverty career in which they cannot achieve normalisation (there were almost no cases in the normalisation/endurance cell). They are caught in a 'poverty trap', but, as we shall show, they have experienced disadvantages in their earlier lives which are merely enhanced by Social Assistance. The critics of the right who believe that claimants do not want to become independent of Social Assistance can find support for their notions in only one small sub-group of the 'welfare-state normalised poverty career', the 'strategic users'. The progress of a Social Assistance career can thus not be ascribed unequivocally to any single pattern of individual behaviour.

The novelty in these major types of poverty career is the apparent paradoxical combination of 'action' with continuous claiming – the 'welfare-state normalised poverty career'. Even the 'optimised poverty management' career is new to traditional poverty research since, irrespective of action or endurance, in this research tradition the possibility of terminating Social Assistance claiming generally has not been conceptualised. The three major types are the components of a contingent model of poverty careers – the 'cross-roads' model – which will be discussed below, after we have elaborated the sub-types shown in table 5.1 (p. 133) to give a more precise picture of the relationships between life courses and individual behaviour patterns.[8]

Entrenched poverty career reflects permanent poverty as a restricted ability to act autonomously. In this type of poverty career, on which previous poverty research has almost exclusively focused, one finds long-lasting continuous Social Assistance combined with endurance. This combination was found among only six of the 31 respondents and was chiefly realised in one sub-type, that of people with discontinuous and critical working lives, all of whom were 'victims' and thus 'endured' the most. Early problems in their working lives were associated with a lack of behavioural control or competence. These behavioural deficits became apparent early in life before they reached working age. In three instances respondents had spent all or part of their childhood in institutional care; another respondent had suffered an accident as a youth with physical as well as psychological consequences. These structural experiences severely constrained the development of their social abilities. The respondents could not reach their goals in life through their own efforts and found themselves trapped in interrupted working careers. Their lives were a matter of 'enduring', something which had not started with the Social Assistance claim but which was exacerbated by it.

Optimised poverty management means 'action' to overcome Social Assistance, even after many years of claiming. For this group, action led to the normalisation of the life course, meaning the permanent termination of Social Assistance, even though most of them had claimed it for many years. This is a very heterogeneous group which could not be so clearly allocated

---

[8] We have defined the major types as combinations of patterns of life courses (critical or normalised) with patterns of behaviour ('endurance' or 'action'), for instance 'normalised life course' with 'action'. Further differentiation of the two dimensions as depicted above produces sub-groups under each major heading, such as 'employment-related normalised life course'/'biographical coper' or 'family-related critical life course'/'victim'.

to specific sub-groups as the two other career types could. We found here almost all the possible combinations of life-course patterns (employment, family and benefit-related normalisation) and methods of coping (pragmatic and biographical copers and strategic users). An obvious grouping was apparent only where 'biographical coping' intersected with 'normalisation through continuous employment'. These are the respondents who were planning their future employment even while they were claiming, and they achieved their objectives by the intended means. Their working lives closely resemble the classical model of the upwardly mobile occupational career.

By contrast, there was another sub-group of respondents who also managed to achieve a working career (whether continuous or not) through their own efforts and thereby secured their futures permanently and independently. But these efforts were not rewarded with success at work in the usual sense, that is, with real promotion corresponding to their occupational qualifications. This group extended over different sub-groups: pragmatic copers, strategic users, continuous or interrupted working careers, as well as benefit careers combined with employment in sheltered workshops.

How far can 'optimised poverty management' be causally ascribed to the behaviour of the respondents? Did the respondents actually achieve the escape from Social Assistance through successful purposive action, or was there no connection between their well-developed management abilities and the successful termination of their poverty careers?

We come closer to an answer if we turn to the only two contrary cases in the lower left-hand cell of table 5.1 (p. 133). Their life courses became normalised even though they were not 'acting' but 'enduring'. In both instances there were exceptional circumstances. The career of respondent 50 was 'normalised' through permanent Unemployment Assistance, as opposed to a pension. This is not really a form of normalisation, a fact to be taken into account in the subsequent analysis. In the case of respondent 42, employment was found even though he passively accepted Social Assistance as a 'mere survivor'. The connection between leaving to a (discontinuous) working career and mere survival management was plausible in this single instance. Sometimes even weak action orientations can lead to success, here overcoming Social Assistance, but this happened in only one case in this study.

At the structural level, this finding suggests there is no relationship between the normalisation of life courses and 'endurance', and that only 'action' may lead to normalisation. This then justifies the assumption that permanent termination of Social Assistance claiming, that is, the normalisation of the life course, requires individual endeavours in addition to other, structural, conditions. Coping matters. And many claimants take their chances. We have shown that claiming does not necessarily imply a loss of a sense of direction in life. Widely shared social values and goals continue to be meaningful for most claimants and contribute to their ability to overcome their dependency on Social Assistance.

Welfare-state normalised poverty career means 'action' in spite of long-term Social Assistance claiming. Traditional social research into poverty did not expect to find claimants who were able to be 'active' even though they had critical life courses, continuing to claim Assistance over many years. We identified two sub-groups. One consisted of men with interrupted working careers who blamed their failure to escape from Social Assistance on themselves in the sense that they were acting as 'strategic users'. They frequently changed jobs when they felt like it, and also stopped working at times. Staying on Assistance was not just forced upon them by structural circumstances, but for them became an objective in its own right. The qualification must be added that all the respondents in this group expressed the intention of changing their lifestyles and reorientating their lives.

The other sub-group consisted of people with continuous employment records who were pragmatic or even biographical copers. By contrast to the strategic users, they were basically interested in pursuing their occupational careers to secure their independent existence without Social Assistance. Their approach was often apparent, long before the Social Assistance claim, in their previous generally long-lasting employment histories. At that time they had deliberately avoided Social Assistance. The unemployment or illness which forced them to claim Social Assistance was an unexpected event. The respondents could not avoid it, but they counteracted marginalisation, trying to retain as much as possible from their previous lives or even to construct a new life. This individual striving is a kind of normalisation, a form of social integration within and through Social Assistance.

Poverty careers between inclusion and exclusion: elements of a non-deterministic approach

What is the theoretical significance of the three chief types of poverty career which we have outlined? These types of career – entrenched, welfare-state normalised, and optimised management – are the components of a contingent career model. This is the 'crossroads' type of career in which neither individual behaviour nor the institutions of the welfare state predetermine a downward career, but instead a diverse range of possible paths is opened up, which we have divided into the three chief types and several sub-groups. Poverty careers cannot be conceptualised adequately in simple terms as 'one-way streets' (as in the deterministic model), nor as 'corridors' which allow various movements in one direction (as in the probabilistic model). They can only be understood properly in the sense of a 'cross-roads' model which allows a number of different paths in various directions. This is a contingent model.

The career models used in current poverty research in Germany are deterministic or at best probabilistic. They can roughly describe some isolated types but are demonstrably insufficient to encompass the whole range of poverty careers. This also shows in the underlying sociological conceptualisations of 'career'. In the beginning of this chapter we distinguished three concepts of career used in sociological research until now: career as downward class mobility, as a process of socialisation into a deviant lifestyle and as social coping. The deterministic model is associated with concepts of downward class mobility and deviance, but these concepts primarily apply to the 'entrenched' poverty career type. The probabilistic model considers processes of coping, allowing for people to react to poverty in a variety of ways, but it does not systematically account for routes out of poverty. The 'contingent' model we propose takes the concept of coping further. Looking not only at reactions of people or even just at the ways they interpret their miserable situation, we are concerned with how they actively deal with the concrete problems they encounter in the family and the workplace, because only this kind of 'socio-economic coping' can help to explain why some people find different ways through and out of poverty than others.

Our three chief types of poverty career differ primarily with regard to the process of coping: whether people cope with their situation at all, and if so, whether they deal with the causes of poverty or only with the consequences, and which of these two challenges they define as the problem to be overcome. Naturally, people who aim to deal with the causes are also confronted with the need to cope with the consequences while they are claimants. Which types of coping distinguish the three chief types of poverty career (see table 5.2)?

In the *entrenched poverty career* challenges are either not confronted at all or only unsuccessfully. Neither the problem that led to claiming in the first place nor the consequences of this situation are overcome or even alleviated. The careers are 'entrenched' in the sense that most of these people's problems remain unresolved and the chances of change are low. Respondent 62 is one of the clearest examples. In the 1970s he was periodically unemployed and received Social Assistance from time to time, but after he started a family at the start of the 1980s he was unemployed over long interrupted periods and generally claimed Social Assistance. He has difficulties with the Social Assistance authorities, feels socially excluded by his lack of money, and discriminated against by potential employers because of his unfavourable work record. His deviant behaviour repeatedly reinforces his downward spiral.

Table 5.2 *Poverty careers between exclusion and inclusion*

	three types of poverty careers		
	entrenched poverty career	welfare-state normalised poverty career	optimised poverty management
sociological career concept	downward class mobility; career in deviance	coping (managing consequences)	coping (managing consequences and causes)
socio-cultural model	negative model: social decline (threat of poverty)	social security, social participation	occupational advancement, marriage as provision
social integration	exclusion	secondary inclusion	inclusion

We also categorise as an entrenched poverty career some of those who manage to terminate their Social Assistance claims but who cannot solve the problem which led to the claim in the first place. That was the situation for respondent 50 who was unemployed for years after ceasing to claim Social Assistance and who by mere survival strategies only dealt with the resulting problems to a limited extent. According to the definition we started with his situation has been 'normalised' in that he has ceased claiming Assistance. However, to retain the validity of the typology respondent 50 had to be regrouped because no real normalisation has taken place in his life. We downgraded him to a critical life course (originally defined as still claiming) even though he is no longer claiming. Our original methodologically conditioned assumption that permanent termination of Social Assistance was evidence of social 'normalisation' had to be qualified on the basis of our own findings.

The *welfare-state normalised poverty career* embraces both successful and unsuccessful management, in that these people cannot overcome the underlying initial problem but manage to cope with the consequences of this situation. A typical instance is that of respondent 11. She worked for 25 years as an employed family member in her father's firm. When it went bankrupt she had to start a new life; she was unemployed, claimed supplementary Social Assistance and had to manage her own household for the first time. She did not define unemployment as a problem to be solved, but rather came to terms with Social Assistance. She coped very well with life on Assistance by adopting deliberate techniques to get by. The course of this 'successful' poverty career is particularly striking because she has no prospects of escaping Assistance.

Respondent 43, who ceased to claim Assistance many years ago but has remained generally unemployed since then, also belongs to this group. She has at least coped with the consequences of her unsolved structural problems. She does a small amount of work as a journalist for low pay, and plans her daily expenditures with great care. Over time, her living conditions have stabilised, but they still reflect a deprived life. In theory her life course has been 'normalised' because she no longer claims, but she has only achieved a kind of secondary normalisation propped up by various social services of the welfare state. We therefore had to regroup her as well, from 'optimised poverty management' to 'welfare-state normalised poverty career'.

Optimised poverty management is the career in which all the poverty problems can be solved. The people in question cope well with Social Assistance and its immediate consequences, and in addition, can overcome the structural cause that led to their claim. By 'optimisation' we mean this double success. But one must not assume that people in this situation are going to have dramatically better lives after they stop claiming. Respondent 14 and his family are typical. When the first child was born, the mother (the respondent's wife) did not want to return to work immediately even though her husband was unemployed at that time after the conclusion of his studies. Her husband decided to pursue further qualifications and claimed Federal Educational Support, while claiming Social Assistance for his wife and child. The family planned to claim Assistance for only a limited period, and they satisfactorily coped with the associated constraints. When he had finished his further studies, the husband found a well-paid job which would ensure a permanent livelihood for his family without requiring his wife to return to employment. This path out of Assistance signals an upwardly mobile occupational career. The remaining cases of 'optimised poverty management' fell into two groups according to how closely they resembled this example.

Behind each of the three types of poverty career lie different socio-cultural models (see table 5.2 above). 'Careers' are the outcome of individual behaviours and institutionalised patterns of expectation. These expectations are related to cultural patterns ingrained in our societies. Sooner or later 'optimised poverty management' leads back to reintegration or even a 'career' in employment or marriage (or both):[9] it is 'optimised' in terms of the dominant upward-mobility ideal of German patriarchal acquisitive society. But people's lives can be normalised in other ways as well. The welfare state can also 'normalise' in a secondary manner

---

[9] This includes transfers to old-age pensions based on previous earnings or on marriage.

when escape from Social Assistance or Unemployment Assistance is impossible (or more rarely is unwanted), but when the claimants know how to deal with their situations in a positive way. Their status can be seen as 'normalised' because it matches the German welfare state's ideals of security and participation, according to which every citizen has the right to the means necessary for a decent and dignified existence. Finally, 'entrenched poverty careers' can only be understood as the mirror image of the ideal of upward social mobility, as downward mobility and social exclusion. As long as there are such careers, they exemplify the threat of poverty which is constantly re-emphasised in the social security system (see chapter 2, p. 34).

The three chief types of poverty career demonstrate the complexity of socio-cultural patterns in modern welfare societies. Social ascent and decline are measured not only in terms of 'success' in the labour or marriage markets. Claiming Social Assistance is not to be equated with social decline, as the 'welfare-state normalisation' career type shows. Conversely, to stop claiming Social Assistance cannot stereotypically be assumed to mean social ascent and normalisation, since some people manage to escape without solving the underlying problem of, e.g., unemployment. In spite of their escape they have not optimised their poverty management, but instead they 'endure' an entrenched poverty career if they cannot alleviate the burdens of their situation, or they have a welfare-state normalised poverty career as long as they continue to depend on social service benefits while coping with their lives under these circumstances.

'Poverty careers' or 'social inequality'? Class, gender and age

Our analysis shows that there is a complex spectrum of poverty careers ranging from social exclusion to social integration, from permanent expulsion into a marginalised existence to re-establishment of 'normal' participatory patterns of life. This heterogeneity of poverty is only revealed when poverty is located in the context of the whole life course, as we have done. From this perspective, poverty is not a fixed characteristic of certain disadvantaged groups such as the unemployed or women ('poverty is female'), nor is it about the delimited 'dregs' of society (as with 'marginal groups'). Instead, poverty is understood as the result of specific events in people's lives, shaped by the ways people cope with their situation. We have described these trajectories as careers. The hitherto dominant deterministic model of a poverty career – the one-way street model – is devoid of the analytic potential which the concept of career embodies and, instead of considering the variety of different poverty careers, it treats behaviour as largely determined by social institutions and structures. Career analyses can then only show how such structures affect the lives of individuals. This perspective has a certain plausibility in the study of those marginal groups from which it was originally derived, although even some studies of seemingly hopeless cases such as 'drug careers' suggest that there are other patterns of life course besides the classical downward spiral (Groenemeyer 1990).

The 'probabilistic' and, even more strongly, the 'contingent' poverty career models, which respectively suggest a corridor or a cross-roads course of poverty, take into account that even socially vulnerable people have some room for their own decisions and action. This enables us to consider a wide range of diverse career patterns.[10] Basic structures of social inequality are mediated and transformed in individual careers. So when we emphasise the variety of individual life courses in our contingent model, we do not mean to imply that structural factors have no significant impact. Socio-structural characteristics such as family background, class, education, occupational status and gender have always been central to the sociological understanding of inequalities. They affect the risk of becoming poor as well as the probability of remaining in poverty or escaping it. These influences are obvious in our findings, too.

We have distinguished several types of critical and normalised life courses (see figure 5.1 p. 133), of which some correspond to the image of lasting structural disadvantage, while in others disadvantages are overcome, a success which we were able to relate to the claimants' own efforts. In conclusion we want to ask: to what extent and in which ways are the three chief types of poverty career which we have identified related to socio-demographic characteristics?[11] We are looking for structural background factors that either positively or negatively influence careers and the scope for individual action.[12] We examine the impact of gender, age and education.

Gender: The 'entrenched' poverty career is largely a male problem, while the other two types, optimised poverty management and welfare-state normalisation, are not more obviously associated with one sex than the other. The

---

[10] The variety of pathways through poverty could also be the result of structural conditions, though. It may derive from the unique position occupied by each individual in the network of social institutions (George Herbert Mead, cited by Kohli 1988, p. 50), and from contingencies which confront some individuals and not others: for instance, the bankruptcy of one's employer.

[11] Since our sample consisted of people who were or had for a time been claimants of Social Assistance, the following comments refer not to the risk of becoming a claimant but to the probability of claimants having a specific poverty career.

[12] In doing so, we again follow the work of Uta Gerhardt, who proposes to relate structural ideal types (in our case the three chief types of poverty career) to structural characteristics (1991) (see also pp. 283f.). We should reiterate that the sub-sample of 31 respondents reported on in this chapter largely reflects both the entire qualitatively interviewed sample of 74 respondents and the representative quantitative sample of 586 case records in all significant factors such as age and gender.

common expression that 'poverty is female' must therefore be qualified in the case of Germany not only with regard to the incidence of poverty but also with regard to poverty careers. Indeed, the life-course perspective evinces how complicated the issue is. Our representative sample of new claimants in a given year shows that the risk of becoming poor (as defined by applying for Social Assistance) is somewhat lower for women than for men. However, since on average women remain claimants longer than men (chiefly because single mothers stay on Assistance longer than unemployed men do), the probability at any point in time of being poor is slightly higher for women – that is, they are over-represented in a cross-sectional view.[13] However, the picture changes again if we look at the careers of claimants beyond the simple objective duration of their claims. We then find, as described above, that although women claim for longer periods of time, they are more likely either to cope with living on Assistance or even to become independent of it, than to get stuck in deprivation as some men do. *Women are better copers* – maybe because they come to terms more easily with being dependent on an external bread-winner, be it a husband or a state agency (see Mädje and Neusüß 1996 with regard to lone mothers).

Age: The 'entrenched' poverty career stands out here as well, since the youngest age group (under 30) is heavily over-represented. The middle age group occurs more frequently among the 'welfare-state normalised' career, while the 'optimised' career is age-neutral.

Education: People with lower school-leaving certificates were more common among those with 'entrenched' and 'welfare-state normalised' poverty careers, while the optimising career was more characteristic of people with full upper school-leaving qualifications (*Abitur*). This finding was to be expected and supports the assumption that educational resources are an important condition for being able to escape from Social Assistance permanently. Against this background it is surprising how occupational training affects the course of Social Assistance claims: people lacking occupational qualifications (who made up almost half of all respondents) were more likely to have 'welfare-state normalised' or 'optimised' careers than 'entrenched' ones. This can be explained by the fact that among this group were those respondents who were planning or had started higher

[13] See the comparison of longitudinal and cross-sectional measures of poverty in chapter 3, p. 67. Of the 31 cases analysed in this chapter and the whole sample of 586 case records, 58 per cent and 60 per cent respectively were men. If we take into account all the people included in the case records, including the partners and other members of claiming units, 53 per cent were male (for further details on the composition of the sample see chapter 3). The official statistics generally reveal slightly more than 50 per cent for females among a cross-section of claimants.

education courses which had not yet been completed, so that in our study they appeared as 'lacking occupational qualifications'.

The three chief types of poverty career are thus related to social characteristics. Entrenched poverty careers more often affect men and young people; welfare-state normalised poverty careers are more often to be found in the middle age group. Only the optimised poverty management careers show no bias in terms of age or gender, but a higher standard of education is more common.

These findings show that socio-structural background factors affect the course of poverty but do not determine it as the deterministic (one-way street) model would suggest. The way in which each individual manages his or her poverty remains of lasting significance. Structural and individual factors are indivisibly linked: entrenched and welfare-state normalised poverty careers can hardly be distinguished in terms of the objective patterns of risk behind them. In both cases long-term unemployment was the principal cause of claiming Social Assistance, often associated with minimal prospects of change. But the respondents dealt with these objective situations differently, and age very clearly played a part in this, as did limitations on ability which had arisen early in life. Experience in life, accumulated life skills and a well-founded sense of personal identity are all resources with which people manage their lives and which may be more developed in older persons. These resources can help people to cope with materially restricted conditions. Education is an important resource among those who are 'optimising poverty managers'. In reflecting on this broad sketch of the relationships among socio-structural factors it must not be forgotten that in individual cases people can overcome poverty with great success even when the objective characteristics might not have predicted such an outcome.

6   Institutional time: does Social Assistance create dependency?

The unintended consequences of social policy have been a subject of lament ever since the beginning of the nineteenth century. The Poor Law was an object of criticism from even earlier times. Both liberals and conservatives have argued that the social institutions which were meant to combat problems instead exacerbated them or indeed caused them in the first place, and should therefore be abolished. The argument is pursued above all in the USA in respect of Welfare,[1] because in that country it does not represent the lowest tier of a fully fledged social security system but in the public debate often stands for the welfare state itself. The catchphrase is *welfarisation*: the assertion that Welfare itself creates dependency by fostering helplessness and even contributing to the development of a culture of dependency.

The topic of the undesirable long-term effects of social welfare is of fundamental importance both to sociology and politics. The question is whether the welfare state has fatal consequences for individual behaviour, in displacing people's capacity and willingness to work for a living and undermining family relationships. The belief that it does unites both right- and some left-wing critics. For the former, the welfare state makes individuals dependent and unfit for labour markets; the latter see it as a means of disciplining and excluding those who stand outside the labour market. In Germany both Christian-Democratic and Liberal politicians warn that benefit levels reach well up to the bottom of the wage scale and thus encourage workshyness, while trade unions and advocates of the poor such as voluntary welfare organisations complain about the danger of a 'two-thirds society'. Unemployed people seem to be doubly cursed in this polarised society: they are victims of an economic policy which accepts mass unemployment, and they are affected by cuts in social services and increas-

---

[1] When capitalised, the term 'Welfare' is used here to mean the US system of residual income maintenance, i.e. Aid to Families with Dependent Children (AFDC; now TANF, Temporary Assistance for Needy Families) and related benefits.

ing control by the unemployment offices. Long-term unemployment holds the danger of a double downward spiral: psycho-social damage as the result of imposed inactivity over time, and the additional effects of continual supervision and control by the state authorities in search of 'welfarisation'. The critics on the right demand stronger controls, benefit restrictions and sharper work incentives; the critics on the left want extended benefits and universal basic social security.

A tradition of criticising the welfare state also exists in the social sciences. Modern institutions such as the state, schools and the health authorities monopolise arrangements for existence and disempower the individual – an example is Ivan Illich's critique of social institutions and the social professions. Norbert Elias's theory of civilisation might support this view as well, and Franz Schultheis (1987) used ideas of the latter in elaborating the 'fatal' consequences of Social Assistance receipt.[2] In asserting that the welfare state furthers a 'functional rationality' (see chapter 2, pp. 38f.), Karl Ulrich Mayer and Walter Müller (1986) drew attention to changes in the structures of meaning of human action as a consequence of the benefits offered by the welfare state. On the basis of our findings about objective and subjective time in German Social Assistance as well as an empirical comparison with the USA, this chapter attempts to bring greater clarity to the question of the long-term effects of Social Assistance.[3]

The welfare state as a poverty risk

The welfare state does not just combat poverty but actually generates poverty itself.[4] Like other great institutional creations which aim to solve problems, it also gives rise to new ones. In a broad sense, any kind of

[2] For a general analysis of the welfare state along the lines of Elias, see Abram de Swaan (1988). For a balanced view of modern welfare institutions see Giddens (1991, chapter 5) (see chapter 2).
[3] David Piachaud (1997) investigates the question of dependency by a correlation analysis of aggregate cross-sectional data in various Western countries (rather than by longitudinal micro data as done in our study). He tests the basic hypothesis of dependency, that is, the assertion that the generosity of social security systems (as measured by the level of benefits) correlates with the incidence of the risk covered – for example generous unemployment benefits leading to a high rate of unemployment. This concept of dependency is a valuable supplement to those concepts that use time and duration to define dependency as system-produced long-term effects arising during individual claiming processes. Piachaud's findings in the fields of unemployment, lone parenthood and inability to work refute the basic hypothesis of dependency. Hartley Dean's and Peter Taylor-Gooby's sociological study *Dependency Culture* (1992) places the issue of dependency in the broader context of social relationships of individuals in labour markets, family and state, all of which imply some kind of dependency. In this light they analyse discourses and policies related to 'dependency' and 'underclass' in Britain.
[4] This section elaborates ideas first outlined in Leisering and Voges (1996).

poverty is (co-)produced by the welfare state. By assuming an all-embracing responsibility for the well-being of its citizens,[5] the welfare state is in principle obliged to abolish poverty, or at least to alleviate it wherever it arises. In this light, poverty which results from (for instance) divorce cannot be blamed on family instability, women's limited employment opportunities or low income alone, but is equally to be ascribed to inadequate social service benefits.

In order to make the concept of state-induced poverty amenable to critical analysis, it should be defined more narrowly. Inadequate state benefits may be counted as a cause of poverty where public provision in such situations may be socially expected: where special institutions exist for the purpose of assisting people in such need situations; where these institutions are embedded in the value system of that welfare state; and where these values and institutions are consistent with the population's attitudes and expectations. Under these conditions the welfare state enters into people's life orientations. As the public welfare sector expands, so state institutions increasingly pattern human lives. This can be seen in its most developed form in the case of 'welfare classes' (see chapter 2, p. 24) such as pensioners. People rely on state old-age pensions with the result that taking out insurance for a private pension becomes less pressing. State pensions are the principal source of income for 90 per cent of old people in Germany. The same applies to handing over one's body to medical experts, which has increased the chances of getting better health care but has reduced the incentive for individuals to see to their own health needs.

The expression 'state-induced poverty' thus covers a wide range of the problematic outcomes of social security systems. The faults may lie in benefit law itself, or may first occur in the benefit delivery system as a consequence of inefficient administration. For example, when benefits in politically vulnerable services such as Unemployment Assistance and Social Assistance are cut for fiscal reasons, as has happened repeatedly since the 1970s, the poverty which this produces must be defined as state induced. As far as benefit delivery is concerned, examples of the problems are Agency staff errors in calculating benefit entitlements, the withholding of information about entitlements (often reported by Social Assistance claimants), and the Agency staff being so overworked that benefit payments are delayed.

The negative consequences of state benefits are usually taken to mean the long-term effects which change the behaviour of people subject to official care or control, for instance dependency on Social Assistance reducing the will to work. However, the negative consequences can also be of a situa-

---

[5] See Girvetz (1968). Joseph Gusfield (1981) speaks of a 'culture of public problems' in democratic welfare states.

tional and selective kind, such as botched medical treatment or a benefit withheld by a social agency, and occur 'mechanically', uninfluenced by the behaviour of the person affected. While critics of the long-term behavioural effects of the welfare state aim to abolish or at least reduce it, deploring the excess of state benefits, the 'mechanistic' generation of poverty by systems such as unemployment insurance is taken by apologists of the welfare state (such as trade unions) as grounds for identifying the paucity of benefits and for demanding the expansion of state provision.

State-induced poverty is a kind of *'secondary' poverty*, in contrast to 'primary' poverty which is immediately caused by, for example, the labour market or disruptions in family life.[6] Which form of state-induced or 'secondary' poverty arises depends on the design of the institutions of the welfare state. One could generalise that, the more complex the institutional arrangements the more likely is the emergence of secondary effects. In this context, complexity refers to the scale of the system, that is, the number of clients and administrative staff, and to the degree of institutional differentiation. Complex systems give citizens a better chance of obtaining effective support, but at the same time they increase the risk of becoming victims of system failure. This paradox is obvious in large social service systems, such as the health or personal social services, but elaborate systems of income maintenance are also liable to malfunction.

The extent and forms of secondary poverty depend not only on organisational complexity but also on what model of welfare state a country has institutionalised. The German welfare state has a dual structure: all-embracing social security systems covering almost the entire population alongside a comparatively small 'residual' Social Assistance system. Under these conditions the receipt of Social Assistance can signify secondary poverty when it is actually the consequence of the inadequacy of higher-rank benefit systems. In countries such as the UK and the USA in which social assistance systems are more highly developed than social insurance, it is less appropriate to view receipt of social assistance as a sign of state-induced poverty. Poverty there is rather induced or at least accepted by society. It follows that in these countries the debate about state-induced poverty centres around the production and reinforcement of poverty in and by Welfare ('welfarisation') rather than by higher-rank systems.

The state production of poverty is criticised not only by outside observers. The review of the changing images of poverty in post-war Germany (chapter 7) reveals with astonishing clarity that even the political actors

---

[6] The concept of 'secondary poverty' is analogous to Edwin Lemert's concept of 'secondary deviance' (1951). It is not related to Rowntree's distinction of 'primary poverty' (physical subsistence) and 'secondary poverty' (above physical subsistence but below social adequacy).

themselves continually treated poverty as having been caused by the welfare state. This began in the debate over 'social reform' in the 1950s and its outcome, the great pension reform which explicitly aimed to relieve the 'pensioners' (*Sozialrentner*) – and not the elderly in general – from the hopelessly inadequate standard of living into which they had been led by an anachronistic Social Insurance system (Hockerts 1980, pp. 197–215). The Federal Social Assistance Act of 1961 was a late outlier of that social reform and was understood as a guarantor for those exceptions which might fall through any remaining gaps in the social security system. In 1975–76 the Christian-Democratic politician Heiner Geißler identified a New Social Question (*Neue Soziale Frage*), tracing back the 'new' poverty of women, the old and large families not just to inadequate benefits but to structural deficiencies of the welfare state: the welfare state in the form of a social-democratic trade-union state was privileging the subjects of 'the old social question', organised labour, at the cost of other groups. Later, it was the cuts in benefits for the unemployed and Social Assistance claimants that led to a recognition (in 1984) of the problem of unemployment as 'the new poverty' in the critical public debate.

The condition of 'poverty' is defined here as the receipt of Social Assistance benefits. This makes sense in a welfare state in which Social Assistance is intended solely as a residual system for emergency situations, one which consequently identifies the claimants as exceptional 'problem cases'. Three types of state-induced poverty can be distinguished: 'frictional poverty', 'transfer poverty' and 'status poverty'. Together these account for half of our sample.

The *frictional poor* are those Social Assistance claimants who have applied for higher-tier benefits, chiefly Unemployment Assistance and Old-Age Pensions, and are waiting for them to be paid. These were described as 'waiting cases' in chapter 3 (pp. 71–82).

The *transfer poor* are those who have to claim supplementary Social Assistance because their transfer payments of higher-tier benefits are inadequate.

The *status poor* are those who suffer from inadequate incomes brought about by state regulations but who are not covered by other social-security benefits, for instance refugees forbidden to take employment or released prisoners.

The possible size of these three groups depends again on the institutional structure of the welfare state in question. In 'residual' welfare states such as the USA, and in the UK, higher-tier security systems are weakly developed, even more so after recent massive cuts, and people in need therefore have to apply for 'welfare': they are the 'transfer poor'. One may find a form of frictional poverty even within such 'welfare systems', as in the USA where claimants may have to wait for benefits longer than in Germany. Status poverty is probably less significant in welfare states based on the principle of citizenship, especially in Sweden, because universal benefits that do not depend on previous contributions effectively counter the processes of exclusion which underlie status poverty. However, the level of a universal benefit may be quite low, so that transfer poverty may occur on a considerable scale. Thus the proportion of old-age pensioners who have their pensions supplemented by Social Assistance is fourteen times higher in the UK than in Germany. In the field of medical provision, the benefits of the National Health Service in the UK are based on universalistic rights, but they are nevertheless accompanied by negative secondary effects and social inequalities attendant on long waiting lists for treatment and administrative inefficiency.

Models of 'dependency'

A sociological examination shows that in the debate on the ways in which the welfare state promotes poverty and dependency, a wide variety of outcomes are described as 'long-term effects'. David Ellwood attempted to provide a more detailed analysis of the diffuse images which are found in the American public's approach to the Welfare system (Bane and Ellwood 1994, chapter 3). He suggested there are three kinds of long-term effects, which may operate independently of each other and together correspond to three theoretical explanatory models of human behaviour. [7]

According to the *rational-choice approach* it is external constraints which above all lead to long-term welfare dependency. An individual's choice between Welfare, employment or marriage (in the case of lone mothers) depends on the level of benefit and the transaction cost of claiming. When the conditions attached to claiming Welfare are attractive compared with the alternatives, it is rational for the individual to choose Welfare. It must already be noted here that this model overlooks important aspects of individual behaviour. We already know that a large proportion of those entitled to claim Social Assistance fail to claim their entitlements because of ignorance or shame (Leibfried 1977, Hartmann 1981, van Oorschot 1995, 1998). Furthermore, there are 'irrational' aspects of behaviour, such as the desire for community and social relationships in the workplace or in the family, which make it unlikely that people give up a job or life with a partner just like that, only to obtain social assistance.[8]

---

[7] For earlier discussions of Ellwood's models see Piachaud (1997) and Leisering and Voges (1992, referring to Ellwood 1987).

[8] A sociological rational-choice model can take these behavioural orientations into account. However, at this point both Ellwood and ourselves are concerned to present the rational-choice model in the form in which it is used in the actual political debate.

The *psycho-social approach* is concerned with factors which reside in the individual. Long-term dependency on Social Assistance is assumed to impair psycho-social competencies such as self-confidence and self-sufficiency. 'Learned helplessness' describes the inability – deriving from repeated experiences of failure – to recognise and seize opportunities for action (Seligman 1975).

The *cultural approach* assumes that long-term claimants develop new, more or less deviant attitudes and behavioural norms, which make it more difficult for them to return to a life without state support. Ellwood locates this type primarily in the inner-city ghettos, in spatially concentrated poverty, in which deviant values are interactively reinforced. We have given this model only scant consideration in our analysis as it seems to have little relevance in Federal German circumstances. In a qualitative analysis of long-term claimants of Income Support in Britain, Dean and Taylor-Gooby (1992, chapter 4) found no evidence of a 'culture of dependency' either. Instead, claimants shared the value-orientations towards work and family prevalent in the rest of society. A cultural explanation model is at work stereotyping East Germans as too slow or incapable of working at a West German tempo because they never learnt how to do so. In this sense the whole of the former German Democratic Republic is characterised as a ghetto of deviant behavioural attitudes.

The cultural model assumes that claimants do not *want* to break their dependency because they have values different from those of the members of core society who pursue an independent mode of being. In the psycho-social model the claimants want to break their dependency but *cannot* manage to do so because they have lost the ability to take the necessary steps required for escape. In the rational-choice model, they similarly do not *want* to break their dependency, but in this case precisely because normal non-deviant orientations of action make Social Assistance appear an acceptable alternative. External factors are decisive in the rational-choice model, but the other two models assume changes within the individual claimant that occur during the claiming period. The cultural model allows in some circumstances for the effects of external stigmatisation, but they may be taken into consideration in the other models as well.

The next sections report what can be said about these three types of long-term effects on the basis of our quantitative and qualitative findings discussed thus far.

The quantitative test of dependency: the impact of objective time

The finding that most claimants receive Social Assistance for only the short or medium term immediately exposes the limitations of the thesis that

Social Assistance creates dependency. This debate thus concerns only a small minority of all claimants: to reiterate, only 6 per cent of all claimants in our representative study received Social Assistance for more than five uninterrupted years (chapter 3, p. 66).

Using multivariate event-history analysis we studied in detail which factors affected the chances that Social Assistance claims would terminate more or less quickly. Our data permitted an analysis of this kind to be carried out for the first time in Germany.[9] The 'welfarisation' thesis implies the hypothesis that the probability of leaving Social Assistance (in technical terms the 'hazard rate') falls with time, because the longer claiming lasts the more difficult it is to escape from Social Assistance. In fact the findings reveal a diminishing hazard rate as duration increases.

However, a hazard rate which falls over time in itself reveals nothing about the reasons for the fall. Is it caused by Social Assistance itself, as if the receipt of state benefits deprives the claimant of will-power to escape? Or does it fall because the falling rate reflects the heterogeneity of the population claiming Social Assistance? In that case the well-qualified unemployed, for example, who possess good escape opportunities, would manage to escape more quickly, leaving behind those such as the disabled with poorer chances of escape. This would cause the transfer rate to fall as the duration of claiming increases. But different durations of claiming would then be based upon different situations of need in which claimants find themselves, rather than being the consequence of Social Assistance itself.

This interpretation has in part been confirmed by quantitative analysis (see chapter 3). The reasons for claiming, especially 'waiting for prior benefits', have a strong influence on how quickly claims are terminated. It is relatively simple to explain the chances of terminating single claiming spells in terms of the structural characteristics of the individuals or households. Longer periods of claiming, however, are often composed of a sequence of several separate spells, and it has turned out to be much more difficult to explain such discontinuous courses. It has thus been harder to predict the overall duration of claiming on the basis of socio-structural background variables.

Other variables which have not until now been considered may therefore be required to explain discontinuous claiming careers of the kind composed of repeated spells with temporary intermissions. These variables may include personal educational and occupational qualifications, integration into social networks, or institutional variables such as the treatment by

---

[9] For full details of the quantitative analysis of duration see Buhr (1995, pp. 149–159). For a summary assessment of welfare dependency in the USA see Blank (1997, pp. 151–156).

Agency staff or participation in activities demanded by the Agency such as employment schemes for claimants like *Hilfe zur Arbeit*. However, our data do not report these variables consistently.[10]

In an in-depth analysis of work exits in our sample, Markus Gangl (1998) found that the chances of ceasing to claim Social Assistance by taking up employment remain about constant during the first two years of claiming, only dropping off slightly thereafter. Families with three or more children, who are deemed susceptible to becoming dependent because Assistance may not be 'less eligible' for them than earning a wage in the labour market, do not achieve fewer work exits than others. Testing common theories of job recruitment in the labour market, Gangl also found that Social Assistance claimants' exits into the labour market follow the 'normal' patterns of job search and selective recruitment prevalent among non-claimants, that is, vocational qualifications, work experience and short periods out of work matter while lone mothers with small children, sick and disabled persons, women and older workers are disadvantaged.

The quantitative analysis has thus not produced substantial evidence that anything like 'welfarisation' exists. Instead, the evidence suggests that a far more credible hypothesis is that the diminishing probability of escape from Social Assistance is largely to be explained by the preceding heterogeneity of the subjects of our survey. In other words, for some claimants it is predictable right from the start that they will remain longer than others – because their problems are of a long-lasting kind and not because they become dependent during the course of claiming.[11] If this hypothesis is correct, the rational explanatory model would be the most appropriate: that is, people continue to claim because in the given circumstances – and in terms of 'normal' and not deviant individual goals – it is rational for them to choose the 'Social Assistance option', because for instance they have a child to care for and alternative solutions such as having a husband as breadwinner are either unavailable or less desirable. They do not remain claimants because (as the psycho-social model suggests) their competence has declined over time or because they have lost self-confidence.

---

[10] Discontinuous Social Assistance careers could be studied using multi-episode models, but their development is still at an early stage (for preliminary approaches in the study of Assistance careers see Leisering and Voges 1992, pp. 467f., Buhr 1995, pp. 157–159, and Weber 1996). They would permit an examination of how far different constellations of reasons might be responsible for spells of different lengths. Models of this kind also allow the duration of intermissions between claiming spells to be taken into account.

[11] This is also found by Walker and Shaw (1998, p. 241) in an analysis of social assistance (Income Support) careers in Britain. Using an explanatory model that distinguishes structural and individualistic determinants of time spent on benefit, they also challenge the notion of dependence.

We have shown that some claimants do in fact weigh up the options between Social Assistance and the alternatives, so that the term *choice* could be applied to a degree. Certain objectives, such as caring for a child, can be achieved under the given conditions only with the help of Social Assistance. But no real choice is available to others such as the 'resigned long-term claimants lacking alternatives', a type to which many of the long-term unemployed may be allocated (chapter 4, pp. 99–101). This stretches the rational model to its limits: external circumstances alone and not the individual's own wishes determine entry to Social Assistance.

If permanent objective circumstances force a person to keep claiming, then there can be no question of time effects: the claim lasts a long time just because the rational grounds which were responsible for entry to Social Assistance in the given circumstances have not changed over time. In other words, there are no genuine long-term effects which would support the image of dependents who have become unfit or even asocial. These cases are far more explicable in terms of a static rational choice model (including the borderline case of 'choices' determined by circumstances). It thus becomes clear that the rational-choice model of dependency is of a static nature and cannot explain processes. In the following passages Ellwood confirms this on the basis of US research findings on Welfare:

A very large part of the evidence on long-term welfare use can be understood without resorting to models emphasizing lack of confidence or adverse values (Bane and Ellwood 1994, p. 119). . . . Dependency needn't be seen as deviance from legitimate and defensible behaviour (Ellwood 1987, p. 92). . . . there is little evidence to date from either statistical or attitudinal work that people really become trapped on welfare in the sense that it becomes harder and harder to escape as duration on the program increases. Finding that some people spend ten or even twenty years on welfare seems to prove that people become trapped. They remain on welfare a long, long time. Yet they may be stuck there as much because they lack alternatives as because they have become passive or unmotivated. (Bane and Ellwood 1994, p. 100)

In these cases long-term claiming is a consequence of insufficient alternatives and is only state-induced in the sense that the social assistance law in some countries permits long periods of claiming under certain circumstances. Claimants make use of what is available and receive maintenance payments over long periods. One can describe this as a dependency effect of the welfare state in only a very loose sense. The concept of welfarisation is thus used in the USA at times to mean no more than that a growing proportion of the population is subsisting with the help of Welfare.

This can point to the conclusion for social policy that alternatives should be provided, for instance that more job opportunities should be created, that women's pay should be raised, or that the arrangements for child care should be expanded. In the USA, the health-insurance bill which President

Clinton proposed would have made a significant contribution, since many people claimed Welfare because it gave access to health services (Bane and Ellwood 1994, p. 123). In a given situation such as lasting mass unemployment or low pay for women, it is a matter of political choice whether or not these spurious long-term effects (that is, long-term claims as the consequence of long-term problem conditions) are unwanted. The question is, for which circumstances of need are state benefits legitimately to be provided? In Germany, the provision of long-lasting or even life-long benefits to those with permanent problems is seen as an expression of the basic values of the welfare state. To allow such decisions to be made, normative criteria are needed to judge what lifestyles and patterns deserve state support and what periods of 'time-off' from the labour market or the family are legitimate. The answer to the question of what is legitimate depends on the prevailing life-course regime and the dominant social policy culture. In the USA the provision of long-lasting benefits or even of benefits as a matter of rights has come to be seen as symbolic of the negativity of the welfare state. Thus the traditional programme structure, which had already been hollowed over the previous two decades, collapsed in August 1996 with Clinton's 'reform' (Lynn 1997).

Dependency profiles: Germany and the USA compared

In the USA, where security for the life course is only offered by the state at a minimal level, public provision can only be justified in extreme situations of need and in the absence of any alternative, and even then only selectively. As Kaufmann puts it: '(The) extremely individualistic American tradition . . . (leads) to a justification of poverty, exclusion and exploitation which is inconceivable in the European tradition' (Kaufmann 1973, p. 94). In its culture this society denies the fundamental and inevitable fact of human dependence – on death, on the family, on the public sphere[12] – and consequently at the deepest level it cannot comprehend the idea of a welfare state: its idea of Welfare is no more than a false image with which to better exorcise the devil. The obsession with which 'welfare mothers' are 'persecuted' in both social science and politics is the supposedly rational garb of a culture in which the relief of the needy can be envisaged only in the form of 'you should sing for your supper'. The neo-conservatives in the USA criticise a Welfare system whose harshness strains the imagination even of those right-wing German politicians who call for restricting Social Assistance.

The German welfare state moulds life courses and is not just their cus-

---

[12] A similar point was made by Dean and Taylor-Gooby (1992) in view of Thatcherite Britain.

todian, and as such it aims to enhance opportunities for choice more strongly. As we have shown, even the lowest tier of the social welfare system, Social Assistance, can be used by citizens in this sense. The availability of Social Assistance enlarges the choices people can make in planning their life projects, and it enables some of them to reject unacceptable alternatives in favour of claiming Assistance long-term.

However, the boundary between active support for the life course and 'nanny-state paralysis of individual initiative' is contested even in the culture of German social policy. There have always been liberal critics of the welfare state but in the mid 1990s their voices became stronger than before in public debate. Unlike the situation in the USA and recently also in Britain, child care in the absence of a breadwinner is still widely recognised as a reason for claiming Social Assistance, but unemployed claimants are confronted with neo-liberals' stereotyped suspicions that they do not want to work or have become workshy while supported by the state's safety net. This reflects the gender-differentiated model of the life course in the German welfare-state regime. Even in the higher-tier systems such as insurance pensions and in the occupational system women are less likely to be treated as participants in the labour market than they are in the USA or in Sweden (chapter 2, p. 50). Whoever uses the rational-choice model in the USA to criticise Welfare, arguing that claiming Welfare is rational because it is more attractive than paid work, is still starting from the assumption that poor people aim to gain employment. By contrast, in the German life-course regime a renunciation of well-paid work in favour of the option of dedicating oneself to full-time child care supported by Social Assistance is to some extent culturally sanctioned and thus rational.

We have examined the effects of social assistance on lone mothers in Germany and the USA in detail in order to compare and clarify the roles of institutional forces. If state support really traps people in social assistance when public support is more attractive than employment as the rational-choice model suggests, then the generous German system of Social Assistance must lead to longer dependence than the US system of Aid to Families with Dependent Children (AFDC, now TANF). To examine this question, a comparative study of the Bremen and American data was carried out with the cooperation of Greg Duncan. The subjects were lone mothers claiming Social Assistance or receiving Welfare (for the following see Duncan and Voges 1993).[13]

Lone mothers can count on only very low Welfare benefits in the USA.

---

[13] The basis of the US data is the Panel Study of Income Dynamics (133 first time lone-mother claimants during the years 1983 to 1986); in Germany it is our Bremen study (108 first time lone-mother claimants during the years 1983 and 1984). The detailed statistical analysis can be found in Duncan and Voges (1993).

In the mid 1980s, for a lone mother with two dependent children these amounted on average to 27 per cent of the national average household income. By contrast, in Germany the proportion ranged between 47 and 67 per cent depending on the age of the children (Duncan *et al.* 1994). Other Western countries similarly exceed the US levels. As a result, income poverty is far more common among dual and single-headed families with children in the USA than in Germany. At the same time, the European welfare systems offer fewer incentives to take paid work than does the system in the USA. Statistically, American Welfare recipients, by taking up work, can raise their incomes relatively more than in most European countries. It follows that longer durations of claiming are to be expected in European systems, if it were only a matter of rational financial calculations on the part of lone mothers.

Nevertheless, our analysis of the durations of claiming show that in spite of the more generous and less stigmatising German system, German lone mothers do not remain claimants for longer than their American counterparts. The reasons are instructive.

First, the waiting-room function of Social Assistance is hardly relevant in the USA, that is, assistance for claimants who are waiting for unemployment insurance or other prior benefits to be paid, since such systems of benefits are less well developed in the USA. The waiting cases lower the average duration of benefit. It also means that women have access to non-discriminating and better endowed entitlement programmes in the German social security system while American women generally have only the choice of full-time employment, marriage or Welfare. If the waiting cases are omitted, it turns out that Social Assistance is paid for longer periods in the German system.

Second, a combination of social factors work together to shorten duration of receipt among German mothers. These include the higher age of both claiming mothers and children, and the lower density of Social Assistance claimants in specific neighbourhoods, for example less ghettoisation. Other factors such as the lower frequency of grandmothers living in the same household tend to act in the opposite direction. Third, German lone mothers have somewhat longer first spells of claiming, but they manage more often to become independent of Social Assistance permanently, while American lone mothers are forced to reapply more frequently (in technical terms 'recidivism'). Fourth, there is some evidence that the better public child-care facilities in Bremen facilitated escape from Social Assistance. All in all, a simulation study showed that if the German system were imposed on the USA the duration of claiming would probably be extended.

We can draw some conclusions. Obviously there are institutional effects on duration, meaning that the length of claims does not depend exclusively on the claimants' objective problems but also on the level of available benefits. Such a finding is hardly surprising when one compares a very generous with an exceedingly restrictive system. At the same time, consideration of the influence of the range and combination of social factors described above leads to the conclusion that if the duration is not wholly dependent on the needs of the claimant it is certainly affected by them. It becomes evident again that the social policy decisions are above all a question of values: whether citizens are prepared, for example, to pay more for a generous system which leads to longer durations but which reduces poverty among children. In spite of certain programme effects this can hardly be interpreted as 'welfarisation'. Seen in an international perspective, the German social security system as a whole keeps poverty relatively low and, by means of higher-tier security systems (and in Bremen also through infrastructural services such as child care), largely prevents people from falling into the lowest safety net, i.e., Social Assistance. This finding is significant in view of the early social policy initiatives by the Clinton administration, especially in the field of health, which aimed to introduce elements of the European social policy tradition (particularly from Germany) into the USA.

The qualitative test of dependency I: the impact of subjective time

The quantitative analysis offers general findings on the duration of Social Assistance claims and hypotheses about the claimants' underlying rationales. However, only the qualitative interviews reveal their actual behavioural attitudes and allow us to distinguish between patterns of action.[14] The analysis of 'subjective time' in Social Assistance (chapter 4) offers us three criteria by which to determine in which cases long-term effects are probable and in which they are not.

The first criterion is the subjective perspective on time. Dependency on Social Assistance is less probable if there is a positive approach to duration, such as the aspiration to escape in the case of the 'subjective bridgers' or a deliberately accepted or even desired long-term perspective in the case of the 'voluntary or calculated long-term claimants'. Conversely, candidates for long-term effects are those with damaged time perspectives, that is the 'unsuccessful bridgers' whose claims became unexpectedly drawn out, and the 'resigned or constrained long-term claimants' who passed into Social Assistance without hope of escape.

The second criterion is the claimants' evaluation of the claim period in

---

[14] Walker and Shaw (1998) use attitudinal data from a standardised survey.

the context of their wider biographies. Long-term effects are unlikely among those who can put the difficult periods of life on Social Assistance into proportion (whether by comparison with an earlier insecure life situation or in relation to even worse current experiences in other aspects of life) or who can even strike a positive overall balance because Social Assistance enabled them to pursue overarching objectives in life. On the contrary, candidates for 'welfarisation' are those who come to an overall negative evaluation, in that they are unable to put the negative aspects of Social Assistance into proportion or compensate for them in the same way.

The third criterion is the intentionality of claiming Social Assistance. Our study confirms that even a discriminating benefit system like Social Assistance can be the object of rational calculation by citizens, and that this is not a matter of benefit abuse but of legitimate entitlement. People not only slide or are pushed into making claims, many make a conscious and deliberate choice. To the extent that claiming is the result of a process of balancing alternatives, one can at least assume that claimants will look out for unexpected dependency effects and will actively struggle against them. This applies to 'calculated (long-term) bridgers' as well as to 'calculated long-term claimants'. In any case the problem of unintended and unexpected consequences remains. According to circumstances these may be unnoticeable or lie beyond people's ability to deal with them: examples are a lack of qualifications or restricted job opportunities after a long period of absence from the labour market.

In order to identify the candidates for long-term effects more precisely, the three criteria have to be taken in combination. There are 'congruent' cases in which two or three criteria point in the same direction. For example people who are bringing up children, or who find themselves at a stage of biographical reorientation, have a good prognosis if they both aim to escape (they are 'subjective bridgers') and have a positive attitude towards the whole of their claiming career because they value the opportunity to care for their child or rearrange their lives. Conversely, the 'incongruent' are those (for instance the 'constrained long-term claimants') who came to Social Assistance without aiming or wanting to, and who have no expectation of escape, but who can put the hopelessness of their fate into proportion by comparing it with the situation before claiming which was even worse. In this instance it is harder to answer the question whether long periods of claiming lead to discouragement and apathy. The incongruent also include those subjective bridgers who have an escape perspective but who nevertheless have been pressured by circumstances into claiming without having made a calculated decision to do so.

We may conclude that long-term effects only arise under specified conditions. They are most likely to occur when claimants are vulnerable in terms of all three criteria: when a negative or interrupted time perspective is present; when in addition the subjects lack overarching biographical points of reference which would help to put claiming into proportion; and furthermore when the claim arose from external pressures and not from an individual decision. By contrast, the ideal type of positive prognosis is the long-term bridger who has deliberately chosen Social Assistance and who can outweigh its negative concomitants with its broader positive functions. The three aspects of subjective time horizon, biographical evaluation and intentionality of claiming are constituents of a *biographisation* of Social Assistance; that is, they locate claiming in the individual's life history and plans.[15] Claiming is invested with a meaning in life. We can therefore conclude that welfarisation is less likely the more claimants achieve a biographisation of Social Assistance. The majority of claimants achieve such a biographisation.

The qualitative test of dependency II: the impact of action by claimants

How about those claimants who are not capable of biographisation? And what happens to those who fail to carry through their life plans relating to Social Assistance, and for whom things develop in ways other than originally planned? To elucidate these questions we must study the actual behaviour of those affected, which we analysed in the previous chapter under the heading of 'coping'. We observed claimants over a period of seven or more years from the time of their first claim. We found five types, distinguished by their ability to cope. In rising order of their ability to cope we have called them victims, mere survivors, pragmatic copers and biographical copers, plus the category of strategic users. At the lowest end of the scale, living with Social Assistance was at best a matter of securing one's material living or surviving the struggle with the Agency; at the highest end it was the biographical objectives which came to the fore and pushed Social Assistance aside, chiefly child care, occupational and personal reorientation or convalescence after illness. We have simplified the scale to three types:
> endurers (people with no ability to cope or chances of doing so): victims and mere survivors
> (active) copers (pragmatic copers and biographical copers)
> strategic users

Within each of these three types or groups there are candidates for a distinct form of dependency. These three types of dependency correspond to a degree to Ellwood's three explanatory models – rational, psycho-social and cultural. These types are commonly confused in the public debate.

---

[15] The concept of 'biographisation' is discussed in chapter 2, p. 36; see also p. 240.

While Ellwood derived his models from an analysis of public debates, we base the three following types of potential dependency on our qualitative micro-analysis of claimants' careers.

(1) Marginalised Social Assistance claimants (affinity to the psycho-social and cultural models)

This is the group of victims and (mere) survivors which in this context we call the 'marginalised claimants' because they have become marginalised in the classic sense. They are vulnerable to the negative long-term effects of Social Assistance. In making sense of their biographies (biographisation) they are unable to associate Social Assistance with anything other than securing basic subsistence or even less. In the public images of poverty and dependency their visible suffering is highlighted especially by social critics from the left, who also blame the welfare state for exacerbating the lot of these people by inadequate provisions and repressive control. In social science this type of claimant is the traditional subject of research into marginal groups.

(2) Subjects of unanticipated outcomes (affinity to the psycho-social and the rational models)

Copers are highly skilled at giving Social Assistance a meaningful place in their biographies (biographisation). They become candidates for long-term effects and permanent dependency when their life plans are thwarted because unanticipated negative effects arise during their period on Social Assistance, such as loss of self-confidence or unforeseen difficulties in re-entering the labour market after years of absence. Critics use this type as evidence that the welfare state may be well intentioned but it has come to create more problems than it solves. Even active and motivated people may lose their self-sufficiency after years of claiming. In social science this view is partly akin to class analysis.

(3) Strategic users (affinity to the rational model)

These people similarly use Social Assistance chiefly to pursue their own plans (a high degree of biographisation), but unlike the copers their aims are potentially illegitimate – for instance, avoiding employment. While the emergence of unintended effects in Social Assistance shows the dangers even of well-intentioned institutions, the strategic use of Social Assistance is often noted by neo-liberal or right-wing critics as evidence that the welfare state is fundamentally flawed because it already negatively influences people's basic action orientations (meanings): it eliminates the pursuit of independent 'substantial' directions in life, leaving only a 'functional rationality' of seeking advantage (Mayer and Müller 1986). Under the label of 'abuse' the strategic use of social welfare benefits has become stylised as a major problem in the welfare state. This type of claimant is akin to a cultural critique of modern institutions expounded by some social scientists and social philosophers.

A more in-depth portrayal of the three types follows.

Type 1: Marginalised claimants

These people display many signs of discouragement, loss of self-sufficiency, and exclusion, but in spite of this the large majority are not welfarisation cases. This is, first, because their long-term claims are primarily the result of an objectively problematic situation, and the chances of escaping from Social Assistance are objectively limited. This relates chiefly to the long-term unemployed, especially younger single men who have additional problems such as sickness or addiction. To that extent this represents a boundary case for Ellwood's rational explanatory model: Social Assistance is 'chosen' because there is no other choice. Under the German welfare-state regime this choice is therefore legitimate and cannot be taken as a sign of dependency. Long-term unemployed people themselves evaluate being unemployed as more significant than claiming Social Assistance.

The second reason is that these people's reduced self-sufficiency stems not from Social Assistance but usually emerged even before they started claiming. Unsuitable socialisation, such as growing up in a multi-problem family or spending long periods in institutional care, beginning in children's homes and continuing into criminality and drug addiction, contribute to the failure to develop stable and independent ways of managing one's life.

In the face of overpowering structural and individual deficits marginalisation is not unexpected, not even by the claimants themselves – by contrast to the second type who use Social Assistance actively in pursuit of biographical goals but unexpectedly get trapped in claiming. The marginalised in fact find themselves in a vicious circle and frequently describe their situation in these terms. In this sense, elements of Ellwood's psycho-social explanatory model are found here, but again not as a sign of dependency but as a description of disintegration processes whose causes lie outside Social Assistance.

However, secondary institutional effects may occur. The Social Assistance Agencies exacerbate these claimants' problems by writing them off as hopeless. As one claimant in our sample expressed it, echoing two further claimants receiving benefit at the Unemployment Agency, 'I was in S's office, he was the top dog of them all, and he said, that's a social case, we'll always have to pay out on that one.' These claimants' situation required more and better targeted help than others, but they received less – a paradox of Social Assistance (Ludwig 1996, p. 283).

Type 2: Subjects of unanticipated outcomes

The 'subjects of unexpected outcomes' are the claimants who enter Social Assistance with an (short- or long-term) escape perspective ('subjective bridgers') or people who accept permanent claiming without becoming resigned to it ('calculated long-term claimants') but who then have to adapt to a wide range of unexpected long-term effects. These include changes in the external conditions such as job opportunities after a long period without regular employment[16] or reductions in self-sufficiency, self-confidence or initiative. Other explanatory models might be used at the same time: the rational model may explain not only entry into Social Assistance but also the diminishing chances of being able to escape from it by taking employment, while the psycho-social and cultural models explain further long-term effects.

The 'unanticipated consequences' type is the object of both right-wing and left-wing criticism, each drawing different conclusions for social policy. Those who support the welfare state in principle focus on the measures which counter the psycho-social and cultural effects, such as advice services, social work and the development of self-help groups for the unemployed and lone mothers (e.g. Bane and Ellwood 1994, p. 119). Conversely, for those who reject anything more than a residual welfare state, such effects merely confirm the prejudice which they have always held against state welfare: the welfare state may be well intentioned but it causes more problems than it solves.

These critics underestimate the 'rational core' of many of these cases: making a claim is a rational response to preceding deprivation conditions which would not disappear if welfare-state support were withdrawn even if this might make them less visible. Even the 'rational' reasons for the increasing difficulty of escape are misunderstood when they are adduced out of context. If job opportunities worsen objectively after years of claiming, the blame cannot be laid unconditionally on the welfare state. Indeed, housewives who are not claimants and who want to return to paid work after their children have left home face the same problem. The conservative critics of the welfare state would surely not conclude from this that the institution of marriage which establishes a relationship between a male breadwinner and a dependent wife should be abolished. A strategy of reducing welfare would risk exacerbating the unwanted consequences of Social Assistance. Mary Jo Bane and David Ellwood therefore recommended – in vain – that the American Welfare reform should demand more effort from claimants but simultaneously should offer them more in services (1994, p. 143), rather than assuming that cutting benefits would facilitate their escape from claiming.

---

[16] Allmendinger (1994, p. 264) labels these as 'duration injuries'.

To what extent do long-term claimants aiming to escape have false expectations about the concomitants of many years on benefit? Our six-year window of observation is insufficient to answer these questions. However, closer examination suggests that long-term bridgers with misconceptions are not very prevalent, as emerges from a small-scale exploratory study by Franz Schultheis (1987). This study in a South German Federal *Land,* investigated an income experiment, a special programme for lone mothers claiming Social Assistance, at the end of the 1970s.[17] The study showed that institutions indeed can lead to welfarisation, but only when the institutional rules disempower the subjects, as was the case in this instance. A comparison with our findings makes the point more explicit.

Out of the 11 subjective long-term bridgers in our study (mainly but not exclusively lone parents), eight were still claimants after six years, so we could not finally establish how realistic their firm intentions of escaping were. Some of them were keeping in contact with their occupations through part-time work, or they had plans to do so which they were just about to carry out. The experimental programme which Schultheis studied was directed against this, aiming to discourage paid employment, meaning that such cases were actively excluded from the study. Three long-term bridgers in our study had already terminated their claims by the time of interview. This 'success' may have something to do with their level of education which was higher than *Hauptschule* (secondary modern school, junior high school) in all three cases. Two of them had first applied when they already had two children, and one woman was living with her student partner. Neither of these situations arose in the Schultheis study; the income experiment excluded cohabitation with a partner and was directed at women who had just given birth to what was presumed to be their first child, the rationale being to dissuade women from choosing abortion. But even in Schultheis' study most of the women managed to escape from Social Assistance: 70 per cent of the participants in the experimental programme managed to achieve this step within six months of the end of the programme. This is a larger number than would have been expected on the basis of our findings.

Type 3: Strategic users
Many claimants could be said to act 'strategically' in the broadest sense, for instance when a lone parent claims Social Assistance in order to care for a child. But when we use the term 'strategic users' we mean only the (few)

---

[17] Schultheis studied lone mothers claiming Social Assistance, mainly 'subjective long-term bridgers', and established that almost all of them suffered from extensive welfarisation such as discouragement and loss of social contacts.

people who deliberately create the conditions through which a claim becomes legitimate. This corresponds to the idea of moral hazard drawn from the field of insurance: the existence of benefits is a temptation (a risk to morality) for people deliberately to create the conditions for a claim, instead of the conditions arising from unpredictable but insurable external risks. Social Assistance in this sense is not a (undesired) means of solving a preceding problem such as unemployment or child care, but is itself part of a strategy. In extreme cases people systematically plan their lives on the basis of the availability of Social Assistance. The value system of such people has effectively been changed under the influence of the welfare state.

'Strategic users' are people who, for instance, keep leaving their jobs and who therefore are excluded from claiming Unemployment Benefits during a three-month waiting period. The availability of Social Assistance allows them to get out of unwanted working situations which may lead to irregular patterns of employment. Another situation is that of women who deliberately avoid a potential partnership in cohabitation with the father of their children and thus create the conditions for claiming Social Assistance. Some of the lone mothers in our study had further children while they were claimants, which might be partially interpreted as a self-induced prolongation of their claiming.

These seem to be classical examples of state-induced dependencies. However, a more detailed analysis points to a disparate picture. It must be noted that this applies to only a limited group of people, particularly young men for whom the irregular employment and repeated Social Assistance claims form only a transitional stage in life before they stabilise their lives occupationally and in marital relationships. Further, the boundary between legitimate use of Social Assistance (for example for child care) and the illegitimate (self-induced eligibility) is a fluid one. According to statute, people who leave their employment 'for good cause' (*aus wichtigem Grund*) have a right to full Social Assistance, because otherwise their constitutionally guaranteed freedom of action would be restricted.[18] If a man leaves an unreasonable job in the knowledge that he will be covered by Social Assistance, this is comparable to a woman who separates from a violent husband knowing that after the separation she has a right to claim Social Assistance. How far Social Assistance ought to empower individuals to choose to leave their employment if it is intolerable or the boss's behaviour

---

[18] Leaving employment without 'good cause' leads, under § 25 II 3 of the Federal Social Assistance Act, to a reduction of benefits to the level of mere absolute essentials. Leaving employment 'for good cause' is permissible without a reduction of benefit under both this Act and the Employment Promotion Act. A 'good cause' exists if the wage rates paid were below the minimum agreed upon by employers and trade unions or below local norms, or the working conditions were illegal or a danger to health or morals (see LPK 1994, section no. 9 and 13 on § 25).

is unreasonable, depends on the current socio-political culture of a country. As far as women are concerned, some in the women's movement demand that Social Assistance should be available on an individual basis instead of depending on the joint income of partners.

The rational model cannot adequately explain the strategic use of Social Assistance either, at any rate not in the current version in which it is asserted that claims are made because employment does not pay. Studies have shown that in Germany, Social Assistance benefits do not exceed the lowest levels of earnings except in some instances of large families with single breadwinners (Breuer and Engels 1994). But we did not find a single example of this (rare) type of household in which employment had been abandoned in favour of Social Assistance. It is obviously not simply a matter of financial calculation.[19] In fact, the strategic users are predominantly young single people, who are always worse off on Social Assistance than in work. It may be that the cultural model applies here, if one wished to describe this as a hedonistic lifestyle. If so, it would be hedonism at a very low level, for example with respondent 24, who repeatedly claimed Social Assistance in order, among other things, to be able to watch as much football on TV as possible, on all European channels. Football gave meaning to his life. When asked during the period of the World Cup games if he had considered taking employment, he replied indignantly, 'then I'd have missed half the matches!'. His was an extreme case which nevertheless shows the kind of modest advantage at stake.

Right-wing critics of the welfare state prefer to treat the strategic user as the dominant type, contrary to our findings, and they therefore call the whole of Social Assistance into question. For sociologists, the type is hardly surprising and even less disturbing, one which occurs in similar forms in many other social institutions.

The politics of dependency

The discussion of the various types of Social Assistance careers in the light of the rational, the psycho-social and the cultural explanatory models reveals a diverse picture of Social Assistance dependency. Long-term effects do exist, but they only appear among very few of the long-term claimants, a group which itself is in any case very small. We have reconstructed three types of effects which are generally confused with each other as 'dependency' in the public debate: the marginalisation of claimants whose lives were already burdened with problems before they claimed; the

---

[19] Low earners in Germany have the right to claim supplementary Social Assistance which then acts as a low-wage subsidy or a minimum wage. This facility was systematically expanded in the 1996 Social Assistance reform.

emergence during longer claims of unanticipated effects affecting claimants with a basic ability to cope; and the 'strategic' use of Social Assistance at the margins between legitimate and illegitimate lifestyles. What appears to be welfarisation is generally not undesirable dependence on institutional services but the legitimate long-term use of welfare-state benefits intended for long-lasting needs. In as far as there are any genuine long-term effects, they mainly reflect the negative dynamic of external contingencies ensuing from structural constraints and individual deficits in socialisation; they are not injuries which Social Assistance itself inflicts.

An element of political culture which distinguishes welfare-state societies from other societies, is the aim of facilitating 'forms of existence outside the labour market' (Offe 1984, p. 94), that is, of liberating citizens from the brute force of the marketplace, from being compelled to sell their labour power in the market even while suffering crises. Esping-Andersen (1990) speaks of 'decommodification'. The welfare state's institutions mediate the impact of market forces – as well as the pressures which accompany family and marriage – and thereby create new forms of social relationship. Even Social Assistance does this – especially, as our findings suggest, in relation to marriage, by enabling women to consider separation without risking material annihilation.

Such cultural changes were the objects of Ivan Illich's critical analysis of modern social institutions. He suggested that public health services have disempowered people and made them incapable of caring for their own bodies, and described this as 'cultural iatrogenesis' (1976). Under these conditions it is both inevitable and rational to seek professional medical services, but only on the precondition of individual helplessness created by the extension of these very services.

However, this cultural critique cannot, without qualification, be presented as a political critique of the welfare state leading to the conclusion that social security should be abolished. The critique is focused on the tense interrelationship between social structures and the individual which characterises all core institutions of modern society such as market, enterprise and association. The critique of modernity does not easily translate into a realistic critique of social policy. It is scarcely possible to tell what an 'independent' or 'substantial' individual orientation to life could be in the light of the structures of meaning in modernity. The individual is constituted by society and is not, as it were, 'corrupted' by social institutions like the welfare state.

Social Assistance is particularly unsuited to be the starting point for criticism of the welfare state. It is as if among all the passengers on the train only those holding the cheapest tickets are made responsible for the problems the whole train experiences. The very large volume of 'latent' poverty, that is, of those who are entitled to claim Social Assistance but do not do so, demonstrates furthermore how unattractive Social Assistance is as a strategic measure, even to the members of the poorer strata.

Long-term effects occur in a few cases – but far fewer than many would like to believe, and with very disparate political significance. Long-term effects could equally well be taken to justify the expansion of welfare benefits, in order to give better support to claimants. Stricter controls aiming to prevent undesirable benefit claims could of course be introduced, but they would only affect a small group of people and lead to minimal savings, although in times of municipal fiscal crisis any savings are welcome. At the time of the German Social Assistance reform of 1996, the responsible Minister, Horst Seehofer, acknowledged that in this field of social security, unlike others, there was little room for savings – unless of course basic human values and the legal requirements of the Federal Constitutional Court were to be abandoned. In the last resort this is a matter of value judgements about which welfare state, what kind of society, which 'forms of existence outside the labour market' are desired. If social policy is to mould patterns of life and not only guarantee a minimal level of existence, then society must give thought to the issues of which kinds of 'time off' from the labour market and family are to be assured, for which people and in which problem situations, for how long, in what circumstances – and with what side effects.

To ask the question whether Social Assistance creates dependency and thereby damages society is therefore not just a matter of considering actual career patterns of the kind we have reported in this chapter, but is rather a question of politics. The fact that the issue is raised in political debates says more about ideological conflicts such as questioning the very existence of the welfare state or party-political confrontations than it does about complex realities. One might wish that such debates could be diverted into open argument about a better and fairer social order.

Right-wing criticisms of Social Assistance come and go irrespective of new scientific findings about the alleged abuses and without connection with the actual scale of the problem. Of a total of DM 52 billion which was spent on Social Assistance in Germany in 1995, only DM 19 billion was for cash benefits (Basic Income Support) – less than the total spent, for instance, on family allowances for civil servants and services for the victims of war (DM 13 billion and DM 14 billion respectively; Breier 1997). Most of the Social Assistance expenditure is not devoted to cash benefits but to benefits in kind (Special Needs Support) (DM 33 billion), above all to care for people who live in residential care (DM17 billion) and for the disabled (DM13 billion) – that is, it is spent on people whose 'time off' is generally uncontested, at least in Germany. Conversely, left-wing assumptions about the hopelessness of poverty and Social Assistance claiming draw on a wealth of scientific studies, but these tend to be biased towards special problem groups among the long-term poor. What is common to both sides is that the discussion about poverty is driven by preconceived images, in which the picture of deep-seated permanent poverty and 'dependency' serves political purposes. The generation and development of public images of poverty is the subject of the next chapter.

Part III
Poverty and social change: debates and policies

Plate 3 'Of Poverty', The Petrarca-Master, Augsburg 1532.

An unnamed artist, active in the first third of the 16th century, created this woodcut *'Von Armut'* to illustrate the first German translation of Francesco Petrarca, *De remediis utriusque fortunae* (1366); *Von der Arzney bayder Glück, des guten und widerwertigen. (Städtische Kunstsammlungen Augsburg)*

Political conditions are slow to change, even – and perhaps particularly – when society is changing. Discourses are dislodged from their well-trodden channels only with difficulty. Poverty is an especially old subject. Ever since the nineteenth century the social risks of industrialised society and the role of the state have been debated, and 'liberal', 'socialist' and 'conservative' ways of thinking have hardened. Even the politically created institutions have their own built-in inertia. Institutionalisation means precisely that: putting social functions on to a long-lasting basis. The response to the collapse of the German Democratic Republic (GDR) was to extend the old well-proven Western institutions to the East.

Hopes for a great new departure, a new constitution in the whole new republic, were soon dissipated. The social policy 'achievements' of the ruined GDR – such as the economically independent role of women, guaranteed employment, pre-school child care, occupational health and social services – were not adopted by the unified country. Instead, the antiquated West German social security institutions were transplanted into the East irrespective of the circumstances. The fact that certain adjustment concessions, such as supplements to the contributory pensions, were temporarily required indicates, however, that legal rules and systems of finance can simply be imposed while the trust in their legitimacy, appropriateness or justice which social institutions need in order to exist cannot be taken for granted. The citizens of the former GDR had different life experiences and attitudes. The subjects of an authoritarian 'provider state' cannot become citizens of a pluralistic welfare state overnight. Heightened sensitivity is required in situations where unemployment and recourse to Social Assistance were unknown. The life careers of the East Germans swing between radical change and continuity (see chapter 8).

However, even the social institutions in the West have been slow in adapting to the social changes and the new forms of poverty of the 1990s. Systems which were created earlier, such as legal structures, administrative apparatuses, the division of power between the various state agencies as well as the citizens' expectations, have a great power of persistence, especially in the democratic welfare state.[1] Hans Achinger, one of the founders of German social policy studies, pointed out decades ago (Achinger 1959) that current social policy is largely concerned with the results of previous social policy activities. In the USA, Morris Janowitz (1976) was among the first to analyse the welfare state comprehensively in terms of its consequences. The welfare state has grown to become a major sector of our society, affecting practically all other sectors. Evidence can be found, for instance, in the lack of innovation in German social politics. Adjustments and consolidation predominate instead, such as in the Pension or Health Insurance systems. It can also be seen in the way that social problems which the welfare state addresses have partially been caused by the welfare state itself. In the field of medical treatment, Ivan Illich has pointed to 'iatrogenesis', the medical generation of illness. Poverty, too, offers examples of this connection (see pp. 32f. and pp. 145–149).[2]

To the extent that the welfare state has expanded and developed its pervasive social activities, monitoring them has become more important. There has been a Federal Social Report in Germany since the 1960s. This Social Budget is collated by the planners in the Federal Ministry for Employment and Social Affairs to give a financial overview of social expenditure. It does not give an account of government departmental expenditure alone, since it includes the expenditures of the independent social insurance institutions which have separate budgets. Government reports on areas such as education, training, health and family matters describe the activities of the welfare state, and to a limited extent report on changes in the circumstances of the beneficiaries of government services. The consequences of social policies are not dealt with in these reports. Poverty is a late-comer as far as social reports are concerned. Local reports on poverty and social conditions were not produced on a wide scale in Germany until the 1980s. The first federal poverty report is planned for 2000. The only previous offering has been the reformed national statistics of Social Assistance available since 1994 (see chapter 9, p. 228).

New ideas in social policy come into conflict with the conservatism of the administrative system, and are received sceptically by the well-worn all-party welfare state. Innovations must be developed from the preceding patterns of

---

[1] Cf. Richard Rose's expression 'inertia of established commitments' (Rose 1984, p. 48). For an analysis of the development of welfare states as a process of institutionalisation see Elmar Rieger (1992).

[2] Similarly, the welfare state has contributed to the 'second-order risk' problems of both contributors and beneficiaries of pension systems following demographic change (Leisering 1992, chapter 6).

organisation and power. Thus during the introduction of the Care Insurance scheme in Germany in 1994, there was a particular argument about whether and how the established contributory principle of financing should be implemented. To introduce a basic income scheme, such as has been demanded by the joint Green-Alliance 90 party and less radically by the Social Democratic Party would involve making allowances for a wide range of ingrained interests and multi-tiered organisational structures.

In order to take account of the dead weight of the existing institutional structures, the next three chapters do not immediately deal with the policy proposals which emerge from the dynamic poverty research findings. Instead, they focus on social change in Germany in the 1980s and 1990s and related policy responses. This includes changes in thinking. Reform of the welfare state demands new ideas or at least an adjustment of the received preconceptions to the changes in reality. Notions of the 'welfare state' and 'poverty' are the subjects of firmly held convictions and ideologies, seemingly hard to change even when conditions alter or new knowledge is brought to light. It would be an exaggeration to say that ideas of social policy have not changed since the establishment of the Federal Republic. The fundamental changes in the economic situation alone – from the post-war collapse, through the reconstruction and the 'economic miracle' of the 1950s to the turbulence of the 1970s and 1980s and finally the impasse of the 1990s – would suggest that there must have been some change in poverty policy, and particularly in the public perception of poverty. In chapter 7 we therefore analyse the images of poverty in post-war Germany, pointing out persistent patterns of thinking as well as changes.

We must emphasise that the types of poverty which we described in the last chapters are not new in every respect. The words which we have used, such as 'temporalisation' and 'individualisation' of poverty, suggest that we are dealing with an increase in short-term claims and, related to that, a widening range of people experiencing poverty conditions. The findings of the Bremen Social Assistance study, like other available longitudinal findings, allow statements to be made only about the 1980s and 1990s. For these years we can trace trends in temporalisation both in the West and the East of Germany (pp. 225–230). For earlier years there are clues which support the generalisations. The unemployed have superseded pensioners as the chief problem group in Germany in the last thirty years, and pensioners stay longer on assistance than do unemployed claimants. Long-term employees of the local Social Assistance Agencies have confirmed that their clients now have a more self-aware approach to Social Assistance.[3] This fits

---

[3] See the analysis by Uwe Schwarze (1994) who, as part of the Bremen Social Assistance study, used intensive interviews with the staff of the Social Assistance Agencies to examine their approaches to poverty.

with our research finding that the increased number of lone mother claimants are often capable of managing autonomously. It was noticeable in our interviews that younger claimants felt less ashamed about claiming Social Assistance than the older claimants did.

7 Between denial and dramatisation: images of poverty in post-war Germany

Social problems such as poverty, unemployment, juvenile delinquency and drug addiction have 'careers' of their own. There are times when they stand in the forefront of public attention and other times when they are ignored even though nothing about the problem itself has changed. Thus, in Germany, the debate about unemployment faded away in the late 1980s though the objective problem remained largely as before. Accordingly, the prevailing perception of a social problem – the assumptions about what it consists of, who is affected by it, what its causes are and so on – do not necessarily reflect its actual characteristics. This simple observation is the basic assumption of the sociological theory of social problems: that social problems are socially 'constructed' and defined.

But is poverty not a clear-cut lack of material resources which leaves little space for social definitions and constructions, unlike, say, psychiatric disorders? Do not 'the facts speak for themselves'? From this point of view, if politicians ignore poverty, it must be for devious reasons, or at best because they lack the information which points to the obvious situation. These questions and assertions underestimate the difficulty of the political debate on poverty. Poverty is a form of social inequality which is particularly liable to controversy. Social inequalities of some kinds such as earnings differentials between more- or less-skilled activities, or the inequalities of earnings-related pensions are basically accepted in society; indeed, they are desired. But poverty describes an extreme form of social inequality; it is that bottom end of the scale of inequality which is considered to be socially unacceptable and to be abolished or at least ameliorated. T. H. Marshall expressed it thus: 'Poverty is a tumour which should be cut out, and theoretically could be; inequality is a vital organ which is functioning badly' (1981, p. 119). What is 'unacceptable', and what kinds of unacceptable situations arouse public attention, change over time and are much argued

Co-authors: Peter Buhr, Monika Ludwig.

175

about in different social circles. Politicians have a particular role in this argument, since combating poverty is a fundamental aim of social policies.

We must therefore ask: to what extent has the problem of poverty in post-war Germany been addressed politically, and what 'images' of poverty have emerged in the public debate? Only on the basis of such stock-taking can the further question be answered: can the ingrained images account for the new forms of poverty which we described in the previous chapters? The history of the approach to poverty taken by West German society is generally presented as one of denial or repression (such as by Colla 1974, pp. 19f., and Döring et al. 1990b, p. 10; for France see Bourdieu 1993). But there must have been more to it than that. In a complex society one would expect to find a variety of ways of expressing the darker sides of social life. Using contemporary political, journalistic and scholarly sources, this chapter offers the first attempt to set out the political history of poverty in post-war Germany.[1]

From the poverty of the people to the poverty of the individual: the fifties

The physical experiences of hunger and cold were the two most urgent problems facing millions of Germans in the first years after the end of the Second World War. War damage, the political developments of the early post-war era and the economic devastation created massive and overwhelming want. In his first government statement (20 September 1949) Konrad Adenauer, the first Federal Chancellor, introduced the list of the most urgent tasks by the simple phrase 'relief of need' (*Linderung der Not*; Adenauer 1949, p. 15) to express forcibly the political poverty problem of his day, the poverty of the whole people. It meant mass poverty affecting all parts of society. Looking back, it could soon be said – as Ludwig Erhard, the 'Father of the German Economic Miracle' expressed it in 1956 – that 'the people were led from poverty to a new well-being'.[2]

Economic policy was correspondingly the poverty policy of the day, an economic policy which aimed at reconstruction, productivity increases and growth. Economic policy acquired a special historical significance as a policy against mass poverty. A further dimension of poverty policy was added to this: redistributive social policies for those who could not immediately share in the fruits of economic policy.

Within the widespread general poverty, certain groups were prioritised

---

[1] For an exhaustive account with extensive references see Buhr et al. (1991) and Leisering (1993). See also Schäfers (1992, section II), whose account is based on Buhr et al. Schulz (1994) offers a selection of historical texts.

[2] See the collection of Erhard's essays (Hohmann 1988, p. 466). Cf. in an international perspective Müller-Armack (1948, pp. 184f.).

by the government's policies while others, who were no less affected by poverty, were disadvantaged. The officially recognised 'poor' in this first period were the war victims who had suffered personal injury or loss – people with disabilities, widows and orphans – and those who suffered from war damage, who had lost their belongings through the effects of war. The latter included exiles and refugees from the previously German territories in the east and in the *Sudetenland*, evacuees and bombed-out homeless people. In dealing with these two groups (war victims and people affected by war damages), social motives were often mixed with judgements about merit. The victims' service to the Fatherland or to the people was to be honoured by them being financially provided for – the so-called 'maintenance principle' (*Versorgungsprinzip*), one of the organising notions of German social policy which is similarly apparent in the non-contributory civil-service pension scheme. Hence a Federal Maintenance Act (*Bundesversorgungsgesetz*) was passed as early as 20 December 1950. For the other group of people who had suffered loss or damage the issue was fair compensation. The Immediate Aid Act (*Soforthilfegesetz*) of 8 August 1948, and the conclusive Compensation Act (*Lastenausgleichsgesetz*) of 14 August 1952, triggered one of 'the greatest economic and financial transactions in German history' (Abelshauser 1987, p. 37). A considerable part consisted and still consists of maintenance and pension payments, and formed a massive downward redistribution, rare in German post-war history (Geisel 1984, Hughes 1991). The key phrase in that first government statement – which in full reads 'the attempt to relieve need, to achieve social justice' – precisely reflects the co-existence of two distinct justifications, need and merit, which acted as guiding principles suggesting directions for policy.

By contrast, other groups which lacked recognised claims fell into the background: workers, large families (benefits for children were not reintroduced until 1954, and then only for workers' families with three or more children[3]) and the unemployed. In spite of the fact that unemployment reached 8.8 per cent in September 1949, and reached its highest point in the history of the FRG before reunification at 12.2 per cent six months later, Adenauer's government statement made no reference to the unemployed. The poverty of this group seems to have been smoothly subsumed as part of the generalised poverty. In addition, during this period it seems to have been unthinkable that people who were in paid work should be treated in some narrower sense as 'poor'. It was somewhat different for the old, whose special needs persisted, even if unmentioned. As pensioners, however, they had fallen within the scope of public social security ever

---

[3] It was significant that the Allied occupiers rejected Child Benefit as typically National-Socialist.

since the nineteenth century, and enjoyed a pension increase of around 30 per cent up to 1953 as the result of some four different adjustment laws which kept pensions in step with the rise in earnings.

The thesis of the concentration of poverty policy on specific social groups must, however, be qualified to the extent that the privileged over-lapped with the disadvantaged groups. Thus in 1949 the *Vertriebene* (exiles: refugees from former German territories in the East) represented quite dis-proportionately some 35 per cent of the unemployed. Almost one-third of all recipients of social security benefits in 1953 received more than one type of benefit. In addition, the privileged groups were particularly large and obvious. In 1950, exiles formed 17 per cent of the whole population. Nevertheless, of all recipients of social security in 1953, 30 per cent received War Victims' Benefits and 6 per cent War Compensation while 31 per cent received workers' Old-Age Insurance Pensions and 'only' 5 per cent were Unemployment Insurance recipients.[4] Not least, poverty policy should also be seen as an aspect of social pacification. Indeed, the exiles in particular presented a politically explosive threat to the new West German democracy for many years.

The economic and social policies of this period were legitimised through the use of the phrase *Social Market Economy*. The expression was coined in 1946 by the economist and sociologist Alfred Müller-Armack, later to become *Staatssekretär*, the highest-ranking government official in the Department of Economic Affairs. It found its chief political protagonist in Ludwig Erhard, during his time as Minister for Economic Affairs from 1949 to 1963, and Federal Chancellor from 1963 to 1966. The Social Market Economy was the trademark of a whole political programme which promised to defeat mass poverty by democratic means within capitalist society. This programme was always aimed at the 'broad masses' and did not focus on any specifically deprived groups. He would 'never tire in the struggle', Erhard assured readers in his best-seller *Wohlstand für alle* (1957, p. 232) (Welfare for All), to ensure 'that the fruits of economic progress should benefit ever wider strata of the population and, if possible, *all* of them in the end'.

The results of this blanket anti-poverty programme were soon apparent, but so too were the limitations of its economic approach and the impro-vised social policies. While the most basic mass needs were relatively quickly met, poverty continued to be widely experienced during the 1950s. The chief population groups affected which were to become the focus of public and political interest from 1955 onwards, were already identified by

---

[4] The percentages refer to cases of receipt, that is, if a person received two types of benefits he or she was counted twice.

the journalists Ilse Elsner and Rüdiger Proske (1953). These were social security benefit recipients, and especially the poor 'social pensioners' (*Sozialrentner*), who had been known as 'small pensioners' in the time of the Weimar Republic. This interest was connected with the extensive discussion of the all-embracing 'social reform' which Adenauer had announced after his re-election in 1953 and which constituted the German equivalent of the renewal of the British welfare state in the 1940s, though it emerged on a more limited scale. The obvious shortcomings of the German social security system fuelled this debate, and permeated the whole social policy discourse of the 1950s. Of the three themes in the debate – simplification of the jungle of legal welfare entitlements, internal reallocation of social expenditures to focus on the 'most deserving', and the raising of benefit levels to adequately meet needs – the latter two both immediately raised poverty policy issues. Hence, the debate over social reform was from the outset confined to groups which were defined in terms of legal entitlements: the issue was the inadequate provision offered to those entitled to welfare benefits, and not the unmet needs of groups in poverty as such, like the old, large families and the unemployed.

However, adequate statistical information about the economic and social situation of pensioners and other benefit recipients was not available in the early 1950s. The first thorough information came when the Federal Government commissioned the Federal Statistical Office to conduct a large-scale investigation of 'the social conditions of pensioners and benefit recipients' in 1953 and 1955. Its findings that 'the social pensioners were the "stepchildren of German progress"' (cited by Hockerts 1980, p. 213) and the numerically most significant group of the poor, were used to justify narrowing the discussion of social reform to focus on pensioners (Hockerts 1980, pp. 307–319).

The *Great Pension Reform of 1957* is a landmark not only in the history of Old-Age Insurance but also in the history of poverty, because it was explicitly intended to deal with poverty: 'the Pension Reform of 1957 was an attempt to break the link between old age and poverty entirely and permanently' (Hockerts 1986, p. 38). As a result, the benefits of about six million pensioners were raised by an average of 60 per cent. In addition, benefits were indexed according to wages ('dynamic pension', *dynamische Rente*). Through this reform, Social Insurance and Social Assistance fully emerged as two separate tiers of the German welfare-state model with distinct rationales. They represented the division between 'policy for workers' (*Arbeiterpolitik*) and 'policy for the poor' (*Armenpolitik*) (Leibfried and Tennstedt 1985c): the pension scheme offered benefits at a level which was to replace previous earnings; the idea of minimum pension payments was rejected; and the income needs of the poor were to be met through means-tested Social Assistance. The reform gave the aging Bismarckian social insurance system its current form and became the legitimating cornerstone of the West German welfare state. It is therefore misleading to refer to this system as Bismarckian. The reform of 1957 was hotly contested at the time, for instance it did not meet with Erhard's support. Forty years later, the very regulations introduced in 1957 are being fundamentally questioned by politicians from all parties.

In the shadow of the debate on social reform and its fulfilment in the pension reform, the system actually intended for the poor, the locally administered Social Assistance scheme, was also fundamentally reformed (see Heisig 1994). Unlike the pension reform, the intention was not the total abolition of the material poverty of a specific group or class, but instead the creation of a comprehensive system of personal support for the contingencies of individual need. This process of reform was accompanied by far less public and political attention; rather, it was the product of thoroughgoing discussion and effort by professional experts and practitioners. It was peripheral to the political process, and this reflected the institutional marginalisation and partition of the administrative struggle with poverty. Thus the welfare reform embodied in the passing of the Federal Social Assistance Act (*Bundessozialhilfegesetz*, generally referred to as BSHG) in 1961 was a significant even if less-noticed achievement of the 'Era of Social Reform', too.

The social history of the FRG and the history of its social policy began as an ascent out of poverty and poor relief. It was no accident that the first consultative meeting, on 13 May 1946, of the German Association for Public and Private Welfare (*Deutscher Verein für öffentliche und private Fürsorge*[5]), whose experts were traditionally engaged in social issues, should have been devoted to 'The Conquest of German Mass Want'. Similarly, in 1949 the theme of their general meeting was 'Public Relief in the Service of the Economic and Social Security of the Population'. As a consequence of the 1949 Immediate Aid Act and the 1952 Compensation Act, the number of households as well as individuals receiving Social Welfare (*Fürsorge*, which later became Social Assistance) declined by more than a third in a year, caused solely by the reduction in Welfare payments related to needs caused by the war. By contrast, the number of recipients of Welfare benefits unrelated to war experiences remained fairly constant till 1955 and only declined slightly until the beginning of the 1960s.

The reform statute introducing *Social Assistance* in the place of Social

---

[5] The term *Fürsorge* carries a general meaning of social care, and a specific meaning of public relief in the traditional poor-law sense. The historical terms Social Welfare (*Fürsorge*) and relief have been used here to distinguish the provisions from those of Social Assistance which was created in 1961.

Welfare, the BSHG, was enacted in 1961 and came into force in 1962. What formerly was poor relief or Social Welfare now became a component of the constitutional state and the welfare state (*Sozialstaat*). The new legal and social status included the individual right to demand help, the statutory objective of ensuring a dignified (*menschenwürdig*) standard of living, and the standardisation of material benefits by means of the new budget standard system (*Warenkorb*) and benefit scales (*Regelsätze*). Also new was the orientation towards case-oriented personal assistance under Special Needs Support (*Hilfe in besonderen Lebenslagen*) as a new category of Social Assistance. This modernising reform was widely accepted politically.

An era of poverty policy ended with the implementation of the BSHG. The collective poverty of the masses, which had been the central issue of the early 1950s, had been solved, and certain groups, chiefly pensioners, were now sharing in the growing affluence, to a greater extent than in most other countries. The only problem left to be solved seemed to be the poverty of certain individuals. Müller-Armack concluded: 'solutions have been found to provide for the broad masses . . . In this classless society the problem is no longer class or status, but the individual' (1960, pp. 270f.).

The 'latency period' of poverty: the sixties

Did the legal definition of poverty embodied in the Social Assistance law match the social realities of poverty? Tales of 'infectious poverty' which had been common in the 1950s became rare in the 1960s. Of course material poverty persisted as before. This can be seen simply from the number of people who continued to claim Social Assistance's Basic Income Support (*Hilfe zum Lebensunterhalt*), which continued to decline but never fell below three quarters of a million. The social pensioners still remained the largest single group of Assistance claimants. Even in the mid 1960s Heinz Strang found, in his study of 'Varieties of Eligibility for Social Assistance' (1970), that almost half of the claimants he interviewed were pensioners.[6] He consequently described them as the 'structure-dominating type'. Two further significant types, each forming about one-fifth of the interviewees, were the 'fatherless families' and the 'singles living alone'.

The social situation of the poor became the subject of journalistic reportage. In 1961, Peter Brügge reported on 'Misery in Wonderland' in the influential weekly journal *Der Spiegel*. He criticised the 'superseded clichés of deprivation in Federal Germany from the 1950s' and 'the almost yearn-

---

[6] It is striking that for nearly two decades the study by Strang was the only empirical survey which did not focus simply on one group of the poor but examined the totality of Social Assistance claimants in one city.

ing search for a kind of poverty that scarcely exists any longer' (*Der Spiegel* 1961, pp. 40f.). He asserted that the crude poverty had vanished, and found the new poverty chiefly:

where illness, accident or other major contingencies break down the carefully balanced budget in low-income families. But chiefly it can be found in the homes of old people living alone and solely dependent on Social Assistance – of course in a manner which is hidden from view. The most acute needs in 1961 no longer consist of material deprivations; they are caused by the lack of love and lack of family security. (1961, p. 44)

The journalists' reports echoed widespread attitudes. In these arguments and illustrations of poverty one finds many parallels with the justificatory notions which influenced the drafting of the BSHG: the assumptions that 'real' or grave poverty no longer existed, and that social problems were instead caused by non-material want.

Besides the elderly, the *Nichtseßhafte* (literally 'unsettled': street people or those sleeping in municipal or other hostels) and the *Obdachlose* (literally 'homeless': those in low-standard municipal housing and deprived of the legal rights of tenants or other residents) were the next group to be discovered as disadvantaged – rather than only poor – in the 1960s. Some interest in this 'rearguard of society' was already being expressed by the middle of the decade (Adams 1971, manuscript 1966). They were described as large families living in cramped circumstances, and special attention was directed at the unmet needs of the children. But it was not until the 1970s that they were categorised together with others suffering disadvantage as 'marginal groups'. This concept became the subject of widespread political discussion and of countless academic studies. Material deprivations and income policies were treated as relatively insignificant. Instead, attention was focused chiefly on the question of thwarted social integration caused by socialisation problems, deviant behaviour and stigmatisation, to be combated through social work. Very little research into material poverty was carried on in the FRG. When it was perceived at all, it was in the context of 'poverty amidst affluence' in other countries, chiefly in the USA.

This 'paradigm shift' from an income-oriented to a social-service-oriented strategy, in the definition of and fight against poverty, introduced by the 1961 Federal Social Assistance Act, was eagerly welcomed and furthered by both academics and practitioners. The redefinition of the problem fitted in well with the thrust towards the professionalisation of social work and its German form *Sozialpädagogik* (social education) as a strategy for the treatment and control of deviant behaviour from the mid 1960s.

'Marginal groups' and other 'disadvantaged groups': the seventies

The trends which had emerged in the 1960s continued to develop strongly during the ensuing decade. However, we can distinguish two phases. In the first phase, the new direction in poverty policies which had begun with the 1961 Social Assistance Act continued with the 'improvements in benefits during the period of economic growth 1969–1974' (Adamy and Naegele 1985, pp. 97f.), supported by improvements in other minimum benefit schemes. But from 1975 on, financial considerations acted as a brake on the development of Social Assistance and ushered in the 'cost-cutting legislation' (Dieter Giese) of the first half of the 1980s. As far as models of poverty are concerned, the treatment of marginal groups and their problems which had emerged in the 1960s now appeared on the official political agenda. Questions of material deprivation and the measurement of poverty came much more to the forefront in the mid 1970s.

In 1969 the Social Democratic Party became the dominant party in the Federal government for the first time in post-war German history (in a coalition with the small liberal Free Democratic Party, after three years of a Grand Coalition with the Christian Democrats). Their social-liberal Politics of Society (*Gesellschaftspolitik*) framed political terms of reference which, using new aspirational formulae such as equality of opportunity and quality of life, aimed at a kind of recapitulated Social Reform (Standfest 1979, p. 50; von Beyme 1979, p. 24; M. G. Schmidt 1978, pp. 209f., 1998, p. 94). This was similar to President Johnson's Great Society Program in the USA, but cast in a social-democratic mould after twenty years of conservative Christian-Democratic hegemony. With historical hindsight, one can detect here for the first time the outlines of a programme for active life-course policies. The programme also aimed for a more equitable income distribution and openings for marginalised and socially weak groups. Nevertheless, an interest in the actual living conditions of specific groups of people was still overlaid by an orientation towards wide-ranging concepts of political planning and direction, and a 'social policy as policy for society as a whole', extending in some quarters like the Young Socialists (*Jungsozialisten*) to a global critique of capitalism (Heimann 1975, pp. 56–58). For instance, in the Social Democratic Party's *Orientation Framework '85*, a comprehensive report from 1975, which included an analysis of society and an agenda for the future, the topics of poverty or Social Assistance were not even mentioned.

Social Assistance experts continued to hold the view that cash benefits were losing weight as compared to personal support geared to individual non-material needs. It is therefore not surprising that the prime target of improvements in Social Assistance during the 1970s was Special Needs

Support, the central feature of the Federal Social Assistance Act, rather than Basic Income Support. Among the most significant changes to Social Assistance was the 1974 revision of the 'help for the vulnerable', which was renamed 'help for overcoming particular social difficulties'. The range of eligible persons was greatly extended to include all those 'whose own capabilities cannot meet the increasing demands of modern industrial society'. The intention was to include especially such groups as the homeless (both *Nichtseßhafte* and *Obdachlose),* alcoholics, drug and narcotic addicts, and discharged prisoners (Federal Parliamentary Papers 7/308, pp. 16f.).

These revisions reflected a general change in the model of poverty: after some delay the politicians now gave special attention to the so-called marginal groups. Towards the end of the 1960s it had fallen to the student movement to sensitise the public and the politicians to this issue. In the government statement of 8 October 1969, Willy Brandt, the first Social-Democratic Federal Chancellor, said that it was now essential to care for the citizens who 'have to live in the shadows in spite of the economic boom and full employment'. On 15 December 1972 Brandt emphasised that more should be done for 'the people whose personal fate it is to live on the margins of society'. This primarily referred to people with disabilities, but elderly and migrant workers were also mentioned.

At the beginning of the 1970s the marginal groups became a topic for the mass media. In 1970 *Der Spiegel* began a series on 'socially disadvantaged groups in the FRG'. It reported on apprentices, the homeless, migrant workers, recidivists, female employees, people with disabilities and mental illnesses, juvenile delinquents and homosexuals. These *Spiegel* reports were published in 1973 as a book, *Underprivileged.* The popular books of Jürgen Roth (1971, revised editions 1974 and 1979) and Ernst Klee, who had been writing about prisoners, psychiatric patients, people with psychological problems or with disabilities, migrant workers and homeless people (Klee 1979) further directed attention to the existence of poverty in the FRG and gave a vivid picture of the circumstances of marginal groups. The problems of marginal groups were also thoroughly researched by academics around this time.[7] Almost all the studies mentioned the effects on children and the consequent processes of downward class mobility and the intergenerational transmission of poverty. Here one can see the foundations of the idea that poverty is a long-term phenomenon and hardens cumulatively in the course of life. Even though other topics have subsequently become more salient in poverty research, the scholarly interest in marginal groups

---

[7] Just as in the 1960s the focus had been on homelessness (*Obdachlosigkeit*) and housing problems. See among others: Albrecht (1973), Iben (1970), Christiansen (1973), Friedrich and Schaufelberger (1975), Friedrich *et al.* (1979), Hess and Mechler (1973), Specht *et al.* (1979) and Vaskovics (1976).

remains to the present day, even if the focus has switched to different groups and aspects. By comparison with the earlier period in which the chief interest was in homeless families in low-standard public housing (*Obdachlose*), the current emphasis is on the more pressing problems of unsettled and single homeless people (*Nichtseßhafte*).

In this debate, the problems of the marginal groups were presented as exceptional and somewhat crude aspects of poverty which could not be explained in terms of inadequate incomes alone or at all. Instead, they comprised complex manifestations of deprivations referring to housing, health and education, as well as to social isolation and stigmatisation. The economist Richard Hauser found that the terms poverty and underprivilege were seldom used synonymously, and he concluded that the inadequate concept of poverty had been superseded by the concept of being underprivileged (Hauser *et al.* 1981, pp. 22f.). Similarly, Claus Offe (1972, first published 1969) referred to new 'horizontal disparities' which cut right across conventional vertical inequalities between classes and income groups.

Until now it has rarely been recognised that the years 1969 to 1974 represent a phase of social policy in which the state introduced new minimum benefits and extended existing ones. In addition to two revisions of the Social Assistance Act, there was legislation for targeted transfer payments for specific purposes. The second Housing Benefit Act considerably improved the first law of 1965. Uniform and more inclusive regulations for educational support were introduced (Federal Educational Support Act for Scholars and Students 1971, Graduate Support Act 1971, parts of the Employment Promotion Act of 1969), together with the 'low earners' top-up pension' (*Rente nach Mindesteinkommen,* 1972) which primarily benefited employed women whose earnings had been too low to allow for sufficient pension contributions (it was not a general minimum pension). Unlike Social Assistance, these minimum benefits were financed by the central government, but they were not as strongly institutionalised, for example they were not indexed. This collection of laws produced an uncoordinated conglomerate of rights to services and implicit poverty lines. This constituted a tacit political acknowledgement that in Germany there were many problems which could not be solved by means of Social Assistance alone. The word 'poverty' was as carefully avoided in these minimum income benefits as it was in Social Assistance. The idea of meeting certain special needs with schemes outside of Social Assistance was part of a new programme for life-course policies – predicated on 'equality of opportunity' and broadened educational access as facilitated by the Federal Educational Support Act – and also a product of fiscal considerations.

In the mid 1970s the New Social Question (*Neue Soziale Frage*) was launched by Heiner Geißler (1976), at that time the Christian-Democratic Minister for Social Affairs in the Rhineland-Palatinate *Land* government. His thesis was to some extent akin to the discussion of marginal groups and the previous work by Claus Offe (1972 [first edition 1969]), in that he suggested that there were new forms of underprivilege, namely the underprivilege of people who were unorganised and not gainfully employed. The New Social Question was a remarkable mixture of two disparate elements. On the one hand it was a party-political attack on the Social Democratic Party, the trade unions and the corporatist welfare state as a whole. On the other, it constituted a social analysis by a politician from a mainstream party in which poverty was for the first time structurally located as a product of the ruling welfare state. At the same time, any connection between poverty and the occupational structure was denied. In retrospect, it is curious that the replacement of the 'old' social question by a 'new' one – which emphasised the old, women and large families – was proclaimed just around the time when the poverty of the elderly began to diminish and that of the unemployed began to increase.

As a result of Geißler's study, poverty increasingly began to be addressed as a matter of income deficiency. That itself introduced a new phase in the poverty business, in which the focus turned to material deprivation and the problems of measuring it. Attempts to measure poverty precisely were undertaken mainly in the context of the social-indicator movement, in particular by the SPES Project (an acronym for the Social-Policy Decision and Indicator System for the FRG, established in 1971) and by researchers trying to improve public social reporting (Zapf 1974, 1976). The spirit of modern social planning managed to stay alive in this form during the first years of fiscal stringency. A variety of concepts and databases were used to try to find out the real extent of poverty in the FRG. In the process, a wide range of estimates were produced for the different types of poverty identified, such as latent or 'hidden', absolute, relative ('strong' or 'weak'), and poverty defined as the receipt of Social Assistance.[8] The study by Hauser *et al.* (1981) stands out here. It was carried out under the auspices of the European Community's First Programme to Combat Poverty, and it can be considered as the first semi-official poverty report for the FRG. One advantage of this line of research was that the scale of the non-take-up of Social Assistance to be evaluated empirically. This 'latent poverty' stood at around 50 per cent of eligible claimants of Social Assistance – a proportion which was confirmed by Helmut Hartmann's sample survey of latent poverty (1981), which

---

[8] See for instance Glatzer and Krupp (1975), Kortmann *et al.* (1975), Scherl (1976), Adam (1977, 1978), Klanberg (1977, 1978, 1979, 1980) and the Transfer-Enquête-Kommission (1981).

remains the most valuable study of its kind to the present day (see chapter 11, pp. 276f.).

Unemployment and the 'new poverty': the eighties

In poverty policy in the decade of the 1980s, as in the 1970s, two phases of development can be distinguished. There was thus both continuity and change. The cost-cutting legislation of 1981 continued the politics of fiscal savings which had started in 1975, but in the mid 1980s a new phase of considerable expansion began. The connection between unemployment and poverty became the focus of approaches to poverty, although naturally some isolated aspects of the material consequences of unemployment had already been considered in the 1970s. Towards the end of the 1980s, then, attention was being directed to new groups in poverty.

Social changes which had begun in the previous decade or earlier became more intense during the 1980s. Unemployment became more widespread in spite of the unexpected return to the path of economic growth. Changes in demography and family structure altered living conditions. The key issues were the decline in the birth rate and the increases in one-parent families, single-person households and divorces. In addition there were socio-cultural changes such as the increasing variation in individual lifestyles which was also noticeable among women with precarious incomes.

In 1982 the Social Democrat–Liberal coalition government in Bonn broke down and a new coalition of Christian Democrats[9] and Liberals, led by Helmut Kohl, took over. In the field of social policy, the ideological shift towards neo-conservatism only intensified the budget-cutting which had begun several years earlier, but from the mid 1980s this shift also gave birth to a substantially new articulation of the scope of the welfare state, oriented towards family policy (Wingen 1993, 1994). Several judgements by the Federal Constitutional Court contributed to this orientation.

The introduction of a Parents' Benefit or Education Benefit (*Erziehungsgeld*) in 1986 was notable because it was disregarded as income in assessing Social Assistance or any other means-tested benefits. It placed single parents, for the first two years of parenthood, in a substantially better position than other Social Assistance recipients. This was a new style of categorical minimum benefit, which for the first time significantly restricted the application of the Social Assistance principle of 'last resort' in relation to other state welfare benefits. The simultaneous introduction in the statutory pension scheme of contribution credits for child-raising years

---

[9] To be more precise, this and other conservative-led governments included two Christian parties, the Christian-Democratic Union (CDU) and its Bavarian twin, the Christian-Social Union (CSU).

also shows how underlying concerns about poverty policy were dealt with at this time, through a deliberate association of family policy and social policy. Poverty was reinterpreted as a handicap to 'the family', and treated accordingly in public and political affairs. This perspective remains strong today, and it constituted a central focus of the poverty debate in the late 1990s.

In the light of numerous cuts in the Employment Promotion Act (Bieback 1985), the interests of both scholars and the critical public turned more strongly to a new group of the poor, the unemployed. The psycho-social and practical consequences of unemployment had of course been analysed since the 1970s. But the New Poverty entered the public's field of vision in 1984 only because, following the cuts in social-security benefits, the material conditions of the unemployed worsened and increasing numbers had to apply for Social Assistance. The result was a flood of publications on the new poverty or the process of impoverishment as a consequence of unemployment (see above all Balsen *et al.* 1984). The contemporary local government reports on poverty similarly emphasised the connections between poverty and unemployment, not least because of the implications for local government finance: higher Unemployment-Insurance benefits would reduce claims for Social Assistance. The public evaluation of poverty had become strongly affected by fiscal considerations since the 1970s.

The New Poverty was new in several respects. For one thing, it was tacitly accepted by politicians, since it was a side-effect of their social and fiscal economies (see Adamy and Naegele 1985, p. 107). For another, it was related to a change among the poverty clientele, from 'ashamed and worried Social-Assistance clients' to 'self-confident and previously relatively well-off family heads' (*Der Spiegel* 1984/29, p. 23), or 'self-assured academics, white-collar employees and rebellious young people, who won't take advice from anyone' (*Der Spiegel* 1988/43, p. 78). The 'active claimant' was discovered, one who knew the ins and outs of Social Assistance and was not afraid of demanding his or her rights. For some claimants, chiefly lone parents, claiming Social Assistance may even be a deliberate decision in planning their lives (see pp. 94–96, 128–130). Collective action by the unemployed and claimants, and the establishment of numerous self-help groups, were started in the latter part of the 1970s and early 1980s. Closely connected with the concept of New Poverty was the notion of the 'two-thirds society' (Glotz 1984, 1985), according to which poverty and under-privilege were leading to increasing structural divisions in society.[10] In fact, both terms were launched in 1984.

[10] See also Natter and Riedlsperger (1988) and Döring *et al.* (1990b, p. 8), as well as Leibfried and Tennstedt (1985b) who identified a 'division of the welfare state'. For a reappraisal of the notion of a 'two-thirds society' see Leisering (1995a) and chapter 10, pp. 251–254.

The concept of 'new poverty' was a means of demonstrating the circumstances of the unemployed. Interest focused on unemployment and not on poverty as such. However, the question of poverty was subsequently able to 'emancipate' itself from unemployment, so that from the end of the 1980s poverty could be studied anew from a wider perspective. The new slogan – calling economic growth into question – was 'poverty amidst affluence' (Döring et al. 1990a). During the 1980s, the Green Party offered the poor a kind of lobby in Parliament for the first time, allowing poverty to be generally discussed once again after an interval of more than thirty years, and in terms not only of Social Assistance but also of new proposed projects like a Basic Income as a citizen's right. Poverty had once again become 'politically respectable' (Schäfers 1992, p. 116).

The tendency to treat poverty and unemployment as largely synonymous had initially overshadowed the increasing poverty risks of other groups. Foreigners, children and lone parents were increasingly overrepresented among Social Assistance claimants, as they continue to be. In general, the 1980s were rich in assumptions about poverty, some of which contrasted with reality, such as the belief in the feminisation of poverty or that old people continued to make up a large proportion of the poor. Mass unemployment, the increase in younger and potentially employable claimants and the growing difficulties of lone parents, put a conclusive end to the hopes of the progenitors of the Federal Social Assistance Act of 1961 that Social Assistance would soon have to provide only for exceptional circumstances. Finally, what was wholly unforeseen was the tidal wave of refugees from all over the world seeking political asylum and of immigrants of German ethnic origin from the communist countries of Eastern Europe and the USSR, as well as the mass influx from the GDR after 1989. During the late 1980s and the early 1990s, these groups alone accounted for most of the increase in the number of claimants (see pp. 225–230). Thus the provision of Social Assistance's Basic Income Support did not steadily decline as had been originally assumed but, on the contrary, both expenditure and the number of claimants continued to rise.

The nineties: two new poverties, East and West

In the 1990s the new poverty in the new East German *Länder* of the former GDR added to the still growing 'New' Poverty in West Germany. The Berlin Wall had been breached on 9 November 1989, and formal unification of the two Germanies was carried out on 3 October 1990, after an intervening period of currency union from 1 July. In the West of Germany, the images of the 'new' poverty from the 1980s (now no longer 'new') continued into the 1990s, with an increasing emphasis on child poverty in the second half of the decade,[11] supplemented by a critical awareness of new immigrants as recipients of Social Assistance. One political response was the transfer of responsibility for financial support for asylum seekers from Social Assistance to a special separate system under the Asylum Seekers Benefit Act (*Asylbewerberleistungsgesetz*, 1993). The motive was not only to impose social controls but also to save money. Heated public debate with strongly racist elements around this time led to a massive legislative restriction on the flow of asylum seekers in 1993, a move which was supported by all the major political parties. But the significance of refugees and of people of German ethnic origin from Eastern Europe and the USSR started to be taken seriously in public arguments about poverty and Social Assistance only in 1996.

The introduction of Care Insurance (1994) was similarly motivated by fiscal considerations, as it was intended to remove a large block of expenditure from Social Assistance budgets of the municipalities and the *Länder* (care was financed under Special Needs Support). In the event, the saving was not as great as expected, but the design of this new branch of Social Insurance was part of the pursuit for a slimmed-down welfare state. This reached its peak in several pieces of legislation for the 'consolidation' of public expenditure in 1993, affecting chiefly the lower tiers of the social security system, including Social Assistance (see pp. 307f.). The pressure on benefit levels increased.

The guarantee of a minimum subsistence income to all citizens has always been one of the legitimating foundations of the German welfare state. A minimum standard of needs therefore had to be established, a socio-cultural minimum as intended by the Federal Social Assistance Act to embody what society understood by a dignified standard of living (Klein 1994). In 1961 the Social Assistance Act introduced a standard of minimum needs in the form of benefit scale rates to be derived from model household budgets constructed by experts (*Warenkorb*). In the pursuit of government expenditure cuts in the 1970s and 1980s, the model budgets were increasingly criticised. In 1990 they were superseded by a self-regulating statistical model (*Statistikmodell*) based on the actual consumption patterns of low-earning households. In 1993 the government suspended even this more modest standard until 1996. This was accompanied by measures aimed at reinforcing the principle of keeping benefit levels below the bottom of the wage scale, known in the UK as 'less-eligibility'. More generally, cost-cutting efforts involved attempts to cut the politically defined minimum subsistence level in the wake of the Supreme Court's ruling that

---

[11] The career of the issue of child poverty started in 1994 (see the valuable study of images of poverty in the 1990s by Peters (1996) based on an analysis of reports by newspapers).

incomes below this level must be free of income tax. Thus, for the first time in dealing with this fundamental question, the criterion of individual need was abandoned.

The Social Assistance Reform Act of 1996 coordinated these developments. The growth in benefit payments was slowed down by linking them to increases in Old-Age Pensions until 1998 (later extended to 2000), and by using a statistical model combined with a muddle of other criteria thereafter. At the same time, incentives to return to work were sharpened by increasing the wage/benefit differential at the lowest levels to 15 per cent, and giving subsidies to employers and return-to-work bonuses for newly employed claimants. The images of poverty used in the public discussion justifying these reforms were the outdated stereotypes of workshy scroungers and abusers of public resources. All in all the 1996 Act was a minor reform which brought few changes, and it even included some positive departures, e.g. for people with rent arrears.

German reunification suddenly created a situation in the East of the country which resembled that of the reconstruction period in West Germany at the start of the 1950s. A whole regionally defined section of the population *collectively* experienced a situation of want and socio-economic insecurity. In both cases the causes were seen as lying in the collapse of an old system and the difficulties of transformation and reconstruction. And in both historical situations some spoke of a transitional situation while others expressed pessimism or at least scepticism about future developments. Under the pressure of overwhelming mass poverty, the idea of some minimum income guarantees to be introduced in Social Insurance gained acceptance, if only as a transitional arrangement. But, in principle, the legal system and the institutions of the West, in this case the Federal Republic's welfare state, were wholly imposed upon East German society, in poverty matters as in all other realms of society. Without it being spelled out, this treated poverty in East Germany as in theory equivalent to that of the West – that is, manageable by redistribution policies – in spite of the fact that it had arisen in entirely different social circumstances. Any departure from this principle was conceived as temporary from the outset, such as the Social Supplement (*Sozialzuschlag*) for pensioners and the unemployed (see chapter 8, p. 220). Such policies work on the assumption that we are dealing with transitional unemployment and poverty which in the foreseeable future will return to 'normal' levels.

The new collective poverty in the East also differed from the old collective poverty of the 1950s in that it implied a notion of poverty as dependency. East Germany was mostly viewed as a passive recipient of aid – just as Simmel had defined individual poverty as an asymmetrical relationship between the poor on the receiving side and the non-poor on the giving side (for the analogy between collective poverty in East Germany and Simmel's concept of individual poverty see Leisering 1997c).

Did the collapse of the GDR mean that the socialist images of poverty vanished from East Germany? As far as the political elites are concerned, this must be true, since they were imported from the West. But for politicians native to the East this might not obtain even if they had coped with the transition by adapting to new ways of thinking. It is also possible that GDR assumptions about poverty, marginal groups and asocial behaviour still persist among ordinary citizens. It is not only because the GDR archives have only recently been opened and research has hardly begun that we know so little about its people's images of poverty. The GDR was a society without a public. When a critical public formed in the late 1980s this already indicated the demise of the regime. In the same way, there was no open discussion of social policy. The implicit but no less effective official models of poverty must therefore be exposed by indirect means.[12]

Poverty certainly had no place in the 'everlasting socialism' which had conquered all the evils of capitalism. Poverty was not just neglected as an issue; it was a non-issue. The system operated on the institutionalised assumption that with the subsidisation of all basic necessities and with full employment it had finally solved the problem of material security for all. Poverty therefore could be recognised in social policy only as a 'health problem', individualised as a physical problem. Similarly, for years there were no independent social welfare associations or social work in the GDR; the system of social work carried out by the church was only a tiny and marginalised exception.[13] Instead, besides the People's Welfare Organisation (*Volksfürsorge*) for the 'Veterans of Labour', there was an extensive healthcare system. Poverty was not a subject of scientific study either – although since the 1970s confidential studies had been carried out for the Party and State to investigate 'inadequate supply of goods' (*Versorgungsmängel*; see chapter 8, p. 212). There was no general wealth standing in obvious contrast to individual deprivation, and poverty was experienced less as individual justice by those affected than as a matter to be combated in 'the common struggle against maintenance deficiencies'. Employment and subsidisation policies were to prevent the emergence of poverty, one of socialism's central objectives.

Denial of poverty? A summary

We can now begin to offer an answer to the question of the career of poverty as an issue in the public debate in the FRG since its foundation.

---

[12] For the following, see Leibfried and Voges (1992b, pp. 16f.) and Voges (1992).
[13] For an overview see Sackmann and Leibfried (1992), and for a theoretically formulated general comparison see Tennstedt (1976b).

Was poverty universally suppressed, and what ideas of poverty were employed? The evidence shows that it is too simple to speak only of suppression or denial. Poverty was recognised and actively addressed as a social problem in both the early and concluding phases of the old Federal Republic, that is, before reunification, and obviously thereafter. One can speak of a kind of latency of the issue only for the period of the 1960s. During the 1970s there were limited periods of more intensified discussion of the problem. The public's ruling images of poverty were anyway different and changeable by comparison with what the denial thesis presupposes. Changing perceptions of poverty, not a thoroughgoing denial of poverty: that is the outcome of our review of the political history of poverty.

Moreover, the denial thesis entirely misses the far-reaching change in the concept of 'poverty' itself. Public talk about 'poverty' referred to something different in each of the four decades, not just with regard to the precise forms of deprivation or particularly affected groups, but fundamentally with regard to the 'social reference unit' in question, the 'possessor' of poverty. When people talked about 'the poor', they could mean very different categories of people. In the 1950s, the whole population or 'the people' constituted the poor; in the 1960s, only individuals; in the 1970s, groups; in the more colourful discourse of the 1980s the concept of the poor included groups, individuals and whole segments of the population; and finally in the 1990s, it was broadened to include a whole regionally defined section of the population once again.

The situation of new immigrants in the 1990s could not be compressed into one image of poverty. On the one hand, they were considered to be a financial burden or even a cultural threat. On the other hand, Germany accepted more political asylum seekers and war refugees from Bosnia than any other European country, thus indicating a recognition of need which nevertheless did not become explicit in the poverty discourse. Table 7.1 summarises the changing images of poverty and the protean career of the issue of poverty.

In summary, the following picture emerges. In the first decade of the FRG, poverty was an openly recognised social problem which was commonly addressed but not treated as implying a criticism of society. It was the everyday pressing want which affected almost all sections of the population and all parts of the country, an all-embracing 'poverty of the *people*'. This was matched by a collective concept of poverty which did not focus on specific groups or individuals in the way characteristic of later concepts of poverty up to the reunification of Germany. Accordingly, the poverty policies of the time were the general measures of economic and housing policy. They attacked the common structural causes of need, the destruction of the housing stock, of the sources of production and of the social infrastructure.

Table 7.1 *Changing images of poverty in the Federal Republic of Germany, 1949–1999*

	the fifties	the sixties	the seventies	the eighties	the nineties
reference unit	poverty of the people (collective poverty)	individual poverty	group poverty	group poverty	regional poverty (East Germany)
causes	structural (effects of war)	individual ('fate')	'society'; welfare state	structural (labour market)	social disruption (German unification)
duration (of individual states of poverty)	transitory	transitory	long-term	long-term	long-term
anti-poverty measures	economic reconstruction, housing policy, Old-Age Pension reform	Social Assistance, social work	'changing society' (*Gesellschaftspolitik*, 'societal policy')	social policy, family policy	regional development, transitional social-security regulations
model of society	Social Market Economy, *Wohlstand für alle*	'middle-class society' *nivellierte Mittelstands-gesellschaft*	'modern welfare state'	'two-thirds society'	society in transformation
public debate (issue cycle)	collective debate	latency of poverty	selective rediscovery	principal rediscovery (New Poverty)	broad debate; 'social exclusion'

In the 1960s poverty was more or less latent. As the contours of the economic miracle and of the welfare-state expansion were becoming apparent at the beginning of the decade, the poverty of the whole population was considered conquered. The concept of poverty now referred to the needs of *individuals* who had fallen through the net of social insurance because of circumstance, often the effects of war. The welfare system, reformed into Social Assistance in 1961, once again became the most important weapon of poverty policy, one which would alleviate the situation of the needy by means of benefits adjusted to individual needs.

A rediscovery of poverty took place in the 1970s – or, to be more precise, a number of unconnected rediscoveries: the attention to 'marginal groups' in the framework of the social-liberal reformist policies; the Christian Democratic Party's politically motivated 'New Social Question'; and in the scientific arena the intensified attempts to measure the extent of income poverty and to prepare a national system of social indicators for monitoring societal development. These ventures shared the reference to particular social *groups*, which were seen as structurally 'underprivileged' in both the economic and social security systems.

The 1980s brought yet another rediscovery of poverty. From around 1984 the focus was on the unemployed against the background of continuous mass unemployment and cuts in social spending. But the debate then broadened and has not ceased since. The concept of poverty used in the debates of the 1980s had many facets. Certain groups were still central to it: besides the unemployed, they included the growing numbers of single mothers. Largely as a result of the findings of social science, the focus on who was most affected by poverty shifted from the elderly to children and young people. At the same time, the expression 'the two-thirds society' acquired a certain resonance, as it once again expressed poverty in terms of the structure of society. The implication was that, over and above some especially affected groups, a whole section of the population was being marginalised. In the 1990s the issue finally returned to a collective concept of poverty, the poverty of (a regionally defined part of) the *people*, namely the East Germans. This also introduced an implicit notion of poverty as dependency, because East Germany was mainly seen as a passive recipient of aid.

The changing frame of reference of the poverty question also documents – further qualifying the denial thesis – that the public views of poverty reflected the basic realities of social life. Social reality and political discourse were not arbitrarily out of step with one another. Economic growth and the welfare state together had indeed ensured that during the 1960s, the 1970s and even the 1980s poverty was no longer a structural problem of West German society. The denial thesis is, however, correct in that poverty was seldom a central issue in political debate and the word 'poverty' was seldom uttered in public discourse; indeed, it became and still is virtually taboo. For instance, there were constant problems in this respect with the implementation of the European Community's Poverty Programme in Germany, leading to the adoption of substitute terms such as 'exclusion'. Germany also played a pivotal role in blocking the European poverty programmes in the second half of the 1990s. When the term 'poverty' is used, it generally refers to Third World countries. This is still the case in Eastern Germany: 'unemployment' and 'housing shortage' sound better and more restricted than 'poverty'.

The two cultures

If poverty was not simply denied: how was it dealt with? What underlying cultural patterns influenced the complex and historically changing images of poverty? Our thesis is that in dealing with poverty West German society mostly stood *between denial and dramatisation* (Leisering 1993). Not only was the subject of poverty not permanently suppressed in the arenas of politics, professional practice and the social sciences, but as in other countries some circles positively dramatised it.

Denial and dramatisation are two extreme points on a continuum. The denial thesis, which prevails among students of the subject, not only ignores the opposing, dramatising interpretation of poverty but also more moderate positions. Denial and dramatisation describe conflicting positions in a debate, but paradoxically they *can* occur simultaneously. A biased dramatisation can be used as a functional component of a denial strategy, for instance when poverty is dismissed as a residual problem of society and the residue of the poor are depicted as deviant or asocial. It is precisely in times of economic crisis that liberal and conservative circles are inclined to be dismissive about the needs of the unemployed and the poor, and yet, by way of negative dramatisation, conjure up an army of the workshy as a threat to the competitiveness of the German economy.

Conversely, dramatisation can also go hand in hand with a denial of less dramatic kinds of poverty. Public concern is often concentrated on the 'visible poverty' (Øyen 1992, p. 620) of groups such as the homeless – the 'street-people syndrome' – overlooking the less obvious poverty of the divorced woman or the pensioner next door. A further example is the short-term and temporary experience of poverty which has been omitted from virtually all discussion so far because attention was focused on long-term and deep-rooted deprivation.[14] Finally, the collective poverty of the post-

---

[14] Busch-Geertsema and Ruhstrat deny or play down the significance of short-term poverty and apparently prefer not to describe it as poverty at all (1992, p. 369). In other words, they try to exclude a less dramatic form of poverty from even being conceptualised as such.

war period has disappeared from any discussion of poverty in Germany. Critics who emphasise the existence of relative poverty even in the welfare state or 'capitalism' have tended to disregard the problem of mass subsistence poverty, which marked the early history of West Germany.[15]

What cultures of social policy, what forms of dramatisation and denial, can we identify in connection with the poverty problem in politics, social-work practice and social science?

The models of poverty used in politics and in the political public do not follow the conventional 'political code' (Niklas Luhmann 1982) in the sense that 'right' can be identified with denial and 'left' with making an issue of or dramatising poverty. These identifications certainly did not apply to the general want of the early 1950s which was attacked from all parts of the political spectrum. However, such a pronounced emphasis on poverty as the 'New Social Question' represented in the 1970s was exceptional for the Christian-Democratic Party. As regards the Social-Democratic Party, one must note that its traditional constituency was the workers and not the poor. 'Policy for workers', not 'policy for the poor' determined the agenda of the SPD (see p. 183), and that meant, in the field of social security, primarily social-insurance policies. Even in the heyday of the social-liberal coalition in the early 1970s, when there was much talk about underprivilege and disadvantaged groups, more general policy issues eclipsed the practical issues of poverty and Social Assistance. If fighting poverty were to cost money then there was not much difference between the political parties anyway. Wolfgang Jaedicke et al. have shown (1991, pp. 58–71) that in the controversy over cutting Social Assistance expenditure, which has been on the political agenda since the 1970s, the decisive lines of conflict lay between central and local government and not between political parties.

The Green Party alone treated the problem of poverty as one of its general social-policy concerns during the 1980s, its first decade of political involvement at the Federal level. After 30 years of an ingrained all-party welfare state, the Green Party temporarily shaped the contours of a new socio-political culture in which poverty found a prominent place beside other unfashionable social issues such as the problems of women and the elderly. While the Green Party's parliamentary inquiries on poverty and Social Assistance addressed the problems in a fairly factual manner, at the grass-roots level among the gamut of Green-alternative social movements the boundaries became blurred in the direction of dramatisation.

---

[15] The important study by Strang (1970) is an exception. Amartya Sen (1983, 1992, especially chapters 3 and 7) has tried to provide foundations for a theoretically informed operational concept of absolute poverty, one which can be applied to any society and not just to those undergoing development. For Sen's criticisms of a narrow focus on relative poverty see the controversy with Peter Townsend (Townsend 1979, Sen 1983, Townsend 1985).

As well as this dramatisation from below, a dramatisation from above has also been part of German political culture, just as much in free-market liberal and neo-conservative circles as in the Social-Democratic camp. Frightening images of poverty can serve the interests of both sides. Neo-liberal politics can more easily be justified if their victims can be defamed as the asocial dregs of society. In this way the allegation of individual fault becomes the means by which poverty can be denied as constituting an occasion for active social policy. Conversely, marginalised groups offer welcome examples to left-wing critics of society, exposing 'unsocial' Christian-Democratic policies.

Dramatising social problems is almost inherent in social-work practice and professional activity. It serves the interests of the social professions to emphasise their clients' needs for support, in order to protect or expand their own jobs. Ethical or emotional motives for helping contribute at a psychological level to portraying as many people as possible as needing help. Professionals dealing with social problems tend to emphasise the need to treat these problems professionally. They also tend to generalise from their limited experience in one field. Their perspectives are confined to problems which as a rule affect only a minority of the population.

This last remark is particularly addressed to the sphere of social work. In its German form it was developed in the 1960s as the historical successor to older traditions of poor relief and municipal welfare administration. It soon acquired a socio-political culture of its own, manifested in professional journals, public statements and related research. In contrast to the older conservative Science of Social Welfare (*Fürsorgewissenschaft*; Matthes 1964), the social-work profession oriented itself during its formative years in the 1970s toward the emancipatory ideals of the left-wing 'critical' social sciences. Representatives of this tendency, who have since advanced in government service or in the non-governmental welfare organisations, continue to make their views heard. The first reports on poverty by such organisations, notably by Caritas (*Caritasverband* 1987), which is affiliated to the Roman Catholic Church, and by the umbrella body of independent local welfare organisations (*Paritätischer Wohlfahrtsverband* 1989), are eloquent examples of an approach tending towards sweeping generalisation and scandalisation. Such an approach was scarcely to be interested in research findings about poverty's heterogeneity and change. Not until the 1990s could one detect some alteration in this position.

In the field of the social sciences (see the overview of German research on poverty by Hauser and Neumann 1992), the methods and findings of the few poverty studies of the 1950s and 1960s lay within the boundaries of mainstream empirical research (such as Münke 1956 and Strang 1970). They were not inclined either to play down or to dramatise their subjects.

The 'critical' social science of the 1970s turned its attention to socially marginalised groups (summary in Karstedt 1975). In that process, the radicalised version of the American theory of social problems, the labelling *approach* (as in Hess and Mechler 1973, see also Iben 1970), and to some extent traditional Marxist approaches (Colla 1974, Zander 1973), were used to articulate a model in which the 'agencies of social control' such as social workers, psychiatrists and the police could be exposed as the true causal agents of deviant behaviour.

Social-indicator research entered this field in the second half of the 1970s. In the spirit of rational social planning, indicators were constructed which could be used to monitor developments in the living conditions of the population. They included differentiated indicators for various types and levels of deprivation (Glatzer 1978). The descendants of both traditions – 'critical' social science and rationalistic 'social reporting' – coexist up to the present day, so that even within poverty research one must speak of 'two cultures'. However, during the 1990s there have been some signs of a rapprochement and cooperation.

8   Disruption and continuity in life courses: poverty in unified Germany

Following German reunification on 3 October 1990, the legal, political and economic institutions of the former Federal Republic were imposed on East Germany. In consequence, the principles of West German social policy, together with its institutional regulations and entitlements, are now applicable throughout unified Germany. This has fundamentally changed the living situation of the East Germans. They understand precarious social situations, especially unemployment and poverty, chiefly as negative consequences of the transformation. There is also a feeling of loss of security, since they are now faced with unfamiliar risks.

But whole societies cannot be changed overnight. Even an abrupt political reversal such as the *Wende* in East Germany (literally: turning point; the 'Change' brought about by reunification) cannot casually shake off the past. This raises several questions. To what extent was there continuity in the process of transformation which seemed like a clean break with the past? The question is posed at two levels: directly, at the material conditions of the population, but also at the institutions which affect living conditions. One might then ask: can the poverty in the new East German *Länder* be ascribed solely to the transformation? After all, was not the GDR a 'poor' country? What new types of poverty were brought about by the transformation which were not already present in the GDR? One might also ask, which types of life course existed before the reunification? How have people's life courses changed, and in what respects did the previous, possibly durable, behavioural orientations fit in with the new institutional circumstances?

To impose institutions from one society on to another involves considerable risks and problems. Institutions are predicated on the existence of certain preconditions in their environment. They rest on normative values and expectations, procedural routines, experiences and competences.

Co-authors: Eva Mädje, Thomas Olk.

200

Institutions which have developed in a particular environment have 'learnt' to live with the situations and circumstances which they find there. Similarly, the people and organisations in that environment have learnt to live with these particular institutions. In a kind of learning process, institutions and environments more or less adapt to each other. But one cannot simply assume a compatibility of this kind between the West German system of social policy and the political, economic and socio-cultural realities in East Germany. During their lives, the people in the East have acquired experiences of a socio-political system which presumed other guiding images and used alternative structures. Friction and conflict are therefore more likely outcomes than harmonic accord.

For these reasons, the question of the transformation of life courses and living conditions in the New Federal Territories can be answered only if the structure and development of society in the GDR are also taken into account. Which processes have been interrupted by the unification; which persist; and which have now been set in motion?

The life-course regime of the German Democratic Republic

The life courses of people in the GDR show a kind of homogeneity which has no parallel in West Germany and which became even more accentuated as the GDR regime matured. To exaggerate, one might describe the whole GDR population as following a one-phase *employment-centred life-course* model.

Some groups of people in the GDR were drawn into this employment-centred life course, even though their careers might have followed a different pattern had they lived in West Germany. This particularly applies to women, many more of whom were employed full time in the GDR. Family ties affected women's employment histories far less than in the West German society, even allowing for the fact that there were differences between the life courses of men and women in the GDR (Trappe 1994, Sørensen and Trappe 1994). Marriage and childbearing did affect the occupational position of women. However, childbearing less frequently turned mothers into 'housewives' whether for a shorter or longer period. 'The typical West German social group of not-employed housewives, together with women pensioners who had not been employed earlier in their lives, hardly existed in the GDR, or only to a far more limited extent' (Landua *et al.* 1993, p. 11).

The proportion of women in employment increased in both German states in the four decades of their divided history. The proportion grew faster in the GDR, and drew in women from different backgrounds earlier than in West Germany. At first, single women, with or without children, were brought into the labour market, followed by married women with children. The strongest growth in employment among married women took place in the GDR in the 1960s, but not until the following decade in the Federal Republic. Women generally interrupted their employment careers with the birth of a child even in the GDR, but such periods of full-time child care became shorter for each new generation of women.

In addition, paid employment determined two other central periods of the life course, the preparation for working life and retirement. The GDR's system of education and training was deliberately aimed at preparation for working life. Education was not seen as a general right of all citizens but was to be firmly directed towards useful work. Both the duration and content of education and training were therefore devoted to the needs of the economy, and were not to be used 'unnecessarily'. Children and young people were to acquire knowledge and skills which would prepare them for the world of work. In the kindergarten they were taught how to work collectively and productively. In the comprehensive schools the general technical education was oriented towards working life. From the age of 13 schoolchildren had to take part in hours of productive work in agriculture or in industry. They began to be systematically informed about occupational careers at the age of 10 and received career guidance from the age of 12. This thorough integration of education and work was also reflected in the direct relationship between education and production. Right up to the end of the school year 1967/68, the school-leaving examination (A-Levels or High School Graduation) could be obtained only in conjunction with a certificate of practical occupational skills. Until the very end of the GDR, schools still provided final-year classes in practical occupational skills (see Anweiler *et al.* 1992, Anweiler 1988).

The period of retirement was similarly affected by occupational careers. Many people deferred their retirement from employment because of the remarkably low pension levels. As a result, one can refer to 'retirement' only with considerable reservation.[1]

Productive work was meant to be the central feature of life. The GDR set full-time employment as the norm, and the state supervised and determined who might be allowed to deviate from this norm and under what conditions. For example, only 27 per cent of all employed women in the GDR worked part time in 1988, compared with 41 per cent in the FRG. It was difficult to obtain permission for reduced working hours if this did not fit in with the requirements of the enterprise.

---

[1] In 1972, 22.7 per cent of all retired people were still working. By 1989 this had fallen to 10.5 per cent (Sackmann and Leibfried 1992, p. 148). This proportion was three times as large as in the West. On the subject of the transformation of the GDR Social Insurance Pension in general, see chiefly Schmähl (1991, 1992).

The concentration on work could chiefly be ascribed to state control. As described in chapter 2, in the communist state the stages of life were defined, the pathways through them were managed and the biographical continuities guaranteed, far more directly than in the Federal Republic. Educational pathways, and therefore occupational opportunities, were regulated and allocated by the state. The GDR's political goal was to emphasise the unbroken working career. State policies aimed to ensure that all groups in the population would be integrated into a life course focused on work as soon as they reached working age. And as the right to social services was linked to the workplace, the occupational orientation was underpinned by the social security system.

The life courses of women in particular were gradually moulded by these policies. By contrast with the gender divisions in the institutionalisation of the life course in West Germany, in which rights to social insurance were founded on both occupation and marriage (chapter 2; Allmendinger 1994), the right to social security based on marriage was restricted from an early stage in the GDR. Social security for women was coupled with their occupational position, while maintenance payments from men to women after the termination of marriage were seldom permitted and then only in well-justified individual cases (Gysi and Meyer 1993, Berghahn and Fritzsche 1991). Widows' pensions were paid only to disabled women or to those with young children in cases in which the women had previously depended primarily on their husbands (Leenen 1985, pp. 12–18). The state provided for the costs of family child-rearing only sparsely through social-security transfer payments. Instead, the gradual extension of state child care, even if of arguable quality, and of inexpensive services were meant to relieve women of family burdens, ease their way into the world of work and in addition to motivate them to bear more children (see Mädje and Neusüß 1996, Frerich and Frey 1993, pp. 391 ff.).

The authoritarian 'provider state' of the GDR always had two faces: it offered security, but at the cost of a densely knit network of social controls. The state did not simply support employment, it demanded it and put a premium on it through its social policies. 'The majority of measures demonstrate the intention of keeping the working population productively occupied, and of offering incentives to those who were temporarily unoccupied to return to work as soon as possible' (Leenen 1985, pp. 12–18). Social security bulwarks were erected against the contingencies of life, such as sickness, measures which resembled those of the Federal Republic and continued the mainly reformist traditions of the Weimar Republic (for the history of these see Tennstedt 1976a). Severe and long-drawn illnesses did not affect the continuity of the working career as easily as in the Federal Republic, as long as the capacity to work was retained or could be restored.

Other groups such as the disabled were integrated into the world of work through a variety of protective measures. Premature retirement pensions were awarded only to those whose capacity for work had been reduced by more than two-thirds. The work orientation of social policy even affected retirement. The minimum wage was appreciably higher than the average old-age pension. Earnings from work after retirement were not offset against the pension, so that continued work remained attractive up to a considerable age.

The focus on occupation in the GDR was emphasised by the way in which many social services depended on the employing enterprise, which in West Germany were instead provided by separate public or voluntary sector organisations (see Backhaus-Maul and Olk 1993). The social-policy responsibilities of the enterprises and the regulations laid down by the Labour Law included housing development, the provision of convenient travel-to-work arrangements, recreational facilities for the *Werktätige* (literally 'those engaged in work' – the socialist term for all employees) and their families, as well as the care of former employees, the pensioners who were treated as 'veterans of labour' (Lohmann 1987, pp. 65 ff.). 'Employment had an even more central importance in the GDR than in the old Bismarckian model [the link between employment and welfare state entitlements – L.L./S.L.] . . . It was not just a formal precondition of receipt of benefits but the primary goal of social policy' (Manow-Borgwardt 1994, p. 49).

A policy of this kind can be pursued only if the state guarantees the provision of employment opportunities to everyone. In this respect the communist path was entirely distinct from that of the Federal Republic's social security system. The 'Right to Work' was the core of the GDR's social policy, anchored in the Labour Law Code of 1961 and the 1968 Constitution (Frerich and Frey 1993, p. 173). The GDR guaranteed the right to work, but only at a price: direct state involvement in the development of the economy and in managing the flow of labour, with restrictions on people's right to chose their career or employer. A 'Duty to Work' was thus established. The state ensured that every male and female citizen would be offered employment corresponding to the 'society's requirements' and individual qualifications. The minimum wage rates were to guarantee an employment income sufficient for existence. The prevention of risk was the guiding principle of social policy.

The Federal Republic's social policies affecting the life course were and are less strictly focused on occupation. Well-paid, life-long jobs are an important prerequisite for social services generally but especially for social insurance. Nevertheless, West Germany, more than most other welfare states, provided for groups which were not economically active (Offe 1990).

Significant threads of the Federal Republic's social security system do not
lead through the eye of the occupational needle; often, for instance, they
lead instead through marriage, a social institution which affects the life
course differently according to gender.

Still, unbroken working careers are rewarded in the Federal Republic, at
least for men. By contrast with the GDR, however, the welfare state does
not directly promote these continuities, although the social security system
treats them as formal requirements. The Federal state even intervenes in the
labour market, but – at least until unification – active labour-market policies were subservient to compensatory social policies. Social policy continues to focus on maintaining people's standard of living and on preventing
poverty in cases where neither the labour market nor marriage can ensure
the means of existence.

Break and continuity: life courses after the 'Change'

The adoption of the Federal Republic's social systems has called old cer-
tainties and practices into question. The new citizens of the East have the
task of finding their way around the new structural and institutional frameworks of the old Federal Republic. With unification, the promise of the
centralised state to provide for the citizens 'from cradle to grave' has evap-
orated. The continuity of the life course, too, is put in question. High
unemployment confronts the East German population with a social phenomenon which they have not known for decades. Mass unemployment,
which has long aroused concern in the Federal Republic, was practically
non-existent in the GDR. No one was involuntarily unemployed in the
GDR. The massive collapse of employment in the GDR was and still
is therefore rightly treated as one of the greatest difficulties in the
transformation.[2]

Unification abruptly changed many people's careers. Unemployment
struck disproportionately women, unskilled workers, young people (20 to
25) and people over 50 (Hanesch et al. 1994, p. 77). The proportion of the
adult population in work in the East quickly adjusted to the levels in the
old Federal territories. In the first half year of 1989, of the 10.97 million
adults available for work in the GDR, 91 per cent (9.93 million) were
working. In the second half year 1993, only 6.13 million were at work.
Forty per cent of all East German workers, more than three million people,
were 'released from employment' within a short period of time – a decline

[2] For a review of the period of social and economic change, see Glatzer and Noll (1995) and
Andreß (1996). For details of the changes in the labour market since unification see the
series of reports commissioned by the European Commission (*Beschäftigungsobservatorium Ostdeutschland*, various editions).

nearly unprecedented in advanced industrial societies. The number of registered unemployed rose from 642,000 in 1990 (after the fall of the Berlin Wall but before unification) to 1.26 million in 1994; the unemployment rate correspondingly rose from 7.3 per cent to 17.7 per cent (21.3 per cent in February 1998).

In the first years after unification, social policy tried to support the continuity of employment as much as possible. Since 1991 roughly one in every four to six unemployed people available for work has been involved in a labour market programme of some sort. In the first half of 1991 some 2 million people took part; in the second half of 1993 it was around 1.4 million. The Federal Labour Agency (*Bundesanstalt für Arbeit*) used about three-quarters of its 1991 and 1992 budgets for active labour market policies in East Germany. 'The Federal Agency thus succeeded in paying chiefly for the avoidance of unemployment instead of passively for its consequences' (Beschäftigungsobservatorium Ostdeutschland, no. 3/4, p. 12).

Early retirement provisions emerged as the most useful means of limiting the shortage of jobs. Already in the second half of 1990 one-third of all labour-market measures covered people undergoing early retirement, and this rose to almost half in the second half of 1993. One must distinguish between Pre-Retirement Benefit (*Vorruhestandsgeld*), which was paid in the final months of the GDR from 1 February 1990 until unification, and was financed half by the enterprises and the state, and Transitional Benefit for the Elderly (*Altersübergangsgeld*), which succeeded the Pre-Retirement Benefit and represented a special form of unemployment benefit. This was paid by the Federal Labour Agency in Nuremberg up to the age of 60, followed by an early Old-Age Pension (Wolf 1991, p. 727, Rosenow 1992).

Short-time work schemes were also introduced to relieve the labour market situation, composing well over half of all measures taken in 1990 and the first half of 1991. From the second half of 1991 a 'second labour market' was established: about a fifth of all measures were job-creation schemes (ABM, *Arbeitsbeschaffungsmaßnahmen*). Access to these programmes was made easy, as it had been with short-time work. Thus unemployed people could receive ABM services even when they had been registered with the Employment Agency for less than six months.[3] From the beginning of 1993 until 1997, Eastern Wage Subsidies (*Lohnkostenzu-*

---

[3] Employers who applied to be included in job-creation schemes received a 100 per cent subsidy to wages whereas in the West this had generally been 50 to 75 per cent. Broad-ranging subsidies for material costs could be added to this. Until the end of 1991, short-time work was also permitted in cases of permanent loss of work: *Kurzarbeit null* was invented for the East German *Länder*, meaning 'short-time work' with zero working hours, to preserve at least a symbolic affiliation of unemployed workers to their former employers (Hanesch *et al.* 1994, p. 59).

schüsse Ost, following § 249h of the Employment Promotion Act) allowed 'the direct use of Unemployment Benefit funds for job creation projects' (Beschäftigungsobservatorium Ostdeutschland, no. 10, p. 8).

The market for further vocational training flourished under the umbrella of the welfare state. The formal qualification levels of the population under the communist regime had been generally high. But these qualifications had often lost their value, thereby diminishing the East Germans' opportunities in the labour market and endangering the continuity of their occupations (Kreckel 1993, Grünert 1993). The Federal Labour Agency was therefore allowed to raise its on-going expenditures for further vocational training to combat this problem. In the first half of 1991, 9 per cent of the labour market measures were devoted to full-time further training; in the second half year it rose to 16 per cent; in 1992 and the first half of 1993 it reached 24 per cent, and it still lay at 20 per cent in the second half of that year (Beschäftigungsobservatorium Ostdeutschland, no. 11, p. 2). In November 1993, the Labour Market Monitor's seventh Labour Market Survey for East Germany revealed that 48 per cent of the employed respondents had taken part in an occupational qualification course since 1991. In East Germany, § 40c of the Employment Promotion Act allowed young people to obtain an apprenticeship in public training centres if no apprenticeships were available in enterprises or their enterprise had gone bankrupt. Almost 35 per cent of all new apprenticeships in 1991 were in the public or para-public sectors, and still about 21 per cent in 1992. The Federal Government paid a one-time subsidy of DM 5,000 for each apprenticeship offered in small businesses (employing fewer than 20 workers) until 1 April, 1992.

This investment in active labour-market policy was unique in the history of the Federal Republic. In some cases even whole branches were supported by job-creation schemes, for example in the field of environmental protection. State-run enterprises and Job Promotion Companies (*Beschäftigungsgesellschaften*), initiated by local governments, were set up with a taken-for-granted abandon which had previously been unthinkable. The Federal Labour Agency did not confine itself to compensating the risks which accompanied the economic transformation, and to paying Unemployment Benefits. Rather, it tried to be actively preventive to limit the collapse in employment and prevent unemployment. It wanted to integrate the unemployed actively into the labour process.

During the 'Change', the GDR, the first welfare state to collapse under the burden of its social services (Mario Rainer Lepsius)[4], fell unpredictably into a condition of *welfare-state gigantism* far exceeding Swedish conditions. Social expenditures reached an historic scale of two-thirds of the

---

[4] See Mayer and Solga (1994, p. 194, note 1).

(East German) regional Gross Domestic Product as a result of the restricted economic activity there and the massive social expenditures subsidised by West Germany, compared with barely 30 per cent in the West (BMAS 1994a, p. 172; 1998, p. 190).

Nevertheless, it would be wrong to speak of a change of direction in West German social policy, for two reasons. First, the measures were mainly carried out within existing institutional frameworks. Second, more significantly, they were intended only to bridge the early gaps in the transformation and then to be terminated. All the measures were limited, based on the expectation that the East German labour market would quickly recover and thus make it unnecessary for the state to continue to provide and finance jobs. The welfare state's management of the flow of human resources, the 'second labour market', was not intended as an institutional innovation, a new response to mass and long-term unemployment, nor to become one in the future. The political management of the transformation was striking for its emphatic 'market optimism',[5] as Lehmbruch has called it (1991, p. 586), and the assumption of a self-sustained recovery.

This is also apparent in that hardly any efforts were made to put the active labour market policies on a long-term and financially sound basis. There was no serious consideration of how the immense financial costs could be met in the long term – for instance in the form of a levy on wealth, as introduced in the 1950s to fund compensation for war-related losses of property (see p. 177). Instead, the Federal Labour Agency, which administers the Unemployment Insurance, and other branches of Social Insurance, which in Germany are independent bodies with self-contained budgets separate from government budgets, were simply overloaded. The repercussions of these policies are still apparent in the late 1990s: there is constant criticism in the political debate that German unification has been financed on a large scale out of social insurance funds and therefore by that part of the population which pays social insurance contributions rather than by all taxpayers. In addition, the public debt incurred by the Federal government and by the *Länder* has soared. In this way, the fiscal problems of unification, or rather the fiscal policy of the Kohl government, have compounded Germany's other financial problems familiar to most Western welfare states in the 1990s.

---

[5] The *Treuhandanstalt* (Public Trustee Agency) was exceptional among Federal Republic institutions and was an anomaly in the market economy system. It was conceived as a huge transitional holding company to privatise the state-owned businesses and establish market institutions instead. At the end of 1990 over a third of all employees were working in enterprises managed by the Public Trustee, but the proportion had fallen to 3 per cent by the second half of 1993 (*Beschäftigungsobservatorium Ostdeutschland*. 11, p. 2). In 1995 the *Treuhandanstalt* was superseded by the BVS (*Bundesanstalt für vereinigungsbedingte Sonderaufgaben*).

The demand for uninterrupted employment – for women and for men, as it was achieved in the GDR – acts as the East German population's chief criterion for evaluating the new social system. Breaks in employment are therefore experienced as an onerous and unwanted fracture in the ability to plan one's life. Observers accordingly offered dramatic accounts of the individual consequences of these changes for the East German population. 'With the loss of their jobs they lost far more than their source of income: they lost the centre of their lives, since the significance of their workplace was far greater in the daily lives of the people in the GDR than in the West' (Wolski-Prenger, quoted by Merten 1994, p. 18).

After unification the chances of achieving life-long employment worsened particularly for women. East Germany now contains significantly more single-earner households than before. If only one of the partners remains in employment, it is more commonly the man, as in the West. Because women in the East cling to their orientation towards paid employment, they are more unwilling to leave it voluntarily than in the West; they are thus in the narrow sense 'unemployed'.

The model of a life course distinguished by uninterrupted employment is still retained as an ideal. But as the transformation processes endanger the realisation of this model for many sections of the population, their fears about the future increase. Ordinary economic and labour-market fluctuations in Germany arouse more anxiety in the East because things are experienced differently there than in the West. The East Germans do not always perceive the risks which confront them simply as transitional problems which bridging measures will quickly overcome. In the face of these risks, some nostalgically view the conditions in the old GDR as 'the good old days'. For those who had hoped for a better life, was unification personally a false beacon?

The advantages of the communist system thus imagined contrast strikingly with the genuine restrictions on personal freedom in the GDR, especially the strict regulation of occupational careers. Many East German citizens nowadays realise plans and wishes which, in the GDR, would have remained unfulfilled or even blocked by the state. This applies in particular to the younger generation who press for voluntary initiatives, as well as to the middle generation whose occupational mobility was restricted and whose expectations of promotion were not fulfilled (see Mayer and Solga 1994). It is also the case for many women with young children, who nowadays have the freedom to spend more time at home with their children if they want to (see Großmann and Huth 1993, Drauschke *et al.* 1993, Meyer and Schulze 1992).

One should also keep in mind that a deeply felt desire to have a meaningful occupation is not to be equated with an unconditional wish for life-long full-time employment. More commonly, while the desire for a career may continue, the form in which it is realised varies widely depending on the circumstances. This was true for at least some East German women, those who would always have taken advantage of provisions for part-time work after the birth of a child if the occupational sector in which they worked had offered the opportunity to them. But by contrast they would not have wanted to follow the West German social-policy model of the 'housewife marriage' and to interrupt or even end their occupational careers. At the same time, the freeing of the choice of career from the guardianship and control of the state is seen as an improvement. Entry to the West's pluralistic society has enabled career choices to be realised outside the ambit of state control and direction. People can realise their individual goals. The changes in the conditions of life in East Germany are multifaceted, as are the criteria by which the citizens judge them. In particular, different generations perceive the opportunities now open to them in quite different ways (Mayer 1994).

Did poverty exist in the GDR?

Even 'real socialism' (*realer Sozialismus*), as the official GDR term went, was striking for its social inequalities. Officially, poverty was a taboo subject in the GDR. Of course there were income differentials, but the issue of inadequate levels of provision which one would classify as poverty was far more suppressed than in the Federal Republic and therefore could not be dealt with using routine social policy measures.[6] Quite apart from the inequality within GDR society, the start of the transformation revealed an enormous differential in living standards between the GDR and the old Federal Republic. We do not know how many poor people there were when development started jointly, and retrospective investigation would not be easy.

In spite of the fact that poverty was not officially recognised in the GDR, both the standard of living and even poverty were the subject of social research. The findings were however not published as long as the GDR existed. The studies reveal that income poverty was widespread in the GDR, though it tended to decline (Manz 1992). In order to determine a poverty line, a GDR research team, whose findings have been reported by Günter Manz (1992), constructed a household budget. This appears

---

[6] For an attempt to study poverty comparatively in the communist countries of Eastern Europe in spite of the suppression of the poverty issue found in all of them see Atkinson and Micklewright (1992); for the first attempt to provide a comprehensive overview of social policy development in the new East German *Länder* see Schmähl (1992); for a broader theoretical approach, see Offe (1994).

Table 8.1. *Poverty in the GDR*

(Employee households below the poverty line, as a percentage of the relevant household type)

Persons in the household	1970	1980	1988
1	5	5	4
2	30	10	10
3	20	9	7.5
4	34	10	6.5
5 or more	45	18	4
Total	30	12	10
Pensioners' households	65	50	45

Source: Manz (1992, p. 88).

exceedingly modest and lies well below the socio-cultural minimum offered by the (West German) Federal Social Assistance Act. Unfortunately the precise construction method has not been published, so that in what follows we can use the data only for general hypotheses and conclusions. The study of poverty in the GDR is still in its infancy and only some preliminary points can be made here. However, survey data collected officially during the GDR period have been found to be fairly reliable.

If we adopt the approach of the survey team and take its household budget (or the cash income which represents it) as the poverty line, and thus define people as poor and lacking resources if they could not afford it, then in 1970 30 per cent of all households were poor. The most severely affected were retired households, 65 per cent of whom lived below the poverty line in that year.

Table 8.1 shows that the proportion in poverty steadily decreased, though by 1988 roughly one-half of all pensioner households were still poor. A reasonably reliable comparison with West Germany emerges if we take the West German elderly whose incomes fell below 40 per cent of the mean income in the West German population. In 1969 this applied to 4.8 per cent of all women over 65 and to 3.4 per cent of all men over 65 (in 1983, 1.7 and 1.9 per cent respectively; Semrau 1990, p. 120).[7] In other words, old people were much more likely to be poor in the GDR than in West Germany, even if it was easier to gather contributory entitlements in the GDR than in the Federal Republic. A minimum pension existed in the GDR (nevertheless

---

[7] These figures refer to persons and do not include foreigners or people living in residential care. Income is measured as per-capita income weighted by the size of the household in which a person lives (equivalence scale).

graduated by the number of contribution years) unlike in the Federal Republic. By granting a minimum the GDR weakened the relationship between working career and the right to social security benefits.

In making a judgement about poverty among the elderly in the GDR, one must take into account the special benefits in kind provided by the state, such as lunches, health care, vacations in holiday homes owned by employers, and domiciliary care services for the housebound. These raised the standard of living for those who could not afford the recommended household budget. In addition, the poverty of the elderly was probably felt as less stigmatising because it was so widely experienced. However, the homes for old people were often in a miserable condition.

Even the pension level itself did not directly depend on the preceding income from employment, but on political considerations. On the whole, the level of social security benefits was low. In addition, pensions in the GDR were not indexed but were raised from time to time by governmental decrees. The systematic socio-political preference for an employment-centred life course was not manifested in social security benefits that rewarded and built on such a life course. In fact any periods of life out of employment were discriminated against, even retirement. The minimum pensions ranged between 300 and 370 GDR Marks per month in 1988; for widows they were 300 Marks (Frerich and Frey 1993, p. 345). By comparison, Manz set the 1988 poverty line for a single-person household at 500 Marks per month (Manz 1992, p. 86). (Corresponding to common usage, *Marks* refers to East German currency; DM to West German Marks.)

As wages and conditions continued to improve in real terms after 1970 in the GDR, Günter Manz assumes that increasing proportions of the population would have been able to afford the minimum budget. Even though the supply situation in the GDR worsened, in that the choice of commodities became more restricted, the poverty rate should have diminished according to Manz. This shows that conventional methods for measuring poverty in Western countries are ineffective for measuring poverty in the GDR: the supply shortage indicated poverty, in that increases in purchasing power did not reflect any increase in the supply of goods. It did not help a private household to be able to afford to rent better accommodation as long as no better accommodation was available.

Any analysis of poverty in the GDR therefore has to consider two aspects: both the level of individual disposable incomes and the general availability of goods and services which the individual could choose to buy (see Tennstedt 1976b). Living conditions in the GDR were marked by an inadequate supply of goods. A considerable part of the 'poverty in socialism' thus appears to have been *collective poverty*, affecting wide sections of the population.

But poverty in the GDR was not solely a matter of the limited supply of goods. As table 8.1 shows, *relative poverty* also existed in the GDR. There were households which could not afford the minimum budget even if all the goods had been available. Collective poverty – the general lack of provision of goods and services – and relative poverty – certain groups' and individuals' lack of income – call for distinct policy responses. One of the instruments of poverty policy in the field of the supply of provisions was the widespread use of price subsidies for basic nutritional foodstuffs.

The study by Günter Manz (table 8.1) does not reveal which household types, for instance single persons, lay at or below the poverty line and we cannot tell how far state transfers reduced the risks or alleviated the conditions of poverty. But in the case of the retired, the following is obvious: their poverty was caused by social policy because pensions were set too low and the social security system did not protect them from poverty. However, the GDR state controlled not only transfer incomes, but also the flow of primary incomes. The state directed the middle stage of the life course far more directly than was ever the case in the former Federal Republic. Insofar as the inequalities in earned incomes in the GDR were determined by the state, the poverty of the employed can also be ascribed to the state.

In short, this research study (Manz 1992) supports the hypothesis that poverty was extensive in the GDR, even if the situation there was better than in other communist countries. In the period immediately before the opening of the Berlin Wall, about one in ten persons in the GDR were poor if measured by the very low standard adopted by Manz. The poverty rate would have appeared much greater if measured by the official Western poverty standard which provided for a higher standard of living. The poverty in East Germany is not something which can therefore simply be blamed on the unification with the Federal Republic. Rather, the GDR seems to have entered the German unification process with a high poverty rate, higher than in the West.

Since the GDR implemented the right to work for women and men alike, the state was not confronted with some of the problems posed for the Federal Republic's system of social security and which affected the struggle against poverty. The Federal Social Assistance Act was launched in 1961 in the hope that its benefits would increasingly be required only for atypical personal contingencies. It was expected that this Assistance would be granted increasingly in non-material form, that is, advice and support to claimants (see pp. 62 and 180–182). These expectations have not been realised.

By contrast, Social Welfare (*Sozialfürsorge*) in the GDR genuinely had the character of individualised casework. The right and duty to work, the statutory minimum wage and the minimum social security benefits all show

Table 8.2 *Social welfare recipients in the GDR* (1947: Soviet Occupation Zone)

	total	fit for work	old-age pensioners	non-pensioners, men	non-pensioners, women	children below age of 18
1947	1,058,000					
1950	530,167	231,301				
1960	166,851	21,045	35,354	16,093	92,885	22,519
1970	56,966	6,935	12,195	4,755	34,145	5,871
1980	17,172		6,435	588	8,611	1,538
1985	8,150		2,298	558	5,024	270
1989	5,535		2,022	477	2,905	131

Source: Frerich and Frey (1993, p. 369).

that Social Welfare was less significant in the whole social welfare system. The official attitude was that Social Welfare in the GDR could be distinguished 'clearly from the previous concept of individual welfare provision, in that it has developed a productive form of Social Welfare whose first steps are taken in the Employment Agency. Thus training or retraining in occupational skills and the offer of employment are in the first rank of individual Social Welfare measures' (Zumpe 1951, quoted by Frerich and Frey 1993, p. 366). The only exceptions to this rule were those who were unfit for work, women over 60 and men over 65, people who had to care for disabled dependents, and mothers with one child under 3 or two children under 8 who could not otherwise care for their children (ibid, p. 368). Table 8.2 shows that the number of Social Welfare recipients fit for work continuously declined. However, in the 1950s and 1960s even this group had to be supported with cash benefits, probably because enough jobs could not be found for them all.

Quite contrary to the experience in the Federal Republic, the total number of Social Welfare recipients in the GDR fell steeply over the years. In 1989, the last year before unification, only 5,535 persons were dependent on relief (see table 8.2), representing only about 0.03 per cent of the GDR population, compared with 5.8 per cent for Social Assistance in the West, including 4.4 per cent for Basic Income Support. The level of cash benefits paid to Social Welfare recipients lay appreciably below the poverty line calculated by Manz. His estimate of the poverty line for a single-person household in 1988 was 500 Marks per month (Manz 1992, p. 86), but the Social Welfare benefit paid 260 Marks (in 1989, 290 Marks; *Law Gazette* of the GDR 1989), plus a limited Housing Benefit in certain cases.

Poverty and Social Assistance claims after the 'Change'

The East Germans do not only look back on the GDR with nostalgia, particularly not as far as the standard of living is concerned, even if the electoral achievements of the PDS (*Partei des Demokratischen Sozialismus*, the renamed former ruling party of the GDR) might suggest otherwise. The end of communism and the incorporation of the Eastern territories into the capitalist system reflected the expressed will of the majority of the population. The standard-of-living differential relative to the Federal Republic was itself a reason for rejecting the old regime, which explains some of the expectations directed towards the social and economic system of the West. The standards used by East Germans to judge their circumstances were less those of the GDR than of West Germany and other Western countries.

The continuity of living circumstances in East Germany after 1989 was seen by many as a curse and an injustice. The people in the East wanted to overcome the conditions associated with the GDR. 'The objective "East–West differences" which existed before 1990 served merely as a comparison between two countries; through the reunification of Germany they have become an intra-national contradiction' (Landua *et al.* 1993, p. 20). From this perspective, poverty and claiming Social Assistance reflected simply the tip of an iceberg of unfulfilled expectations connected with unification with the Federal Republic.

Poverty is seen as indicative of the social problems of the transformation. This is apparent when one considers that in East Germany social distinctions and inequalities have developed which were unknown in the GDR (see Joas and Kohli 1993b, Geißler 1993, 1996). These inequalities are augmented by the backlog in relation to the West. It is easy to find poverty on a considerable scale in the East. Still, one must ask about the degree of continuity or change among those affected by poverty. In what ways has the very process of unification contributed to the income poverty in East Germany? Most studies are devoted to developments after the opening of the Berlin Wall or unification. However, the effect of the transformation on developments in the East can only be adequately clarified when prior developments in the GDR have first been studied. Only then can one judge how far the unification started the process of impoverishment, or advanced it, or even reduced it.

One cannot use Manz's data on the GDR given above for a direct comparison with the present day. But since the poverty line used by Manz fell so far below the Social Assistance level, some crude conclusions may be permissible. The income data of the Socio-Economic Panel study also give a point of reference. Its first survey in the East was carried out in June 1990,

Table 8.3 *Poverty in Germany, 1990–1997* (People in poverty as per cent of total population)

	1990	1991	1992	1993	1994	1995	1996	1997
Total	14.0	12.2	11.5	12.1	11.6	12.8	10.0	9.1
West Germany	10.5	10.0	10.0	11.1	11.1	13.0	9.6	8.4
East Germany	26.7	20.3	19.4	17.9	16.1	13.2	11.6	11.6

Note: Poverty line: 50 per cent of the mean equivalent income in West Germany (from 1996 in the whole of Germany); incomes in the East corrected for purchasing power parity.
Sources: Krause (1993, 1994b; personal communication), Habich and Krause (1997); Socio-Economic Panel.

which was during the last months of the GDR and in particular before currency union which came into force on 1 July. A further question is how the GDR might have developed if unification had not taken place. We cannot know how many people who are now poor might not have been impoverished under GDR conditions, and, conversely, how many people who are not poor today might have been impoverished by the decline of the GDR's economy.

Three aspects of the development of poverty in East Germany are of special interest: the extent and composition of the population in poverty; the number of Social Assistance claimants and their characteristics; and the evolution of the welfare differential between West and East. The chief research findings are as follows: by comparison with the GDR era, we may assume that significantly fewer people in the East live in income poverty in the mid and late 1990s; nevertheless, there are many more Social Assistance claimants than previously received Social Welfare. Poverty is more openly apparent, and the gap in incomes by comparison with the West has not been closed.[8]

In table 8.3,[9] the West German poverty standard is used for both West and East Germany. The higher average income[10] in the West is thus used as

[8] For an integrated conceptual analysis in a Simmelean perspective of these three types of poverty in unified Germany – relative income poverty, institutionally acknowledged poverty (Social Assistance) and collective poverty (the situation of the East compared to the West) – see Leisering and Mädje (1996).
[9] For data on income poverty in the Federal Republic since 1962 see Hauser (1997a).
[10] Income is measured as 'equivalent' income to account for different household sizes and household compositions (e.g., age of household members). By definition, the poverty of individuals then coincides with the poverty of the respective households although poor persons are used as counting units.

a yardstick for the development of income. If East and West were simply regions of a homogeneous country, one would naturally use a single country-wide all-German poverty line, as is customary in international comparisons. The Western standard, however, has been the policy target (Krause 1993, p. 31). If the lower all-German standard were used, it would be reduced by the same lower Eastern incomes which themselves have to be raised. Instead, by using the West German standard, as in this instance, one can determine how the welfare differential is changing as regards poverty. (From 1996, however, we use an all-German poverty line because the new Germany is increasingly perceived as a whole).

The poverty rate in the West as measured by the West German standard has remained fairly constant: roughly one person in ten lived below this poverty line, with a slight increase since 1993 and again since 1995. The risk of poverty in East Germany was disproportionately higher, although the total number in income poverty has continued to fall. Where one in four people in the East were poor before unification (the data for 1990 were collected in June), the proportion sank continuously after the 'Change', so that by 1995 only about one person in eight was poor. Thus while people in the East have not yet equalled those in the West in possessing money and goods, they are catching up.

For a contrasting picture, let us take the *East* German poverty standard, which is preferred by some authors, e.g. by Hauser (1997a, b) (for the following see Peter Krause 1994b, pp. 19–21, and personal communication). By this standard a household counts as poor if it had less than half of the average equivalent income of East German households. Not surprisingly, by this lower poverty yardstick considerably fewer people were poor than when we use the Western standard, that is, only 8.0 per cent of the East German population were poor in 1995. While the extent of poverty was more limited using the Eastern measure, an opposite picture emerges if we consider the trends in poverty between 1990 and 1995. By the Eastern standard poverty increased in the East (in annual percentage steps from 3.5 to 4.3, 6.0, 6.3, 7.9 and 8.0 per cent), although by the Western standard it decreased, as shown in table 8.3. In other words, by the Western standard poverty in the East was high but falling, while from the perspective of the Eastern standard it was low but rising. The highest poverty rate by the Eastern measure in 1995 still lay well below the lowest rate by the Western measure, at 8.0 per cent compared with 13.2 per cent respectively. The explanation for this surprising outcome is that the Eastern standard lay far below the Western but was rising towards it as earned incomes in the East rose faster than those in the West.

The duration of spells of individual poverty is as important as the extent of poverty overall. The public may assume that poverty in the East has solidified into a long-term prospect for those affected by it (Hanesch *et al.* 1994, p. 255). But the findings of the Socio-Economic Panel study show that even during the first years after unification, while the risk of being poor in the New *Länder* was greater than in the old, the odds of escaping from a spell of poverty were better than in the West. Of those people who were poor in 1990, two-thirds had escaped from poverty by 1992 in the East compared with only half in the West.[11] Our analysis of the duration of Social Assistance claims in an East German city (see pp. 232–235) reveals that short-term claims are as frequent as they are in the West. On the whole, poverty in the East is not a long-term condition for most people affected – at any rate as long as the pace of social change is maintained and a further disproportionate growth in incomes is achieved; as long as the massive transitional social-policy programmes for the East continue; and finally as long as unemployment in the East is less likely to lead to poverty than it is in the West (see pp. 219–221). These very conditions have become critical since 1997. Longitudinal studies of the duration and entrenchment of poverty conditions during the late 1990s, however, are not yet available.

As in the West, the groups most affected by poverty in the East include the unemployed, the divorced, single parents and large families. Old people in the East have been particularly successful in avoiding poverty. They can be counted among the winners of unification, since they benefited by the change to a welfare state from a society in which retirement was only minimally supported. Eastern pensioners are profiting from the Western pay-as-you-go pension scheme. The advantages offered by the Western pension legislation before 1989 to the small band of immigrants and refugees from the GDR are extended to all previously working generations in the GDR. Without having paid contributions to West German pension funds, they are now entitled to benefits based on their life-long employment records. This leads for instance to higher pensions for East German women, based on their longer periods of paid work.

The Federal Social Assistance Act has been in force in East Germany since 1 January 1991, initially with some exceptions. From the currency union until that date, i.e. during the second half of 1990, a Social Assistance Act, which in many respects anticipated the Federal Act, was in force. The number of people who applied for Social Assistance exploded in 1991. The number of claims for Social Assistance lies well above the number of earlier claims for the Social Welfare programme of the GDR and has been rising gradually since, but remains well below the Western level (see table 8.4). The Social Assistance benefit scales remain lower in the

---

[11] These findings are based on a poverty standard of 50 per cent of mean equivalent income in the whole of Germany; see Krause (1994a, p. 198).

Table 8.4 *Claiming Social Assistance in Germany, 1990–1997* (Claimants of Basic Income Support as per cent of total population)

	1990	1991	1992	1993	1994	1995	1996	1997
Total	—	3.9 (2.5)	4.4 (2.9)	4,7 (3.0)	(2.8)	(3.1)	(3.3)	(3.5)
West Germany	4.4 (2.8)	4.3 (2.8)	4.7 (3.2)	5.1 (3.3)	(3.1)	(3.4)	(3.6)	(3.8)
East Germany	0.8 (—)	2.0 (1.4)	2.8 (1.8)	3.2 (1.8)	(1.6)	(1.8)	(2.0)	(2.5)

Note: Claimants not living in residential care or homes. From 1994 asylum seekers are not included.
Claimants 1 January to 31 December of each year (in brackets: claimants on 31 December only).
—: figures not available.
Source: Statistisches Bundesamt (1998c, 1992b–1998b).

East. While the claims rate in the West grew in the 1980s chiefly because of immigration (see pp. 226ff.) and levelled out at the beginning of the 1990s, a new increase in claims started in 1992. Besides the falling, though still significant, proportion of immigrants claiming Social Assistance, the chief cause has been the rapid increase in unemployment. For the first time, the unemployment rate in 1996 reached the peak of 1950.

The fall in claimants' numbers in 1994 reflects the introduction of Asylum Seekers Benefit in November 1993. As a consequence, 450,000 persons were transferred from Social Assistance to the new benefit scheme. Table 8.4 also shows that in the East the number of people who claimed Assistance at any time of the year (all-year measure) increased faster than the (necessarily lower) number of people who made claims on 31 December in each year (single-day measure). This means that there were more and more short-term claims, at least until 1993, the last year for which all-year figures were given in the official statistics.

The enduringly high level of unemployment in the East has thus far not led to a dramatic increase in the rate of claims for Social Assistance, because as suggested above a large part of the potential unemployment was prevented through labour-market measures such as job creation and early retirement. Where straightforward unemployment occurred it was less liable to cause poverty than in West Germany. Klaus Müller *et al.* (1996) found, drawing on the Socio-Economic Panel study in the East, that the households of the unemployed there were less often poor and remained poor for shorter periods than in the West. The main reason is that more women were (and still are) in paid employment in the East, so that usually only one earner in the household was unemployed at a time. If all the adults in the household were not struck by unemployment simultaneously, the likelihood of having to claim Social Assistance was reduced. In addition, unemployment in the East has been more likely than in the West to affect people with higher qualifications, whose income level on earnings-related Unemployment Benefit was more likely to lie above the Social Assistance means test. Furthermore, East German unemployed persons were more likely to be receiving the higher Unemployment Benefit than the lower tier of means-tested Unemployment Assistance. One may assume, however, that these peculiarities of Eastern unemployment have diminished.

Unification was also accompanied by social security legislation which helped to relieve the Social Assistance agencies. The Pension Insurance Benefits were supplemented, like those of Unemployment Insurance. These Top-up Supplements (*Sozialzuschläge*) were payable if the pension benefits fell below a defined level[12] and were raised in step with increases in the Social Assistance benefit scales. On-going Unemployment Insurance claims were eligible for supplements until 1995, though new claims from the beginning of 1992 were not supplemented. On-going pensions were similarly supplemented until 1996, although new pension claims from January 1994 were not eligible. The pension level for a single person was set at DM 495 per month by the Pension Adjustment Act of 1990. Since January 1992, the income of a partner has been taken into account in assessing eligibility for a Pension Supplement.

The restriction on the payment of supplements is further evidence that the transformation was interpreted in policy terms as a process that required only transitional make shift arrangements rather than radical institutional innovations. According to those responsible for the unification negotiations (BMAS 1994b, p. 68), the Social Supplements were introduced as a response to the absence in 1990 of effective local Social Assistance Agencies in the GDR to which old or unemployed people in poverty could turn for help. After 1994, the number of cases in which Supplements were paid to Unemployment Benefits decreased dramatically, and entitlements among pensioners also declined. While 23 per cent of all pensioners had their pensions increased by Supplements (662,570 people) in 1991, by 1993 this had fallen to 2.5 per cent (101,843 people).

The enormous problems of the labour market did of course have their effects on Social Assistance. Unemployment is an even more important reason for Social Assistance entitlement in the East than the West. Over half of all East German households (54 per cent) claimed Basic Income Support for this reason, compared with 29 per cent in the West. In the West

---

[12] The Top-up Supplements did not preclude application for Social Assistance benefits if the total household requirements were greater.

it has chiefly been couples with children, together with single people, who have been beneficiaries primarily for this reason, but other causes have been at work in the case of single mothers (1992; Statistisches Bundesamt 1994b, p. 72; see also Hauser and Hübinger 1993, pp. 193ff.; since 1994 separate figures for East and West Germany are no longer available). The apparent peculiarities in the East may be seen as part of the belated consequences of the work-centred life courses in the GDR. As in the West, children and young people are particularly affected.

It seems that at the outset of the transformation the people in the East themselves inclined to the view that this was a matter of a short but possibly painful transition to Western standards and goals. Living conditions improved soon for about half the East German population, and for a further 29 per cent they did not deteriorate (Landua *et al.* 1993, p. 118). Satisfaction with the standard of living, rising income levels and social security in the East rose, in appreciation of the improvements of recent years. Nevertheless, the levels of satisfaction with all three aspects remained below those in the West. As before, the East German population compared itself 'from a perspective of underprivilege and relative deprivation with the West German population' (Landua *et al.* 1993, p. 17).

Optimism about the future noticeably slackened during the first years after unification, and the economic situation has again become more tense since 1996/1997. The feeling of relative disadvantage can also be detected in the view shared by most East Germans that the West Germans ought to be prepared to sacrifice more in the unification process. They seem to interpret the income differential as a distributive injustice and not as a problem of inadequate resources.

These findings allow us to conclude that major inroads in the entrenched conditions of the GDR could be achieved. On the other hand, in the short run it was impossible to reach the inevitably unrealistic goal of catching up with the West's standard of living – to create a 'thriving landscape' (*blühende Landschaften*) as Chancellor Kohl's much criticised formula of 1990 goes. These unrealistic expectations may be predicated on overly rosy recollections of living conditions in the GDR. In 1992, half of the East Germans still believed that pay and prices had been more satisfactory at the time of the GDR (SFZ 1992, p. 6).

Conclusion

People in East Germany desire a high and rising standard of well-being no less than those in the West. On central issues, principally housing but also incomes, the promises of unification have not been fulfilled. The West's lead has been reduced but it has not yet been done away with. The people in the

East are poorer and see themselves as deprived by comparison with those in the West. There was more continuity than expected where the wish for a break with the old regime was most pronounced, in the field of the material standard of living.

By contrast, the rupture in the institutional life-course regime which followed political unification was more marked than expected. Individual patterns of behaviour and assumptions about life did not keep up with the speed of change. Ideals which had illuminated the whole life course in the GDR affected expectations towards the Federal Republic's social policy. This is one source of insoluble tensions. The Federal Republic's welfare state cannot guarantee a 'right to work'. Such a right would contradict fundamental assumptions about the relationship between politics and economy in welfare capitalism. However, the gendered differentiation in life courses – that is, the institutionalised incentive for women to marry and have families instead of working full-time for life (see pp. 34, 50f.) – is a peculiarity of the West German life-course pattern which could in principle be changed, and indeed has not been fully transferred to the East. The example of other countries shows that women in Western society certainly can arrange their lives to accommodate occupational careers.

The pessimistic diagnoses and predictions that the New Federal Territories would become a poor region in the unified Germany, a kind of German *mezzogiorno*, the equivalent of the permanently underdeveloped southern region of Italy, may have been exaggerated. Relative income poverty as measured by the Western standard has fallen in the East since 1990 and no longer exceeds that in the West. The extent of Social Assistance claiming in the East is still significantly above the number of recipients of the GDR's earlier Social Welfare, but it has remained well below the level in the West. Longitudinal data of Social Assistance careers in the first half of the 1990s do not indicate far-reaching processes of marginalisation either (see pp. 230–235). In addition, poverty in the East cannot be seen simply as a consequence of the imposition of the West German model of society; to some extent it is an inheritance from the GDR, in which income poverty was considerable and even more extensive than in the West. However, the overall inequality of net incomes in the East German population, as measured, e.g., by the Gini and the Atkinson coefficients, has increased markedly during the years 1990–1995, although it still has not reached the West German level (Hauser 1997b). Wages have become more unequal and revenue from self-employment and assets has become more important while welfare state transfers may have evened out some of the new inequalities.

On the whole, a favourable prognosis for the East would presuppose accelerated economic development, continued labour-market support measures and cash transfers from the West. In the last third of the 1990s these needs have become critical: there are cuts in Unemployment Benefit and labour-market measures such as job-creation schemes; transitory schemes like the Old-Age Pension Supplement are no longer available; the Solidarity Surcharge (*Solidaritätszuschlag*) a special tax raised for the East German *Länder* was reduced in 1998; and economic conditions remain difficult. Unemployment, in particular, continued to rise, abating slightly (later than unemployment in the West) in 1998 (17.1 per cent in August 1998 as compared to 9.0 per cent in the West) and in 1997 the economic growth rate fell below the growth rate in the old *Länder*. As a reaction, spending on employment schemes has not been cut in 1998 as originally planned (19.9 billion DM, that is 1.6 billion DM more than 1997). This included special schemes for the long-term unemployed to be extended until 2001.

A new structure of poverty might be emerging in these years. Until now, the transitional social policy measures have been able only to limit the disturbances in the occupational system and to neutralise the social side effects brought by the transformation, not to overcome these problems. Nevertheless, social unrest in East Germany could thus be prevented. But it seems increasingly difficult to sustain such a gigantic 'welfare state in transition', which absorbs more than half of the regional gross domestic product, unless its finances are put on a firmer footing. During the years 1991–1997, 1.186 billion DM were transferred from West to East (net cash flow 895 billion), including 806 billion by the Federal government and 283 billion by social insurance funds. For years to come, annual net transfers of c. 150 billion are expected.[13] Attempts at a large-scale tax reform, which would also have benefited the economy, failed dramatically in 1997 and have been revitalised by the new goverment led by the Social Democrats in 1999. The reform of the institutional structure of the German welfare state is still moving slowly.

---

[13] Bundesfinanzministerium (1998). For a discussion of the financial aspects of unification see Weidenfeld and Korte (1996, pp. 294–307, 630).

9   Increasingly dynamic? The impact of social change on Social Assistance dynamics

Is the dynamic character of poverty a new phenomenon in an era of accelerated social change and increasing discontinuities in individual lives? Or, on the contrary, is it an old phenomenon destined to fade in the course of growing social exclusion and polarisation? The question is whether and how the time patterns of poverty risks have changed over historical time. Few studies have asked about the impact of social change on poverty and Social Assistance with regard to the duration of claims, e.g., whether the extent of short-term or long-term claiming has changed over historical time. In this chapter we investigate this question in two ways: first, we compare Social Assistance careers in West Germany in the mid 1980s to careers in the late 1980s and early 1990s; second, we compare East German to West German Social Assistance careers to trace the impact of the unique transformation triggered by unification in 1990.

For the USA Huff Stevens (1994), using data from the Michigan Panel Study of Income Dynamics (PSID), found that changes in exit rates from Social Assistance corresponded to economic conditions. In the recession years of 1985 and 1983, for example, the exit rates were 0.47 and 0.45, while in 1984 the exit rate was 0.58. Hoynes and MaCurdy (1994) report that the duration of welfare spells in the USA decreased between the mid 1970s and early 1980s, but increased during the 1980s. The proportion of welfare spells lasting seven or more years, for example, decreased from 22 per cent in 1975 to 15 per cent in 1980 and increased again to 21 per cent in 1985. Labour-market conditions would appear to have played only a minor role here, whereas some of the shift in exit rates could be explained by changes in benefit levels. Several other authors in the USA have analysed the influence of changes in programme characteristics and participation rates on duration of claiming, but without being able to reach clear conclusions (cf. Moffit 1985, 1987).

Co-authors: Petra Buhr, Doris Rentzsch, Andreas Weber.

'New poverty'? – the 1980s and the 1990s compared

In Germany a widespread assumption is that the duration of Social Assistance claims has increased during the 1980s due to the economic crisis and an increase in long-term unemployment. However, the scarce empirical evidence points in a different direction: Andreß (1994) and Samson (1992) report for the City of Bielefeld that time on Social Assistance has decreased continuously since 1977. A study by Hagen and Hock (1996a and b) shows little overall variation in duration between 1988 and 1992 in a small city in mid Germany.

In chapter 3 we looked at people who first claimed Social Assistance in 1989 and followed them through to 1994. In this section we compare this applicant cohort with an earlier cohort, to people who first applied for Assistance in 1983, followed through to 1989. The Social Assistance careers of the earlier cohort reflect the social conditions of the 1980s whereas the careers of the later cohort reflect the conditions at the end of the 1980s and during the early 1990s. A comparison of these two cohorts should reveal the impact of social change on poverty and Social Assistance.

After a temporary relaxation towards the end of the 1980s, unemployment started to rise again in the early 1990s and even more dramatically from the mid 1990s. The long-term unemployed again made up one-third of all unemployed persons, as they did in the mid 1980s (33.4 per cent in January 1998). Social security benefits were further cut during the 1980s, especially in the field of unemployment insurance, but new benefits were introduced at the same time, e.g. Education Benefit for parents of small children in 1986. The Old-Age Pension system was also consolidated in the 1992 Reform Act. Changes in family formation and related cultural changes such as individualisation and pluralisation of lifestyles have continued, along with a further increase in lone parent families and singles. In addition, as described in chapter 3, immigration rose dramatically from the late 1980s.

The term *New Poverty* was coined in the public debate in Germany in 1984 to draw attention to the new poverty of the unemployed under conditions of stepped-up cuts in social security benefits (see chapter 7, pp. 188f.). The term is still current today. 'New Poverty' as used in this debate expresses assumptions about the nature of poverty and about changes in poverty in the 1980s and in the 1990s:

that the number of the poor and of claimants of Social Assistance is continuously rising;

that this rise is mainly due to unemployment; and

that the key problem is increasing long-term claiming.

In this section we put these assumptions to the test, that is, we ask: Have

Social Assistance claims really increased? What are the main structural causes? Have long-term claims increased?

The main difference between the two applicant cohorts (first application for assistance in 1983 versus first application in 1989) is the proportion of *new immigrants*. Almost half of the 1989 applicants belonged to this group (see figure 3.3 on p. 68). (By 'immigrants' we always mean people who newly immigrated in the year of application for Assistance, not 'foreigners' as such. Moreover, 'immigrants' may include persons of German nationality.) Among the 1983 applicants, immigrants accounted for only 8 per cent, one-half being refugees (asylum seekers), the other half 'settlers', i.e., ethnic Germans from Eastern Europe and the Soviet Union. Contrary to all expectations the group of resident applicants (resident Germans as well as resident foreigners who immigrated earlier) diminished during the 1980s, not only proportionally but even in absolute numbers. Without the immigration of the 1980s there would have been fewer new applicants in 1989 than in 1983. This corresponds to the finding from the German Socio-Economic Panel that income poverty among the resident population of West Germany did not rise in the 1980s (see Krause 1994b).

In 1989 most of the 'settlers' only waited for prior benefits to be paid – Unemployment Benefit or Old-Age Pensions – and therefore left Social Assistance after a short time. Since 1993, however, newly arrived settlers are no longer entitled to Unemployment Benefit. They only receive Transition Benefit (*Übergangsgeld*) while they attend a language course, the duration of which has also been shortened.

Apart from the proportion of immigrants, the earlier and the later applicant cohort do not differ much. This is a surprise considering the social changes that occurred during the 1980s and the early 1990s. Rather than explaining change we face the task of explaining non-change. Among resident claimants the proportion of lone parents was higher in 1989 than in 1983, as could have been expected. Unemployment remained the key cause of claiming among resident applicants. Moreover, about one-third of the applicants in both cohorts were only using Social Assistance to bridge the waiting period until prior benefits were paid.

We can conclude that the rise in claimant numbers cannot be attributed to unemployment as suggested by the discussion about New Poverty. Neither can rising numbers and costs be taken as evidence of increasing 'dependency' as reiterated in the discussion about abuse of benefits and the negative effects of Social Assistance on clients. By contrast, the rise in claimant numbers was only due to immigration: between 1986 and 1992 the incidence of Social Assistance among Germans ceased to rise (2.2/2.3 per cent) while the incidence among foreigners doubled (5.1 to 11.0 per cent) (Statistisches Bundesamt 1998c, p. 48; figures for West Germany). Until the present day, new immigrants composed a significant part of the clientele of

Social Assistance and (from November 1993) of Asylum Seekers Benefit. The official Federal statistics, however, do not reveal the number of 'settlers' on Assistance. Discounting settlers, who figure as Germans, the incidence of Social Assistance among native Germans has probably fallen between 1986 and 1992.

Has the duration of claiming Social Assistance changed? Have the chances of leaving Assistance deteriorated during the 1980s and early 1990s? Again, contrary to widely held beliefs, Social Assistance careers at the end of the 1980s and in the beginning of the 1990s did not last longer than in the mid 1980s. The proportion of short termers even increased from 47 per cent in 1983 to 50 per cent in 1989 (referring to the observation windows 1983–1989 and 1989–1994 respectively, as before; for 1989 see figure 3.1 on p. 63). At the same time, long-term claims of more than five years decreased from 19 per cent to 16 per cent. A slightly different picture, however, emerges when we disregard new immigrants. Resident claimants – Germans and foreigners who have lived in Germany for a longer period of time – had slightly longer durations in the 1989 cohort than in the 1983 cohort. Short-term claims decreased from 45 per cent to 41 per cent, while long-term claims increased from 21 per cent to 22 per cent. Looking at specific social groups we find that many of them had slightly longer durations of claiming. However, there is no clear-cut trend, e.g., although lone parents' average single claiming spell was longer, their average overall period of claiming was shorter than among other social groups because second spells among lone parents were less frequent.

Among young people, couples with children and 'waiting' clients, multiple claiming – periods of claiming interrupted by periods off benefits – was even more widespread in 1989 than in 1983. This indicates that it has become more difficult to leave Social Assistance permanently. However, leaving Social Assistance by taking up work seemed to be easier at the end of the 1980s and at the beginning of the 1990s: among the 1983 applicants more than half of those who had left Assistance by taking up work had to reapply for Assistance after a while. Among the 1989 applicants only 36 per cent reapplied.

When the findings on short-term claiming among the 1983 cohort were first published in Germany, critics asserted that these results were dated and could not be expected to be replicated for later years under conditions of rising unemployment and social exclusion. The analysis of the 1989 cohort, however, has shown that the duration of claiming has not increased. Looking back to decades before 1980 we can assume that claims lasted even longer:[1] in the 1960s the old-age pensioners, especially elderly widows, constituted the main clientele of Social Assistance. Although longitudinal data

---

[1] Special surveys conducted by the Federal Bureau of Statistics in 1972 and 1981 show a pronounced fall in duration during that period of time (Statistisches Bundesamt 1974a, 1983b, c).

about these years are lacking, there is every reason to believe that old-age pensioners claimed Assistance for long periods of time. In the late 1970s and in the 1980s, the elderly were superseded by the unemployed as the main claimant group. Our study has shown that the unemployed rank among the groups with shorter claims, that is the switch from the elderly to the unemployed should have decreased average durations.

What can we expect of the dynamics of Social Assistance careers in the mid and late 1990s? A true longitudinal analysis would require an 'observation window' of several years, so that current careers can only be fully analysed in retrospect after 2000. Since 1994 the reformed Federal Social Assistance Statistics include some information on duration (referring to a point-in-time sample of current claimants), but they do not suggest that short-term claims are a thing of the past: on 31 December 1996, half the caseload (48 per cent) were short-termers (duration up to one year; Statistisches Bundesamt 1998c, pp. 30f.).[2] Some groups, e.g., young people and couples with children, may face deteriorating chances of becoming independent of Assistance if the trend found in the two cohorts discussed above continues. Unemployment has been rising from the second third of the 1990s, while immigration has been restricted.

Social Assistance claims by immigrants are state produced: they depend on political decisions about who is welcome in Germany and who is not and on regulations of work permits and entitlements to non-means-tested benefits. In an all-party parliamentary compromise the influx of refugees (asylum seekers) was seriously restricted from 1993, and the number of 'settlers' from Eastern Europe and the former Soviet Union was fixed at around 200,000 per year (figure 9.1). In the mid 1990s, however, new refugees, in this case people fleeing the civil war in Bosnia, added to the Social Assistance caseload. In 1998 most of them were still living in Germany, because even after the Dayton agreement the situation in Bosnia had not sufficiently stabilised to allow people to return to their home towns.

Furthermore, Social Assistance claims in East Germany have been rising since re-unification in 1990, although income poverty has been rapidly falling in terms of the mean West German income. As we will show in the next section, Social Assistance claims in East Germany – surprisingly – are more often short term than long term just as they are in the West. The unification of the two Germanies in 1990 and the subsequent transforma-

---

[2] On the one hand, this figure underestimates overall duration because it refers only to the current claiming spell (that is, previous times on Assistance are not counted) and because the current spell has not yet been terminated. On the other hand, the figure overestimates duration because point-in-time sampling is biased towards long-term cases (see chapter 3, pp. 67f.). Both effects seem to roughly offset each other.

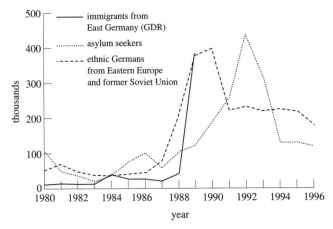

Figure 9.1 *Immigration in Germany, 1980–1996*
(number of new immigrants in each year)
Note: 1980–1990 figures for West Germany
Source: Statistisches Bundesamt (1982a–1997a).

tion of East Germany, therefore, have not increased the proportion of long-term clients.

The results of our comparison of the 1983 and the 1989 applicant cohorts question key assumptions which underpin the notion of New Poverty. The findings suggest that this notion is too simple in many ways. Social Assistance claims have indeed increased in the 1980s – but mostly due to factors not addressed by the debate on New Poverty and hardly discussed even nowadays, namely immigration ensuing from political decisions. For several years immigration even exceeded unemployment as a cause of rising claimant numbers and it still accounts for a massive proportion of the caseload. When the New Poverty was proclaimed in 1984 the phrase highlighted something which really was new in Germany at the time, the poverty of the unemployed, which had emerged in the 1970s. In 1970 the category 'unemployment' was not even included in the official statistics on the causes of claiming Social Assistance. Paradoxically in those very years after 1984 when the New Poverty was being broadly debated, other factors began to gain importance, especially immigration. This, too, is 'new poverty'.

Immigration by East Germans to the West after the fall of the Berlin Wall on 9 November 1989 until re-unification on 3 October 1990, was a short-lived type of immigration which nevertheless put considerable pressure on the West German system of Social Assistance (see figure 3.3 on p. 68). Internal migration from the East to the West continued thereafter, but from

Unification Day these people were no longer considered immigrants. While the fall of the Berlin Wall produced a wave of (mostly) short-term claims, the erection of the wall in 1961 did likewise. This is revealed by remarkable Federal statistics of that year which, unlike the ordinary Federal statistics until 1993, give information on flows rather than only on stocks. There was an enormous turnover of 'immigrants' among the claimants of Social Assistance, with 71 per cent of the 1961 claimants being new applicants and 83.5 per cent of the new applicants terminating Assistance in the same year (Statistisches Bundesamt 1962, p. 13). This strong fluctuation can only be accounted for by the erection of the Berlin Wall on 13 August 1961. The figures give evidence of the massive influx of East Germans into West Germany and West Berlin immediately before the building of the Wall, and of their rapid subsequent integration into West German society.

The assumption of rising long-term claims which is associated with the concept of New Poverty is equally shaky. Even long-term unemployment, which is normally seen as the main source of long-lasting Social Assistance claims, has not had this effect because the long-term unemployed as a percentage of all unemployed people did not rise from the mid 1980s to the late 1990s and because the majority of the unemployed are short termers, in terms of the receipt of both Unemployment Benefit and Social Assistance.

Poverty and Social Assistance in the late 1990s are shaped by three main factors which had emerged by the late 1980s: the labour market, changes in family life and immigration. 'Labour market' means unemployment and, possibly, insufficient wages and the emergence of a group of 'working poor' hitherto unknown in Germany. 'Family changes' means lone parenthood, divorce, remaining single and the erosion of ties between the generations. And 'immigration' reflects political persecution, civil war and misery in many parts of the world – and also the moral power of our society to show solidarity with foreigners. All in all, a complex picture of the poverty of the 1990s emerges. Social exclusion and rigid social cleavages coexist with a remarkable fluidity in life situations and life styles (see chapter 10).

Social transformation in East Germany: a 'poor house' or society in transition?

The unique transformation of East Germany after unification, by which the entire legal and institutional system of a country was replaced in one day, offers unrivalled opportunities for sociologists to observe and analyse social change. It is a live experiment in social development. This applies in particular to the institutions of the welfare state. Following the history of Social Assistance in East Germany offers a rare opportunity to observe a benefit scheme from its very start in a new region. The old Social Welfare system (*Sozialfürsorge*) in the GDR had faded to virtual irrelevance by the time of the collapse of the old regime (see pp. 213f.). Among the people in our East German sample who first applied for Social Assistance in 1990 only 5.2 per cent had received Social Welfare at the time of the GDR. Among those who first applied in 1991 it was even fewer, only 1 per cent. This means that the great majority of claimants had never been in touch with social assistance in their previous lives.

In this section we analyse a 10 per cent sample from the East German city of Halle, followed for almost five years.[3] We compare the situation in Halle with the situation in Bremen. This makes sense because Bremen and Halle share basic characteristics: both are middle-sized towns by the standards of West Germany and East Germany respectively and in both cities the incidence of Social Assistance is above average. The year 1989 was the last year of the 'old' Federal Republic, and the year 1991 was the first full year of re-unified Germany (Unification Day was 3 October 1990). While 1991 was a special year for the East Germans because it was then that they first experienced the full thrust of mass unemployment and social dislocation, the social conditions in West Germany changed little between 1989 and 1991. We may, therefore, reasonably assume that West German Social Assistance careers which started in 1991 do not fundamentally differ from those that started in 1989. In this light, it makes sense to compare the applicant cohort 1989 (West) with the applicant cohort 1991 (East), followed for almost five years each, up to 1993 and 1995 respectively.[4]

Although most claimants had no previous experience of social assistance, the influence of past factors dating from GDR times had to be considered beside the impact of the current social transformation. Attitudes and behaviours, regarding work or the state, were still influenced by biographical experiences dating from the Communist period. Two hypotheses compete: some scholars describe the process of transformation as 'delayed modernisation' (*nachholende Modernisierung*; Wolfgang Zapf, cf. pp. 221f.) implying that social conditions in East Germany will gradually come to resemble those in the West. Others assume that the East will take

---

[3] We do not report the results of the analysis of the 1990 entry cohort because they refer to a provisional kind of Social Assistance scheme set up in the second half of 1990, that is, after the monetary union between the two Germanies. There were few applicants in those early months. The figures exploded in 1991 and declined considerably in subsequent years.

[4] To compare Assistance careers in both cities we had to adjust the lengths of the observation windows. Since the observation window in Halle was 58 months compared to 69 months in Bremen, we had to cut the window artificially by 11 months in the Bremen case. The cut-off point for Halle, then, was October 1995; for Bremen it was October 1993. For this reason the figures in this section do not fully compare with the figures given in chapter 3 because the latter are based on the full observation window of 69 months which ended in September 1994.

an independent path of development, either as a new underdeveloped region or as an area with distinct social patterns. The analysis of poverty rates and groups in poverty in chapter 8 showed that elements can be found of both, i.e. of similar and dissimilar development. A key difference we found was the massive size of transitory social security schemes and labour-market policies unknown in the West.

Which temporal patterns of Social Assistance claiming can we expect to find in East Germany? In the public debate, which inclines to dramatisation, many people assume that large parts of the Eastern population are being marginalised. This would imply that people claim Social Assistance in East Germany for longer periods of time than in the West. The unprecedented scale of unemployment and social dislocation and the obsolescence of occupational qualifications among many members of the workforce make such an assumption plausible. This would apply particularly to the elderly who learn new patterns of behaviour less easily and adapt to new circumstances with greater difficulty. This might lead us to expect long durations of claiming Assistance in this group.

As regards the role of attitudes, two contradictory hypotheses seem equally plausible: since people were used to living under comprehensive state provision from the Communist regime one might assume that they do not resent receiving Assistance and do not actively seek to terminate claiming. On the other hand, however, East Germans might associate Social Assistance with old images of oppressive and humiliating poor relief under early capitalism because they lack the experience of a modernised scheme as introduced in West Germany in 1961. This might make stigma a bigger problem in the East. The data showed that people in the East, especially women, remain more work-oriented than West Germans. This work culture could exert a strong pressure, e.g., on lone parents, to try to escape Social Assistance as early as possible. Similarly, child-care facilities remain better in the East, a factor which could also encourage early exits.

One major difference between Bremen and Halle is the proportion of new immigrants among the clientele of Social Assistance. Whereas in Bremen immigration accounted for almost half of the new claims in 1989, in Halle in 1991 it was only 7 per cent, and these consisted exclusively of refugees seeking asylum. Immigrants recognised as ethnic Germans from Eastern Europe and the former Soviet Union did not figure at all in Halle. To make a meaningful comparison we therefore restrict the analysis in the remainder of this chapter to resident claimants, i.e., to Germans and foreigners who have lived in Bremen or Halle for a longer period of time. We compare the new applicants in Bremen in 1989 with the new applicants in Halle in 1991, the first full year of Social Assistance in East Germany. In Bremen there were 493 cases, and in Halle 287.

In both cities most people managed to leave Assistance after a limited period of time. The escape routes, however, differ greatly: exits into paid work were much less common in Halle than in Bremen. In Bremen twice as many people left by work (20 per cent of all reasons for ending Social Assistance as compared to 10 per cent in Halle). At the same time, Halle claimants were much more likely to claim prior benefits immediately following Social Assistance termination (41 per cent as compared to 25 per cent in Bremen). The different escape routes from Assistance testify to the condition of the East German labour market, which was and remains even worse than in West Germany, and at the same time, to the importance of social security benefits as crisis management in the lives of East Germans (see chapter 8, pp. 218–221).

The most surprising finding is that Social Assistance careers in the East do not last longer than in the West: short-term claims are even more frequent and long-term claims occur less often. In Halle short-term claims (up to one year) account for almost half of the clientele (49 per cent), compared to 42 per cent in Bremen. Over one-third of claims were long term (more than three years) in Bremen (35 per cent) compared with a quarter (25 per cent) in Halle. These figures refer to 'gross duration' as defined in chapter 3, that is, the overall duration of claiming including periods off Assistance which may occur in a discontinuous Assistance career. Using the other measures of duration, net duration or single spell duration (see figure 3.2 on p. 65), we obtain an even higher proportion of short-term claims. Measuring only the duration of the first spell on Assistance, the difference between Bremen and Halle is less pronounced. One explanation for the great discrepancy in gross duration between the two cities, therefore, is that multiple spells are less frequent in Halle than in Bremen. Claims among the 1990 application cohort in Halle (see note 3 on p. 231) are equally short.

Looking at specific groups among the clientele we get a clearer view of the differences between East and West. First, we find that duration relates to *age* in different ways in Bremen and Halle: in Bremen young people below 20 years of age are more often found among the claimants and they stay on Assistance for a particularly long time (36 months as compared to 12 months in Halle). This indicates problems of entry into the labour market. In Halle, by contrast, it is primarily people in their thirties who are disproportionately represented among the claimants and who make very long claims (22 months as compared to 17 months in Bremen; for people in their forties it is 14 per cent as compared to 9 per cent). This might hint at the difficulties and slowness of adaptation of people who had already settled in their occupational career in the GDR and who are now forced to acquire new skills and adapt to new exigencies of working life. For people in their fifties, however, the picture is reversed (mean duration of seven months in Halle as compared to 13 months in Bremen). We assume that this is not the result of a higher ability to adapt to occupational changes or of better labour-market chances among these older workers. Shorter claims by older East German workers rather seem to be a result of the employment and social security policies which included massive early retirement schemes.

Looking at different *household* types, we find first that lone parents claim Assistance for a long time, both in the East and the West. However, East German families and lone parents terminate claiming earlier: the mean duration of the first spell is nine months among lone parents, compared with 13 months in the West. In terms of gross duration, it is 18 months in the East and 26 months in the West. West German couples with children even claim Assistance for twice as long (24 months) as their counterparts in the East. These differences seem to be related to differences in starting and ending Social Assistance claims: East German lone parents were more often unemployed and they terminated Assistance more often through prior benefits. This result seems to corroborate the hypothesis of a stronger work-orientation among East German lone parents. Earlier exits by families may equally be due to the stronger work-orientation of East German women, because the East still has more households with two earners than the West. It is difficult to judge whether these data also reflect better child-care facilities. People who received Social Assistance only because they were waiting for prior benefits to be paid, such as Unemployment Benefit or Old-Age Pensions, on average had short claims in both cities. Unemployed claimants who were not 'waiting', however, claimed for much longer periods of time in Halle. This corresponds to our finding that taking up a new job is a less frequent escape route in Halle.

All in all, we found both similarities and differences between East and West. Some of these were unexpected, above all the even higher incidence of short claims in the East. The below average durations among older workers (over 50) and among pensioners was equally unexpected and supports the view that the elderly were the winners of unification in the East. The difference in escape routes from Social Assistance, however, matches our expectations: work exits are less frequent in the East, while escape to higher-tier welfare-state benefits are more frequent, an indication of the massive integrative function of the welfare state in the course of the social transformation in the East. Shorter claims among lone parents match our expectations of differing work orientations. Differences regarding age – longest durations among young people under 20 in the West, compared with longest durations among people in their thirties and forties in the East – neither confirm nor refute our expectations.

Clearly, East Germany has not become the 'poor house' of the Federal

Republic of Germany. Comprehensive labour market policies and social policies – in conjunction with economic growth rates which were higher than in the West during the first five years after unification – have successfully restrained processes of marginalisation. This is reflected in the small proportion of long-term Social Assistance claims. Data from the Socio-Economic Panel show that income poverty is equally often short term (see p. 218). There is also no evidence of a social polarisation between winners or losers, or, in terms of Social Assistance, between short-term and long-term claimants, because between these two extremes we identified a sizeable group of middle cases whose multiple claims indicate a precarious, discontinuous life course and suggest that this is a special problem group apart from the permanently marginalised.

The high proportion of short claims shows that Social Assistance has acted as a measure of social integration and adaptation during the historical transition from a Communist command economy to a free market society: even in East Germany, Assistance acted as a transitory bridge at critical periods in the lives of the citizens. However, Social Assistance could only play this role because higher-order social security schemes and labour-market policies were highly developed and even enhanced for a limited period of transition. Had these schemes, such as mass early retirement, job-creation schemes and shorter working hours, not existed, then East Germany might actually have become a huge poor house, with millions of people being forced on to Social Assistance for longer periods of time. Politically, this would have been totally unacceptable. Preventing precisely this scenario was one of the justifications used by policy makers for the introduction of the Old-Age Pension Supplement which was paid till 1996.

The positive role of the welfare state, however, also entails problems. High expectations have built up and people may have difficulties in accepting a slowing down or partial dismantling of state support measures. As Wolfgang Zapf once remarked, East Germans tend to attribute successful developments in their part of Germany to the market economy while failures are put down to the state. From 1997 some changes hint at a possible deterioration of socio-economic conditions in the East which might result in a rise in Social Assistance claims and their duration (see p. 223).

Part IV
Poverty and society:
Towards a new welfare state?

Plate 4 'The Tree of Estates'. The Petrarca-Master. Augsburg 1532.
An unnamed artist, active in the first third of the 16th century, created this
woodcut *'Der Ständebaum'* to illustrate the first German translation of Francesco
Petrarca, *De remediis utriusque fortunae* (1366); *Von der Arzney bayder Glück, des
guten und widerwertigen.* (*Staats- und Stadtbibliothek Augsburg*)

10 Time and poverty: towards a new picture of poverty and social exclusion

Individual poverty situations are more liable to change and the people affected are more capable of coping than has hitherto been assumed. This has been demonstrated in chapters 3–6. There are signs of changes in the forms of poverty and its place in society, especially with regard to the 'officially' poor, the claimants of Social Assistance. Poverty is no longer (if ever it was) a fixed condition or a personal or group characteristic, but rather it is an experience or a stage in the life course. It is not necessarily associated with a marginal position in society but reaches well into the middle class. Poverty is specifically located in time and individual biographies, and, by implication, has come to transcend traditional social boundaries of class. These characteristics of present-day poverty can be referred to as *temporalisation*, *biographisation* and *democratisation* (or 'transcendence') of poverty.

The new dynamic perspective does not just mean standing the old idea of poverty on its head, focussing on short-term poverty instead of long-term poverty. The new insight is, rather, that poverty has many faces.[1] Nor does our study aim to present poverty as unproblematic, as might be at first glance assumed in the light of our rejection of the dark picture painted by many conventional studies. The life-course approach set out in this book seeks to show that poverty is more complex, and is harder to grasp and to combat, than it may have been at a time when easily comprehensible categories of people in need could be identified, whose conditions could be changed and ameliorated in obvious ways by wholesale cash benefits and social services provided by the state.

---

[1] Similarly, Pete Alcock (1997, p. 110) emphasises that the 'message from poverty dynamics can . . . cut two ways' – transience of poverty in many cases as well as cumulative deprivation in case of long-term poverty. In our study we found further differentiations, between entrenched and normalised varieties of long-term poverty, and we also emphasised the other side of short-term poverty, namely the broadening range of people affected by poverty at some point in their lives ('transcendence', see pp. 240, 242f.).

'Temporalisation', 'biographisation' and 'democratisation'

Temporalisation means that experiences of poverty occur in many temporal forms – short, medium and long, and in single or repeated spells. This may be related to a variety of meanings of poverty in the lives of the people affected. The time dimension – the objective duration and continuity of being poor, as well as the subjective location of spells in poverty in one's life history – is an important aspect of the poverty problem which has previously been neglected. Poverty must no longer be readily equated with pre-ordained economic categories – such as the unskilled – or with conventional marginalised groups – such as the homeless or even the 'asocial' – nor with welfare classes whose members live 'on welfare' for long periods. Rather, poverty more commonly occurs at certain junctures in people's lives. The risk of poverty is obviously higher for families in the lower economic classes, but the new poverty looms as a permanent risk facing middle-class families, if only as a temporary condition.

This is what we term the *democratisation* or *transcendence* of poverty. Ulrich Beck in his Risk Society (1992 [German edition, 1986, p. 149]) first spoke of a 'democratisation' of poverty and unemployment to point out that in advanced modern societies ever larger sections of the population share in the risks – and not only in the benefits – of modern society. He also described what his disciple Peter Berger later (1990) called 'temporalisation' (*Verzeitlichung*). The term 'transcendence' (*Entgrenzung*) was coined by Ulrike Nagel (1993, p. 150) in a study of the professional concepts of social workers. She found that many younger social workers conceive the social problems they are dealing with in their work as transcending social boundaries: in their view, these problems do not indicate marginality but could equally arise in their own lives, such as a mental crisis after divorce or periods of unemployment.

The third concept, *biographisation* of poverty, refers to the subjective meaning of temporalised poverty in individual biographies. The concept is based on three assumptions: first, that poverty is tied to specific life events and biographical episodes; second, that objective disadvantages are shaped by the biographical meaning individuals attach to them – the fact that being poor is perceived and evaluated in the light of other experiences in life, whether before, contemporaneously or later; and, third, that the objective duration of being poor is overlain by a person's subjective time orientation, framing the poverty experience in the perspective of the whole lifetime.

Temporary poverty reflects biographical transitions in life, triggered by such events as divorce, illness, leaving the parental home, having a gap between finishing education and starting work, or losing a job. Glaser and Strauss spoke of status passages in the life courses (1971; s.a. Heinz 1991a,

1991b). When critical biographical episodes are dynamically linked and gain momentum, they may give rise to careers or may even determine whole phases of life. In spite of the fact that transitional poverty tied to critical status passages has become very common, it has only recently been analysed in its own right, by dynamic poverty researchers. Poverty 'careers', too, have only recently been analysed in a comprehensive way, that is, not restricted to specific groups such as the homeless (chapter 5; Ludwig 1996). These configurations of being poor – passages, phases, careers – are not necessarily associated with downward social mobility or with psycho-social decline, not even over longer periods of time.

How far other forms of poverty – not just entitlement to Social Assistance – are subject to 'biographisation' still remains to be researched. In principle, it seems plausible to assume that our findings are not confined to Social Assistance claimants. A theoretical concept which may be relevant here is that of 'deferred gratification' (Schneider and Lysgaard 1953). It involves postponing rewards in life, as young people do when they accept hardship as students in order to achieve higher incomes later, or as employees do when they save in order to set up their own business. Besides external restrictions on incomes following the model of the poverty cycle – poverty arising during periods of childhood, child-rearing and inability to work – people may also voluntarily accept poverty if it cannot be avoided on their path to future rewards.

If poverty is sometimes deliberately and strategically adopted, this does not imply unnecessary or fraudulent benefit claims, nor does it mean that poverty is the poor's own 'fault'. It is rather a matter of planning one's life in a way which is meaningful for the individual and legitimate for society. Our study provides evidence of this in the context of Social Assistance claims, some of which involved reducing material consumption in favour of other more highly valued goals in life (chapters 4 and 5). These included bringing up one's children, especially among female claimants; bridging a period of vocational training to enjoy higher income and more satisfying work later on in life; and pursuing an independent life among some young single male claimants. Claiming Social Assistance is generally treated as legitimate by German society in the first two examples. In the case of child-rearing, this is partly because of the value placed on encouraging population growth at a time of decline, tied up with traditional assumptions among the conservative Christian parties about the proper role of women. Job training is justified by the requirements of a dynamic market in an achieving society, especially in Germany with its strong emphasis on formal training and certificates (see p. 51). But using Social Assistance to lead a free and unsettled lifestyle is seen as legitimate by only a small minority of citizens, mainly in the Green Party and 'alternative' social movements.

The risk of becoming poor is not as obviously distributed across the life course nowadays as it was at the beginning of the century when Benjamin Seebohm Rowntree described the poverty cycle of unskilled workers (1901; see figure on p. 15 above). Life courses in Western countries are to varying degrees shaped by the welfare state (see pp. 47–53), so that stages of life which were prone to poverty in earlier times, such as old age, no longer are, for instance in Germany. Moreover, individuals vary their life courses more, for example postponing their entry into the labour market or the birth of their first child. There are a wide variety of options nowadays – different individual arrangements in the realms of education, work, partnerships and the engagement of welfare-state services. Temporalisation and bio-graphisation of poverty are part of the Risk Society, in which both structures and individuals' life projects rapidly and flexibly change, and in which breakdowns and transitional life crises are more likely to hit even the middle classes.

The *democratisation* of poverty refers to the ways in which poverty has come in recent decades to transcend traditional boundaries. This development is familiar but its significance often goes unnoticed. It is well known that unemployment nowadays also hits better-off families who previously felt secure. We also know that the poverty associated with certain stages in life, such as during higher education or between vocational training and employment, affects not only marginalised groups. Social change, for instance, the increasing number of single mothers or growing youth unemployment, together with changes in lifestyles, have led to new forms of transitional poverty. Clearly, 'democratisation' or 'transcendence' does not mean that poverty is equally common in all strata of society. In Beck's view this only applies to some ecological and technological risks such as the global warming effect or environmental pollution. No social stratum is protected from them. Beck speaks of 'the end of "the others"' (1986, p. 7) to express that the line between 'us' – living in security – and 'them'/'the others' – living in risk and being the object of help by 'us' – can no longer be drawn. In the case of social risks such as poverty and unemployment the boundary between 'us' and 'them' has become blurred but, much more than in the case of environmental risks, structures of inequality are still pronounced.

The slackening of the social boundaries of poverty has political consequences, especially in terms of the possibility of political protest (see Beck 1992 and Vobruba 1995). Socially unbounded poverty is harder to detect because it is more widely spread and thus more diffuse. Perhaps this was one of the reasons why the Kohl government was so profitably able to ignore the high and growing extent of unemployment and poverty up to the mid 1990s. The new character of poverty means that those affected by it find it hard to organise either socially or spatially. This may even apply to countries where larger groups of poor people live in concentrated deprived areas than in Germany.

On the other hand, middle-class poverty can also provide a stronger basis for collective action. For instance, academics among the Social Assistance claimants play an important part in local claimants' initiatives. However, collective action of a more political kind at the national level is scarce, maybe because poverty among middle-class people is mostly transitory and they tend to strive for individual solutions rather than to appear on the public stage.

The fabric of poverty

Is poverty in the Risk Society so diverse, so amorphous and classless, that its structure cannot be comprehended any longer? Or can we detect specific types of poverty? If the (material) victims of the war, the pensioners and the unemployed were the poor of the late 1940s and the early 1950s, and old women were the poor of the 1960s, who are the typical poor of our decade?

The categories of poor who currently figure in social policy discussions are clearly compelling: the *unemployed, single mothers, children* and *foreigners* (new immigrants as well as people who have lived in Germany for many years, the former being rarely referred to with respect to their poverty). All four groups indicate crises or changes of traditional social institutions and relationships, whether national or international, and all four present challenges to new policy thinking: the unemployed reflect the structural crisis in the social organisation of work; single mothers reflect changes in family relationships and women's goals; the unmet needs of children as well as of others who need personal care reflect changes in the contract between the generations; and foreigners reflect the problems of multi-ethnic societies, in Germany especially the problems of international migration and of the social integration of second and third generation immigrants.

Tracing social divisions primarly to mass unemployment – as implied in the German debate by the phrase 'two-thirds society'[2] – underplays the problematic of the new poverty for society. If instead one thinks in terms of Risk Society, it becomes apparent that changes in poverty can be understood only in terms of a broader range of economic and socio-cultural processes of change. Several distinct strands of development have worked

---

[2] By contrast, in its original version as proposed by Peter Glotz (1984) the formula was not restricted to unemployment but emphasised the variegated nature of this new bottom segment of society (see chapter 10, pp. 251f.).

together to cause impoverishment over the last two decades (Beck 1986, p. 153).

A dynamic perspective on poverty sheds new light on these social groups, especially the unemployed, single mothers and immigrants. *Unemployed* claimants of Social Assistance are a very heterogeneous group. By contrast with the public perception of the unemployed, short spells of claiming are by far the most common among this group. Hence, the growth of unemployment, which includes an increase in long-term unemployment (in absolute, not in relative terms), is not simply a sign of an increasing social exclusion of disadvantaged members of society. Since short-term claims among the unemployed are growing simultaneously and significantly faster, mass unemployment is as much evidence of the volatility of the labour market in our time. Thomas Klein (1987) showed that in (West) Germany the material situation of the unemployed depends largely on the circumstances of their households, chiefly on how many people they contain and whether there are any second earners. This applies even more strongly in East Germany (Müller *et al.* 1996). Our study shows that the unemployed are also very heterogeneous in the temporal dimension – their duration of claiming Social Assistance. Thus the relevance of claiming Social Assistance in the lives of the unemployed varies greatly. In our sample it ranged from a completely unproblematic temporary spell, generally perceived as simply transitional by the claimant (a 'subjective bridger'), to long-term claiming because of a lack of alternatives, which can lead to resignation and hopelessness, to the few cases in which Social Assistance was used in a deliberate manner, for instance to facilitate frequent job changes.

Lone parents who claim Social Assistance also appear in a different light in our study, similar to the study by Mädje and Neusüß (1996). A not inconsiderable number of these single mothers could be described as actively using benefits as a resource to enable them to pursue some overarching goal. For some, the goal is to devote themselves to child-rearing; for others the intention is to buy time to reorientate themselves personally and occupationally.

Poverty among *foreigners* has only recently become a subject of German political debate. The focus, however, has largely been on foreigners who have lived in Germany for many years (see for instance von Freyberg 1995) – termed 'resident foreigners' in chapter 3 – rather than on new immigrants. We have shown (see pp. 68–90 and 226–230) that two groups of new immigrants – asylum seekers from all over the world, and people from Eastern Europe and the former Soviet Union recognised as German nationals (*Aussiedler* or 'settlers') – accounted up to 1992 for a large part of the rapid increase in Social Assistance claimants and still compose a sizeable proportion of claimants since. By contrast, the incidence of Social Assistance among resident foreigners seems to be overestimated in the critical debate (in our sample their claiming rate did not increase at all during the 1980s) because the official Social Assistance statistics lump resident foreigners into the same category of 'foreigners' as new immigrants of foreign nationality. In our sample, immigrants who had settled in Bremen in 1989 and were followed through to 1994 had mainly very short spells on Assistance. However, this may change, since from the early 1990s the integrative measures for settlers (such as language courses and entitlement to Unemployment Insurance Benefits and Old-Age Pensions) have been reduced, and changes have taken place in both the level of qualifications among settlers and in labour markets.

Besides the new identification of these conventional types of poor people, the dynamic approach to poverty exposes other cross-cutting types, especially the *temporarily poor*. This poverty of our times has been overlooked in both social-scientific and public debates – although short spells of poverty cannot simply be disregarded as unimportant. Who these people are changes as society changes. In Germany in the 1990s it has principally been the unemployed and immigrants. *Repeatedly poor* people form another type defined by temporal criteria. We may assume that this not inconsiderable section of the population, which traditionally hovers just above the poverty line, falls more frequently below it in times of economic insecurity and changing life projects. *Permanent or long-term poverty* is a further contemporary type existing beside the temporarily poor, which is no contradiction when poverty in general is on the rise.

These types of poverty defined merely by duration are statistical categories, not social types. What social types do the findings about the heterogeneous temporality of being poor suggest? The 'old' social inequalities defined by occupational class have not necessarily been superseded; they are modified and transformed by other dimensions of inequality. These include social divisions created by the welfare state, differences in household structure and, not least, temporal inequalities between different stages in the life course (see pp. 279–285). Social exclusion has not only a class dimension but also a time dimension.

The spectrum of poverty ranges from a temporary interruption of social integration (or social inclusion) to permanent exclusion. The spectrum can be divided into four types, plus two special kinds which cut across these categories:

Relatively secure members of the middle class. The higher risk of poverty in these circles may be a new phenomenon of our time, evidence of a rising tide of social insecurity.

People with permanently low incomes. Living just above official poverty lines[3] this group is easily overlooked in public debates on poverty, but it makes up a substantial part of the population even in affluent societies.

The long-term deprived. People who suffer significant material or non-material deprivations without being necessarily and comprehensively excluded from participating in social life.

The long-term socially excluded. People who are not only deprived by some statistical measure but who are excluded from social participation because of discrimination by social systems and social actors and because of insufficient coping.

The two cross-cutting special types of poverty are:

People with an unsettled mode of existence. Their degree of exclusion from social participation is around the middle of the inclusion–exclusion scale but their lifestyle on the edge of society is in part an expression of a deliberate choice.

New immigrants. They are by definition in a transitional situation and do not know what social status in German society they will be able to attain. Therefore, it would not make sense to rank them in the above inclusion–exclusion spectrum.

The range of the four or six types of poverty exposes the diversity of conditions between exclusion in a strict sense and full inclusion. Narrowing down the meaning of the concept exclusion helps to get a clearer picture of the varieties of poverty. *Exclusion* as used in this typology differs from mere 'deprivation' or 'low income' in three respects: first, it is not a matter of degree – having something but less than others – but of all or nothing, of being in or out – for instance being legally banned from working by immigration law. The deprived are losers but the excluded do not even take part in the game (cf. Claus Offe 1994).[4] Second, exclusion does not just mean lack of resources as measured statistically by researchers but refers to social relationships, to reduced chances of participation in social life and in social institutions. These chances result in part from deficient resources, but they also depend on the action strategies of the individuals concerned, especially their coping behaviour, and on the reactions, expectations and social definitions of others – state agencies, law, neighbours, social workers, etc. Third, exclusion should be confined to meaning the condition of wide-ranging restrictions affecting a person's entire life, and not used to mean the

---

[3] The definition of 'low income' used in the German literature refers to levels significantly below average income, but above the prevailing official minimum income standards taken to be the poverty line (see Hauser *et al.* 1981, p. 30).

[4] Both concepts of poverty can be found in Georg Simmel's essay 'The poor' (1908, 1965) although the common reading of the essay focuses on the latter (see the reinterpretation in Leisering 1997c).

lack of minor resources of one kind or another. Naturally, 'exclusion' and 'deprivation' may shade into one another, but they remain conceptually distinct. For example, as shown below, claiming Social Assistance long-term may simply indicate 'deprivation', without exclusion in the strict sense described here; depending on the individual case, it may also involve exclusion.

The following description of the six types of poverty makes use of the categories introduced in the qualitative analysis in chapters 4 and 5. We enquired into the respondents' orientations towards time, and distinguished between the 'subjective bridgers', the 'calculated' and the 'resigned' long-term claimants (pp. 91–101). We also investigated poverty careers and described the 'entrenched poverty career', the 'welfare state normalised poverty career' and 'optimised poverty management', corresponding to exclusion, 'secondary' inclusion and (full) inclusion or integration (chapter 5, pp. 131–136).

Relatively secure members of the middle class risk becoming temporarily poor under certain critical conditions such as the early stages of family formation and occupational life, or later interruptions of these, as well as in the pursuit of deliberate personal life-projects involving risk. If longer periods occur, they may give rise to social exclusion, but in general these persons head for full inclusion in society. The experience of poverty generally follows the pattern of 'optimised poverty management' in which the poor actively combat their situation and overcome the need to claim Social Assistance. These people's perspective on time is that of the 'subjective bridgers': from the outset, benefit claiming is seen as temporary, even if it lasts longer than expected.

People with permanently low incomes who have a modest standard of living 'when it's going well' can easily be tipped into poverty temporarily or repeatedly even by minor crises. They lack a cushion of protective resources because of their structural position or stage in life. This social category is integrated into society at a low level but its integration is constantly threatened, even if those threatened are not always aware of it or have even actively repressed the idea. These people live at the lower end of the scale of legitimate inequality, just above the poverty line defined by Social Assistance. The study by Werner Hübinger (1996) suggests that they may suffer deprivations similar to the actual poor. He therefore describes their position as 'precarious well-being' *(prekärer Wohlstand)*, an intermediate status between genuine poverty and genuine well-being. When people accustomed to a low level of income are forced to claim Social Assistance, their time perspective is usually that of the 'subjective bridgers'. Their claiming careers usually culminate in 'optimised poverty management', but some end up in the next type, in long-term deprivation.

The *long-term deprived* are people for whom crisis situations become prolonged even though they may have seemed to be temporary at the outset, or for whom an accumulation of problems such as age, illness or disqualification, or other exceptional circumstances reduce the chances of changing their situations. Their subjective perceptions of time range between 'resigned long-term claimants' and 'calculated long-term claimants'. The progress of their poverty typically follows the pattern of the 'welfare-state normalised poverty career' – the underlying problem remains unsolved, but they actively manage life on Assistance, and exclusion from participation in social life can be avoided, although it is a kind of 'secondary' inclusion by the welfare state. In as far as there is any psychosocial decline, it generally manifests itself in private, and thus escapes the neighbours' gaze and awareness.

Long-term deprivation may shade into *long-term social exclusion*, a situation where social problems, sometimes deviant forms of behaviour, and a cumulation of disadvantage which started early in life coincide with material deprivations. This background contributes to the absence of a time perspective ('resigned long-term claimants') and results in an 'entrenched poverty career'. These people can neither solve the problem that led to their application for Social Assistance nor do they cope with their current situation. Social isolation and emotional problems are likely to ensue. Included in this group are many of the unsettled, homeless, mentally ill and small-time criminals. In the form of 'visible poverty' (Øyen 1992, p. 620) these 'marginal groups' dominate the German public's image of the poor. Joining these traditional marginal groups in the 1990s are new ones such as illegal immigrants, who live in Germany without rights and formal allegiances, street children and especially some of the long-term unemployed whom we would expect to range between deprivation and exclusion. The study by Martin Kronauer *et al.* (1993) suggested that (a sub-group of) the long-term unemployed were emerging as a new 'marginal group' in Germany. It must be remembered though that, contrary to widely held views, the long-term unemployed form only a small fraction of all those without employment, most of whom are out of work for less than a year. Moreover, many of the unemployed are not poor in terms of income.

People with an *unsettled* mode of existence, such as some young single men who repeatedly claim Social Assistance, could be seen as 'commuters' between normal life courses and social decline. They often seem to find themselves in an extended hiatus in the transition to regular employment and family formation. They correspond to the 'strategic user' type of Social Assistance claimant (see pp. 130f., and pp. 159–165) who deliberately uses Assistance over a lengthy period of time, perhaps with intermissions. The time perspective is that of a 'voluntary long-term claimant'. The poverty careers of unsettled people are a special case of 'welfare-state normalised poverty careers' and as such are an expression of the individualisation of lifestyles in the lower social classes.

New immigrants. What was an integral part of the experience of nation-building in the USA is new in post-war Germany, at least in the public debate: the poverty of new immigrants. Although post-war Germany has a history of immigration, beginning with the huge influx from the Eastern part of the former German Reich into West Germany in the 1940s and 1950s and the migrant labourers *(Gastarbeiter)* from Mediterranean countries from the late 1950s, immigration has not shaped the self-image of German society.[5] Ideally, this poverty should be a transitional phenomenon. When Robert Ezra Park, one of the founders of the Chicago school of sociology, introduced the concept of 'marginal man' (1928), he had the social situation of the immigrant in mind. In the US discourse, marginality has never lost the association with immigration, usually thought of – with Park – as being of limited duration and perceived positively as a productive factor in socio-cultural change. By contrast, in the German discourse, established by Friedrich Fürstenberg (1965), the term *Randgruppe* (marginal group) is generally used to refer to economically or socially deprived groups in the resident population. It carries the implication of lasting structural exclusion and is normally seen negatively as a failure of capitalist society or of the welfare state's agencies of social control.

Beyond social exclusion

'Social exclusion' has become a fashionable term in the new European discourse of social problems and it influences much of the European Union's agenda for action and research in the poverty field (see p. 8 for references). The common vague use of the term covers a wide range of issues related to poverty, deprivation, unemployment and discriminations of various kinds. In contrast to this, our typology aims to show the heterogeneity of states of poverty on a scale between full social inclusion (integration) and social exclusion proper as defined above. In this view, poverty does not necessarily imply social exclusion (and, vice versa, exclusion does not necessarily or not only refer to poverty). Exclusion is only one extreme type at the end of the spectrum of four or six types of poverty. This differentiated view is suggested by the empirical findings of the dynamic life-course approach to poverty employed in this study. While the American debate on the existence of an 'underclass' is widely cited in Europe, the no less substantial body of research on the dynamics of poverty by American scholars, now joined by

---

[5] For immigration to Germany see Münz, Seifert and Ulrich (1997).

Europeans, is hardly mentioned in debates on social exclusion.[6] The concept of exclusion is used both for the micro-sociological analysis of certain groups and for the macro-sociological analysis of the structure of inequality or even for societal diagnosis at large. Shortcomings of an unrestricted use of the concept are apparent on both levels, and they are connected.

The German debate on unemployment illustrates this point. Socially engaged scholars see social divisions and polarisation as the most important problem of social and economic policy in the 1990s, and the nationwide unemployment and its consequences stand at the forefront of the problem. While this perspective treats the trend towards the permanent detachment of a section of the population as an indubitable fact, the empirically based longitudinal research into living conditions supports with equal confidence the contrary position: 'For two decades, short-term unemployment in West Germany has been a mass phenomenon. For the overwhelming majority of those affected in the old Federal *Länder,* unemployment is a hard but relatively short transitory experience' (Landua and Habich 1994, p. 7).[7] In this connection, the widely used figurative concept of 'hard-core unemployment' (*Sockelarbeitslosigkeit*) can be misleading because it confuses two issues: on the one hand, a high and rising unemployment rate in Germany which has not significantly declined after periods of recession during the last two decades, and, on the other, a cumulative core of permanently excluded and unemployed persons. Thus the declaration 'Solidarity and Competitiveness in Germany' *(Solidarität am Standort Deutschland)* by committed social scientists and theologians stated that: 'over the past fifteen years the core of unemployment has grown after every economic downturn and has entrenched joblessness as a permanent fate of the victims' (Oswald von Nell-Breuning-Institut 1994, p. 4). In reality, the core of permanently excluded *persons* is fairly small, in contrast to the statistical core composed of changing people.

The detachment or division thesis only partially corresponds to social reality. The changing social structure of poverty is characterised by at least three aspects. First, there actually is a social division but it affects far fewer people than widely assumed. Thus, as shown above, the proportion of long-term Social Assistance claimants has fallen from the 1980s to the 1990s, and long-term unemployment accounts for one third of all people without

---

[6] See Neckel (1997) and the critical social-science journal *Leviathan* (1997, no. 1, special issue on poverty and underclass) as examples of the German reception of the American debate.

[7] The findings of dynamic research into poverty and unemployment have so far scarcely been taken into account by theoretical sociological analyses of society. Exceptions can be found in Georg Vobruba (1995) and the theory of the Risk Society which itself was a source of the dynamic approach (see Beck 1992 [1986, pp. 143–151] and Berger 1990).

employment in 1998 as it did in the mid 1980s. At a time of rising overall unemployment and poverty this may nevertheless mean that the number of long-term cases has increased. Second and more importantly, there has been a simultaneous democratisation of poverty and unemployment that runs contrary to exclusion and cleavage, that is, middle-class people beyond the traditionally marginalised are temporarily affected. This democratisation or 'transcendence' not only applies to income poverty but also to deprivations in other areas of life (Hübinger 1996). Third, there has been a pluralisation of social divisions and lines of conflict, as exemplified even by the four well-known problem groups described earlier: the unemployed stand for economic inequalities; single parents represent divisions between families and the sexes; children and others in need of care indicate problems of intergenerational relationships; while foreigners exemplify ethnic divisions. Divisions conditioned by the labour market are only one among at least four dimensions of precarious social changes.

The social-divisions hypothesis therefore underestimates the complexity of the changes in poverty and inequality. The accelerating rate of social change is leading not only to a permanent exclusion of 'useless' members of society but also and at the same time to the creation of a fluctuating mass in society, people who experience insecurity rather than exclusion. In a rapidly changing world this poverty seems to act as a buffer against radical social change and adjustment. Chapter 12 offers an attempt at a theoretical interpretation of the new structures of social inequality.

A 'two-thirds society'?

Before the concept of exclusion came to the fore in the 1990s, the idea of a two-thirds society was influential in the political debate in Germany. Like 'exclusion', this idea suggests permanent separation of a lower section of the population: 'The path of modern industrial society leads to segmentation . . . the coagulation of social change into new quasi-classes' (Glotz 1985, p. 38). In the mid 1980s this seemed a plausible scenario to us as well: ' the majority of those affected (have) no real chance of being absorbed into the working population . . . the boundaries between the working and the poor population (are) increasingly demarcated' (Leibfried and Tennstedt 1985b, pp. 14f.); 'increasing numbers of people (are being) uncoupled from the growing affluence and are being pushed into marginal positions' (Döring et al. 1990b, p. 7).

The concept of the two-thirds society implies that a third of the population is sunk in relatively long-lasting and comprehensive deprivation. Three assumptions can be traced: *stability* assumes that the people in question are deprived for long periods if not permanently; *marginalisation* assumes that these people experience cumulative processes of deprivation and find themselves in a situation of social exclusion; and *dualism* assumes that this social division leads to an antagonistic structure in which the upper two-thirds stand in conflict with the lower third. This new segmentation remodels the old dualism of capital and labour; it divides 'normal' workers from people on the margins of the labour market. Peter Glotz and other adherents of the 'two-thirds society' school of thought remain attached to models of society which presuppose dualistic antagonisms between social role players, the strong and the weak, winners and losers, the guilty and the victims. Thus Ehrenfried Natter and Alois Riedlsperger (1988, p. 12) see the concept of the two-thirds society as 'a more or less explicit "political programme": the defence of one's own social position by in effect excluding other social groups or even doing so deliberately'. In this way, the upper two-thirds live 'in relative affluence at the expense of this excluded third'. The apparent paradox of growing poverty at a time of growing affluence is explained here as a result of cleavages between sections of society.

On closer examination, these assumptions appear open to criticism. Against the background of the findings of dynamic poverty research, the suggestion that there is an unchanging section of society condemned to its margins becomes questionable. Even in those cases where people have remained in the lower segment for a long time, social marginalisation is not inevitable, as people in poverty or claiming Social Assistance deal with their situations in many different ways. There are of course some permanently marginalised people, but they are far fewer than has hitherto been assumed.

In statistical terms, national income data reveal that West Germany is not a 'two-thirds society' but a '70–20–10 society',[8] composed of 70 per cent who were never poor, 20 per cent who were occasionally in poverty and 10 per cent who were poor more frequently (figure 10.1). A 'mere' 2.7 per cent of the population were poor almost throughout the 11-year period studied – in other words, only a small part of the 10 per cent who were poor more frequently. This can only be seen in the findings of a longitudinal panel study: the same people were interviewed in the period from 1984 to 1994 to see who was poor in each year. If the poverty line is drawn at 50 per cent of mean equivalent income, almost one-third (32 per cent) of the whole population was poor in some year. If the line is drawn at 60 per cent, it was almost half of the population (47 per cent).

These panel data are adjusted for misrepresentation of lower-income

[8] This expression was coined by Headey *et al.* (1990, p. 12) originally as the '75–15–10 society' based on the more limited panel data for 1984–1989 which were available in 1990. The source of the data is the Socio-Economic Panel study, which includes foreigners but only those who had immigrated by 1984.

years in
poverty

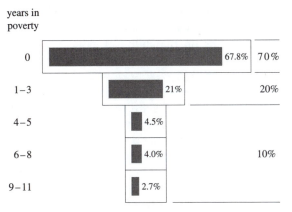

Figure 10.1 *The '70-20-10 society': income poverty in West Germany, 1984–1994*
Source: Krause (1998); Socio-Economic Panel Study (SOEP).

strata although people at the very bottom such as the homeless or illegal immigrants cannot be adequately represented in such surveys.[9] However, the numbers of groups of this kind are too small to distort the overall picture. It is also important to keep in mind that national income surveys do not normally reveal the spatial concentration of poverty. Clearly, in deprived areas we can expect to find more long-term poverty. Research on urban poverty, which has been revitalised in Germany in the 1990s, tends to emphasise processes of exclusion.[10]

Are we sounding the 'all clear' signal to the current state of society? We are not. Some of the empirical foundations on which the model of the two-thirds society stands are justified. Social Assistance claims have risen considerably in the last 25 years, including long-term claims (which have increased in absolute terms even if not in relative terms). Unemployment plays a significant and central role in this trend, unlike in the 1960s. There are lasting structural causes of unemployment and social disruption which have proved hard to tackle. Poverty has in fact acquired a social relevance again, but not in the sense suggested by the 'two-thirds society'. The social divisions referred to in the notion of a two-thirds society are better described as a growing but fluctuating core of unemployment, poverty and homelessness. Within this core there are fluid and less fluid sections,

[9] See the critique by Dangschat (1994). A large new income panel study concentrating on people with a low income has been started in 1998 by the Federal Ministry of Health to overcome the limitations of the general Socio-Economic Panel Study.
[10] See the analyses of concentrated urban poverty by Dangschat (1995) and Friedrichs (1998a). Some increase in spatial segregation of the poor is even suggested by our own Bremen data on Social Assistance when disaggregated by quarters (Farwick 1998).

including a hardened section of a limited size (which is a hard core composed of specific individuals, not a fluctuating statistical core). This situation makes greater demands on the ability of policy-makers to devise alternative approaches than does the idea of a permanently deprived section of the population.

Dynamic research is sometimes accused of playing down poverty. Indeed, finding that poverty is often short term is good news. However, there is also bad news: poverty is more widely spread in the population than generally believed. The risk of becoming poor is underestimated from the conventional point of view: the normal cross-sectional measure of the extent of poverty, used also by social critics, shows that 10–11 per cent of the population were poor in any one year around 1990 in terms of the 50 per cent of mean income measure (19 per cent at the 60 per cent line). Thus, a cross-sectional view reveals only a third (or less than half) of all those liable to be poor as measured by longitudinal data (32 per cent and 47 per cent respectively).[11]

Not only are divisions between people less clear-cut but also structural divisions have become fuzzy. Does, for instance, the increasing statistical core of unemployment reflect a cleavage in the labour market, between core and peripheral employment, in which the latter is the fluctuating recruiting ground for the unemployed? Martin Osterland has suggested (1990, p. 355) that the idea of a two-thirds society is contradicted not only by the extensive flux of individuals between the employed and the unemployed, but also by the blurring of the structural distinction between 'being employed' and 'not being employed'. He refers to the grey zone between employment and non-employment which embraces a range of working conditions such as part-time work, marginal self-employment and governmental make-work schemes.

To conclude, it seems that if people refer to social exclusion, polarisation or a two-thirds society, they often just seek to draw attention to increases and changes in poverty and social inequality. But poverty and inequality have many forms and rigid divisions are only one of them, as demonstrated by the spectrum between full inclusion and exclusion depicted above. These findings are based on a fairly broad cross-section of the poor found among the clientele of a comprehensive and little stigmatising social assistance scheme, corroborated by research on income poverty based on the German Socio-Economic Panel Study. Looking at specific groups such as the homeless or at deprived areas, as done by most poverty researchers, some forms of poverty may be found to be more pronounced than others.

[11] The difference between cross-sectional and longitudinal measures is described in chapter 3.

Reappraising Social Assistance: how the welfare state shapes the lives of the poor

The findings of dynamic research also suggest a new picture of a key institution of the welfare state, Social Assistance, and its effects. German Social Assistance not only 'manages' social marginality and stigmatises its clientele, but it also plays a positive role in the lives of many claimants and is used and valued accordingly. For instance, it allows single mothers to devote themselves to their children; it supports women in breaking away from unbearable marriages; and it underpins a personal or occupational reorientation after an illness or a psychological crisis. In short, Social Assistance is better than its reputation.

Social Assistance is not simply a form of *ad hoc* emergency help: it also shapes people's life courses. The three basic principles of the Federal Social Assistance Act – subsidiarity in relation to state and other benefits, support tailored to individual need and help with self-help – provide the programme a flexible timeframe in which to deal with poverty: benefit should be paid 'as briefly as possible and as long as necessary' (see p. 62). The large number of short-term claims shows how well help to self-help works in re-establishing people's ability to run their own lives. However, the Social Assistance Agencies do not primarily provide specific support through counselling, job offers or support of child care. Rather, most claimants 'only' get cash benefits to be able to mobilise new sources of income on their own, or to wait until they are in a position to do so, as in the case of a convalescence. Moreover, even short periods of receiving benefits may have long-lasting effects on autonomy and personal identity.

Our study of Social Assistance claimants shows that people are making use of state benefits more confidently than ever before. It seems that claimants are not only using their legal rights but are consciously acting as 'citizens of the welfare state' and rejecting the ascribed role of 'welfare recipients'. Thus even a marginalised system such as Social Assistance supports the thesis we set forth in chapter 2: that the modern life course is formed not only by the educational and pension systems but also by the diverse systems of social risk management in the welfare state, such as Unemployment Insurance, Health Insurance, Social Assistance and social work. The way in which these systems affect life courses is, however, less apparent because they do not intervene at pre-defined fixed points in the life course and they directly affect most people only during brief stages in life and for periods which vary widely among individuals. Their biographical impact may be less discernible but it is not less momentous than the impact of other welfare-state institutions. Jutta Allmendinger's view (1994; Allmendinger and Hinz 1998, p. 64) that Social Assistance is unrelated to the wider biographies of the claimants – that Social Assistance is a 'situational programme' characterised by 'life-course indifference' in contrast to Old-Age Pensions held to be a 'continuous' or 'biographical programme' – needs qualification.

The relatively positive evaluation of Social Assistance which our study supports does not signal that there is no room for improvement. Most of the claimants as well as many of the social workers we interviewed (Schwarze 1994) told us about the negative aspects of claiming: about insufficient benefits and especially about relations between officialdom and claimants. A standard criticism was, for instance, the restrictive approach towards giving information adopted in many offices and by a few higher officials. This testifies to the 'passive institutionalisation' of Social Assistance asserted as early as two decades ago (Leibfried 1977, p. 54). More generally, the new picture of poverty which emerges from the dynamic research – above all the temporalisation and democratisation of poverty and the high degree of activity among the poor – suggests a new approach to anti-poverty policy. This is the subject of the next chapter.

11 Paths out of poverty: perspectives on active policy

What new perspectives on policies against poverty are suggested by the life-course approach? Our first such conclusion in the early 1990s was that municipalities ought to include data on the duration and course of poverty and other conditions in their social reports (Buhr, Ludwig and Leibfried 1990, 1992; Voges and Leibfried 1990). The dynamic approach soon struck roots in politics and administration. Temporal aspects were included in the 1993 reform of the national Social Assistance statistics (implemented from 1994 onwards; see Beck and Seewald 1994, Buhr *et al.* 1992). The findings of the Bremen study, that many Social Assistance claimants were only waiting for Unemployment Benefits to be paid, led the Bremen Employment Department to take steps to increase its efficiency; changes in national labour law followed (see below). Our research also influenced the concept of a basic income scheme submitted by Andrea Fischer of the Green Party in 1997. This proposal conceives of claimants as full citizens and autonomous agents, entitled to a basic income as a right but also obliged to assume basic responsibilities such as budgeting on their own with standardised lump-sum payments. The findings about short-term claiming and poverty transcending marginal groups were referred to by speakers from all parties in a heated debate on poverty in the Federal Parliament (Proceedings 1996, pp. 11352–11374, see esp. 11355f., 11359f., 11363).

The new dynamic approach had its greatest influence on policy-making in the USA, its country of origin. President Clinton's plan for the reform of Welfare (AFDC) was deeply influenced by the dynamic perspective. Two leading dynamic researchers from Harvard University, Mary Jo Bane and David Ellwood (see Bane and Ellwood 1994), were appointed as senior officials in the Clinton administration to carry out the reform. Their efforts, however, were eventually vitiated by the 'November revolution' of the Republicans in Congress in 1994.

Dynamic research suggests four new policy orientations to be discussed in this chapter:

The time dimension of poverty and Social Assistance ('temporalisation') suggests the need to reconceptualise anti-poverty policy as *life-course policy*.

The action potential of the poor, which is the driving force behind the dynamics of poverty (see chapter 5 on coping), implies the need for – and the feasibility of – an *enabling approach*, focusing on paths out of Social Assistance, rather than just administering cases and paying benefits.

When poverty spreads beyond traditional marginal groups ('democratisation'), then the barriers between 'policies for the poor' and 'policies for workers' or 'policies for citizens', between the lower and the higher tiers of the welfare state (which are particularly pronounced in comprehensive European welfare states of the conservative and social-democratic variety) lose their meaning. An *integrated social policy* is thus called for.

Dynamic research, which evaluates the impact of Social Assistance on people's lives, is itself part of a new *reflexive social policy*. The latter relies on continual social reporting as well as the monitoring of its own effects, quite unlike traditional Social Assistance.

Life-course policy

The poverty of the late twentieth century has many faces: to shed light on these we elaborated several temporal typologies of poverty, based on different categories of time, within which useful distinctions can be made among patterns of Social Assistance claiming. We developed typologies of the duration and continuity of claiming (objective time, chapter 3), of claimants' own time perspectives and their biographical evaluation of claiming (subjective time, chapter 4), of life courses, of coping patterns and 'careers' (living time, chapter 5), of dependency (institutional time, chapter 6) and of inclusion/exclusion (chapter 10). Some of these distinctions have been researched previously and figured in political debates while others have received little or no attention in earlier studies and debates. Some important types have been invisible or suppressed in public discourse. The heterogeneity of poverty argues for a differentiated approach to anti-poverty policy.

Until the end of the 1980s, German Social Assistance evinced hardly any policy differentiation. The official statistics of course distinguished various categories of claimants, but they did not give rise to measures geared to these groups' specific needs. In the more general social policy arena – and at least in the critical debate on Social Assistance – there is a common way of differentiating policies, notably by identifying *'problem groups'* or *'target groups'*, such as 'the unemployed', 'the elderly' or 'the homeless', and to devote policy measures to them. This approach is of limited use.

The first problematic issue is that the people in these groups experience such wide differences in the *duration* of poverty and other problems that a uniform policy can scarcely hope to offer solutions to the whole group. In fact, the dynamic approach seems to suggest that anti-poverty policies ought to be differentiated according to the duration of poverty – whether it is short or long term in the simplest case. In a study of relative income poverty among children in the USA, Robert Walker (1994) argued for distinct policies for groups according to duration. For example, he proposed state loans for the temporarily poor and for those with repeated short-term spells. A provision of this kind would lift 35 per cent of poor US children out of poverty. For those who repeatedly experienced longer spells of poverty he proposed a package of conventional social policy measures, including the support of employment opportunities and health insurance coverage. By contrast, only structural reform of the socio-economic system could promise relief to the long-term poor.

Closer examination shows, however, that the temporal structure of poverty cannot be easily translated into a meaningful and effective policy design: the members of a given group interpret their experience of poverty differently. The second problematic issue in differentiating policies, therefore, is that objective, chronological time ('how long does poverty last') is modified by *subjective* and *biographical time*. It is politically difficult to identify and influence these dimensions of time. The efficacy of policy measures depends to a great extent on how those targeted react to the policies and actively participate in them – and thus on their subjective orientations of action. The complexity of these problematic situations exceeds the precision of the measures normally available for policy use.

A policy perspective which uses life-course theory to temporally distinguish different life situations does not escape the underlying dilemma of target group policies. Faced with the amorphous mass of problems among the general population, political strategies to combat poverty cannot avoid selecting certain groups for action, identifying them and targeting their measures on them, even though these groups are very heterogeneous in composition and the intended beneficiaries may possibly be missed. The groups which are identified in practice are chiefly marginalised groups in the lower social strata and socio-structurally defined 'problem groups' in the core population.[1] The temporal analyses have offered a new cross-cutting dimension, which shows how changeable the life circumstances of

---

[1] For an analysis of 'problem groups' in the German population, see Landua and Habich (1994).

the members of such groups can be. This increases the dilemma of social policy between universal measures based on standardised services intended for large social groups, and selective measures aimed at smaller sections or even designed for individual circumstances.

The third problematic issue is, then, that even when aimed at small groups, social policy can take temporal aspects into account only in a way amenable to the administration. We might call this *administrative time*. A Social Assistance official cannot normally predict if a new claimant will be long or short term. Unlike the hindsight of social science analysis, prognostic tools would be required to identify potential long-term claimants – or, equally, short-term claimants.[2] In order to be practicable, such predictive measures would have to be restricted to basic socio-demographic indicators such as being female, young or a single parent, each of which identifies a target group (see Bane and Ellwood 1994, p. 47).

Furthermore, it is not only hard to determine how long poverty will last, both objectively and subjectively, and how duration can be handled by the administration, but – the fourth problematic issue – we have to clarify how long Social Assistance ought to last. This involves normative questions about the legitimate duration of receiving Social Assistance or other social benefits, which have to be answered in the democratic process. For instance, should long-term claims be totally prohibited, as in the Clinton Reform Act of 1996, and, if so, for which groups? Which sections of the population should be allowed to have time out at the expense of the state, that is the taxpayers, and in what circumstances and for how long? This is a question of how legitimate certain lifestyles are, and such questions go far beyond those who are poor. While the subjective and the administrative dimensions of time tend to show the limits of policy, this normative dimension suggests scope for political action to shape living time — to define *political time* with regard to individual life courses. This is life-course policy.

In practice, poverty policy always implies some sort of life-course policy. In particular, it regulates how periods of employment and non-employment are arranged in the life course, and which periods out of the labour market are recognised by the state as worthy of support. Policies rarely reflect this life-course perspective explicitly. But before devising specific measures, poverty policy must lay down which life stages and events are to be supported at all, and which periods of non-employment are to be treated as legitimate.

Even the Federal Social Assistance Act does not define 'need' as a criter-

---

[2] According to §15b of the Federal Social Assistance Act, the official must make a judgement if someone will be claiming Social Assistance 'predictably for only a short period'. The claimant may then be offered Social Assistance as a loan. If the official does not anticipate that a claim will be short-term, but it turns out to be, then the benefits do not have to be repaid.

ion of eligibility without restriction. The general requirement that people should secure their livelihoods by paid work is suspended only in precisely defined situations (BSHG sections 18, 25). Should, for instance, lone parents be relieved of the obligation to take paid work, as stipulated in the Act, and be entitled to welfare-state provisions? If so, for how long, up to what parental age, until the child is how old, and under what conditions? Should this continue to be realised under Social Assistance, or in the form of an independent categorical social-security scheme, or through a combination of need-based benefits for children and for divorced or lone parents? The spectrum of stages and activities in life to be so acknowledged as worthy of support could be extended to include housework, caring for sick or elderly family members, education and training, voluntary and honorary activities, and so on.

In this way 'political time' is defined. Constructs of this kind can already be found in many social security systems. Thus, quite apart from Social Assistance, child-rearing has been increasingly recognised in Germany as giving entitlement to benefits in the Old-Age Pension system. The postulate of an integrated anti-poverty policy (see below) would then require that the criterion for periods of non-employment during one's life should be open to debate in all parts of the social security system and should be reframed on a unified basis. This would replace the present situation in which 'time out' is treated differently in different policy fields (such as income maintenance or health insurance), in different security systems (such as the Old-Age Pensions for workers and employees, which are insurance based, and the civil service pensions, which are tax financed) and at different levels (such as Social Insurance and Social Assistance).

By putting a premium on particular life-course patterns, Social Assistance and other social security systems presuppose fundamental political decisions about models of life in our society. In reforming Social Assistance, society has to decide: what patterns of life does it want to open up for – or impose on – women and men, families and lone parents, the low-paid and the well-off, children and old people? Does it want to perpetuate the German model of the 'male breadwinner' and consequently discriminate against women in the pension system – and therefore, if the breadwinner is absent, force them into the safety net of Social Assistance? Does it want to continue to pursue the ideal of the two-parent family at the cost of allowing the children of lone parents to spend their first formative years in poverty? Should the fiction of male life-long full-time employment be maintained, and should the unemployed be punished by unfavourable social policies? These issues demand nothing less than a new definition of living time, comparable and intertwined with similar debates in industrial relations about new patterns of spreading working hours over the week, over the year and in the life span. Fundamental social arrangements have to be rethought: the relationship between the sexes, the extension of the concept of productive work beyond paid work in the market, and the relationship between the generations, as manifested in questions of poverty among children or the reduction in social services for the increasing proportion of elderly people.

'Objective time', 'subjective-biographical time', 'administrative time' and 'political time' – these highlight the complexity of the time dimension in social risks, challenging social policy and simultaneously creating openings for choices and action. Poverty located in real time and real lives – as encapsulated in the concepts 'temporalisation' and 'biographisation' – makes serious demands on those involved in political action. Poverty policy defined as life-course policy takes account of its own impact on life patterns, and entertains debates on the models of male and female life courses on which it is predicated.

On the basis of the typology of poverty careers developed in chapter 5 we can give an example of how poverty policies can be differentiated according to objective and biographical time.[3] We distinguished three types of career. Long-term receipt of Social Assistance, combined with multiple and cumulative deprivations and a loss of direction, gives rise to an entrenched poverty career. This career mostly affects young single men. The welfare-state normalised career also involves long-term receipt with little chance of escaping but the people affected cope better and they have a wider temporal horizon of action than those in entrenched poverty. In the case of the optimised career, coping helps people even to escape Assistance.

Entrenched poverty careers constitute a genuine field for social case work, normally on a long-term basis. Social problems such as isolation, addiction or chronic illness matter more than the mere lack of income. In our qualitative study we found that this group of people, who need more help than others, actually get less – a Social Assistance paradox. In this sense, the Assistance Agencies can even be said to exacerbate the predicament of this hard core of the poor. They constitute a long-term 'welfare class' in the sense of a 'foster class'.

In the case of the normalised career, the cash transfer function of Social Assistance is more important than social work. People with this type of career constitute a welfare class in the sense of a 'benefit class' because their standard of living depends on the rates of benefits, just like that of old-age pensioners depends on their pensions. In fact, Social Assistance assumes the character of pension-like benefits. In view of this group there is a good case for maintaining benefit rates at an adequate level rather than cutting

---

[3] The following is based on Ludwig (1996, chapter 8).

them to get people off Assistance. An extended social assistance scheme like the German one provides a fairly good service for them although higher-tier benefit systems could do even better, either categorical systems, for example for people with disabilities, or minimum provisions within social insurance. This would put benefits on a more regular footing without stigma attached. In addition to cash, counselling services are also beneficial because they engage the action potential of claimants. This, too, is a field for an enabling approach – helping claimants help themselves – though not through escape from Assistance. The type of enabling needed, however, varies widely because this group is more heterogeneous than the entrenched group.

For those who manage to optimise their poverty career through escape, Social Assistance assumes its ideal function of a transitory bridge at critical life stages – help to self-help in the purest sense. Again, cash benefits are the most important type of aid. In principle, these people – for example unemployed persons with good employment chances or new immigrants with adequate training and a good command of the German language – can help themselves: they just need money to bridge a difficult phase in their life and to regain independence. In an age of social upheaval, of employment crisis, familial instability and ethnic cleavages, enabling policies make sense even for this group of people, precisely because they are willing and able to make use of support. Enabling would not involve traditional social work but, for example, may support their job-search in the first labour market or help with child care. This group also includes 'long-term bridgers', especially some lone mothers. Enabling measures would aim to sustain their action potential during the years of claiming Assistance in order to facilitate the eventual escape.

An enabling approach

A key issue of reform is the action potential of the poor. In sociology, especially in the study of marginal groups, the agency of the poor has often been denied (see pp. 19f., pp. 39f., pp. 123f.).[4] Social policy makers have either equally denied agency, sometimes blaming its extinction on ill-designed social security systems, or they have emphasised the negative side of it – scrounging, abuse of benefits, pursuit of hedonistic or deviant ends – to justify repression, social control and cuts in benefits. However, the dynamic approach to poverty and on-going social assistance reforms in several countries during the second half of the 1990s have converged in vindicating the

---

[4] For a reappraisal of the aspect of agency in Georg Simmel's essay 'The poor' (1908), which has sometimes served as a basis for this denial, see Hvinden (1995) and Leisering (1997c).

poor as agents: active claimants require active, enabling policies, poverty dynamics require 'dynamic policies' (Leisering and Walker 1998c). Dynamic research has revealed a degree of agency among the poor which conventional poverty policies have not fully exploited. Although longitudinal analyses do not support the notion of social assistance making claimants passive and dependent (see chapter 6), improved assistance could even further their activity.

The finding that claimants are generally more active than widely believed and that most of them manage either to terminate claiming or to cope while claiming, might tempt politicians to save money by reducing support, because 'claimants are able to help themselves'. On closer examination our findings suggest the contrary: investing in claimants pays, because most of them are both able and determined to make use of support to become independent or in order to secure a decent living if they are unable to become independent. This would make a case for maintaining and extending support services and limiting control measures. Enabling policies are in fact being introduced, even if driven by fiscal pressure.

The current transnational political emphasis on 'getting people off welfare' should, however, be put into perspective. Many claimants cannot terminate claiming within a given period or are not expected to do so by cultural norms specific to each country, because they are sick, old, young (children) or objectively have no chance of returning to work or because society does not expect them to work, as in Germany in the case of lone parents with younger children. Ignoring these people would add to the Social Assistance paradox described above. In fact, of the three principal types of Social Assistance careers identified by qualitative dynamic research, two are characterised by medium- or long-term claiming (pp. 131–136). Investing in them will also pay – getting many of them off Assistance in the long run, and securing a decent level of living 'worthy of human dignity' (*menschenwürdig*) as the Federal Social Assistance Act requires in accordance with the Federal Constitution.

In 1996 and 1997 new approaches to social assistance reform emerged in Germany, Britain and the USA that went beyond a mere readjustment of the levels of wages and benefits or of controls. These new departures aim to exploit the claimants' potential for action by offering active support rather than merely creating incentives by making work pay. This diverse set of measures is multi-faceted: some include coercion, deterrence and a reduction of entitlements, others provide new real routes to independence, and many blend coercion and support.

In Britain, even before Tony Blair took office, the Job Seekers' Allowance was introduced in 1996 to supersede both Unemployment Benefit and Income Support for the unemployed. This includes compulsory re-training and participation in work schemes. After his landslide electoral victory in May 1997, Blair appointed Frank Field Minister for Welfare Reform. Field tried to design policies that incite people to get off assistance, embedded, though, in a moral crusade against 'dependence' and 'abuse' of benefits. While Field's hopes of recasting the welfare state in general and even solving the problems of unemployment and lone parenthood on this basis seem elusive (he quit after a year of office), we may realistically expect to see more people leaving social assistance than before, possibly an extra 10 per cent or even 20 per cent of the clientele. More could only be achieved if benefits were curtailed and access further restricted. This, however, would be a different story altogether: not an active policy forging imaginative links between benefit and labour market but simply a value-based decision against the social rights of certain groups, like lone mothers whose benefits were cut in Britain in 1998.

In Germany, too,[5] Social Assistance has traditionally only 'administered', not empowered the poor so that we could speak of 'passive institutionalisation' (Leibfried 1977, p. 54). But from the mid 1990s a minor revolution has been taking place in major municipalities. Driven by budgetary pressures the move towards modernising public administration has eventually reached Social Assistance, that marginal component of the welfare state. For the first time, the prime objective of Social Assistance, to 'help claimants help themselves', is being taken seriously and the effectiveness of measures is being evaluated. Computerised processing of file records, New Control Models (*Neue Steuerungsmodelle*) to rationalise the administration and new instruments for supporting claimants are being introduced to boost efficiency and effectiveness. Above all, getting claimants off benefit has become a primary goal.

Ideally such measures can reduce costs as well as help the poor. Clients, staff and local employers are mobilised to avert long-term claims. While conventional work schemes within and without Social Assistance led to a 'secondary labour market' propped up by the government, some of the new initiatives aim at the 'real' primary labour market. The city of Hamburg, for example, has charged a private Dutch company *Bureau Maatwerk* (Dutch for 'work to measure') to get long-term unemployed claimants of Social Assistance back to work. The method operates on precise knowledge of the characteristics of each unemployed person and of the needs of individual local employers. On this basis many people found a job, even new

---

[5] For more on the novel active policies in Germany described below see Leisering, Buhr and Gangl (1997). On enabling policies in the Nordic welfare states see Hvinden (1999). New 'welfare to work' schemes in several European countries are analysed in a research project (1997–1999) led by Ivar Lødemel, Oslo, and funded by the EU under its Targeted Socio-Economic Research (TSER) scheme.

jobs were created and millions of DMs were saved (Landessozialamt Hamburg 1997). Conventional labour exchanges do not normally collect and use knowledge to this extent. In the Christian-Democratic Party innovators like Ulf Fink have taken up this and other ideas as ways out of the employment crisis.

In the reform movement exit policies are generally restricted to labour market outlets, but it is necessary to go further. Our research finding that many people only claim Social Assistance because they are waiting for prior benefits to be paid (see chapter 3) induced the German government to change the Employment Promotion Act (*Arbeitsförderungsgesetz*, AFG) in 1996 to speed up the delivery of Unemployment Benefit (AFG §147,1). Immigrants' chances of leaving Social Assistance largely depend on political regulations. For example, cutting language courses for ethnic Germans coming from Eastern Europe and Russia, as was done in the mid 1990s, is bound to lengthen rather than shorten dependency on public funds. Further, lone mothers need help to combine work and child rearing, for instance via better child-care facilities or 'full half-day schooling' (which means that, unlike today, school should finish at the same hour every day). Some long-term Social Assistance claimants need intensive support by social workers. Specific problem groups such as people in debt also need targeted help. To cut counselling services for people in debt and other problem groups may prove costly in the long run. Counselling is a classical and comparatively cheap way of enabling people to help themselves.

The new municipal reforms have grown out of local initiatives, although communication networks between municipalities are developing. The general political debate at the Federal level has been slow to notice this reform movement, although the latter promises to be more significant both for clients and the administration than legislative changes, such as the reform of the Social Assistance Law of 23 July 1996. Improvements in social services at the local level geared to a diversity of individual needs seem to be more effective than intricate uniform systems of monetary incentives. Empowering claimants through support measures may increase social spending but is likely to pay off before long.

Integrated social policy

Social policy and social administration in the field of poverty in Germany suffer from a modernisation lag. This also applies to the dominant images of poverty and to the basic assumptions about how to combat poverty in politics. Poverty has traditionally been pushed to the margins in the political system, it has been effectively residualised. Poverty issues are not treated as a significant element in strategic social-policy planning, but instead they are concentrated into a separate system (Social Assistance) outside the regular social security system. Social Assistance did not assume a more central position in politics until fiscal and labour-market pressure mounted in the 1990s. The poor are seen as a negligible residual category of modern society. The finding that poverty transcends traditional social boundaries and reaches into the middle classes fundamentally calls such residualising assumptions and institutionalisations into question. Instead, it demands modernisation, a differentiation and normalisation of poverty policies and images appropriate to the new kinds of poverty.

In considering poverty policy, developments in Social Assistance must be distinguished from developments in higher-tier social security systems. The German social security system has a dual structure: a central core, composed chiefly of Social Insurance schemes, and a peripheral field of social services at the heart of which lies Social Assistance. The core programmes are not intended to address poverty risks; for example, as a matter of principle, there is no minimum pension. Entitlements are based on the individual employment record and on marriage. Nor does family policy recognise the minimum needs of children or of divorced women. Deviations from this model are only tolerated temporarily during periods of collective want, such as at the outset of the 1950s in the case of Old-Age Pensions, or in the form of the limited Social Supplements to social security in Eastern Germany until 1996.

The last attempt to introduce minimum benefits failed in 1989 when the Pension Reform Bill for 1992 was passed in the *Bundestag*. The dualistic model has always presupposed and tolerated that the core institutions would allow a certain amount of poverty which then had to be dealt with at the periphery. Problems arose when this 'state-produced poverty' began to increase faster than expected, as it did at the end of the 1970s. By contrast with the 'poverty approach' of the Anglo-Saxon welfare states, the principal aim of the German system is to secure a person's achieved standard of living by means of earnings-related benefits. This benefits the middle classes most, thus creating strong political support for the welfare state. Conversely, means-tested benefits are claimed by only a small section of the population. Under these circumstances, Social Assistance plays a much smaller role in the debate about the future of the welfare state than it does for instance in the USA.

Within Social Assistance there is already a trend towards closing the gap to the higher-level 'regular' social security system. The Federal Administrative Court's 1954 judgement established the individual's right to claim welfare benefits and thus abolished one of the most conspicuous relics of the old Poor Law. The reform of the Federal Social Assistance Law in 1974 restricted the range of relatives who could be held liable to repay benefits which their parents and children had received, and thus further individualised the right to Social Assistance. Since the 1980s the job creation scheme under Social Assistance has increasingly offered regular employment contracts tied to Social Insurance entitlements, instead of the notorious and badly paid 'workfare', which nevertheless continues to be used as a lower level of Assistance. This, too, shows signs of alignment with other parts of the income maintenance system.

The form and style of the Social Assistance Agency – such aspects as the furnishing of the buildings, communication with claimants and the qualifications of the staff – continue to be widely experienced as inferior and discriminatory by those eligible for benefits. The stereotypes of claimants and of unemployed people which pervade political debates in Bonn also require modernisation and normalisation. This ought to change when the German Parliament moves to Berlin, which is, unlike Bonn, an arena of Germany's modernisation conflicts. Although abuse occurs in all social service and benefit systems, not to mention the widespread evasion of taxes, the debate usually focuses righteously on the socially weak. This contrasts notably with the total silence about the far greater problem of the non-take-up of Social Assistance entitlements – the 'latent poor'.

The position of Social Assistance in Germany's dual system of social security must be rethought. The more that poverty is recognised as transcending social boundaries, the less difference can be seen between the claimants of Social Insurance programmes and those of Social Assistance, in spite of the total policy separation between these two tiers maintained by administrative structures. The widespread criticism that Social Assistance has degenerated to a pension-like benefit for relevant social groups instead of being a marginal system of last resort for 'atypical cases', cannot be supported on the basis of the duration of claims. It is, however, true that Social Assistance extends to specific groups in society and not just to atypical individuals. We can distinguish three options or strategies to respond to this situation.

The first option would be to integrate some of the Social Assistance claimants into the normal social insurance system. This could be called a social policy of *upward integration*. The long-standing demand that Social Assistance be confined to 'atypical life courses' (see, for example, Hauser and Hübinger 1993, p. 424) could be achieved by building minimum benefit scales into the system of social insurance, something which is also discussed as giving a 'minimum basis' or a 'floor' (*Sockelung*) to Social Insurance. This is the model envisaged in the platform of the Social Democratic Party for the 1998 Federal Election. As far as Special Needs Benefit is concerned, the new long-term Care Insurance has partially removed typical situations which occur on a mass scale from the scope of this marginal means-tested scheme. But many of those affected will still have to claim regular benefits from Social Assistance since the Care Insurance neither covers high accommodation costs nor addresses more limited care needs.

Another way of transferring a whole section of Social Assistance claimants into a higher storey of the social security system would be the idea, discussed since the 1980s, of distinct pension entitlements for women within the general Old-Age Pension Insurance (Rolf and Wagner 1994). This model offers widows an entitlement to a pension in their own right, and not simply, as at present, a survivor pension based on their late husband's contributions. Furthermore, running joint training schemes and job creation programmes for the unemployed, irrespective of their status as claimants of Unemployment Benefit or Social Assistance, would also be a form of upward integration. This idea has increasingly met with support in the late 1990s.

A second option, which is somewhat contrary to the first, would be a kind of *socio-cultural integration* or harmonisation of social policies, that is, retaining and even strengthening the lower tier of social security while raising its standards in the realms of entitlement, client-orientation and service quality to a level hitherto reserved for the higher tiers. Social Assistance claimants would be recognised as full citizens. This kind of modernised 'citizen's Social Assistance' is the core of the Basic Income Scheme (*Grundsicherung*) of the Green Party which was part of their platform for the 1998 Federal election. It is much more restricted in scope than the fundamentalist concepts discussed in this party during the 1980s and has therefore been difficult to swallow by its left wing. It is open to question whether a modernised version of Social Assistance will remove its residual and stigmatising character. Moreover, a tension remains between the aim of catering for people in (sometimes permanent) need and the aim of getting people out by providing routes to higher tiers or self-sufficiency. Since the latter aim will always be of prime importance, Social Assistance can never achieve a fully equal status among the range of social security schemes. There is a limit to socio-cultural integration. The Green's model even includes an element of institutional downward integration: Unemployment Assistance, the means-tested lower echelon of Unemployment Benefit, is to be fully incorporated in the Basic Income.

While the Green Party aims to retain a (reformed) higher tier of social security, a third option would be *downward integration*, that is dismantling the dual structure by reducing the higher-tier schemes to minimum provisions. Kurt Biedenkopf, the Prime Minister of Saxony, has long advocated the idea of a universal minimum pension to replace the ingrained earnings-related pay-as-you-go scheme. This would be a step towards a residual welfare state, although the minimum provisions would not necessarily have to be means-tested. This is conceived as a response to current challenges faced by the welfare state at large (see the discussion in chapter 13) and not only to problems of poverty policy.

In all political parties in Germany there are groups and persons who propose a basic income scheme or a minimum basis of one sort or another, often presented as a panacea for the current problems of poverty policy or even of social policy at large (for a critique of basic income schemes as a strategy of general welfare-state reform see pp. 312–317). The terms used are similar but their meanings differ greatly. The three types of 'integrated' social policy just described all involve some concept of minimum provisions. While any anti-poverty policy will have to include some provision of basic income,[6] basic income schemes are only one component of a strategy to fight poverty and social exclusion. In a pluralistic and individualised society there is a diversity of needs and demands that require a broad range of specific benefits and services in addition to Social Assistance or other general basic income provisions. The challenge for the reform of poverty policy is to achieve both a differentiated and well-coordinated social security system.

Therefore, besides vertical integration of lower and higher tiers of social security, a kind of horizontal differentiation and integration within each tier is of equal importance. Indeed, new social problems like overindebtedness of consumers cut across the established institutional fragmentation of social services, pointing at gaps and lack of coordination in the public welfare sector. In the 1990s Germany has responded to the need to integrate social policies, especially by coordinating income maintenance policies, tax policies and family policies. In the rest of this section these issues are further delineated, starting with a blueprint of integrated social policy by Richard Hauser (1994; Hauser and Hübinger 1993, part VI) which covers both vertical and horizontal integration.

Richard Hauser and Werner Hübinger's concept seeks to turn the fight against poverty into a prime objective of the entire social security system and beyond, in labour promotion policy, in the tax system and in civil law. Anti-poverty policies should not be confined to Social Assistance. Hauser and Hübinger argue that most poverty can be abolished in this way. This would support the notion that poverty can be combated with the standard instruments of government – law, money and bureaucracy – and that only a small number of persons remain who need non-standardised forms of support.

---

[6] For different concepts of a basic income – during the 1980s this was a much discussed issue – see van Parijs (1992, 1995) and, related to the employed, Scharpf (1993, 1994). Concepts with a more restricted scope were presented by Leibfried (1990), Schmähl (1993) and Bäcker (1994).

Hauser and Hübinger depict the current system of social welfare production in three tiers: the highest tier is the labour market which provides people with income, the second consists of the 'regular' systems of social security, and the lowest tier is Social Assistance. The proposal works on the assumption that the three tiers should be reformed and coordinated with the aim of pushing as many people as possible to higher tiers, that is, off of Social Assistance (upward integration). Social Insurance and other second-tier schemes should be made 'poverty proof' (Hauser and Hübinger 1993, p. 420) to minimise the need to apply for Social Assistance. The concept implies that all 'able-bodied' are to be catered for by the Labour Agency, even those persons whose 'time out' from the labour market is socially accepted, such as lone parents. This new comprehensive Labour Agency would be responsible for integrating the able-bodied into the labour market or facilitating self-employment. It would also administer Unemployment Benefit and Unemployment Assistance. Minimum benefits would be introduced in the regular social security systems, for example in Old-Age Pensions.

Child Benefit would be raised to cover the minimum needs of children, the Advance Alimony Law would be extended to advance money to divorced women in case of unpaid alimony up to the child's eighteenth birthday, and Housing Benefit would relieve household income from the extra burden of high rent. Such benefits which address specific needs not covered by Social Insurance are an essential part of poverty policy even today, although they are not explicitly viewed by policy makers as parts of a coordinated anti-poverty policy (see p. 185). Raising Child Benefit and Housing Benefit for the lower third in the income hierarchy alone would lead to a considerable reduction of the number of Social Assistance clients in Germany. All in all, 'integrated' models of social policy have to take account of several institutional levels as well as of a multitude of areas of life. There remain aspects of life which cannot be covered by standardised cash benefits; targeted measures and specific income support systems are required instead.

In particular, poverty policy, tax policy and family policy are closely interconnected in the question of a minimum income, since the latter mostly affects families. The Federal Constitutional Court's judgements, implemented by Parliament in 1995, dictate that a family's minimum subsistence income may not be taxed. This was a considerable opening for an integration of social and poverty policies which could be developed further. The High Court is still struggling with the issue (see the November 1998 decision: Bundesverfassungsgericht 1999). At the same time, because the non-taxable minimum subsistence income is defined by Social Assistance levels, there is a noticeable political tendency to suppress Social Assistance scales in order to minimise the loss of revenue resulting from this tax exemption. In the last resort, the Constitutional Court itself may have to take remedial action by setting guidelines for the minimum subsistence income which would prevent the Federal Finance Ministry from intervening. Otherwise, the objective of giving fiscal protection to the minimum income could be vitiated. The Federal Constitutional Court ruled that a taxpayer must have enough left after the deduction of all taxes 'as is required to meet his essential living expenses and . . . those of his family (minimum subsistence)' (Rulings of the Federal Constitutional Court, BVerfGE, vol. 87, p. 153). The Court has not yet gone so far as to lay down a general rule to be observed by the state, that not only 'taking' (taxes) but also 'giving' (transfer payments) must be consistent with a social minimum, for instance that the various forms of state support for the costs of children ought to take the level of Social Assistance as a guideline. To do so would make a significant contribution to poverty policy.

Empirical research findings have shown that Social Assistance only exceeds wage levels among some families with three or more children (Breuer and Engels 1994, Hanesch and Bäcker 1993). If Germany had a form of state support for the child-related expenses (for an international comparison see Schultheis 1992), at least at the level of the Social Assistance children's scales, then the overlap with earning levels would not occur. The perennial arguments about the relationship between Social Assistance and wage rates ('less eligibility') are a kind of 'shadow boxing' and reveal yet another failure of the welfare state, that it does not redistribute the costs of children fairly among the citizenry.

Taken together, models of 'integrated' social policy of whatever variety would make poverty policy an integral part of general social policy for the first time in Germany. But even an integrated policy would have its limits. It is doubtful whether it would make the welfare state 'poverty proof' in a social sense, since legal and administrative integration of the poor would not do away with social differentiation. As long as benefits for 'the poor' are restricted to minimum standards, 'policy for workers' and 'policy for the poor' will remain distinct, even if they are jointly provided within the framework of the Social Insurance system, Child Benefit and so on. To that extent, the negative status of the poor is maintained as those who have no valid claims other than their need, and thus, as Georg Simmel showed (1908, p. 362), will receive nothing more than minimum subsistence benefits.

Minimum benefits for the unemployed, for example, if integrated into the general Unemployment Benefit scheme, would probably not differ much from Social Assistance as regards the level of benefits, means-testing and the stigma attached. Higher levels of benefit in pursuit of wider social policy goals can normally be justified politically only on the basis of criteria of demonstrable merit. This leads to fundamental questions of values and choices. Benefit entitlements could be based on a wide range of positively evaluated 'life-time contributions', such as bringing up children, acting as a care-giver or other socially valued work. Obviously, this would involve positive and negative discriminations and create new inequalities.

Reflexive policy

Reflexive poverty policies take conscious account of the consequences of their own operations. Eligibility for Social Assistance is often a result of the failure of prior income maintenance systems such as social insurance or family benefits (cf. the concept of 'welfare-state produced poverty', pp. 145–149). Efforts must be increased to report statistically on social conditions and poverty and to monitor the effects of policies. Monitoring, programme evaluation or even income experiments are little developed in Germany, not only in Social Assistance but also in the higher-tier social security schemes. More information about the temporal aspects of poverty situations is of particular importance. In this section we first deal with social reporting and then with the issue of monitoring.

The public debate on poverty is coloured by underestimation and exaggeration, by denial and dramatisation (see pp. 196–199). A normalisation of the political treatment of poverty presupposes the institutionalised social reporting, routine collection of relevant information. National social reports (*Sozialberichte*) were introduced at the Federal level at the end of the 1960s, but they only cover social law and social budgets, not social conditions. To the present day there is no national poverty report. Reports on poverty and social problem groups at the *Land* and local levels started to be produced in the 1980s and 1990s. The reform of the Social Assistance statistics came into force in 1994 (Wolff and Beck 1993).

A dynamic approach to poverty is very important for social reporting as well. Until recently the official statistics gave no information on the duration of Social Assistance claims. Even the municipal poverty reports rarely gave such information. But academics had from an early stage called for such information (Glatzer and Krupp 1975, p. 223). In the 1990s, the scholarly findings on the temporal structure of income poverty penetrated the social reports of the Federal Statistical Bureau (Datenreport 1997) as well as of the national non-governmental welfare organisations (Hanesch *et al.* 1994). The reform of the Social Assistance statistics, too, has opened up a more dynamic perspective (see also Buhr *et al.* 1992).

Conventional cross-sectional counts of the number of Social Assistance claimants still remain useful for fiscal purposes from an accountancy perspective. They reflect the actual case-load of the Social Assistance agency. But longitudinal and other temporal data are often indispensable even for resource planning purposes. Jill Vincent and others give an example from the United Kingdom (1991, pp. 3ff.), where it was planned to transfer resources from the elderly to families, based on the greater susceptibility of families to being poor. But it was also observed that families were on average poor for a much shorter period than the elderly were, and thus each family cost the welfare state less.

To meet its objectives a report on social conditions must give information on the following topics: the extent of poverty measured both cross-sectionally and longitudinally, that is the 'incidence' as well as the 'prevalence' of poverty (see Walker and Leisering 1998); the duration and patterns of poverty measured in terms of objective chronological time; the subjective perceptions of time of those affected by poverty and the biographical significance of poverty; and finally poverty careers as defined and propelled by public institutions, above all Social Assistance. The latter point increases the welfare state's own knowledge of itself. The extent to which the information can be assembled is subject to the restrictions of ethics, cost and the legal requirements of data confidentiality. In any case, some aspects of dynamic analysis are much more matters for scholarly research than the responsibilities of local official reports. This is especially the case for qualitative research into subjective and biographical aspects. Researchers, however, need support by local governments.

Just as the welfare state's regulation systems and welfare-state produced poverty have increased in complexity, so the state must concern itself more with inspecting and monitoring its operations. The very idea of evaluating or monitoring the effects of political measures and institutions has hardly been expressed in the German political system as a whole, let alone in social policy. Unlike the USA, where many statutory programmes are time-limited from the outset and may continue only if positively evaluated, in Germany measures which have once been introduced tend to have high staying power. This deficit is particularly noticeable in the field of poverty policy. Evaluation and the monitoring of effects were a blind spot in German poverty policies up to the mid 1990s and at the level of Federal government they still are. In the course of the small revolution in local government mentioned above, major municipalities have been introducing measures for monitoring the effectiveness of administrative processes as well as policy programmes, for example by use of benchmarking techniques. The general absence of any evaluative measures in poverty policy – or in any other policies with knock-on effects for poverty – is just one more sign of the residual character of this policy field.

By contrast, the Revenu Minimum d'Insertion (RMI), the lowest level income maintenance scheme in France, was deliberately introduced in 1989 on an experimental basis in order to amass experience of this type of measure and to provide for a systematic evaluation of the effects on the target population (Castel and Lae 1992, Schulte 1993, pp. 604–606). The first report was published and debated in the French Assembly in 1992. Similar examples in the USA include the Income Maintenance Experiments with new kinds of income and tax in Seattle and Denver (see Wiseman 1991a, Manski and Garfinkel 1992, Blank 1994) and earlier in New Jersey. The dynamic perspective on poverty is especially well designed – indeed, necessary – to help improve monitoring. Collecting process data is expensive but it is more suitable than static data as a basis for effective socio-political intervention: movies reveal more than stills do.

Two fields can be distinguished: the effects of Social Assistance itself, and the poverty-relevant effects of prior social security systems. Taking the latter first, German Social Insurance aims to maintain the income levels of people with 'standard' contribution records above the poverty line. However, the need to apply for Social Assistance can sometimes be ascribed to the inadequacy of prior insurance benefits.[7] More generally, we can distinguish three types of failure of prior systems which correspond to the three kinds of poverty caused by the welfare state analysed earlier (chapter 6, pp. 148f.):

administrative delay and *inefficiency* in delivering insurance benefits to the unemployed and old, who therefore have to wait for benefits which will eventually be paid;

the structural *ineffectiveness* of the insurance system showing inadequate benefits to people whose work records fall below the norm, for instance pensioners whose level and amount of contributions are not up to standard;

poor coordination between the social security systems themselves, and between them and other fields of policy or law. Notable examples include tax policy and the problem of coordination between the tax threshold and the minimum subsistence level according to Social Assistance law; policies applying to foreigners and asylum seekers and the prohibition of taking paid work; legal policy and the coordination of minimum income levels protected against attachment and the Social Assistance scales; and the question of benefits for released prisoners.[8]

---

[7] Contrary to a widely held belief, the proportion of claims caused by insufficient insurance benefits need not rise. For example, it did not rise between 1978 and 1991, mainly because insufficient Old-Age Pensions decreased in number (Leisering 1995c). This may change, however, with the lowering of Pensions ensuing from the 1997 Reform Act and with the increasing range of health services no longer publicly mandated.

[8] On the question of the coordination of different legal minima see Leibfried (1990).

In the 1990s the question of insufficient coordination has, however, been tackled in some fields, for example the prohibition of employment by asylum seekers has been relaxed, and the minimum subsistence income level has been declared tax-free according to a high court ruling. But no improvement in the effectiveness of income maintenance policies has been apparent. In order to test if a system achieves its goal of ensuring a given income replacement level for the standard citizen, one must discover how far reality deviates from the ideal of the 'standard pensioner' (*Eckrentner*; defined as a person with 45 years of full employment and average income). No such monitoring of the effectiveness of Social Insurance has yet been institutionalised. One policy conclusion which could be drawn is that the abolition of poverty or at least its minimisation should be firmly established as a goal of the Social Insurance system. Standards would have to be laid down to define the boundaries at which deviations from the 'normal' work record would be treated as problematic. For the first time this would offer criteria for identifying the poverty-relevant consequences of Social Insurance, and thus help to derive ideas for reform.

The effects of Social Assistance, the second field in which poverty policies can be monitored, also demand attention. In chapter 6 we already examined the question of whether Social Assistance makes its claimants passive and dependent, and answered it for the most part negatively. The most notable gap in the official analysis of the effects of the Federal Social Assistance Act is the absence of any information on 'latent poverty' or 'the hidden numbers in poverty': people who fail to claim Assistance although they are entitled to it. The total failure of politics to confront the problem of latent poverty stands in stark contrast to the fundamental significance of the state's guarantee of a minimum subsistence income for all citizens. The welfare state actually contributes to latent poverty through its 'passive institutionalisation' of Social Assistance (Leibfried 1977, p. 54), that is, the authorities make no outreach-effort to offer help to those who need it but who, out of ignorance or shame, avoid claiming. Outreach-efforts are interestingly more pronounced in Anglo-Saxon countries, especially when new programmes are legislated, like Supplemental Security Income (SSI) in the USA which aimed at the elderly and the disabled. The problem has hardly been taken up by the social sciences. Studies were mainly confined to the 1970s and 1980s, and suggest hidden poverty figures of around 50 per cent of those entitled (see the summary in Hauser and Hübinger 1993, pp. 52–54). One might assume that the numbers of the hidden would have tended to fall considerably, since those eligible for Social Assistance increasingly see it as their right. However, there are no recent empirical studies of the problem.

Active anti-poverty policies must expose not only the extent but also the causes of the failure to claim, if they are to identify the critical points for locating countermeasures. Apart from our filter model of selective Social Assistance claiming (Leibfried 1977, p. 62) there are few German contributions, chiefly Hauser and Hübinger (1993, pp. 122–129) and BMAS (1990, pp. 86–88). The situation is different in the UK. Jill Vincent *et al.* have shown (1991, pp. 11–20) how the circumstances of non-claiming behaviour can be explained by process analyses.

Regular reports on poverty and social conditions together with systematic monitoring would add up to what we termed 'reflexive policy'. In political terms, poverty policy would become aligned with other, more modernised, government departments in which a self-awareness of this kind has been institutionalised for far longer. In this way, too, the German welfare state's institutional and cultural division into a core indifferent to poverty and a neglected and marginalised poverty sector could be overcome. This would be a step in the direction of integrating anti-poverty policy with social policy as a whole.

Perspectives on reform: Germany and the USA compared

When comparing the concept of poverty policy outlined in this chapter – integrated and reflexive life-course policy – with the ideas of reform which Mary Jo Bane and David Ellwood developed for the USA on the basis of their dynamic analysis of poverty, the peculiarities of the German welfare state's approach to the life course are revealed. Bane and Ellwood put forward three demands: those who work should not be poor; both parents should remain responsible for the child's support even if they live apart; and the state's social services, above all Welfare benefits, ought to contain clear incentives to obtain paid work, both by offering the poor more support and by expecting more from them (1994, p. 143).

The work-centred model of the life course promoted by the American welfare-state regime was endorsed by Bane and Ellwood's proposals for reform. But they proposed to reduce the punitive aspects of workfare – the provision of compulsory work – in favour of a version similar to the original Swedish model based on active labour-market and family policy (see table 2.1 on p. 49). It is not universalistically aimed at the life-course patterns of the mass of the population, though, but, true to the American tradition, only offers minimal security for the lowest income groups in the population; it does not offer a full-blown life-course policy. The demand that poverty policy should be integrated into social policy also hardly plays a role in the USA, since the higher tiers of social security above the welfare level are only weakly developed (in the face of better private and occupational schemes). President Clinton's attempts to introduce a universal health insurance system would have changed this and relieved the Welfare system, which some claim only to obtain or maintain access to medical treatment, but the health reform was defeated (Hacker 1997, Skocpol 1997). Finally, Bane and Ellwood do not call for reflexive poverty policies, maybe because in America it is taken for granted far more that policy monitoring, or even income experiments, will be carried out than it is in Germany.

The routes out of poverty, as envisaged by Bane and Ellwood, always lead into the labour market, which means that long-term benefits for the able-bodied must be totally avoided. By contrast, in accordance with the assumptions of the German state-oriented approach to managing the life course, our model includes routes into the higher tiers of the welfare state and allows some individual cases to remain in a reformed Social Assistance system for longer periods or even for good. Periods of absence from the labour market caused by external forces such as the lack of job opportunities or sickness, or the demands of housework, care-giving or child-rearing, would all count as fundamentally legitimate and creating entitlements to support. Underpinning this is a broader conception of 'work' and of the state's involvement in the life course.

The condition set by Bane and Ellwood, that employment must pay adequately, is less urgent in Germany where there still are fewer 'working poor'. What however needs reform is women's pay. This point may become relevant to poverty in the future, since there are increasing political pressures for more low-paid jobs, and wage reductions in real terms can already be seen. The proposal that fathers living apart from their children should be compelled to contribute to their support, as guaranteed by the state, corresponds to the family policy aspects of our proposal for the integration of social and poverty policies, though it aims at a level of provisions already implemented in Germany. Finally, we subscribe to Bane and Ellwood's idea of offering welfare claimants more but also expecting more from them. Reducing support while expecting increased individual initiative is not a reasonable policy for Germany either.

12   Social inequality in transition

What does the fluidity of individual experiences of poverty tell us about the structures and processes of social inequality? If being in poverty is often just a phase, indicating horizontal inequalities in the life course, does this mean that vertical class inequalities have become irrelevant?

The changes which have taken place in the risks of poverty are connected to structural changes in our society, the consequences of which cannot yet be foreseen. The examination of life courses in a dynamic manner indicates deep-seated changes in the structure of social inequality. Traditional concepts such as 'class society', 'capitalism' or 'industrial society' no longer adequately encompass the new realities. The social sciences have not yet addressed these changes sufficiently to develop concepts with which these new emergent social structures can be analysed. The common terminology of 'post-industrial' or 'post-modern' society is used only to describe what no longer exists – without giving a precise picture of what is developing instead.

Among German sociologists, Ulrich Beck tried, in the mid 1980s, to describe the new perils inherent in post-industrial society with the term *Risk Society* (Beck 1992 [German edition, 1986]). In his view, the social question of the nineteenth century concerned the unequal distribution of material resources and has since been overtaken by the question of ecological risks and scientific-technological diswelfares. Unlike the 'old' social risks, the new risks affect all citizens irrespective of their social position: 'You can isolate want, but you cannot isolate the perils of the atomic age any longer' (1992 [German edition, 1986, p. 7]). At the same time, Beck suggests, there has been an individualisation of ways of living which cannot be put down to traditional class differences but which shows itself in a plurality of life plans and life courses. This also applies to social problem situations such as poverty or unemployment which have reappeared as major problems, though in a different form: they have become 'temporalised' and 'democratised'. This implies a new concept of social inequality seen as the outcome of fluctuations and breaks in life courses, whereby class differences are remodelled and vertical inequalities are obscured or even superseded by horizontal inequalities. Beck speaks of an *individualisation of inequality.*

By contrast, vertical inequalities have been emphasised in the German social policy debate under the name 'two-thirds society'. The phrase was coined in the 1980s by the social-democratic thinker and politician Peter Glotz (1984, 1985) to imply social polarisation (see pp. 188, 194f., 251–254). In the 1990s the discussion merged with the broader European debate on 'social exclusion', with increasing references to the earlier American debate over an *underclass* (see pp. 8, 249f.). In addition, the concept of 'global cities' (Sassen 1991) has been used by Jens Dangschat to examine segregated poverty in Germany (1994, 1995), and there is talk of an urban underclass (Häußermann and Kronauer 1999).

It has largely gone unnoticed that the theory of the Risk Society shares the assumption underlying these other approaches, namely that poverty is once again a structural feature of our society, and that it is not just a problem of traditional marginalised groups as it was during the years of the 'economic miracle' of the 1960s and early 1970s. Still, two diagnoses of our time are competing with each other (Leisering 1995a): advocates of the 'two-thirds society' model assume that risks are concentrated among a bottom third of the population doomed to stay there, while the Risk Society model assumes highly mobile individualised life courses in all sections of the population.

In sociology, Beck's view has been questioned by Karl Ulrich Mayer's quantitative analysis of life histories. Moreover, the concept of exclusion, besides its use in the social policy debate, has also received more attention in sociological theory (for Germany see, for example, Luhmann 1994 and Stichweh 1997). The concept seems to have assumed the role of a new approach to social inequality in general, maybe, amongst other reasons, because it seems better suited to account for divisions of gender and ethnicity than the traditional approaches which revolve around class.

'Inequality' or 'life course'? Rigidity and fluidity

From a life-course perspective, Martin Kohli maintains that inequalities in the life course call into question traditional models of inequality among social strata or classes. Often the life stage or age group in which individuals find themselves can explain social differences which cannot be ascribed to vertical occupationally defined inequalities (see Kohli 1986b, p. 186; 1990). Social inequality must be reconceptualised. Karl Ulrich Mayer (1991b) has even noted critically that proponents of the concept of individualisation actually replace 'inequality' by 'life course' as the chief structuring principle of society. But Kohli is less concerned to pose horizontal differences based on life courses in contradistinction to vertical class-based models of inequality than to try to integrate the two.

Traditional research into inequality has not excluded changes in life courses but has treated them as aspects of social mobility. Studies of social mobility pursue life courses usually by way of broad variables associated with occupation, such as father's job and one's own education and job. Using this framework Mayer and Blossfeld showed empirically (1990) that the life course reinforces and even creates – 'constructs' – vertical inequalities of class. In other words, there is no tension between class position and status change in the course of life but, instead, a close association. This fits in with Mayer's concept of the life course as a closed causal nexus (see pp. 37, 41). While students of class and occupational mobility emphasise the determination of social processes, the broader life-course perspective emphasises individual agency, change, choice and dynamics. For the vast majority of people thrown into poverty or forced on to benefit the experience is short-lived. While the deterministic view reminds us of the rigidities of class and gender that act as barriers or constraints to people's life trajectories, the alternative view emphasises the fluidity of social life, opening up chances for individual self-expression and life plans, for changing the direction of your life after periods of disruption.

These two conceptions, the latter also espoused by Giddens (1991), may appear to be diametrically opposed. However, there is a way to recognise the value of both perspectives and to deny that they are mutually exclusive. The two approaches focus on different aspects of social reality and rely on different levels of analysis.[1]

The conventional deterministic approach rests on statistical correlations of aggregate variables with a low temporal resolution such as 'class origin' and 'class destination' (e.g., Wright 1997), whereas the opponent approach typically employs high resolution measures of time and makes fine distinctions between different social states. Crossing the poverty line, for example increasing equivalent income from 45 per cent of the mean to 70 per cent, need not impact significantly on a person's class position nor set them on a trajectory to the top half of the income distribution. In Germany, most movers do not seem to make it much further, staying below mean income in the medium term (Krause 1998). Nevertheless, such changes usually have

---

[1] The rest of this section also shows that dynamic research does not neglect or even deny class or structural constraints on individual action, as claimed by some German critics of our study (e.g. Butterwegge 1996, Dangschat 1994, p. 880, and Gerstenberger 1994). Class analysis is of little avail when it comes to the study of poverty and marginality (see also chapter 1, pp. 12f., 17) and of complex life trajectories.

great personal significance for the individuals concerned and may well have major consequences for the roles they play within other social domains. Moves off social assistance also mark significant biographical changes as people break free from the associated stigma and attain self-sufficiency. From a policy perspective, moves of both types can be counted as relevant successes. Deterministic studies neglect changes of this order. 'Small' changes matter for the individuals and for politics even if some of them may not affect the overall pattern of social structure.

Inequality as a basic characteristic of Western societies is only acceptable under conditions of social mobility. The ideal of an open society requires removing barriers for social ascent. In a comprehensive comparative study Erikson and Goldthorpe (1992) found that historically there has indeed been more upward than downward mobility, resulting in a general upgrading of the stratification structure. That is, mobility has increased in absolute terms. But the openness or fluidity of the social hierarchy has not increased. That is, the rate of mobility has remained constant in relative terms: a 'constant flux' (Erikson and Goldthorpe 1992).

But again, small differences matter. Rather than stories of rags to riches embedded in the American dream we find 'changing fortunes' (see Duncan 1984), diverse risks and chances in individual lives. On the basis of the Michigan Panel Study of Income Dynamics (PSID), for example, Martha and Daniel Hill and Robert Walker (1998) found some general evidence of intergenerational transfer of poverty. But looking more closely at individual trajectories of young people during adolescence, following them through from the age of 15 to 30 years of age, they identified considerable upward and downward moves. Differences in mobility could in part be explained by individual behaviours of the youth as against parental background. Similarly, Esping-Andersen (1993, p. 232) emphasised significant occupational mobility among unskilled service workers, even if the broader picture is one of mainly short-range or medium-range moves.

In the 1980s and 1990s some students of class analysis began to use life-history data, panel data and event-history analysis that allow for a high temporal resolution in analysing individual processes (see Walker and Leisering 1998 for an overview of dynamic research methods). Karl Ulrich Mayer, for example, established the German Life-Course Study as a quantitative approach to life-course research. This elaborate type of analysis, however, has a specific focus:

the emphasis is on isolated strands of the life course, above all on occupational careers of men (for recent examples see Allmendinger and Hinz 1998 and DiPrete *et al.* 1997), or on marital careers;

there is more interest in general patterns of careers than in specific risks like unemployment, poverty, illness or deviance (see chapter 1, p. 17);

the approach is based on quantitative data;

and the data analysis is variable-oriented rather than case-oriented.

In this way, broader patterns of social structure are well captured, but much of the complexity and fluidity of individual life courses is missed.

An alternative approach would seek to combine two or more strands of the life course, to tune to risks rather than general career patterns, to use qualitative data in addition, and to analyse single cases and group them in typologies. This type of approach also adopted in this study exposes more fluidity of social life. Examples include Uta Gerhardt's analysis of 'patient careers' (1986a), the study by Frank Furstenberg *et al.* on 'Adolescent Mothers in Later Life' (1987) and Judith Wallerstein and Sandra Blakeslee's longitudinal study of the consequences of divorce, *Second Chances* (1989), which by the title already suggests the approach adopted. It is not by coincidence that Anthony Giddens (1991) starts his first chapter with a depiction of the optimistic results of the latter study.

Uta Gerhardt, in particular, has developed an elaborate methodology, rooted in Weber and structural functionalism, that has been used in medical sociology although it has a broader scope (Gerhardt 1999b; for further references and an application to Social Assistance careers see chapter 5). This methodology enables researchers to analyse social inequality from a biographical perspective, to link structure and action. In Gerhardt's study of patient careers (1986a) the biographical analysis of individual cases (patients) is linked to structural aspects of society in several ways.

First, the life of each person in the sample is analysed by way of differentiating several biographical strands: the occupational biography, the financial biography, the familial biography and the course of medical treatment. This reflects the structural differentiation of modern society in different functional spheres. Second, the action of each person is analysed in the light of the normative models prevalent in society, for example occupational advancement for men of working age. This reflects socio-cultural structures of society. Third, by a complex process of analysing and comparing single cases, ideal types or rather typologies are constructed at various stages of the analysis, culminating in structural types of 'careers' as the essence of the study. These career types typify the ways in which individual action and social institutions or structures interact. Fourth, the structural types are correlated with conventional socio-demographic variables such as class, gender, age, etc. to see how social inequalities affect the types. These aggregate variables only come in at the final stage of the analysis to leave room for diversity in the case-oriented empirical analysis done at a previous stage. The action-theoretical types can be expected to correlate to a degree with the conventional variables but they do not normally coincide with any of them (for analyses of inequalities of social risks see also Gerhardt 1985, 1987).

Ulrich Beck does not deny class or the persistence of income inequality either. In his *Risk Society* he rather pointed at changes in social structure 'beyond class and status', as the title of an earlier article (1983) goes, that is changes not adequately accounted for in class analysis (although Beck traced the germs of his individualisation thesis to Weber and Marx). The factors that in his view cut across the categories of class analysis include the 'elevator effect' by which the entire hierarchy of incomes and patterns of consumption is lifted; changes in the time structure of the life course, above all the decrease of paid work as a share in the (male) life span; and the expansion of higher education which has especially benefitted women. These changes, which derive from an analysis of Germany's economic rise and the expansion of its welfare state in the post-war period, add up to new ways of living (*Lebensformen*) that coexist with class but qualify the social relevance of class inequality for individual lives. This results in what Beck terms the 'individualisation of inequality' which includes a pluralisation of life styles and a 'temporalisation' of risks such as poverty and unemployment.

Martin Kohli has outlined a model for the study of inequality that elaborates the time dimension of individual life situations and the subjective meaning attached to them while retaining an interest in the structural foundations of inequality. The aim is to link 'life course' and 'inequality', life-course research and traditional class analysis, action and structure, fluidity and rigidity.[2]

When Kohli calls for *'a biographical concept of social inequality'* (1990, p. 399), he aims to provide an integrative model of the structure of inequality which is more refined and related to action than allowed by the traditional sociological variables used in class analysis. What must be investigated are 'the structural conditions and processes which maintain continuity or permit discontinuity' (ibid.). In order to 'imbue its theoretical apparatus with a sense of time', four aspects of inequality must in Kohli's view be given more weight than hitherto: the duration of a status position (because inequality at the individual level is always measured in terms of duration); the sequences of changes in position, whether rising or falling in the social scale; the ways in which such changes are structured, especially by institutional control; and the biographical perspective of those affected: how they locate their lives in relation to class and reference groups.

Kohli's integrative approach derived from his research on the standardised life course and its major discontinuities, above all the transition to old

---

[2] As a conclusion of their study, Erikson and Goldthorpe (1992, p. 397) similarly plead for extending the scope of class mobility analysis to include microsociological process analysis, coping strategies of the individuals in question, and case studies.

age. The findings of our research into poverty situations suggest extending the scope of Kohli's idea: 'minor' and less standardised discontinuities such as the risks of poverty, illness and unemployment, also contribute to moulding socio-economic inequality in temporal and biographical terms ('temporalisation', 'biographisation'); and this temporal structure, as in the case of the major breaks between the age-related stages of life, is largely shaped by the institutions of the welfare state. In chapter 2 we treated these institutions as aspects of the welfare state's 'risk management' – managing individual contingencies through Unemployment Insurances, Health Insurance, Social Assistance or social work -, in contrast to those institutions that deal with the major breaks and long-term perspectives in people's lives, chiefly educational and training services and insurance for old age.

In chapters 1 and 2 we showed that the study of marginalised groups in Germany has been isolated from the general study of social inequality in, for instance, education and occupation. Our work seeks to link the two by showing that even research into the margins of society can profit from an awareness of the time dimension and individual biographical aspects of inequality, beyond the common focus on downward careers. Indeed, such an awareness is indispensable if the long-underestimated heterogeneity of marginal groups is to be acknowledged. To the extent that higher social classes are also affected by those non-standardised perilous contingencies of life, their life courses too are significantly marked by the timing and course of such perils.

In our study, all four of Kohli's temporal dimensions figure as important to an understanding of the situation of poverty: the duration of being poor is highly variable and often short. The sequences of status change also proved to be multifarious: 'careers' in this field do not necessarily reflect downward mobility, even when those affected remain in a low economic position for a long time. The welfare state is a significant institutional director in structuring life courses. Among our respondents we also found a variety of biographical orientations which were not determined by their exiguous material circumstances. Some respondents aspired towards wider horizons in the future; they were not fixed immovably by their problems into one social position. Uta Gerhardt's methodology of qualitative analysis also implies a comprehensive biographical concept of social inequality already tried in several studies.

Periods of transition: the politics of functional poverty

Individual biographical perspectives are related to collective perspectives of reference groups or society at large. In particular, socio-economic aspirations are influenced by the future prospects of the economy and social development. The experience of poverty and disadvantage, therefore, is not only located in one's own biography (individual time) but also in the context of on-going social change (historical time). In fact, individuals seem to be more inclined to accept living in poverty and cope better with it when they interpret it as the effect of some larger social change assumed to be transitional. In this case a critical life stage (individual time) is seen to be related to a critical stage of social development (historical time).

This would apply, for example, to times of want during war and post-war reconstruction. Generally, poverty or increased inequality could be considered inevitable or even necessary during a critical historical phase. A link between individual and societal prospects could also be observed during the years of unbroken economic growth in the 1960s and early 1970s in Germany when poorer people could realistically hope for betterment in years to come. Poverty may even be deemed 'productive' if the critical phase is expected to be transitional, leading to a state of society beneficial to all citizens. Such poverty could be politically justified by reference to a *productivist concept of justice* that would temporarily allow to relieve the *distributive concept of justice* which dominates much of welfare-state thinking (Vobruba 1996). In the field of poverty, the idea of 'productive' or *'functional' poverty* has a long tradition.

The functionalist approach to poverty set forth by Herbert Gans in the *Positive Functions of Poverty* (1972, 1992) suggests that poverty persists because the poor fulfill a variety of functions for the rest of society. They consume, for example, spoilt and devalued consumption goods and do the dirty work. These functions are still carried out smoothly even when there is constant change in the composition of those doing them. In the USA, low-paid jobs may be a staging post in the careers of new immigrants. From this perspective, at times of far-reaching change in the social and economic systems there is a 'functional need' to shift the burden of the costs of social change on to the lower social groups, for instance in making workers redundant when industries decline, or as a result of people being uprooted and forced to move elsewhere. John Kenneth Galbraith linked the functionalist view to the underclass debate by speaking of a 'functional underclass' (1992). We could interpret this concept as describing a fluctuating lower section of the population, on to whom the undesirable concomitants of social change are dumped.[3] In this way, the critical impetus of the idea of an underclass can be retained and combined with the dynamic view. 'Temporalised' poverty would then appear as a buffer in times of drastic social change, during a period of societal transition.

---

[3] Galbraith himself mixes assumptions about permanent membership in the 'functional underclass' with assumptions about fluctuation (1992, pp. 30–41).

The notion of 'functional' or 'productive' poverty is not just a theoretical concept devised by Herbert Gans or John Kenneth Galbraith, but it is an important strategic tool in the political process. The suggestion that thoroughgoing economic restructuring is accompanied by social upheaval and deprivation, and indeed is impossible without it, was already developed in the early Industrial Revolution in England, for example by thinkers like Frederick Eden (Leisering 1989, pp. 136f.). Poverty was not, or not only, seen as a regrettable concomitant of social transformation, but it was considered functionally requisite to economic growth. Thus wages had to be forced down, as early economists such as David Ricardo and Thomas Malthus claimed. Political indifference to poverty could thus be rationalised. There was also a movement to abolish the Poor Law, climaxing in the 1810s, which led to considerable social unrest among the labouring population. Karl Polanyi (1945, pp. 44–46) critically analysed the calculated optimism of the liberal economic justification of poverty. The current poverty of some people was justified in terms of the (expected) future welfare of all.

Drawing on Niklas Luhmann we can trace the idea of 'productive poverty' back historically to a 'functional primacy' of the economic system. In an analysis of the differentiation of the economic system in the nineteenth century, Luhmann claimed that a societal sub-system, in this case the economy, could for a limited period of time assume a functional precedence over the other functional sub-systems, that is, impose its function on them. This would only be feasible during an 'evolutionary bottle-neck' phase, identified by Luhmann in the breakthrough of industrial capitalism in the nineteenth century. During this transitional period, the widespread suffering of the working classes was ignored by the economic elites – and from this functionalist viewpoint had to be ignored in order to facilitate economic development (Luhmann 1970, p. 227).

In contemporary German society, poverty is linked to three momentous social transitions: to economic and political deregulation, designed to adapt the German economy to the demands of globalisation; to the social transformation of a totalitarian socialist society to democratic welfare capitalism in East Germany; and to repeated waves of international crisis which result in masses of refugees and migrants coming into Germany.

In the first field, *deregulation*, competitiveness in the world market is claimed by economic liberals to require lower wages, lower standards of social security and a relaxation of industrial law both to increase incentives to take up employment and to shift parts of national income from consumption to investment. The underlying notion is that reductions in material welfare will be transitional, since low wages and insecure employment are expected to create new jobs and kindle economic growth to benefit all.

The *transformation in East Germany*, the second field in which functional poverty is at issue, was emphatically defined as transitory by the Kohl government. In fact, no 'blood, sweat and tears' speech was deemed necessary by the Chancellor, and no special taxes or levies were introduced to meet the massive cost, with the exception of the Solidarity Surcharge (*Solidaritätszuschlag*) of 5.5 per cent on income tax. Likewise, planners in the Federal Ministry of Labour and Social Affairs expected that social spending could be reduced from the exceptional 73 per cent of Gross Social Product in 1992 to 48 per cent in 1997 (BMAS 1994a, p. 173). By promising normalisation of the situation in this way, the attendant diswelfares both for East Germans and West Germans could be depicted as limited in scope and duration. In actual fact, the figure only fell to 55 per cent (BMAS 1998, p. 190). Wages were (and still are) fixed by industrial agreement at significantly lower levels than in the West to account for low productivity and to facilitate competitiveness. Even public sector employees receive only 86.5 per cent of Western salaries (1998).

The constitutional debate in the wake of unification illustrates our point. The introduction of basic social rights – the right to work, the right to adequate housing and the right to social security – was rejected by the Joint Constitutional Commission of both Chambers of Parliament (*Gemeinsame Verfassungskommission von Bundestag und Bundesrat*) in 1992/93. The government welcomed this decision because social rights would have meant 'significant dangers for the Social Market Economy with its open organisation of economic, industrial and social relations and its characteristic capacity of adapting to new and changing conditions in a flexible way' (BMAS 1994a, p. 23). This implies a notion of functional inequality, the assumption that social diswelfares have to be accepted because economic growth would be stifled by too high levels of wages and social services (cf. Leisering and Mädje 1996). However, this was a strategy of functional inequality, not of functional poverty as can be seen from the massive increase in social spending that prevented poverty and dependence on Social Assistance to emerge on a larger scale (see chapter 8).

In the third field, *migration*, the situation has also been mostly defined as transitional. The early migrant workers coming to Germany from Mediterranean countries since the late 1950s were referred to as 'guest workers' (*Gastarbeiter*). This may have helped to ignore the often miserable conditions of work and housing to which they were subjected. In the 1990s, war refugees from Bosnia were also expected to return to their home country in due course. Asylum seekers as well as some war refugees receive Asylum Seekers Benefit, which is inferior to Social Assistance. In many cases, however, the assumption of a limited stay in Germany proves to be erroneous, yet discriminatory benefits are retained (even if the level of benefits may be raised in individual cases). This also applies to the numerous people whose applications for asylum were rejected but who are tolerated to live in Germany. Even if poverty among immigrants continues to be justified, among other reasons, by the transitional nature of their stay in Germany and the low standard of living in their home countries, this poverty can hardly be seen as 'productive'. It is produced or at least tolerated by the state, but rather with a view to deter future immigrants than to act as an incentive to work hard and integrate oneself into German society. The 'multi-cultural society' invoked by intellectuals and some municipal governments never materialised.

What follows for the politics of inequality and poverty? Strategies for social change that rely on poverty as a resource to facilitate societal transitions, justified by a productivist concept of justice, are to be judged on their own premises: do they succeed in making diswelfares – low wages, low social security benefits, discontinuous 'flexible' employment, low-skill jobs and mass unemployment – transitional phenomena that lead to increased welfare for all after a period of social reconstruction? Or, if some of these diswelfares turn out to persist longer than expected or are even accepted as a permanent structural requisite of society, do they affect people only at certain life stages, that is, are they transitory in individual lives even if not in the historical 'life' of society at large? We delineate two criteria for the evaluation of strategies that build on functional poverty, followed by four conditions or premises of their success.

First of all, the evaluation of policies of 'productive' diswelfares depends on whether such diswelfares can be confined to transitional periods in people's lives. With regard to unskilled service jobs, for instance Gøsta Esping-Andersen (1993, p. 241) argues in a similar way: such jobs may offer opportunities for youth entering the labour market, for women lacking skills or for immigrants. As long as they remain stopgaps in the lives of these persons, social exclusion can be avoided. The debate on the social consequences of deregulation has been marred by simplistic confrontations. Looking at the problems involved in this dynamic way might provide a common ground for economic liberals and social democrats to discuss the issues in a productive manner.

The second criterion for policies based on the concept of functional poverty refers to the welfare state. Countries differ with regard to the support and protection they offer to people in lower social positions. 'Functional poverty', if seen from a neoliberal perspective, may just mean leaving people to fend for themselves. But it may also imply institutional support for these people to ensure that their situation is confined to a transitional period. From this point of view, those who call for more functional poverty must be prepared to invest more, not less in institutional support for the poor. As Katherine McFate put it in her article 'Trampolines, Safety Nets, or Free Fall' (1995, p. 657): 'Trampolines require strong, flexible safety nets. To bounce back into the mainstream, one cannot be allowed to fall too close to the ground or languish there too long.' Similarly, Esping-Andersen (1996, p. 17) emphasised that a low-pay sector in the economy requires 'active social investment' in the skills of the workers if the emergence of a class of permanent working poor, disincentives to work and rising expenditure on social assistance are to be avoided.

Advocates of the welfare state have always emphasised its positive functions for a capitalist economy (Vobruba 1989, 1991). Building bridges for people at critical stages of their lives, and in particular offering pathways out of poverty (see chapter 11), could be an increasingly important function of the welfare state in an age of deregulation and flexibilisation: a strategy of 'productive poverty' would elicit the 'productive welfare state' (Leisering and Leibfried 1996).

In practice, historical transitions will always produce winners and losers. Some people will suffer permanent losses. It may take a generation to take full advantage of newly emerging opportunities. Some historical transitions only impinge upon a phase in the lifetime of the people affected while more far-reaching transitions require adaptations that cannot be achieved during the life of one generation. The impact of the transformation in East Germany, for instance, is graded by generation (Mayer 1994). For the middle-aged it was too late to adapt their careers to the needs and opportunities of a market economy. The elderly fared well at least with respect to security of income because the West German Old-Age Insurance scheme was readily extended to the East.

Whether functional poverty is made a transitional experience in people's lives, and whether institutional support is offered during these transitions – these are two key criteria for evaluating policies that use poverty strategically. In addition, there are four conditions or prerequisites for the success of such policies.

First, their success obviously depends on socio-economic conditions that cannot be fully controlled by politics. If the economy does not provide enough openings, individual periods of socio-economic deprivation may drag on. For example, Esping-Andersen (1993, p. 231) reports that unskilled service jobs are transitional stopgap jobs in all advanced Western countries, except in Germany, where mobility among this group is low. In these countries the alleged new service proletariat is, therefore, 'not a class, but people temporarily willing or forced to take unpleasant jobs' (p. 239). We should add that even in countries hailed as models of job creation such as Britain or The Netherlands, unemployment is still high if judged by standards common in Western democracies only ten years ago.

The second prerequisite to successful strategic poverty management is a clear-cut and open definition of the situation in question as either transitional or of a more long-term nature. Policies will differ depending on which of the two definitions is adopted. Depicting German unification as a short-lived period of transition may have helped to sustain confidence among both East and West Germans to put up with the burdens of this sudden and unforeseen change. After almost a decade, with East Germany still lagging behind economically and the tension between Western and Eastern lifestyles and mentalities still existing, the drawbacks of this strategy show. Discontentments among the East Germans linger, and the economy and the public administration in the East continue to require considerable cash transfers from the West, making it even more difficult to reduce the soaring public debt.

The immigration by workers from Turkey and other Mediterranean countries in the 1960s and 1970s was similarly misinterpreted as transitory. Although many of these workers and their families stayed, their social integration has never been a major political issue at the Federal level. Hence in the 1990s Germany is still faced with problems of social integration – unemployment, behavioural problems, emerging religious fundamentalism and segregation – even among the third generation of the former immigrants. So not even the succession of generations could accomplish the transition to settling in German society.

The third prerequisite to successful policies of transition is related to the decision about the level and degree of poverty to be inflicted on a part of the population. If the poverty threshold is set at a fairly high level, the strategy of functional poverty turns into a strategy of functional inequality: accepting an increase in inequality for the sake of societal restructuring but avoiding poverty in a strict sense by adequate institutional support. This strategy has by and large been adopted during the transformation in East Germany (see chapters 8 and 9).

The fourth point refers to the people affected. Societal transitions, individual transitions, generational transitions – any policy confronting these challenges must take into account the perceptions and interpretations by the citizens as the agents of social change. The schedules laid down by planners in public departments may be at variance with the biographical horizons and views to be found in the population. While the people immediately affected, such as Social Assistance claimants, tend to have a fairly clear picture of the (mostly) transitional or (less frequently) long-term nature of their situation of need (see the qualitative analysis in chapter 4, above all the 'subjective bridger'), the general public is saturated with the image that entrenched long-term poverty and unemployment are the typical case. It seems to be difficult to comprehend that far-reaching social changes as indicated by the long-term rise of aggregate indicators such as the rate of unemployment may impinge on most individuals only during limited life phases. Using terms of the sociological debate: growing insecurity and instability of life courses – signalling fluidity – is often mistaken as wholesale social exclusion – signalling rigidity (see pp. 249–251).

Among politicians distorted perceptions of this kind go hand in hand with a strategic use of images of poverty. These may vary on a scale between denial and dramatisation (see pp. 196–199). When society is in the midst of a transition laden with social problems, politicians may resort to a strategy of denying or playing down poverty. This approach can be used to justify some drastic economic cure, even when it is clear that not all of the poverty of the transformation will be temporary and that even transient periods of poverty may leave their traces in some people's lives. This sort of denial is compatible with a negative dramatisation in which economic problems are blamed on the victims. An example is the claim that unemployed workers prevent the labour market from clearing (as simple market theory expresses it) by refusing to work at wages below the agreed rate. In such cases, poverty is being treated as a necessary condition for economic growth.

13 Individual lives and the welfare state: recasting the German welfare regime

New kinds of social inequality are not unquestionable givens. They are susceptible to political action. Even if poverty risks are related to structural social change, this still does not justify acquiescence. Ulrich Beck himself does not treat the identification of a Risk Society as grounds for pessimism. He would much rather emphasise the necessity of political debate and offer openings for argument about alternative perspectives for society. This is what he calls *'political self-reflection about risk'* (Beck 1991, p. 11).

From the mid 1990s the welfare state has been under more pressure than ever before. Fiscal constraints foster cuts in social spending, demographic changes endanger the viability of social security systems, and poor economic performance and mass unemployment are traced to disincentives and high labour costs created by the welfare state, especially in the context of intensified European integration and economic globalisation. Political support for comprehensive state welfare has reached a low. While in some quarters the concept of the welfare state has always been rejected as such, in others, represented for instance by Franz-Xaver Kaufmann (1997), it is asked more precisely which changes over the last 25 years may have transformed the positive economic, social and political effects of the welfare state, which explain its historical success in Europe, into negative ones.[1] Some of these changes are external to the welfare state, while others are produced by the welfare state itself. From this point of view, Kaufmann identifies a set of heterogeneous challenges currently facing the welfare state, in contrast both to a wholesale rejection of the welfare state and to Social-Democratic – and Christian-Democratic – conservativism of the German variety which until the mid 1990s insisted on preserving the status quo.

When welfare states shape individual life courses (chapter 2), the debates about reforming or dismantling the welfare state are at the same time

---

[1] Manfred G. Schmidt (1998, pp. 293f.) balances positive against negative effects by taking stock of the existing empirical studies. See also Lampert (1995) and Leibfried (1998).

debates about reshaping life courses. The common argument in the political debate asserts that the mobilisation of labour, capital and knowledge requires more open, more flexible, and more fluid ways of life. Current socio-economic challenges clearly bear upon individual life trajectories: economic challenges raise the issue of redefining phases of work and non-work and their linkages in the life course; gender challenges require rethinking the differences between male and female 'normal biographies' (pp. 34, 50f.); and demographic challenges urge revisions of the age structuration of the life span as defined by social norms and institutions.

In this concluding chapter we sketch a potential path of movement from welfare state to welfare society as a response to current challenges. With the term 'welfare society' we do not mean to reduce society to the economic market (more or less explicitly supplemented by the family) as some liberals have done ever since the nineteenth century (see Pinker 1979, p. 81). Rather we think of new welfare mixes in a pluralist, differentiated society with a variety of social actors, norms, relationships and institutions. Common, simplistic oppositions of an omnicompetent state with an unfettered free market, of the 'state' versus the 'individual', of 'public' and 'private' are less than helpful in tackling the current task of recasting the social contract. We delineate three challenges for policy-makers and citizens, three interrelated fields and levels of reform and innovation in social policy. These challenges are:

> to renew the commitment to *citizenship* as a basic value of our society: to secure social rights for both old and new disadvantaged groups, to make clear decisions about which forms of inequality are unacceptable and which are tolerable;
>
> complementary to this first challenge, to redefine *social responsibilities*: to require accountability for social diswelfares and to impose duties both on holders of social rights and on those who cause diswelfares;
>
> to reform and create *institutions* that shield citizens against the increasing risks of life and, at the same time, are adapted to new flexible ways of living – leading to an integrated structure of state and non-state institutions, of welfare policies and more general regulatory policies that serve as a framework for non-state welfare production.

Renewing social citizenship

The first challenge to the welfare state is to ascertain what social inequalities and exclusions ought to be readdressed or overcome. Women in particular continue to be more disadvantaged in Germany than in other Western countries: in the labour market, in insurance for old age, and in attempts to combine employment with family life, often because of inadequate child-care provision. Politicians and citizens have got to make up their minds what opportunities in life they want to offer disadvantaged groups among women, children, foreigners and people with low incomes. Are they prepared to mobilise resources – cash and personnel – in order to ensure that the poor and those who lack occupational qualifications are enabled to take a decent part in social life, that women are guaranteed equal opportunities throughout life and that children get their full rights? These are value choices. Rather than, as is done for example in the case of lone mothers claiming social assistance, blaming social problems on 'dependence' or moral degradation – notions largely refuted by dynamic poverty research (see chapter 6) – we are called upon to make choices about the ways we want to live.

Privileges and disadvantages are often introduced and entrenched without public debate or decision. Tax allowances often create much greater costs and inequities than direct welfare benefits about which there is so much public dispute. Inequalities which result from political decisions and may even be their hidden goal, ought to be laid open so that they can be publicly evaluated in terms of the basic values of our society.

During the 1950s and 1960s broader sections of the population succeeded in gaining economic and social rights and opportunities. The German Old-Age Pensions Reform Act of 1957 aimed for the first time to secure for the elderly an independent life at a financial level comparable to that which they enjoyed during working life. The poor came closer to full citizen status through the introduction of modern Social Assistance in 1962. Women have been among the winners of the boom in higher education which started in the 1960s.

But we have to recognize that citizenship continues to present political challenges. New problem groups face barriers to social inclusion assumed to have been removed long ago. These include groups such as the unemployed and foreigners, both long-time residents and new immigrants. A section of the long-term unemployed forms a new marginal group while other people affected by social problems cannot be easily grouped under old labels like 'marginal' or 'disadvantaged' group. Temporary situations of need in the lives of citizens, insecure life trajectories that reach well into the middle classes – the 'social transcendence' of poverty (chapter 10) – are new challenges to the quest for citizenship. Overindebtedness among consumers, the need for care in old age which even members of the middle classes find hard to afford, and the new poverty of children are examples of this diverse set of social problems. They require new, imaginative policies – 'life-course policies' – rather than conventional welfare policies directed to well-defined disadvantaged groups (cf. chapter 11). The 'working poor' – a term hitherto unknown in the German debate – might also become a problem group (Strengmann-Kuhn 1997, Schäfer 1997). In a German study the situation of working people whose income is just above the Social Assistance level has been described as 'precarious welfare' (Hübinger 1996). At a time when real incomes stagnate or even fall and demands on individuals and families to cope with rapidly changing social conditions increase, this last group is especially likely to need attention.

It usually takes time before new problem situations become politically acknowledged as issues requiring action. In Bonn, unemployment took two decades, from 1974 to 1994, to become a key political platform issue – and it was a similar story at the European level. The attention paid to foreigners still focuses on asylum seekers, war refugees, illegal immigrants and crime, but little has been done to further the integration of resident foreigners in educational, occupational and socio-cultural life, even though Germany has in the meantime acquired the largest proportion of foreigners in Europe after Luxembourg – an extreme and special case – and Belgium. And children remain outsiders, irrespective of rhetorical declarations to the contrary.

Extending social accountability

State intervention in people's lives can only be justified and promoted if the rights of citizens are balanced by social duties and responsibilities. This is the second challenge to the policies of the welfare state.[2] Decisions about social rights incur costs. The redistribution of social resources will require encroachments on the privileges of ownership. During radical social change, fundamental value commitments are put to a severe test. For instance, as medical costs and the number of old people both rose in recent years, we soon saw apparently undisputed basic assumptions about society melting away, including the idea that all citizens have an equal stake in the essential security of their existence. The elderly were then suddenly treated as no more than a 'burden' which 'cannot be financed'. Are we prepared to accept the putative or actual negative side effects of social policy measures on the economy or on public finance? These questions reach beyond technical matters of finance. They concern the underlying collective beliefs of society, the 'moral economy' of social relationships. They demand a new 'social contract'.

The idea of duty is commonly used in the social policy debate in a narrow sense, referring to obligations to (paid) work, to individuals (rather than companies or other corporate actors) and to claimants of state services

---

[2] Compare this with the North American discussion on entitlements and obligations in social policy (Mead 1986, 1992). On the question of responsibility see Kaufmann (1992).

(rather than taxpayers). The basic idea is that people have a duty to work to support themselves, while admitting to a varying degree that those who are not fit for work may be supported by society (for the USA see Mead 1986). 'Work' conventionally means paid employment, and only on second thought is household work taken into account, and then usually (in this context) referring only to the care of dependants.

But people's life courses are not defined, in Germany at least, solely by their employment and family. People are integrated into society through a wide range of roles, and in developed welfare societies their solidarity is enhanced by their roles as tax and contribution payers, as volunteers in a wide range of activities and generally as socially engaged citizens. In addition, the state lays down laws which emphasise and even constitute the individual's duty to fulfill prior obligations, such as the duty of parents to support an adult child who becomes poor, or of a man to pay alimony to his divorced wife.

Who is challenged by the new kinds of poverty problems? Ulrich Beck claims that the new ecological and technological risks are harder to attribute to their causes than the old questions of social welfare were (1991, p. 10). Cause, blame and responsibility cannot be so clearly determined. He therefore calls for political debate about new forms of accountability. In this section we aim to show that causal attribution is similarly difficult for social risks under conditions of advanced modernity. The expansion and the restructuring of the welfare state historically always went together with shifts in the public discourse about whom or what to hold responsible (see Ewald 1993). New discourses over attribution are on the agenda – and therefore also new conflicts over distribution: who can be held liable for the new types of poverty and who should contribute to financing redistributive measures?

Even in Germany, the state is not the only body with authority to deal with social problems. There is no state 'social monopoly' for the implementation of social measures, even if a long tradition of German thought and welfare policy might suggest otherwise. However, the state does have a monopoly of accountability. It has the exclusive responsibility for laying down who has which duty and what is necessary to ensure the wellbeing of its citizens. The state does not itself have to act; it has done its duty when it ensures that social forces can reliably deal with problems by laying down and safeguarding private duties. The state thus acts only as regulator.[3]

---

[3] With 'regulation' we refer to the Anglo-American usage of the term: the creation of legal rights and duties for third parties, involving the state only as an overseer and standard-setter (see, e.g., Majone 1994b,c; for a similar German usage see Mayntz 1983). This usage has become quite important at the EU level – and for European social policy – due to the peculiar multi-level construction of the European Union (see Majone 1994a, b, 1993). See section 'Reforming and Creating Institutions' below.

Similar monopolies over the ascription of responsibility exist in all welfare states (Girvetz 1968), even to a degree in the USA. This corresponds with Kaufmann's (1997) conceptualisation of the welfare state as consisting of two components: state responsibility for the wellbeing of its citizens as a general political goal – in Germany even mandated by the constitution – and the actual social services designed to implement this goal. The welfare goal itself does not prescribe any particular benefit schemes or services.

If material problems are to be solved, there must be some redistribution among social groups. The costs of dealing with the problems facing certain groups must be attributed to someone. This is done when, so to speak, 'the rich', 'those at the top' or 'the better-off' are asked to give more, such as paying higher taxes so that social services can be expanded. But this idea is limited, since redistribution in the welfare state, especially as the basis of social insurance, is mainly a horizontal redistribution across the life course. It has been called 'redistribution within one class' because the benefit claimants themselves pay for their benefits before or afterwards (partially or wholly) through taxes and contributions. It is hardly conceivable how it could be otherwise in a welfare state which insures the majority of the population at a high level. In effect, the welfare state smoothes out individuals' income fluctuations over the life cycle (for evidence from the UK see Falkingham and Hills 1995, chapter 5).

Social Assistance corresponds most closely to the old model of redistribution from the top downwards. But because of the wider class boundaries of need and the fact that most episodes are only temporary, the reality here, too, is that most claimants have paid taxes for their own benefits. Moreover, in Germany, Social Assistance cash benefits for periods of six months or less can be administered as repayable loans.

The new kinds of poverty raise questions of attribution which cannot adequately be answered by simply calling for more (or less) top–down redistribution by the state. Four examples from real life suggest some new approaches to attribution and accountability: (a) *debt,* (b) *child poverty,* (c) the material consequences of *divorce,* and (d) collective social problems such as the social disruptions in *East Germany* after unification and *mass unemployment* in the whole of Germany.

One can see the range of potential forms of causal attribution in these examples, and the kinds of arguments they raise. The old contradistinctions between 'individual fault' and 'social environment', or between 'state provision' and 'self-help' are simplistic and contribute little to finding solutions. Poverty can also be attributed to third parties, whether to individuals such as marriage partners (in the case of divorce) or to collectivities such as businesses, banks or even the state (in the case of debt). Or the attempt to attribute causation or responsibility to individuals or institutions could be dropped altogether, and the community as a whole be unequivocally charged with dealing with the risks (for instance in the case of the transformation in East Germany).

Many problems which can no longer be attributed to individuals, such as child poverty or mass unemployment, are currently treated in an ambiguous manner and thus located in an unstable grey zone: many people still cling to the notion of individual responsibility while others accept collective responsibility. Simply dismantling the welfare state implies wholesale attribution to the individuals in need, forcing them to bear the ensuing diswelfares or even to accept the blame for them and thus ignoring the intricate web of accountability that underlies the social problem in question and which might suggest avenues – actors, interests and resources – of dealing with it in a preventive or curative way.

(a) Debt

The debate on the debt problem shows that, under the pressure of conditions, new attributions have become plausible which in the past were treated as unrealistic. Indebtedness[4] was for a long time treated as a classical sign of individual failure, as the extreme form of economic misbehaviour in a society based on the idea of consumer sovereignty (as liberal economists characterise it) which included in its creed the individual's freedom to spend. Social policy in Germany has long responded to this problem in an equally individualistic manner, at best by debt counselling. By contrast, business debt traditionally has been dealt with in an institutionalised way, by settling with creditors or by employing a receiver in bankruptcy, which allow for a relatively secure new start with a clean slate, free of debt.

In Germany, a Reform of the Insolvency Law, which has been effective from 1 January 1999 (Schmidt-Räntsch 1994), regulates the insolvencies of both businesses and individuals. The extension of the bankruptcy provisions to private households is a fundamental change of attitude, recognising the social context which leads people into debt. This raises the question of the duty of creditors, chiefly the banks. Those who, in the course of business, used to offer 'generous' credit to people with insecure incomes, are now required, subject to legal regulation, to surrender some of their claims, something which previously had to be individually negotiated and was granted as a mercy. Debts remaining after seven years will be liquidated.

---

[4] *Debt* or *indebtedness*, being in debt, are terms used in this context for the problematic situation in which a person is unable to meet scheduled repayments on credit, loan or mortgage arrangements (overindebtedness). It is not generally used for the normal situation of being 'in debt' by reason simply of having such arrangements, as long as scheduled repayments are being made as agreed.

There is a generalised, institutionalised 'product liability' which is designed to relieve people in their struggle to get out of debt. However, the statutory provisions go nowhere near as far as the demands during the policy debate calling for the banks to accept extensive responsibility. Nevertheless, in the Länder of North Rhine-Westphalia and Rhineland-Palatinate, regional laws at least require the banks to contribute to the cost of debt counselling agencies.

This introduces causal attribution into social policy. Until recently this was discussed almost exclusively with regard to ecological damages and has occasionally been introduced as a legal principle there. Such a principle of causality has rarely been implemented in the social policy realm – who would want to make employers responsible for the Unemployment Benefits of the workers they make redundant (beyond regulated redundancy settlements in the case of major lay-offs which include compensation payments)?[5] Externalising the social cost of private businesses has long been a key rationale of the welfare state. The example of redundancy settlements emphasises a kind of collective attribution which also increasingly plays a role with regard to debt: the phenomenon must be very widely experienced before it becomes recognised as structural, even though there is no logical reason for supposing that an infrequent risk must be caused by the individuals affected.

There is an important historical precedent for introducing causation into social policy: the German Accident Insurance which was established in 1884 under Bismarck's government.[6] It is the only branch of Social Insurance which is financed entirely by the employers' side; in all other branches (Old Age, Health, Unemployment and Care Insurance) the employers and employees each pay half of the costs. The Employers' Liability Insurance Associations (*Berufsgenossenschaften*) are statutorily obliged to carry the risks of industrial injuries. What was decisive is that this introduced collective responsibility and freed the victims of injury from having to seek compensation via individual settlements with employers or by proving the latter's negligence in court. Thus certain illnesses became and continue to be recognised as standard 'occupational diseases' (*Berufskrankheiten*) in certain trades and activities, and carry the right to insurance benefits.

To attribute responsibility through causation has its limits. Primary attribution to a causal agent may fail for several reasons, such as that the

[5] Experience rating is commonplace in the USA, especially in the field of Workers' Compensation Insurance (Marmor *et al.* 1990). By contrast, cause and liability in German Accident Insurance is collectively attributed to the employers according to branches (see below).

[6] François Ewald reconstructed the ideas of risk insurance by welfare states in his historical case study of Accident Insurance (1993). See also Ulrich Beck's (1993) observations in the context of the Risk Society.

liability of the agent is too uncertain or cannot be proven in court (as often happens in the case of divorce settlements); because the causal agent cannot be identified; or because several different causes inseparably interact. Such cases justify recourse to the adjudicator of last instance, the state, to deal with certain risks. This raises the question of secondary attribution, the attribution of responsibility which does not necessarily imply attribution of causality.

In distinguishing between primary and secondary attribution it is clear that little can be gained from the outworn ideological antitheses of more or less state intervention. If the supporters of less state intervention plausibly want to combat poverty and social disadvantage, they must accept a thorough-going primary attribution. This is emphasised by the example of the complicity of the banks in the risk of debt. Conversely, secondary attributions to the state are not necessarily synonymous with demands for more state intervention in the sense of state control or provision. Rather, the state acts as reinsurer when the primary causal agent fails to compensate. The state then appears as legal guarantor or provides financial surety. An example is when the state guarantees legal support to divorced women seeking maintenance payments, or advances money to divorced individuals in cases in which the spouse fails to pay maintenance. Non-means-tested schemes of this kind like the Advance Alimony Law (*Unterhaltsvorschuß-gesetz*) only act as a temporary bridging support.

(b) Child poverty

Like debt, poverty among children has grown massively in Western countries,[7] and primary attribution is similarly problematic. For a long time the poverty of children was not treated as a social problem in its own right. Neither the legal system nor (German) social science recognises children as full subjects: statistical studies generally treat them like housewives to be included in the household in which they live. Poverty measurements focus on households or individuals, and in both cases assume that resources are distributed equally or according to need. A household member thus counts as poor only if the household as a whole falls below the poverty line relevant to its size and composition.[8]

It is true that from this perspective poverty among large families was often deplored, but the underlying reasons were more commonly political concerns about population growth rather than commitment to the welfare

[7] See Smeeding *et al.* (1988), Burkhauser and Duncan (1988), Otto (1997), Cornia and Danziger (1997), Mansel and Neubauer (1998) and Klocke and Hurrelmann (1998).

[8] For a discussion of the distribution of resources within households and the consequences for the measurement of poverty see Stephen Jenkins (1991).

of children. The individualistic creed of Western societies is biased towards the adult male, compared with whom other family members seem less important. The current criticism of high Social Assistance benefit levels obscures the fact that cuts would significantly affect children. The argument that benefit levels above low wages weaken work incentives applies only to the family's breadwinner – but the social policy consequences affect children to an equal and possibly greater extent. Social Assistance policy is also family policy. To simultaneously demand more generous family policies and cuts in Social Assistance for poor families is contradictory. It is only when children are seen as the bearers of individual rights that the question of child poverty gains a stronger significance.

Who can be blamed for child poverty? Certainly not the children themselves. Blaming the family does not take us much further. Even when the poverty of the children is simply subsumed under the poverty of their parents, we still have to ask how the parents' poverty arose and what remedies there may be. A political strategy must start with the children and take account of their fundamental need for protection.[9] Social policy approaches have to be underpinned by legal measures, such as integrating the UN Declaration of the Rights of the Child of 1989 into domestic law. Germany is one of the last countries in which this has not yet been done, since German family law would then have to be revamped. In addition, children should routinely have a legal advocate in their own right. The state could solve the social policy problem of the responsibility for child poverty if it provided needs-oriented resources outside the framework of Social Assistance. A considerable redistribution of resources would be required, such as a restriction on the preferential treatment of married couples (as compared to non-married couples) in the German tax law.

(c) Divorce

Similar questions are raised by the need to safeguard economic security in divorce. It makes sense to connect policy solutions for children in lone parent families with the protection of divorced women (and men). The current state scheme in Germany, the Advance Alimony Law, provides very limited support (basically advancing money) if the liable spouse pays insufficient maintenance. An integrated poverty policy aiming to secure life courses (pp. 266–273) would have to guarantee full maintenance until the children are 18; currently money is paid only until the children are 12, and only for six years. The state could thus contribute to the struggle against child poverty.

[9] Franz-Xaver Kaufmann (1980) refers to a 'structural irresponsibility' towards children in highly stratified societies.

In the models discussed so far, poverty is referred to collectivities: the poor are neither blamed individually nor are they required to take private legal action against liable third parties. The standardised administrative programmes of Social Insurance, personal bankruptcy law and Advance Alimony Funds step in to do this or they offer solutions irrespective of causation or primary liability. In one respect, however, the models continue to be individualistically oriented (Accident Insurance least of all): the assumption persists that each case of poverty must be dealt with individually. The individuals who are directly involved have to be seen as responsible – such as the divorced husbands and fathers, or the state in their absence, or some institutional participant, such as a bank which has contributed to a particular case of debt. But there are forms of poverty in which ascribing responsibility to individuals or to discrete organisations is to border on the absurd. In the case of poverty which is collectively experienced and structurally caused, especially in times of vast historical social change, as in the East German transformation, it makes sense to seek new, stronger, ways of allocating responsibility to society more broadly.

(d) Collective social problems

The most immediate example of collective social problems is the poverty in the New Federal Territories of East Germany. The attribution of causality here is difficult: should the causes of this poverty be sought in the policies of the former communist regime or in the unification policies of the West German government? Can it be blamed on the failure of socialism or the deficiencies of the capitalist market? Whatever the answer, responsibility for this poverty can only be attributed to collectivities, not to individuals. So should the poverty in the New Federal Territories be paid for by 'society', in other words by all taxpayers, or, as has happened to a considerable extent, by the contributors to Social Insurance, thus sparing the wealthy and the civil servants, neither of whom contribute to Social Insurance? In practice, the social risks in East Germany were dealt with by the 'normal' institutions for risk management – and indirectly by massively extending the normal process of revenue sharing between the *Länder*. Nevertheless, one step towards the recognition of collective responsibility was the major use of the instruments of Social Insurance and labour-market policy, and secondly to resort to Social Assistance (pp. 205–210). This approach was probably unavoidable if reunification was to be accepted. It would have been politically unthinkable to treat the East as a giant 'poor house', a pool of Social Assistance claimants.

More extensive redistributive measures between social classes were not adopted, however. The Herculean political act of financial compensation

(*Lastenausgleich*), paid from the 1950s onwards, by which billions of DMs were redistributed to German refugees and others who had suffered material damage as a result of the Second World War (pp. 177f.) was not repeated in the course of German reunification. A levy on wealth in the West or on recovered property in the East was not imposed – on the contrary, the soaring public debt benefited the creditors. Reunification was celebrated as an historical event, but an 'historic' remedy to deal with its social consequences was not ventured, even though the quantity of money transferred was considerable. Unlike the 1950s, in the 1990s no 'social contract' was achieved to provide for a new start together.

We should look for new kinds of non-individualistic attribution of other types of collective deprivations as well. Trying to combat mass unemployment exclusively by means of Unemployment Insurance, as has been firmly maintained for two decades, simply gives rise to further problems. A universal labour-market levy which would include civil servants – who in Germany cannot be fired – would be a step towards collective acceptance of responsibility for a risk which is far more than a 'normal' insurable risk occuring infrequently in life. The structural causes of unemployment have to an increasing extent been recognised by officialdom since the 1980s, in Germany as throughout Europe (see the European Union's White Paper, EC 1993, also Beam 1994), and some thought has been given to remedies. This has called the social consensus on individualistic explanations into question and prepared the ground for initiatives which would pass greater responsibility to collectivities, even at the European level. This cause is especially espoused by the French socialist government and since 1998 also by the German government led by the social democrats. Moving towards larger collectivities is easiest to achieve where social risks have already been collectively allocated for other reasons. Such has been the case in East Germany, where active labour-market policies have been pursued to an extent previously unthinkable in the West.

The idea of a net product levy (*Wertschöpfungsabgabe*), also known as a 'machine tax', represents an interesting conceptual attempt at a structural attribution. In Social Insurance, risks are traditionally allocated to the employees and their employers, and they are framed in an individualised manner: employers pay contributions (half of total contributions) for the workers they employ. By contrast, the machine tax is meant to be born more heavily by businesses which dispense with workers by using advanced production technology. A tax of this kind to bolster Pension and Unemployment Insurance funds was demanded at the end of the 1970s, inspired chiefly by concerns about unemployment, in order to oppose the trend towards the elimination of jobs by rationalisation and technology. In the 1980s, a further aim was to use these means to counter a demographically shrinking working-age population (Leisering 1992, pp. 273 ff.). But the demand was originally raised in the 1960s, explicitly formulated as a question of a fair and just allocation of social risks. Lobbyists for small and medium-sized entrepreneurs saw the traditional contributory basis of social insurance as a distortion of competition, benefiting the larger enterprises with better opportunities for replacing workers by machinery and reducing their insurance contributions, and thus avoiding this social responsibility.

In principle, if a net product levy could replace or complement contribution financing by taxing enterprises, then the social risks would be attributed to global economic and technological change and become a collective responsibility of enterprises, including those which are not involved in causing individual cases of unemployment and poverty. But the overall effects of a machine tax might nevertheless be problematic.

In the 1998 Federal election in Germany, the Green Party made an 'ecological tax' (*Ökosteuer*) a cornerstone of their platform. A levy on energy consumption and petrol is supposed to solve the crisis of social budgets and of high labour costs due to high insurance contributions. Unlike the machine tax, this scheme cannot be justified on grounds of collective attribution of social problems. Rather, it is an instrument of ecological policy which would yield revenue to finance the Greens' plans for a new basic income and reformed old-age pensions. Their call for tripling the price of petrol within a period of ten years (to reach DM5 per litre) triggered a heated debate in early 1998. A much reduced version of an ecological tax is part of the agenda of the social democratic green government that came to power in late 1998.

To summarise, we can see that there are indeed opportunities for new foundations of social responsibility during periods of crisis. There is scope for new policies beyond the extremes of dismantling the welfare state or preserving it as it is. A variety of new ways of attributing causation and responsibility beyond traditional class politics of top–down redistribution is conceivable to respond to changes in social risks. 'Primary' attribution aims to introduce the principle of causal attribution into social policy. 'Secondary' attribution focuses on the state, not as 'provider' but as mediator, guarantor and enabler of last resort if primary attribution seems inappropriate or unpromising. Collective accountability can offer greater security to plaintiffs than do individual liability claims which have to be fought through the courts. For large-scale risks such as mass unemployment and the problems in East Germany, one must locate both causes and responsibility in social structures, i.e., in society itself. This places the duty on society, or rather on the abilities of all of its members, instead of simply on those directly affected. This demands political imagination and the will to use unconventional methods based on more than entrenched ideological presumptions.

New ascriptions and attributions should not be confined to social security policies; they ought to extend into economic policy, family policy, legal policy and constitutional law. Examples include the bankruptcy laws for debt, the demand for full human rights for children, the regulation of maintenance payments and divorce settlements, and integration of an independently determined minimum income standard into the broader income maintenance system for children and families, that is, into the tax system as well as into the system of social transfer payments. This would require not just the coordination of social and poverty policy as outlined in chapter 11 (pp. 266–273), but an integrated policy in all social realms which would embed the welfare state in a wider welfare society. An integrated strategy, however, would multiply the potential for resistance by broadening the range of social groups affected by reforms. Proceeding in piecemeal fashion could limit resistance by dealing with one group at a time.

Attributions are the products of political argument rather than reflections of the objective structures of causation. The question is, who has the power to define the social situation and to make the corresponding ascriptions stick across society? As the discussion of new types of poverty attribution has shown, the resulting arguments over the distribution of resources have less to do with class struggle than with a multitude of overlapping fields of conflict, both overt and latent: children against adults; contributors against taxpayers; private companies against public agencies; public against private-sector employees; small against big business; women against men; the unemployed against those in work; the elderly against those of working age; claimants of social services against professionals in these fields; state against private liability – and so on. We may expect groups in fear of losing out to use denial or active negative dramatisation of the situation of the deprived in order to defend themselves against the latters' claims. Conversely, the disadvantaged and their advocates will resort to dramatising of situations of need (see chapter 7, pp. 196–199).

Reforming and creating institutions

New rights and duties, newly defined entitlements and liabilities, require institutions to secure them and to put them on a permanent footing. The third challenge to future social policy is therefore the development – not the dismantling – of institutions. This assertion seems to run against the major current of present-day politics and policy. In Germany, the current catchphrase is 'reconstruction' (*Umbau*) of the welfare state, a vague term used in different political quarters with varying meanings ranging from a straightforward reduction of all benefit schemes to a minimum level (residual welfare state), to curtailments that preserve the basic structure of social security (*Rückbau*), to structural reform geared to the needs of a changing society.

Since the reunification of the two Germanies in 1990, especially since the end of the attendant economic boom in 1993, German social politics has resembled its US counterpart in that social provisions have not been actively developed, but were instead cut in the interest of reducing the national budgetary deficit ('cost reduction strategy', *Kostendämpfung*; see Borchert 1994; 1996; but Alber 1998). The general reduction in available resources as a result of tax cuts automatically restricts social policy options (for the USA see Pierson 1994). Jens Borchert described the situation as 'a transformation of the welfare state through incurring debt' (1994, p. 18), in effect a conservative 'reform' of social policy by the back door, made possible only by the exigencies of the moment. This condition was reached in Germany in 1990. The enforced 'slimming therapy' which the Kohl administration was unable to introduce when it came into office in the early 1980s was surreptitiously implemented in the wake of the growing reunification deficits. The statutory expenditure cuts in the 'package' laws were explicitly introduced under the label of 'the social union of Germany' (BMAS 1994a, p. 117; now Manow and Seils 1999).

In fact, the same Chancellor who excelled in seizing the historical moment in 1990 to bring about unification failed on a similarly historical scale when it came to financing the subsequent transformation in East Germany. The national debt has soared and Social Insurance budgets have been heavily burdened till the present day. The Social Democrats rightly point out that this atmosphere of financial constraint is welcomed by the liberals, who depict the impasse as evidence that the welfare state is inherently rotten. Furthermore, unification has produced large regional earnings differentials unknown in Germany for a long time, as the wage rates in the East were set at a lower level; these differentials are diminishing only gradually. This limits the power of the trade unions, and also of employers' organisations, nationwide – and has become a major fault line for the organisational capacity and effectiveness of Germany's 'coordinated economy' (Soskice 1991). These political factors conditioning the current crisis of the German welfare state are sometimes overlooked in debates about purely 'objective' economic, demographic and social challenges.

By grouping Germany with the USA as a type of welfare state in retrenchment, however, Jens Borchert misses the ambivalence of German 'economising' policies, since cuts and consolidation, sometimes involving expansion, go hand in hand. Family policy in particular is being enhanced, lately by use of tax law changes, and the Old-Age Pension system was thoroughly consolidated in the Reform Act of 1992 and, accompanied by structural cuts, in the Reform Act of 1997, which would have gone into effect in 1999 (*Rentenreform '99;* see Leisering and Motel 1997) had the Schröder government not suspended it until December 2000 (Schmähl 1998b). Moreover, Care Insurance (*Gesetzliche Pflegeversicherung*), a new branch of Social Insurance, was introduced in 1994/5 (Rothgang 1997).

The attempts at curtailing social policy may be based on cleavages in the political culture. Surveys have shown that the population as a whole strongly supports the welfare state. Even when this support flags, it revives markedly when cuts are implemented (see Pierson 1995). But support for the welfare state by elites throughout the OECD has fallen since the 1970s – in Germany all the major parties are affected, including the social democrats, albeit less noticeably. A lot is known about building welfare states, also from a comparative perspective (Schmidt 1998), but very little is known about the process of dismantling them (see Pierson 1996). Paul Pierson has warned against a kind of (welfare-state) crisis illusion which feeds above all on the idea that collapse is imminent since the social forces that built the welfare state are withering away. This crisis view overlooks the fact that the institutionalisation of the welfare state has led to the development of new forces – interests of clients, providers and institutional constellations – which sustain the welfare state.

Indeed, we maintain that current pressures on the welfare state do not necessitate dismantling it, but that a reformed welfare state as an integral part of a welfare society can even be a productive response to the challenges of a rapidly changing society. We delineate two characteristics of such a future welfare state: *flexible risk management* and *regulatory control of non-state welfare production.*

Flexible risk management

It is misleading to assume that the increasing speed and variability of social life, the mobility and 'fluidity' of present-day life courses, require de-institutionalisation. The tendencies towards greater variety in life courses do not indicate that people increasingly pursue freely chosen life plans, or that they have been atomised by the sheer power of socio-structural changes. These changes do not imply that social institutions play a diminished role in affecting life courses. When in chapter 2 we described the individual as a 'life-course runner' pursuing his or her own 'life-course policy', what we meant was that people follow the paths of their own lives within the framework of state and civil institutions. Even if modern institutions such as educational authorities, social security and health services do not influence individual behaviour as directly as the localised economic and residential communities in which people were primarily embedded up to the nineteenth century, they do significantly condition individual action. If individual 'life-course policies' change, then the institutions must also change.

The current challenge, therefore, is not the abolition but the reform and expansion of institutions. Greater variety and increased risk in life courses and life plans necessitate more differentiated and more flexible forms of institutionalisation. We witness a 'de-standardisation' of life courses but not their de-institutionalisation.[10]

Flexible retirement is a case in point. In many countries, schemes of early retirement (more recently shifting to later retirement) have been introduced in state and occupational pension systems either by statute or by corporatist agreements between employers and employees (Delsen and Reday-Mulvey 1996). A greater flexibility of choice about when and how to retire was introduced in the German Reform Acts of 1972 and 1992. The latter Act established new 'partial pensions' which allow work and retirement to be combined (Leisering 1992, pp. 276 f.). Other schemes of the 1990s combine reduced working hours with supplementary unemployment benefits to be negotiated between employers and trade unions (*Altersteilzeit,* from 1996). Complex legal and actuarial rules create an increased flexibility while taking account of fiscal and labour-market interests. In this instance, institutionalisation does not mean rigidity but, on the contrary, ensures dynamic life courses. In the near future we can therefore expect the three major domains of life-course policy in the welfare state – education, pensions, and social-risk management as depicted in chapter 2 (pp. 24f.) – to develop in such a way that the inherently flexible systems of *risk management* become more significant and the more standardised systems of education and pensions become more flexible and address social risks as well. We have already mentioned examples of the new types of security against risks or proposals for reform in the fields of long-term care, housing, debt, children and divorce in the context of integrated social policies against poverty (chapter 11, p. 271) and in the above discussion of extending social accountability.

The strategy of flexible risk management does justice to the dynamics of international and domestic markets while not subscribing to the liberal response of economic and social deregulation. Increasing economic mobility requires stepped-up social and institutional mobility. Institutions convert the uncertainty and discontinuity of life courses into calculable risks (Kaufmann 1973, Beck 1992/1986, Giddens 1991). According to Wolfgang Zapf (1994), the strains imposed on the East Germans by the accelerated modernisation of East Germany after unification did not primarily arise because production and incomes did not increase fast enough

---

[10] For the early debate on the de-institutionalisation of life courses see Kohli (1986a) and Wohlrab-Sahr (1992, 1993).

– they did increase fast – but rather because the people had to adapt to new
and uncertain conditions. Even if the unprecedented scale of social risk
absorption by the welfare state in East Germany (see pp. 205ff.) was not
able to relieve all anxieties, it did reduce social tensions considerably.

The success of far-reaching structural transformations of society, then,
is conditional on implementing active life-course policies. Ideally, state
support for individuals should only act as a *stop-gap* in the lives of recipients (leaving aside more lengthy contingencies like disability or old age).
While flexible state support may help to bridge biographical breaks, the
chances of getting back to self-support ultimately rest on the performance
of markets, families and social networks. To introduce a low-pay sector into
the economy – as proposed by liberal politicians and employers' associations in Germany in the late 1990s to combat unemployment – is only
acceptable when it does not contribute to the permanent exclusion of an
ever larger part of the population (see p. 289). In the US tradition, the
model of transitory poverty as a route to economic success and social
integration is embodied in the immigrant, but this model does not always
work. Countries differ with regard to an individual's chance of moving up
the social ladder from a marginal position like that of low-skill employment
(Esping-Anderson 1993). Liberal concepts of 'functional poverty' and
'productivist justice' (see chapter 12, pp. 285ff.) are only viable politically
as long as episodes of poverty actually remain stop-gap periods for most
people. Only then can sacrifices for the expected future benefits for society
be justified and social bonds and peace be preserved.

Regulatory control of non-state welfare production

The second characteristic of a new welfare state in a new welfare society is
regulatory control of non-state welfare production. The idea of the state as
a mere regulator has a long tradition. It lies at the heart of the liberal
concept of the constitutional state (*Verfassungsstaat*) or the rule of law.
From its inception in Locke and other philosophers, it has assumed various
shapes at different points in history and in different countries. The mere
idea of restricting the scope of government to regulatory functions (or at
least of emphasising these functions) does not provide us with a blueprint
of policies and institutions. Historically, the idea of the constitutional state
was to contain government, as a precondition of a free society. But regulatory concepts have also been used to justify the extension of state action.
The German concept of the Social Market Economy, for example, grew out
of the 'ordo-liberal' school of economics that developed in Germany in the
1930s and 1940s. This doctrine assigned to the state the role of regulatory
economic policy to secure the 'order' of the economic market. Government

should take measures and establish institutions, for example, to secure monetary stability or to preserve competition in the market by anti-trust legislation.

Even Western welfare states have not normally assumed more than regulatory powers. Only some advocates of far-reaching state welfare, like Jeremy Bentham or Sidney and Beatrice Webb, and liberal welfare state critics have imagined otherwise.[11] Welfare statism rests on the idea that society cannot be based on the institutions of the market, the family and local social networks alone. In this view appeals to community values must be underpinned by a legal and institutional infrastructure to enable and empower individuals to pursue their objectives (see the concept of an 'enabling state' by Neil and Barbara Gilbert 1989). The current challenge is to redesign the shape of regulatory policies and institutions in the face of social changes and to make choices about policy goals and the scope of government action.

Insurance is a case in point. In the mid 1990s the German Old-Age Pension system was more strongly attacked than it had been for three decades, i.e., since the great Reform Act of 1957. Booming share markets promised to yield higher returns for private provision for old age. This was seen as a case for deregulation by strong factions in the political debate. Young people, in particular, no longer unanimously trusted state pensions as their parents had done. However, as the 1997 crash in share and money markets made clear, private systems depend on sound basic regulations, on basic control by public institutions. As a consequence of the breakdown of its country's banking system, Japanese pension funds announced in early 1998 that they could no longer guarantee the promised rate of return on contributions. A major extension of state controls of Japanese banking was called for.

Private insurance in Western countries could not have acquired a relevant and growing share of provision for social risks without tax deductions favouring private provision, without a state regulatory authority, without consumer protection and without a final safety net provided by the state, such as social assistance. The political infrastructure for private systems becomes even more important and, at the same time, more difficult to establish at a time when insurance markets become international in the course of European unification and economic and financial globalisation. In essence, 'private' systems have a substantial public side. Final responsibility for the

---

[11] This applies to Bentham's totalitarian blueprints of prisons, hospitals, schools and poor houses. His general utilitarian concept of social welfare, however, marks a shift in the history of political thought: in view of the emerging markets and modern politico-administrative systems he reinterpreted the older concept of 'political society' to mean delegated control by governments indicating regulatory policies (Leisering 1989, chapter 4).

welfare of the people, especially in times of socio-economic crisis, still rests with the state.

As a consequence, 'going private' does not bypass questions of social justice and inclusion. The moral economy of private schemes is far from being clear: who justifies such arrangements, who loses, who wins, who has to care for losers, how secure are the social bonds and the trust relations on which insurance markets and capital markets are built? Recent developments in Germany, such as the call for ombudsmen in the insurance business or the increasing attention paid by consumer protection associations to financial markets, suggest that a new institutional framework or even culture of private provision seems to be developing without which 'private' systems could lose the acceptance necessary for their operation.

Flexible, imaginative welfare-state institutions – geared both to the requirements of a new, more 'flexible' society and to the increasing plurality of lifestyles – and new state institutions regulating the ever-broadening range of private welfare provisions are both characteristics of a new welfare society. They share a focus on supporting the individual, on exploiting his or her action potential and quest for self-expression, while at the same time securing the institutional requisites of social citizenship for all. This adds up to a vision of a 'civil society', a variety of civil society, however, that relies not only on markets, families and values.

The politics of the social minimum

Would not a strategy of minimum provision – restricting state benefits and services to minimum standards – be the obvious solution to the current problems, a solution that combines flexibility with preserving a basic welfare-state structure? While in the 1980s the idea of a basic income loomed large among social critics and the Greens in Germany, Britain and France, in the 1990s it is most forcefully propagated by economic liberals. The idea is not seldom presented as a panacea to the illnesses of our time, the meaning and institutional design of specific schemes varying widely among and within political quarters. [12] Minimum standard strategies seem to be the easy way out of fiscal pressures and labour-market problems while sustaining political support. On closer examination, however, all three gains expected to ensue from such a strategy – *fiscal*, *political* and *economic* – turn out to be elusive.

Fiscal. Social assistance and other basic income schemes are a safety net of last resort. They largely mirror failures of prior systems, above all labour-

---

[12] See Richard Hauser's comparative analysis (1996); see also chapter 11, pp. 266–273.

market, family and higher-tier welfare-state schemes. Restricting state benefits to a minimum, therefore, cannot shield against the pressures stemming from social problems brought by social change. Most Western countries have experienced an explosion in the number of clients of social assistance and of related social spending. The reforms that took place in the second half of the 1990s could slow down but not reverse that development. In advanced capitalist democracies poverty is conceived in relative terms so that a minimum income standard tends to be based on a relative poverty line that reflects the changing requirements of living in a society like ours.[13] At least in the European tradition of social responsibility, inroads into this basic social standard, as they occurred in the US welfare reforms of 1996, are less likely to be achieved.

In Germany the clientele of social assistance is comparatively small – 3 per cent of the population in 1994 as compared to 23 per cent in Britain. This is largely due to more developed higher-tier benefit schemes like old-age pensions and unemployment benefit: 13 per cent of German unemployed people fall on to social assistance while 71 per cent of the British do; for the elderly the percentage is 2 per cent as compared to 24 per cent (Leisering and Walker 1998d). This shows that in a welfare state with weak higher tiers, social assistance tends to be overburdened by social problems left unsolved by prior schemes.

In Germany, as in other countries, the critical debate centres on the level of social assistance benefits (standard rate of maintenance payments, *Regelsatz*), while housing allowances within social assistance are not touched upon even though their cost equals the amount spent on maintenance.[14] Housing is an essential component of a social minimum. As long as social assistance includes a full housing allowance, spending will continue to rise with rising numbers of clients and higher rents paid in the housing market.

In addition, a basic income strategy ignores the specific fiscal problems stemming from social services (or benefits in kind), especially health services and care for the elderly. The problem of containing health costs ensuing from advances in medical science and technology and from Baumol's 'cost disease' of social services is beginning to creep into social assistance. The financing of health services for Social Assistance claimants in Germany is currently under revision. The system might end up spending one-third of its budget on basic maintenance, another third on housing and

---

[13] For an analysis of how governments in 10 Western societies define minimum income standards see John Veit-Wilson (1998).

[14] Each accounts for 40 per cent of total expenditure; the remaining 20 per cent stem from one-time payments (*einmalige Beihilfen*) for, e.g., clothing or needs on special occasions like a wedding or house repairs (Wenzel 1995).

the remaining third on health. In the USA welfare legislation has always faced the problem that there is no general health insurance; the special schemes of medical care for welfare recipients (and the elderly) constantly pose problems. In Germany a key rationale in introducing the new statutory long-term Care Insurance was to take pressure off Social Assistance: it was here that the costs of care for the aged were covered. Spending on Special Needs Support (*Hilfe in besonderen Lebenslagen*), the branch of Social Assistance that includes care for the elderly and the disabled, amounted to twice the money spent on Basic Income Support (and is still higher after the introduction of Care Insurance in 1994/95).

A consistent minimum provision strategy would also have to define general minimum standards for health and other services, not only for claimants of social assistance – unless it would be considered acceptable to drive increasing numbers of middle-class people into social assistance only because they cannot afford health and long-term care. This was the prospect for the German middle class before the introduction of Care Insurance.

In fact, establishing minimum standards is also under discussion in the German debate on health provisions. The ingrained norm of providing everybody with the full standard of treatment according to the current state of medical science is under attack. This is most tangible in Care Insurance which is the first branch of Social Insurance which does without any legally defined standard of services, even a minimum standard. Only graded flat-rate payments are provided (Rothgang 1997). In Old-Age Pensions, benefit standards are also eroding. The reform which was to become effective in 1999 included a reduction of standard benefits to a level below wage replacement (introduced in 1957) but above the level of Social Assistance.[15] But this reform was suspended in 1998.

In contrast to cash benefits, health services face the insurmountable problem of defining minimum standards that result in substantial spending cuts while avoiding doing physical harm to those patients who get less than the state-of-the-art in medical treatment. Any substantial denial of available treatment is prone not just to make life less comfortable for the patients concerned but to lengthen illnesses and shorten life expectancy, or even cause death. Non-state provisions can partially make up for this, but inequalities according to the ability to pay and the vicissitudes of financial markets are bound to emerge. Formulas like 'targeting benefits to those really in need' or 'guaranteeing basic provisions for all' sound comforting, but they are saddled with much less comforting consequences.

[15] For a comparative analysis of the erosion of legislative benefit standards in several fields of German social security in the 1990s see Leisering (1997b); for Old-Age Pensions see Leisering and Motel (1997).

Political. The political repercussions of a minimum strategy could be no less damaging. The crucial legitimisation of the welfare state resides in the middle class, flowing from the higher-tier benefits that accrue to the average worker and employee, rather than from the benefits that go to the poor (Esping-Andersen 1990). In this sense Social Insurance (for old age, health and unemployment) is the pillar of the German welfare state. The National Health Service (NHS) plays a similar role in Britain. Dismantling higher-tier benefit schemes could, therefore, erode the political support for the welfare state provided by the middle classes. A welfare state which only caters for the poor will have poor support. Weak higher-tier systems will weaken the lower tiers. This can be seen from the extremely low standard (see chapter 2, pp. 47–50) and the political vulnerability of the US welfare system which culminated in the 1996 reform. The very notion of minimum or 'basic' security so forcefully advocated by present-day German liberals is likely to be self-defeating. In the transformation of East Germany after reunification, politicians raised Social Insurance spending to unprecedented levels because they knew that turning East Germany into a poor house with masses of people living on Social Assistance would have put unification at risk (see above).

Economic. New basic income schemes have been proposed and tested in the 1990s in the USA, Britain and Germany to solve problems of the labour market. For decades Social Assistance has been a side issue of the German social policy debate, or only soaring costs were discussed – quite unlike the US or British debate. But from the mid 1990s it has assumed a pivotal role in the controversy about growing unemployment and revitalising the labour market. The levels of wages and state benefits, so the argument goes, ought to be better coordinated to move more people into the market. This would produce incentives for both workers and employers to take up or supply work respectively. One option is to create a low-pay sector in the economy hitherto little known in Germany. Social Assistance benefits would have to be reduced to ensure 'less eligibility' or, alternatively, wage subsidies would have to be paid by the Social Assistance authorities. Wage subsidies were prominently proposed by Fritz W. Scharpf in the mid 1990s and also by a Commission on the Future of Society inspired by the Social Democratic Party (Zukunfts-kommission 1998). They were partially enacted in the Social Assistance Reform Act of 1996 (§18, (4), (5)), to little avail, however. Another option is to smooth the transition between benefit and work by way of a demogrant (*Bürgergeld*, 'citizens' wage') envisaged by the Liberal Party or by way of a negative income tax. Even the President of the German Trade Union Congress, Dieter Schulte, when coming back from a trip to the USA in 1997, considered the idea of an Earned Income Tax Credit (EITC).

Such concepts are riddled with problems. They tend to be expensive. The new benefits might be used by workers or employers who would have taken up work or offered a job without a state subsidy (our research has shown that many people leave Social Assistance anyway, see chapters 3–5). And the means test that would have to be applied even more forcefully than before applies to households, not to individuals. Since German Social Assistance is paid to anyone below an income threshold, including the employed (but since 1993 excluding asylum seekers), it could have always been used as a subsidy for low-paid jobs, but apparently neither the employers nor the trade unions or individual workers have been inclined to do so to a relevant extent.

This testifies to the mechanical and rationalistic nature of the belief that a mere modification of monetary parameters like the level of wages or the level of benefits could solve the problems of the labour market. This belief rests on the assumption by pure economic theory of a self-regulating labour market which reaches a perfect balance if only the parameters are right. For Britain, Robert Walker and Michael Wiseman (1997) have used quantitative models to test whether the US-type Earned Income Tax Credit could be successfully transplanted to Europe. They conclude that this scheme, which is costly and not very efficient in the USA, would not suit the British situation. A partial tax credit to individuals supplemented by a means-tested family allowance is considered more appropriate.[16]

From the mid 1990s new approaches have been tried in Germany and Britain. Rather than adjusting monetary parameters such as wages, tax rates and benefit levels, new social services are designed to exploit the action potential of the claimants. These 'enabling policies' offer active support instead of creating passive incentives only by making work pay (see section 'An Enabling Approach' in chapter 11, pp. 263–266). This approach promises to be more effective.

The discussion of recent innovations in social assistance policies illustrates several points we made on the new welfare state in a new welfare society: First, designing new and more flexible institutions rather than simply down-sizing seems to be the more promising response to the current challenges. Second, even in poverty policy, reforms point towards strengthening income support systems and services prior to traditional minimum-oriented social assistance. In the process both tiers of social security systems ought to be better coordinated (see section 'Integrated Social Policy' in chapter 11, pp. 266–273). Third, enabling people through local

---

[16] For an assessment of an early income experiment in South Germany see Franz Schultheis (1987) (see p. 163).

social services geared to a diversity of needs promises more success than intricate uniform systems of monetary incentives based on a readjustment of tax rates and benefit levels in income maintenance schemes. Fourth, the confrontation of public or state versus private agencies is of little avail. Even in a country with a strong state tradition like Germany, private companies like *Bureau Maatwerk* operate to move Social Assistance claimants into work (Hamburg) while other municipalities plan to use the same methods via local government agencies. Fifth, much of the reform debate is not about functions and dysfunctions of the welfare state but about values, choices and national cultures. Lone motherhood, for example, meets with considerable moral contempt in the USA and increasingly in Britain while in Germany lone mothers on Social Assistance are not the preferred scapegoats for welfare state critics. In general poverty is accepted to a considerable degree in the USA (and in Britain) while unemployment is not. In Germany and some other European countries it is rather the other way round, as Amartya Sen (1997, p. 160) observed.

Beyond the nation state

The international system sets limits for domestic policies.[17] However, the changing structure of the international economic order also provides national policy makers with new incentives for a shift from state-oriented to societal solutions both for traditional and new welfare problems. Pressures to contain policy reactions as well as increased demands for social and economic security loom large in today's political discourse in Western Europe. Dani Rodrik sums up the present state of the national–international interface for the welfare state in an OECD perspective:

In essence, governments have used their fiscal powers to insulate domestic groups from excessive market risks. . . . At the present, however, international economic integration is taking place against the background of receding governments and diminished social obligations. . . . Yet the need for social insurance for the vast majority of the population that remain internationally immobile has not diminished. If anything, this need has become greater as a consequence of increased integration. The question therefore is how the tension between globalization and the pressures for socialization of risk can be eased. (1997, p. 6)

In addition to the world-wide competitive pressures of 'globalisation' since the mid 1980s the pressures of European unification make themselves

---

[17] For an overview see Rhodes (1996), Leibfried and Rieger (1995), Rieger and Leibfried (1997 [Revised English version 1998]; 1999), Zürn (1998, part IV), Beisheim *et al.* (1999) as well as Scharpf and V. A. Schmidt (2000).

felt domestically, directly and also indirectly.[18] One may illustrate the direct pressures with the case of the rejection of a nationwide minimum pension in Germany by Norbert Blüm, the country's long-serving Minister for Labour and Social Affairs until September 1998. On 30 May 1990, he refused to adopt the GDR's minimum pension system lest an exportable right for a minimum pension were to arise among those citizens of other EU countries who had spent a few years of work – also contributing to Social Insurance – in Germany: 'That would be an invitation to finance a European welfare state using German social funds . . . I just wanted to refer to this European aspect of the minimum pension question' (cited by BMAS 1994b, p. 69). More recent examples of major influences of European integration would refer to the massive consequences of the 'free mobility of services' on national welfare states, be it on transborder health services (cf. Becker 1998) or on Care Insurance (Sieveking 1998). Such developments in the European Union – effects of the integration of markets for goods, services,[19] capital and labour on social policy – could inspire a 'race to the bottom' and thus lead to a 'social union' based on the lowest common denominator; or it could feed an incremental, slow process of European disintegration (Leibfried 1997).

Economic migration from Eastern Europe and other places in the world, which is likely to increase (Ireland 1995), is accelerating such a race. Thus contract labourers from Poland create problems for the German welfare state, provoking fierce arguments since 1996 between political parties and trade unions about wage dumping and low pay on German building sites. Since 1997 a new national law protects wages and social rights in Germany's construction industry, and the access of labourers from Eastern Europe has been restricted significantly. In addition, data from the SOPEMI data base of the OECD show a clear trend: rates of immigration of foreign labour are decreasing in all member states of the European Union. As European integration has been topped off by free capital movement within and beyond Europe since the mid 1980s, the political consequences of globalisation pose harder questions for all member states of the European Union, including Germany. The issue is whether the modern state's autonomy has been restricted and whether it has also lost its formal sovereignty in many spheres (Held 1991, p. 213), consequently becoming increasingly inable or incompetent respectively to develop relevant social policies. The European Monetary Union may push such combined losses

[18] For an overview on social policy cf. Leibfried and Pierson (1995, chapter 13), as well as Rhodes (1996); on unemployment Scharpf (1997/1999); on industrial policy V. A. Schmidt (1996); for a comparative assessment of general institutional predispositions and approaches V. A. Schmidt (1997).

[19] This includes the European private insurance market which has been integrated since 1994.

in autonomy and sovereignty beyond a critical threshold. On the other hand, such a Union would substantially increase the European welfare states' aggregate counterweight in the competition within the 'triad', that is with North America and the Asian region.

If we follow the US political scientist Miles Kahler, the on-going global conflict should be interpreted as taking place between a distinct Western European 'world of welfare' and at least two alternative world models:

Perhaps the most pessimistic reading of effects of regionalization in transatlantic relations concerns the underlying sources of economic conflict between Europe and the United States. Rather than simple protectionism, conflict increasingly might center on 'unfair competition' and 'level playing fields' – terms defined less by any measurable barriers to market access than by presumed differences between two distinct capitalist political economies. (If one adds Japan, then the clash of systems involves at least three distinct models.) The European Union, in this view, represents more than a collection of coordinated policies or even a set of distinct institutions: it incorporates a distinctive social and economic order, in contradistinction to 'Northamerica'. (1995, p. 41)

Dani Rodrik points to two opposing modes of levelling such playing fields in the world economy: 'Free trade among countries with very different domestic practices requires either a willingness to countenance the erosion of domestic structures or the acceptance of a certain degree of harmonization (convergence)' (1997, p. 37). The latter option points towards reshaping supranational as well as intranational institutions such that citizens may be shielded effectively and more flexibly from the social risks stemming from the international system.

The states' welfare institutions, especially in Western Europe, are coming to be regarded as barriers against adjusting to the new structures and functional requirements of today's world economy, in line with the erosive mode just mentioned. This tendency is more pronounced in Germany than in other European states because traditionally in Germany 'transfer state' issues have been divorced from matters of education, i.e. the former are considered 'welfare-state' or 'social-state' issues in contradistinction to educational policy (*Bildungspolitik*) (see Heidenheimer 1981).[20] This makes a truly coordinated response to the challenge of globalisation facing high-skill economies more difficult. Critics see the German welfare state in its current state as incompatible with the demands of global economic institutions. This is a new situation for national policy.

But the welfare state has not yet become a historical phenomenon of so little significance that it can casually be put aside simply to adapt to some

---

[20] In the Anglo-American world as well as at the supranational European level, in contrast to Germany, education policy is seen as part and parcel of social policy.

exaggerated 'world market trends'. Surveys show that people's expectations of politics have changed in the second half of the twentieth century, leading to the current noticeable 'social-policy nationalism'. Thus there have been attempts, against the tide of public opinion, to bring the institutional foundations of the new world economic order into line with national welfare requirements via 'social clauses', as shown by several developments in the ILO, GATT and now the WTO (see Kapstein 1996), as well as in other international agreements.

All three of the challenges to the welfare state's life-course policies discussed above are also relevant on an international level – the need to renew the commitment to social citizenship, to extend social responsibility as well as accountability, and to reform and create institutions that shield citizens more flexibly. Citizens' rights can no longer be understood exclusively as a matter of national citizenship rights, as was originally the case when welfare provisions were established in nation states. Furthermore, citizenship rights are no longer state centered as regards the sources of welfare and its administration.

Since the Maastricht Treaty of 1992, a post-national European citizenship status has been emerging which would perforate the nation-state shell (Meehan 1993, sceptical: Preuß 1997, Schnapper 1997). The quotation from Norbert Blüm places the issue of entitlement to security in old age in the context of European integration and supranational politics. Today, citizens' rights in Europe can be enforced nationally and regionally by supranational organisations as in many EU regulations, for example on gender equality. Numerous decisions of the European Court of Justice (ECJ) have led to amendments and reinterpretations of national law. The supranational location of social accountability plays a significant role in domestic policy nowadays. At the European level, this includes programmes for poorer regions which also affect richer member states such as Germany (Anderson 1995) or sectoral redistributive policies as for agriculture (see Rieger 1995).[21]

Citizens' rights can also be upheld against national governments globally by international institutions as in the case of ILO standards or the UN Declaration of the Rights of the Child, which is not compatible with current German law (see above). In general that also poses the question of how to remodel social policy institutions on a supranational and an international level. Is anything like a European or even world-wide welfare state conceivable (Leibfried 1994a, de Swaan 1992, 1994)? Or can we develop more flexible 'regulatory' functional equivalents to welfare states, region-

---

[21] On the process of supranationalisation in Europe cf. Wallace and Wallace (1996); Marks *et al.* (1996), and Majone (1993, 1994a, b); on the future of European welfare see also Mény and Rhodes (1998).

ally or globally, which do not monopolise risk-solving but farm risks out to third parties – be they public or private – at other levels in multi-tiered political and social systems like the EU or beyond?[22] Will the world welfare 'state' be a decentralised multi-level and multi-sectoral network of agencies and regulations with loose coupling between its components?

What is thinkable – particularly as a consequence of Monetary Union – is that pressures will build up for Europe-wide 'Brussels-directed' redistributive as well as regulatory policies which could also focus on combating unemployment and social exclusion (Leibfried 1992, 1994a, b, Leibfried and Pierson 1995).[23] Such pressure is particularly exerted by the French socialists who came into power unexpectedly in 1997 and since October 1998 by the German Social Democratic Green government. Related policies could build on European Commission initiatives pursued since the 1970s. Also, European nation states might more offensively turn into 'laboratories of democracy', learning from each other and racing more towards some middle ground and even higher in welfare state reform rather than to the bottom – if properly 'reinsured' by European standards. Actors in the German political sphere are hardly aware that there have been a series of EU poverty programmes based on experimental projects in which poverty and marginalisation were studied even in Germany.[24] Even the first systematic study of poverty (Hauser *et al.* 1981), the only quasi-official German poverty report so far, was part of these programmes. In addition, a foundation for comparative poverty reports was laid, managed by the EU's Statistical Bureau in Luxembourg. In 1992, the European Commission formulated national poverty policy guidelines, not to determine the level of minimum standards but to emphasise the legal right to minimum security provisions and due process (Schulte 1991, 1993).

It remains to be seen if in these social, political and international contexts the potential and necessary reforms of the German welfare state can be carried out on the basis of the existing governmental arrangements. In short, the issues are to make clear and unequivocal value judgements about the *citizen rights* of old as well as new disadvantaged groups, to allocate new social *accountability* and responsibilities, and to form innovative and

---

[22] At the EC level this is already the typical pattern of intervention (cf. Leibfried and Pierson 1995). The EC itself does not provide any welfare-state services to the citizens of its member states. Rather, Brussels 'regulates' private sector or lower-tier public provision of such services and shifts the costs for such provision to lower levels, too.

[23] On the European dimension of the poverty debate see Atkinson (1991, 1992); Atkinson and Cazes (1990); Henningsen and Room (1990); Leibfried (1992); Smeeding *et al.* (1990); and Kohl (1994). On the subject of poverty problematics world-wide, see Øyen, Miller and Samad (1996).

[24] Poverty is an unwanted issue in official politics in Germany so that the German Federal government even effectively blocked the last, the 'Poverty 4' programme of the EU.

flexible *institutions*. At a time when far-reaching social changes erode the ingrained assumptions – particularly pronounced in the German welfare-state model – of unbroken employment careers, stable marriages and negligible immigration, new life-course policies and politics are called for: a new welfare regime that would permit a wider variety of lifestyles and, more than ever before, would build bridges to lead people in crises to escape routes from poverty and marginalisation. Such a welfare state would have to go beyond the traditional or newly advocated residual model of fighting marginalisation by marginal policies, like social assistance or 'welfare'. Rather, poverty policies would have to be integrated in a larger social-policy setting in a citizens' state.

A social order of this kind is not just a question of more or less government action, of reducing or retaining the welfare state. It demands a genuine transformation anchored in a new social contract. It requires a changed 'moral economy' at a time when the idea of universal participation is being subjected to severe endurance tests. As Hugh Heclo put it, in the context of the USA with her lack of a tradition of social citizenship:

... anti-poverty policy is an act of collective self-confidence. The basic question is, why should we care about each other, care in any concrete action-forcing way? These 'why should' questions ultimately only find answers within the moral will of a political community. It is 'moral' because the questions are about valuations, not facts, about judgements of worthiness applied not only to individuals but also to how a society comports itself. It is 'political' because we are the subject, a collective enterprise aimed at expressing itself through joint action. ... A new beginning? Moral commitments to a politics of inclusion and anti-poverty policy will have to grow from inside our national life and cannot be remembered, shamed or blamed into being. (Heclo 1994, pp. 433, 435, and 437.)

References

Abelshauser, W. 1987. *Die Langen Fünfziger Jahre. Wirtschaft und Gesellschaft der Bundesrepublik Deutschland 1949–1966.* Düsseldorf: Schwann

Achinger, H. 1959. Soziologie und Sozialreform, in *Soziologie und moderne Gesellschaft. Verhandlungen des 14. deutschen Soziologentages.* Stuttgart: Enke, pp. 39–52

Adam, H. 1977. Zur Armutsdiskussion in der Bundesrepublik Deutschland. *Sozialer Fortschritt*, **26**, 2: 37–39

1978. Einkommensarmut und Armutspotentiale. *Sozialer Fortschritt*, **27**, 1: 17–20

Adams, U. 1971. *Nachhut der Gesellschaft. Untersuchung einer Obdachlosensiedlung in einer westdeutschen Großstadt.* Freiburg i.B.: Lambertus

Adamy, W. and Naegele, G. 1985. *Armenpolitik in der Krise. Bestandsaufnahme und Entwicklungstrends*, in Leibfried and Tennstedt (eds.) 1985a, pp. 94–121

Adenauer, K. 1949. *Regierungserklärung vom 20. September 1949*, in Behn, H. U. (ed.) 1971, *Die Regierungserklärungen der Bundesrepublik Deutschland.* Munich/Wien: Olzog (Deutsches Handbuch der Politik, vol. 5), pp. 11–33

Alba, R.D., Handl, J. and Müller, W. 1994. Ethnische Ungleichheit im deutschen Bildungssystem. *Kölner Zeitschrift für Soziologie und Sozialpsychologie*, **46**: 209–237

Alber, J. 1984. Versorgungsklassen im Wohlfahrtsstaat. Überlegungen und Daten zur Situation in der Bundesrepublik. *Kölner Zeitschrift für Soziologie und Sozialpsychologie*, **36**: 225–251

1986a. Der Wohlfahrtsstaat in der Wirtschaftskrise – Eine Bilanz der Sozialpolitik in der Bundesrepublik seit den frühen siebziger Jahren. *Politische Vierteljahresschrift*, **27**: 28–60

1986b. Germany, in Flora, P. (ed.), *Growth to Limits. The Western European Welfare State Since World War II*, Vol. II. Berlin: de Gruyter, pp. 1–154

1989. *Der Sozialstaat in der Bundesrepublik 1950–1983.* Frankfurt a.M./New York: Campus

1998. Der deutsche Sozialstaat im Licht international vergleichender Daten. *Leviathan*, **26**, 2: 199–227

Albrecht, G. 1973. Obdachlose in Köln. Bericht über eine Längsschnittstudie, in Arbeitskreis junger Kriminologen (ed.), *Randgruppenarbeit. Analysen und*

324   **References**

Projekte aus der Arbeit mit Obdachlosen. Munich: Juventa, pp. 29–58 (mimeo 1970)

Albrecht, G., Specht, T., Goergen, G. and Großkopf, H. 1990. *Lebensläufe – Von der Armut zur 'Nichtseßhaftigkeit'.* Bielefeld: Verlag Soziale Hilfe (mimeo 1979)

Alcock, P. 1997. *Understanding Poverty.* Houndmills: Macmillan (second edn)

Allmendinger, J. 1989a. *Career Mobility Dynamics. A Comparative Analysis of the United States, Norway and West Germany.* Berlin: Sigma (Max-Planck-Institute for Human Development and Education, Section Education, Work and Social Change, Reports, vol. 49)

1989b. Educational Systems and Labor Market Outcomes. *European Sociological Review,* **5**: 231–250

1994. *Lebensverlauf und Sozialpolitik. Die Ungleichheit von Mann und Frau und ihr öffentlicher Ertrag.* Frankfurt a.M./New York: Campus

1999. Bildungsarmut. Zur Verschränkung von Bildungs- und Sozialpolitik. *Soziale Welt,* **50**, 1: 35–50

Allmendinger, J., Brückner, H. and Brückner, E. 1993. The Production of Gender Disparities over the Life Course and their Effects in Old Age – Results from the West German Life History Study, in Atkinson, A.B. and Rein, M. (eds.), *Age, Work and Social Security.* New York: St. Martins Press, pp. 188–223

Allmendinger, J. and Hinz, T. 1998. Occupational Careers under Different Welfare Regimes: West Germany, Great Britain and Sweden, in Leisering and Walker (eds.) 1998a, pp. 63–84

Allmendinger, J. and Leibfried, S. 1991. Risks of Marginalization in Comparative Perspective. Paris, mimeo.

Anderson, J. J. 1995. Structural Funds and the Social Dimension of EU Policy: Springboard or Stumbling Block? in Leibfried and Pierson (eds.), pp. 123–158

Andorka, R. and Spéder, Z. 1996. Armut im Transformationsprozeß – am Beispiel Ungarns, in Clausen (ed.), pp. 520–532

Andreß, H.-J. 1994. Steigende Sozialhilfezahlen. Wer bleibt, wer geht und wie sollte die Sozialverwaltung darauf reagieren? in Zwick (ed.), pp. 75–105

(ed.) 1996. *Fünf Jahre danach. Zur Entwicklung von Arbeitsmarkt und Sozialstruktur im vereinten Deutschland.* Berlin/New York: Walter de Gruyter

(ed.) 1998. *Empirical Poverty Research in a Comparative Perspective.* Aldershot: Ashgate

Andreß, H.-J. and Schulte, K. 1998. Poverty Risks and the Life Cycle: The Individualization Thesis Reconsidered, in Andreß (ed.), pp. 331–356

Anweiler, O. 1988. *Schulpolitik und Schulsystem in der DDR.* Opladen: Leske und Budrich

Anweiler, O., Fuchs, H.J., Dorner, M. and Petermann, E. 1992. *Bildungspolitik in Deutschland 1945–1990. Ein historisch vergleichender Quellenband.* Opladen: Leske und Budrich

Ashworth, K., Hill, M. and Walker, R. 1992. Patterns of Childhood Poverty: New Challenges for Policy. Centre for Research in Social Policy, Loughborough University of Technology (CRSP Working Paper No. 169)

Ashworth, K. and Walker, R. 1992. The Dynamics of Family Credit. Centre for Research in Social Policy, Loughborough University of Technology (CRSP Working Paper No. 172)

Ashworth, K., Walker, R., Trinder, P. and Jenkins, S. 1995. The Dynamics of Income Support and Unemployment Benefit. Centre for Research in Social Policy, Loughborough University of Technology (Working Paper No. 242)

Atkinson, A. B. 1989. *Poverty and Social Security.* London: Harvester Wheatsheaf

1991. Comparing Poverty Rates Internationally: Lessons From Recent Studies in Developed Countries. *The World-Bank Economic Review*, **5**, 1: 3–21

1992. Towards a European Social Safety Net? London: London School of Economics, Welfare State Programme, STICERD (Discussion Paper WSP/78)

Atkinson, A. B. and Cazes, S. 1990. Measures de la pauvreté et politiques sociales: une étude comparative de la France, de la RFA et du Royaume-Uni. *Observations et Diagnostiques Économiques,* No. 33, October: 105–130

Atkinson, A. B. and Micklewright, J. 1992. *Economic Transformation in Eastern Europe and the Distribution of Income.* Cambridge: Cambridge University Press

Backhaus-Maul, H. and Olk, T. 1993. Von der 'staatssozialistischen' zur kommunalen Sozialpolitik, Gestaltungsspielräume und -probleme bei der Entwicklung der Sozial-, Alten- und Jugendhilfe in den neuen Bundesländern. *Archiv für Kommunalwissenschaften*, **32**: 300–330

Bäcker, G. 1994. Soziale Sicherung und Arbeitslosigkeit. Soziale Ausgrenzung, Negativsteuer und Grundsicherung. Düsseldorf: Wirtschafts- und Sozialwissenschaftliches Institut der Gewerkschaften (WSI-discussion paper No. 18)

Balsen, W., Nakielski, H., Rössel, K. and Winkel, R. 1984. *Die Neue Armut – Ausgrenzung von Arbeitslosen aus der Arbeitslosenunterstützung.* Cologne: Bund Verlag

Bane, M.J. and Ellwood, D.T. 1986. Slipping into and out of Poverty: The Dynamics of Spells. *The Journal of Human Ressources*, **12**: 1–23

1994. *Welfare Realities: From Rhetoric to Reform.* Cambridge, MA: Harvard University Press

Beam, C.R. 1994. European Unemployment: A Survey. *Journal of Economic Literature*, **32**: 573–619

Beck, M. and Seewald, H. 1994. Zur Reform der amtlichen Sozialhilfestatistik. *Nachrichtendienst des Deutschen Vereins für öffentliche und private Fürsorge*, **74**: 27–31

Beck, U. 1983: Jenseits von Klasse und Stand? in Kreckel, R. (ed.), *Soziale Ungleichheiten.* Göttingen: Schwartz (*Soziale Welt*, special issue No. 2) pp. 35–74

1991. Einleitung, in Beck, U. *Politik in der Risikogesellschaft.* Frankfurt a.M.: Suhrkamp, pp. 9–29

1992. *Risk Society. Towards a New Modernity.* London: Sage (German 1986. *Risikogesellschaft. Auf dem Weg in eine andere Moderne.* Frankfurt a.M.: Suhrkamp)

1993. Risikogesellschaft und Vorsorgestaat – Zwischenbilanz einer Diskussion, in Ewald, pp. 535–558

Beck, U. and Beck-Gernsheim, E. 1993. Nicht Autonomie, sondern Bastelbiographie. Anmerkung zur Individualisierungsdiskussion am Beispiel des Aufsatzes von Günter Burkart. *Zeitschrift für Soziologie*, **22**: 178–187

Beck, U. and Beck-Gernsheim, E. (eds.) 1994. *Riskante Freiheiten. Individualisierung in modernen Gesellschaften*. Frankfurt a.M.: Suhrkamp

Beck, U., Giddens, A. and Lash, S. 1995. *Reflexive Modernisation. Politics, Tradition and Aesthetics in the Modern Social Order*. Cambridge: Polity Press (German version, with new contributions by Beck: *Reflexive Modernisierung. Eine Kontroverse*. Frankfurt a.M.: Suhrkamp 1996)

Beck, U. and Sopp, P. (eds.) 1997. *Individualisierung und Integration. Neue Konfliktlinien und neuer Integrationsmodus?* Opladen: Leske und Budrich

Becker, H. S. 1963. *Outsiders. Studies in the Sociology of Deviance*. New York: The Free Press

Becker, I. 1997. Die Entwicklung von Einkommensverteilung und Einkommensarmut in den alten Bundesländern von 1962 bis 1988, in Becker and Hauser (eds.), pp. 43–62

Becker, I. and Hauser, R. (eds.) 1997. *Einkommensverteilung und Armut. Deutschland auf dem Weg zur Vierfünftel-Gesellschaft*. Frankfurt a.M./New York: Campus

Becker, U. 1998. Brillen aus Luxemburg und Zahnbehandlung in Brüssel – die gesetzliche Krankenversicherung und der Binnenmarkt. *Neue Zeitschrift für Sozialrecht*, **7**, 8: 359–364.

Behrens, J. and Voges, W. (eds.) 1996. *Kritische Übergänge. Lebensläufe im Sozialstaat. Statuspassagen und sozialpolitische Institutionalisierung*. Frankfurt a.M./New York: Campus

Beisheim, M., Dreher, S., Walter, G., Zangl, B. and Zürn, M. 1999. *Im Zeitalter der Globalisierung? Thesen und Daten zur gesellschaftlichen und politischen Denationalisierung*. Baden-Baden: Nomos

Bellebaum, A., Becher, H. and Greven, M.H. (eds.) 1985. *Helfen und Helfende Berufe als soziale Kontrolle*. Opladen: Westdeutscher Verlag

Benner, M., Vad, T. and Schludi, M. 2000. Sweden and Denmark: Changing Places in Defense of the Welfare State, in Scharpf and V. A. Schmidt (eds.) (in preparation)

Berger, P. A. 1990. Ungleichheitsphasen. Stabilität und Instabilität als Aspekte ungleicher Lebenslagen, in Berger and Hradil (eds.) 1990a, pp. 319–350

1994. Individualisierung und Armut, in Zwick (ed.), pp. 21–46

1996. *Individualisierung. Statusunsicherheit und Erfahrungsvielfalt*. Opladen: Westdeutscher Verlag

Berger, P. A. and Hradil, S. (eds.) 1990a. *Lebenslagen, Lebensläufe, Lebensstile*. Göttingen: Schwartz (*Soziale Welt*, special issue No. 7)

1990b. Die Modernisierung sozialer Ungleichheit – und die neuen Konturen ihrer Erforschung, in Berger and Hradil (eds.), 1990a, pp. 3–24

Berghahn, S. and Fritzsche, A. 1991. *Frauen in Ost und West. Bilanz und Ausblick*. Berlin: Basis Druck

Berntsen, R. and Rendtel, U. 1991. Zur Stabilität von Einkommensarmut im Längsschnitt, in Rendtel and Wagner (eds.), pp. 457–485

Beschäftigungsobservatorium Ostdeutschland 1990ff. (No.1ff.): Wissenschaftszentrum Berlin für Sozialforschung, Forschungsschwerpunkt Arbeitsmarkt
und Beschäftigung (ed.), im Auftrag der Europäischen Kommission, General-
direktion Beschäftigung, Arbeitsbeziehungen und Soziale Angelegenheiten,
Berlin

Beyme, K. von, 1979. Einleitung, in Beyme (ed.). *Die großen Regierungserklärungen
der deutschen Bundeskanzler von Adenauer bis Schmidt*. Munich: Hanser, pp.
7–50

Bieback, K.-J. 1985. Das Sozialleistungssystem in der Krise. Bestandsaufnahme
der Sparaktionen, ihre strukturellen Auswirkungen und ihre verfas-
sungsrechtlichen Probleme. *Zeitschrift für Sozialreform*, **31**: 577–590 (part I),
641–655 (part II), 705–722 (part III)

Blank, Rebecca M. 1994. The Employment Strategy: Public Policies to Increase
Work and Earnings, in Danziger *et al.* (eds.), pp. 168–204

   1997. *It Takes a Nation. A New Agenda for Fighting Poverty*. New York: Russell
Sage Foundation

Blum, R. 1964. *Soziologische Konzepte der Sozialarbeit. Mit besonderer
Berücksichtigung des Social Casework*. Freiburg i.B.: Lambertus

Blume, O. 1960. *Die Obdachlosen in Köln. Sozialstrukturelle Untersuchung der
Bewohnerschaft von Obdachlosen-Unterkünften im Kölner Raum*. Göttingen:
Schwartz

BMAS (Bundesministerium für Arbeit und Sozialordnung, Federal Ministry of
Labour and Social Affairs) 1990. *Alterssicherung in Deutschland 1986*; Infratest
Sozialforschung. Munich, Band Z. *Zusammenfassender Bericht*, Munich:
Infratest Sozialforschung

   1994a. *Sozialbericht 1993*. Bonn: BMAS (Series: Berichte und Dokumentationen)

   (ed.) 1994b. *Der Sozialstaat eint. Eine Aufzeichnung von Hans-Ulrich Spree. Zur
sozialen Einheit Deutschlands – Entwicklungen und Eindrücke*. Baden-Baden:
Nomos

   1998. *Sozialbericht 1997*. Bonn: BMAS (Series: Berichte und Dokumentationen)

Bolte, K. M. 1990. Strukturtypen sozialer Ungleichheit. Soziale Ungleichheit in der
Bundesrepublik Deutschland im historischen Vergleich, in Berger and Hradil
(eds.) 1990a, pp. 27–50

Bonß, W. and Plum, W. 1990. Gesellschaftliche Differenzierung und sozialpolitische Normalitätsfiktion. *Zeitschrift für Sozialreform*, **36**: 692–715

Borchert, J. 1995. *Die konservative Transformation des Wohlfahrtsstaates:
Großbritannien, Kanada, die USA und Deutschland im Vergleich*. Frankfurt
a.M./New York: Campus

   1996. Playing the National Card, *Critical Review*, **10**, 1: 63–94

Borjas, G. J. and Hilton, L. 1996. Immigration and the Welfare State: Immigrant
Participation in Means-tested Entitlement Programs. *The Quarterly Journal of
Economics*, **111**, 2: 575–604

Bourdieu, P. 1986. L'illusion biographique. *Actes de la recherche en sciences sociales*,
No. **62/63**: 69–72

   1993. *La misère du monde*. Paris: Editions du Seuil

Breier, B. 1997. Sozialbudget 1995. Neue statistische Ergebnisse. *Bundesarbeitsblatt.* 3: 5–7, 136–142

Breuer, W. and Engels, D. 1994. *Bericht und Gutachten zum Lohnabstandsgebot.* Stuttgart: Kohlhammer (Reports of die Federal Ministry of the Familiy and Senior Citizens, Vol. 29)

Brose, H.-G. and Hildenbrand, B. (eds.) 1988a. *Vom Ende des Individuums zur Individualität ohne Ende.* Opladen: Leske und Budrich

Brose, H.-G. and Hildenbrand, B. 1988b. Biographisierung von Erleben und Handeln, in Brose and Hildenbrand 1988a, pp. 11–32

Brück, G.W. 1976. *Allgemeine Sozialpolitik.* Cologne: Bund-Verlag

Büchel, F., Frick, J. and Voges, W. 1997. Der Sozialhilfebezug von Zuwanderern in Westdeutschland. *Kölner Zeitschrift für Soziologie und Sozialpsychologie,* **49,** 2: 272–290

Buhr, P. 1991. Plädoyer für eine dynamische Armutsforschung – das Modell der USA. *Zeitschrift für Sozialreform,* **37**: 415–433

 1995. *Dynamik von Armut. Dauer und biographische Bedeutung von Sozialhilfe.* Opladen: Westdeutscher Verlag

 1998. Armut im Wunderland? Wege in die und aus der Sozialhilfe in Schweden und Deutschland. Working Paper No. 51, Sfb 186, Bremen (published in: Leviathan, 1999)

Buhr, P., Leibfried, S., Ludwig, M. and Voges, W. 1989. Passages through Welfare. The Bremen Approach to the Analysis of Claimants' Careers in 'Publicly Administered Poverty'. Bremen University, mimeo (German 1990. Wege durch die Sozialhilfe. Der Bremer Ansatz zur Untersuchung 'bekämpfter' Armut im zeitlichen Verlauf, in Dressel, W. *et al.* (ed.) 1990. *Lebenslauf, Arbeitsmarkt und Sozialpolitik.* Nürnberg: IAB (Beiträge aus der Arbeitsmarkt- und Berufsforschung 133), pp. 175–199)

Buhr, P., Leisering, L., Ludwig, M. and Zwick, M. 1991. Armut und Sozialhilfe in vier Jahrzehnten, in Blanke, B. and Wollmann, H. (eds.) *Die alte Bundesrepublik. Kontinuität und Wandel.* Opladen: Westdeutscher Verlag *(Leviathan,* special issue No. 11), pp. 502–546

Buhr, P., Ludwig, M., and Leibfried, S. 1990. Armutspolitik im Blindflug. Zur Notwendigkeit einer Erweiterung der Armutsberichterstattung, in Döring *et al.* 1990a, pp. 79–107

 1992. Sind wir auf dem Weg zu einer verbesserten Armutsberichterstattung? Anmerkungen zur geplanten Reform der Sozialhilfestatistik. *Nachrichtendienst des Deutschen Vereins für öffentliche und private Fürsorge,* **72**: 215–221

Buhr, P., Voges, W. 1991. Eine Ursache kommt selten allein . . . – Ursachen und Ursachenwechsel in der Sozialhilfe. *Sozialer Fortschritt,* **40**: 261–270

Bujard, O. and Lange, U. 1978. *Armut im Alter. Ursachen, Erscheinungsformen, politisch-administrative Reaktionen.* Weinheim/Basle: Beltz

Bundesfinanzministerium [Federal Ministry of Finance] 1998. Öffentliche Leistungen für Deutschland. *Sozialpolitische Umschau,* No. 11, 23 March, p. 20

Bundesministerium für innerdeutsche Beziehungen [Federal Ministry for Inter-German Relations] (ed.) 1985. *DDR Handbuch,* 2 vols., Cologne: Verlag Wissenschaft und Politik

Burkart, G. 1993. Individualisierung und Elternschaft – Das Beispiel USA. *Zeitschrift für Soziologie*, **22**: 159–177

Burkhauser, R. V. and Duncan, G. J. 1988. Life Events, Public Policy, and the Economic Vulnerability of Children and the Elderly, in Palmer *et al.* (eds.), pp. 55–88.

Busch-Geertsema, V. and Ruhstraat, E.-U. 1992. Kein Schattendasein für Langzeitarme! Wider die Verharmlosung von Langzeitarmut im Zusammenhang mit der 'dynamischen' Armutsforschung. *Nachrichtendienst des Deutschen Vereins für öffentliche und private Fürsorge*, **72**: 366–370

Butterwegge, C. 1996. Nutzen und Nachteile der dynamischen Armutsforschung. Kritische Bemerkungen zu einer neueren Forschungsrichtung. *Zeitschrift für Sozialreform*, **42**, 2: 69–92.

Bundesverfassungsgericht 1999, Decision of 10 November 1998. *Neue Juristische Wochenschrift*, 8: 557–561

BVerfGE (Entscheidungen des Bundesverfassungsgerichts [Rulings of the Federal Constitutional Court]), ed. by the members of the Federal Constitutional Court *et al.*, Vol. 87 (1993), Tübingen: J.C.B. Mohr (Paul Siebeck)

Caritasverband (ed.) 1987. *Arme haben keine Lobby. Caritas-Report zur Armut.* Freiburg i.B.: Lambertus

Castel, R. and Lae, J.-F. (eds.) 1992. *Le revenu minimum d'insertion. Une dette sociale.* Paris: L'Harmattan

Christiansen, U. 1973. *Obdachlos weil arm. Gesellschaftliche Reaktionen auf die Armut.* Giessen: Edition 2000

Clausen, L. (ed.) 1996. *Gesellschaften im Umbruch. Verhandlungen des 27. Kongresses der Deutschen Gesellschaft für Soziologie in Halle an der Saale 1995.* Frankfurt a.M. and New York: Campus

Coffield, F., Robinson, P. and Sarsby, J. 1980. *A Cycle of Deprivation? A Case Study of Four Families.* London: Heinemann Educational

Colla, H.-E. 1974. Armut im Wohlfahrtsstaat, in Bellebaum, A. and Braun, H. (eds.) *Reader Soziale Probleme 1. Empirische Befunde.* Frankfurt a.M. and New York: Herder & Herder, pp. 19–33

Conrad, C. 1994. *Vom Greis zum Rentner. Der Strukturwandel des Alters in Deutschland zwischen 1830 und 1930.* Göttingen: Vandenhoeck & Ruprecht

Cornia, G.A. and Danziger, S. (eds.) 1997. *Child Poverty and Deprivation in the Industrialized Countries 1945–1995. A UNICEF International Child Development Centre Study.* Oxford: Clarendon Press

Dahrendorf, R. 1979. *Lebenschancen. Anläufe zur sozialen und politischen Theorie.* Frankfurt a.M.: Suhrkamp

1984. *Reisen nach innen und außen. Aspekte der Zeit.* Stuttgart: Deutsche Verlags-Anstalt

1988. *The Modern Social Conflict. An Essay on the Politics of Liberty.* London: Weidenfeld and Nicolson (German 1992. *Der moderne soziale Konflikt: Essay zur Politik der Freiheit.* Stuttgart: Deutsche Verlags-Anstalt)

1997. An der Schwelle zum autoritären Jahrhundert. Die Globalisierung und ihre sozialen Folgen werden zur nächsten Herausforderung einer Politik der Freiheit. *DIE ZEIT* No. 47, November 14, pp. 14–15

330   **References**

Daly, M. 1997. Armut unterwegs – wohin? *Soziologische Revue*, **20**, 4: 433–441

Dangschat, J.S. 1994. Soziale Ungleichheit und die Armut der Soziologie. *Blätter für deutsche und internationale Politik*, **39**: 872–885

1995. 'Stadt' als Ort und als Ursache von Armut und sozialer Ausgrenzung. *Aus Politik und Zeitgeschichte. Beilage zur Wochenzeitschrift Das Parlament*, B31–32/95: 50–62

Danziger, S.S., Sandefur, G.D. and Weinberg, D.H. (eds.) 1994. *Confronting Poverty: Prescriptions for Change*. Cambridge, MA: Harvard University Press

Datenreport 1994, 1997. *Zahlen und Fakten über die Bundesrepublik Deutschland*, ed. by the Federal Bureau of Statistics (Statistisches Bundesamt) in co-operation with the Social Science Research Center Berlin (Wissenschaftszentrum Berlin für Sozialforschung). Bonn: Bundeszentrale für politische Bildung

Day, B. 1992. Income Source as a Social Barometer. *Journal of Social Policy*, **21**: 469–487

Dean, H. and Taylor-Gooby, P. 1992. *Dependency Culture: The Explosion of a Myth*. New York/London: Harvester Wheatsheaf

Delsen, L.O. and Reday-Mulvey, G. 1996. *Gradual Retirements in the OECD Countries. Macro and Micro Issues and Policies*. Aldershot: Dartmouth

DeParle, J. 1996. Mugged by Reality. *The New York Time Magazine*, 8 December: 64–67, 99–100

Der Spiegel, 1961. 'Unsere Armen haben das nicht nötig!' Elend im Wunderland. *Der Spiegel*, **15**, 52: 40–47

1984. Neue Armut. Druck unterm Deckel. *Der Spiegel*, **39**, 29: 21–22

1988. Einfach hinlangen. *Der Spiegel*, **43**, 43: 74–78

de Swaan, A. 1988. *In Care of the State*. Oxford: Polity Press

1992. Perspectives for Transnational Social Policy. *Government and Opposition*, **27**: 33–52

1994. Perspectives for Transnational Social Policy in Europe: Social Transfers from West to East, in ibid. (ed.) *Social Policy Beyond Borders. The Social Question in Transnational Perspective*. Amsterdam: Amsterdam University Press, pp. 101–115

DFG (Deutsche Forschungsgemeinschaft [German National Research Council]) (ed.) 1994. *Mikroanalytische Grundlagen der Gesellschaftspolitik. Ergebnisse aus dem gleichnamigen Sonderforschungsbereich an den Universitäten Frankfurt am Main und Mannheim*, vol. I: *Ausgewählte Probleme und Lösungsansätze*, ed. by Hauser, R., Hochmuth, U. and Schwarze, J., vol. II: *Erhebungsverfahren, Analyseverfahren und Mikrosimulation*, ed. by Hauser, R., Ott, N. and Wagner, G. Berlin: Akademie Verlag

Ditch, J., Bradshaw, J., Clasen, J., Huby, M. and Moodie, M. 1996. Comparative Social Assistance: Localisation and Discretion. York/Stirling: mimeo

DiPrete, T. A., Graaf, P. M., de Luijkx, R., Tåhlin, M. and Blossfeld, H.-P. 1997. Collectivist versus Individualist Mobility Regimes? Structural Change and Job Mobility in Four Countries. *American Journal of Sociology*, **103**, 2: 318–358

Döring, D., Hanesch, W. and Huster, E.-U. (eds.) 1990a. *Armut im Wohlstand.* Frankfurt a.M.: Suhrkamp

1990b. Armut als Lebenslage. Ein Konzept für Armutsberichterstattung und Armutspolitik. Einleitung, in Döring *et al.* (eds.), 1990a, pp. 7–27

Drauschke, P., Mädje, E., Neusüß, C. and Stolzenburg, M. 1993. Alleinerziehende Frauen in Berlin, in Meulemann, H. and Elting-Camus, A. (eds.) *26. Deutscher Soziologentag Düsseldorf 28.9.–2.10.1992, Tagungsband II.* Opladen: Westdeutscher Verlag, pp. 304–307

Duncan, G.J. 1984. *Years of Poverty, Years of Plenty. The Changing Economic Fortunes of American Workers and Families.* Ann Arbor, MI: Institute for Social Research, The University of Michigan

Duncan, G. J., Gustafsson, B., Hauser, R., Schmaus, G., Jenkins, S., Messinger, H., Muffels, R., Nolan, B., Ray, J.-C., Voges, W. 1995. Poverty and Social-Assistance Dynamics in the United States, Canada, and Europe, in McFate *et al.* (eds.), pp. 67–108

Duncan, G. and Hoffmann, S. 1988. The Use and Effects of Welfare: A Survey of Recent Evidence. *Social Service Review*, **62**: June: 238–257.

Duncan, G. J. and Voges, W. 1993. Do Generous Social Assistance Programs lead to Dependence? A Comparative Study of Lone-parent Families in Germany and the United States. Centre for Social Policy Research, University of Bremen. (Working Paper No. 11/1993)

Duncan, G.J., Voges, W., Hauser, R., Gustafsson, B., Jenkins, S., Messinger, H., Nolan, B., Ray, J.-C and Schmaus, G. 1994. Armuts- und Sozialhilfedynamiken in Europa und Nordamerika, *Zeitschrift für Sozialreform*, **40**: 281–313

Eardley, T., Bradshaw, J., Ditch, J., Gough, I. and Whiteford, P. 1996. *Social Assistance in OECD Countries* (Vol. I: *Synthesis report*, Vol. II: *Country reports*). London: HMSO (Department of Social Security, Research Report No. 46)

EC (European Communities – Commission) 1993. Growth, Competitiveness, Employment – The Challenges and Ways Forward into the 21st Century (White Paper). Luxembourg: Office for Official Publications of the European Communities

Eichhorst, W. 1998. European Social Policy between National and Supranational Regulation. Posted Workers in the Framework of Liberalized Service Provision. Cologne: Max-Planck-Institute for Social Research (DP 98/6)

Ellwood, D. T. 1987. Understanding Dependency: Choices, Confidence, or Culture? Waltham, MA: Brandeis University, mimeo

Elsner, I. and Proske, R. 1953. Der Fünfte Stand. Eine Untersuchung über die Armut in Westdeutschland. *Frankfurter Hefte*, **8**: 101–111

Engbersen, G., Schuyt, K., Timmer, J. and van Waarden, F. 1993. *Cultures of Employment. A Comparative Look at Long-Term Unemployment and Urban Poverty.* Boulder, CO: Westview Press

Erhard, L. 1957. *Wohlstand für alle.* Düsseldorf: Econ (reprint 1990)

Erikson, R. and Goldthorpe, J. H. 1992. *The Constant Flux. A Study of Class Mobility in Industrial Societies.* Oxford: Clarendon Press

Esping-Andersen, G. 1990. *The Three Worlds of Welfare Capitalism.* Cambridge: Polity Press

1993. Post-industrial Class Structures: An Analytical Framework, in Esping-Andersen, G. (ed.), *Changing Classes. Stratification and Mobility in Post-industrial Societies.* London: Sage, pp. 7–31

1996. After the Golden Age? Welfare State Dilemmas in the Global Economy, in Esping-Andersen, G. (ed.) 1996. *Welfare States in Transition. National Adaptions in Global Economics.* London: Sage, pp. 1–31

Ewald, F. 1993. *Der Vorsorgestaat.* Frankfurt a.M.: Suhrkamp

Falkingham, J. and Hills, J. (eds.) 1995. *The Dynamic of Welfare. The Welfare State and the Life Cycle.* London: Harvester Wheatsheaf

Farwick, A. 1998. Soziale Ausgrenzung in der Stadt. Struktur und Verlauf der Sozialhilfebedürftigkeit in städtischen Armutsgebieten. *Geographische Rundschau,* **50**, 3: 146–153

Federal Parliament Proceedings (*Deutscher Bundestag, Stenographische Berichte*) 1960

1996 [Poverty Debate], pp. 11352–11374

Federal Parliamentary Papers (*Bundestagsdrucksache*) 3/1799 of April 20, 1960. Entwurf eines Bundessozialhilfegesetzes. [Draft of a Federal Social Assistance Act]

3/308 of 1974 [Social Assistance Reform of 1974]

Ferber, C.v. and Kaufmann, F.-X. (eds.) 1977. *Soziologie und Sozialpolitik.* Opladen: Westdeutscher Verlag. (*Kölner Zeitschrift für Soziologie und Sozialpsychologie,* Special Issue No. 19)

Ferrera, M. 1998. The Four 'Social Europes': Between Universalism and Selectivity, in Meny and Rhodes (eds.), pp. 79–96

Ferrera, M. and Gualmini, S. 2000. Italy: Rescue from Without? in Scharpf and V.A. Schmidt.

Frerich, J. and Frey, M. 1993. *Handbuch der Geschichte der Sozialpolitik,* vol. 2: *Sozialpolitik in der Deutschen Demokratischen Republik.* Munich/Wien: Oldenbourg

Freyberg, T. v. 1995. '. . . im ganzen also sehr widerwärtig . . .' Verleugnen, Verleumden, Ausgrenzen: Vom Umgang mit der Armut, in Hengsbach, F. and Möhring-Hesse, M. (eds.), *Eure Armut kotzt uns an! Solidarität in der Krise.* Frankfurt a.M.: Fischer, pp. 23–37

Fridberg, T. (ed.) 1993. *On Social Assistance in the Nordic Capitals.* Copenhagen: Socialforskningsinstituttet

Friedrich, H., Fränkel-Dahmann, I., Schaufelberger, H.-J. and Streeck, U. 1979. *Soziale Deprivation und Familiendynamik. Studien zur psychosozialen Realität von unterprivilegierten Familien und ihrer Veränderung durch ausgewählte Formen sozialer Praxis.* Göttingen: Verlag für medizinische Psychologie/ Vandenhoek und Ruprecht

Friedrich, H. and Schaufelberger, H.-J. 1975. Armut und soziale Unterprivilegierung. Zum Verhältnis von sozialer Lage und Familiendynamik bei sozialen Randgruppen, in Osterland, M. (ed.), *Arbeitssituation, Lebenslage und Konfliktpotential. Festschrift für Max E. Graf zu Solms-Roedelheim.* Cologne: EVA, pp. 185–212

Friedrichs, J. 1998a. Do Poor Neighborhoods Make their Residents Poorer? Context Effects of Poverty Neighborhoods on Residents, in Andreß, H.-J. (ed.), pp. 77–99

(ed.) 1998b. *Die Individualisierungs-These*. Opladen: Leske und Budrich

Fürstenberg, F. 1965. Randgruppen in der modernen Gesellschaft. *Soziale Welt,* **16**: 236–245

Furstenberg, F.F., Brooks-Gunn, J. and Morgan, S. P. 1987. *Adolescent Mothers in Later Life*. Cambridge: Cambridge University Press

Galbraith, J. K. 1992. *The Culture of Contentment*. Boston/New York: Houghton Mifflin

Gangl, M. 1998. Sozialhilfebezug und Arbeitsmarktverhalten. Eine Längsschnittanalyse der Übergänge aus der Sozialhilfe in den Arbeitsmarkt. *Zeitschrift für Soziologie,* **27**, 3: 212–232

Gans, H.J. 1972. The Positive Functions of Poverty. *American Journal of Sociology,* **78**: 275–289

1992. Über die positiven Funktionen der unwürdigen Armen. Zur Bedeutung der 'underclass' in den USA, in Leibfried and Voges (eds.) 1992a, pp. 48–62

Gebhardt, T. 1998. *Arbeit gegen Armut. Die Reform der Sozialhilfe in den USA*. Opladen: Westdeutscher Verlag

Gebhardt, T. and Jacobs, H. 1997. Amerikanische Verhältnisse? Sozialhilfe in den USA und Deutschland: Ein Vergleich aus historischer, institutioneller und rechtlicher Perspektive. *Zeitschrift für Sozialreform,* **43**, 8: 597–633

Geisel, E. 1984. *Lastenausgleich, Umschuldung. Die Wiedergutwerdung der Deutschen. Essays, Polemiken, Stichworte*. Berlin: Tiamat

Geißler, H. 1976. *Die Neue Soziale Frage. Analysen und Dokumente*. Freiburg i.B.: Herder

Geißler, R. 1993 (ed.). *Sozialer Umbruch in Ostdeutschland*. Opladen: Westdeutscher Verlag

1996. *Die Sozialstruktur Deutschlands, zur gesellschaftlichen Entwicklung mit einer Zwischenbilanz zur Vereinigung*. Rev. edn, Opladen: Westdeutscher Verlag

Gerhardt, U. 1979. Coping and Social Action: Theoretical Reconstruction of the Life-Event Approach. *Social Health and Illness,* **1**: 195–225

1985. Introduction. Stress and Stigma – the Dilemma of Explanantion, in Gerhardt, U. and Wadsworth, M.E.J. (eds.), *Stress and Stigma*. Frankfurt a.M./New York: Campus; London: Macmillan; New York: St. James' Press, pp. 15–36

1986a. *Patientenkarrieren. Eine medizinsoziologische Studie*. Frankfurt a.M.: Suhrkamp

1986b. Verstehende Strukturanalyse: Die Konstruktion von Idealtypen als Analyseschritt bei der Auswertung qualitativer Forschungsmaterialien, in Soeffner, H.-G. (ed.), *Sozialstruktur und soziale Typik*. Frankfurt a.M./New York: Campus, pp. 31–83

1987. Soziologische Erklärung gesundheitlicher Ungleichheit. Probleme der theoretischen Rekonstruktion empirischer Befunde, in Giesen, B. and Haferkamp, H. (eds.), *Soziologie der sozialen Ungleichheit.* Opladen: Westdeutscher Verlag, pp. 393–426

1990. Patient Careers in End-Stage Renal Failure. *Social Science and Medicine,* **30,** 11: 1211–1224

1991. Idealtypische Analyse von Statusbiographien bei chronisch Kranken, in Gerhardt, U., *Gesellschaft und Gesundheit. Begründung der Medizinsoziologie.* Frankfurt a.M.: Suhrkamp, pp. 9–60

1994. The Use of Weberian Ideal-Type Methodology in Qualitative Data Interpretation, An Outline of Ideal-Type Analysis, *BMIMEO Bulletin Méthodologie Sociologique,* No. 4, December: 74–126

1996. 'Ideal-Type' and the Construction of the Life-Course, in Heinz, W. and Weymann, A. (eds.), *Society and Biography.* Weinheim: Psychologie Verlags Union, pp. 21–50

1998. Die Verwendung von Idealtypen in der fallvergleichenden biographischen Forschung, in Jüttemann, G. and Thomae, H. (eds.), *Biographische Methoden in den Humanwissenschaften.* Weinheim: Psychologie Verlags Union, pp. 195–213

1999a *Herz und Handlungsrationalität. Biographische Verläufe nach koronarer Bypassoperation zwischen Beruf und Berentung. Eine idealtypenanalytische Studie.* Frankfurt a.M.: Suhrkamp

1999b *Ideal-Type Analysis. Linking Case and Structure in Qualitative Data Interpretation,* mimeo

Gerstenberger, H. 1994. Die dynamische Armutsforschung und das Elend der Welt. *Leviathan,* **22,** 1: 7–16

Giddens, A. 1991. *Modernity and Self-Identity. Self and Society in the Late Modern Age.* Cambridge: Polity Press.

Giesbrecht, A. 1987. *Wohnungslos, Arbeitslos, Mittellos. Lebensläufe und Situation von Nichtseßhaften.* Opladen: Leske und Budrich

Giese, D. 1993. Die Änderungen des Sozialhilferechts durch das Gesetz zur Umsetzung des Föderalen Konsolidierungsprogramms (FKPG). *Zeitschrift für das Fürsorgewesen,* **45:** 145–164

Gilbert, N. and Gilbert, B. 1989. *The Enabling State. Modern Welfare Capitalism in America.* New York/Oxford: Oxford University Press

Girvetz, H. 1968. Welfare State. *International Encyclopedia of the Social Sciences,* **16:** 512–521

Glaser, B.C. and Strauss, A.L. 1971. *Status Passage.* Chicago: Aldine

Glatzer, W. 1978. Einkommenspolitische Zielsetzungen und Einkommensverteilung, in Zapf, W. (ed.), *Lebensbedingungen in der Bundesrepublik Deutschland. Sozialer Wandel und Wohlfahrtsentwicklung,* 2nd edn, Frankfurt a.M./New York: Campus, pp. 323–384

Glatzer, W. and Hübinger, W. 1990. Lebenslagen und Armut, in Döring *et al.* (eds.) 1990a, pp. 31–55

Glatzer, W. and Krupp, H.-J. 1975. Soziale Indikatoren des Einkommens und seiner Verteilung in der Bundesrepublik Deutschland, in Zapf, W. (ed.), *Soziale Indikatoren. Konzepte und Forschungsansätze III.* Frankfurt a.M./New York: Campus, pp. 193–238

Glatzer, W. and Noll, H.-H. 1995. *Getrennt Vereint: Lebensverhältnisse in Deutschland seit der Wiedervereinigung*. Frankfurt a.M./New York: Campus

Glotz, P. 1984. *Die Arbeit der Zuspitzung: Über die Organisation einer regierungsfähigen Linken*. Berlin: Siedler

1985. *Manifest für eine Neue Europäische Linke*. Berlin: Siedler

Göckenjan, G. 1999. Das Alter würdigen. Altersbilder und Bedeutungswandel des Alters. Frankfurt a.M.: Suhrkamp

Groenemeyer, A. 1990. *Drogenkarriere und Sozialpolitik*. Pfaffenweiler: Centaurus

Großmann, H. and Huth, S. 1993. Wandel sozialer Ungleichheit: Subjektive Erfahrungen ostdeutscher Alleinerziehender in der Sozialhilfesituation, in Hanesch, W. (ed.), *Lebenslageforschung und Sozialberichterstattung in den neuen Bundesländern*. Düsseldorf: Hans-Böckler-Stiftung, pp. 137–150

Grünert, H. 1993. Weiterbildungsbedarf bei kaufmännischen Industrieangestellten in den neuen Ländern, ed. by the AG Qualifikations- und Entwicklungsmanagement, Berlin (*Quem-report 4*)

Gusfield, J.R. 1981. *The Culture of Public Problems. Drinking-Driving and the Symbolic Order*. Chicago, IL, London: University of Chicago Press

Gustafsson, B. and Voges, W. 1998. Contrasting Welfare Dynamics: Germany and Sweden, in Leisering and Walker (eds.), 1998a, pp. 243–261

Gysi, J. and Meyer, D. 1993. Leitbild: berufstätige Mutter, DDR-Frauen in Familie, Partnerschaft und Ehe, in Helwig, G. *et al.* (eds.), *Frauen in Deutschland: 1945–1992*. Berlin: Akademie-Verlag, pp. 139–165

Habich, R. and Krause, P. 1994. Armut, in *Datenreport 1994*, pp. 598–607

1997. Armut, in *Datenreport 1997*, pp. 515–525

Habich, R. and Noll, H.-H. 1993. *Soziale Indikatoren und Sozialberichterstattung. Internationale Erfahrungen und gegenwärtiger Forschungsstand, Expertise für das Bundesamt für Statistik*. Bern, Schweiz, Berlin und Mannheim

Hacker, J. 1997. *The Road to Nowhere: The Genesis of President Clinton's Plan for Health Security*. Princeton: Princeton University Press

Häußermann, H., Kronauer, M. and Siebel, W. (ed.) 1999. *Eine neue Unterklasse? Armut und Ausgrenzung und die neue 'Urban Underclass'*. Frankfurt a.M.: Suhrkamp (forthcoming)

Haferkamp, H. 1977. Von der alltagsweltlichen zur sozialwissenschaftlichen Begründung der Soziologie sozialer Probleme und sozialer Kontrolle, in von Ferber and Kaufmann (eds.), pp. 186–212

Hagen, C. and Hock, B. 1996a. *Dynamik von Armut in einer hessischen Kleinstadt. Sozialhilfeverläufe und -karrieren*. Frankfurt a.M.: Eigenverlag des Deutschen Vereins für öffentliche und private Fürsorge

1996b. Stabilität und Mobilität – Dynamische Armutsforschung in einer hessischen Kleinstadt. *Nachrichtendienst des Deutschen Vereins für öffentliche und private Fürsorge*, **76**, 3: 95–100

Hagenaars, A.J.M. 1986. *The Perception of Poverty*. Amsterdam: North-Holland

Hall, P. 1997. The Political Economy of Adjustment in Germany, in Naschold, F. *et al.* (eds.), *Ökonomische Leistungsfähigkeit und institutionelle Innovation. Das deutsche Produktions- und Politikregime im globalen Wettbewerb*. Berlin: Edition Sigma (WZB-Yearbook), pp. 293–318

336 References

Halleröd, B. and Heikkilä, B. 1999. Poverty and Social Exclusion in the Nordic Countries, in Kautto *et al.* (in print)

Handler, J.F. and Hasenfeld, Y. 1991. *Poverty and Welfare Reform: A Moral Issue.* London: Sage

Hanesch, W. 1991. Der halbierte Wohlstand: Zur sozialen Lage in den neuen Bundesländern. *Sozialer Fortschritt*, **40**: 242–248

Hanesch, W., Adamy, W., Martens, R., Rentzsch, D., Schneider, U., Schubert, U. and Wißkirchen, M. 1994. *Armut in Deutschland. Der Armutsbericht des DGB und des Paritätischen Wohlfahrtsverbandes.* Reinbek: Rowohlt

Hanesch, W. and Bäcker, G. 1993. Sozialhilfeniveau und untere Arbeitnehmereinkommen. Eine Expertise im Rahmen der Landessozial-berichterstattung NRW. Düsseldorf: Ministerium für Arbeit, Gesundheit und Soziales des Landes Nordrhein-Westfalen, mimeo

Hartmann, H. 1981. *Sozialhilfebedürftigkeit und 'Dunkelziffer der Armut'.* Stuttgart: Kohlhammer

1992. Lebenslage Armut – ein Konzept zur Armutsbeschreibung und Armutspolitik. *Theorie und Praxis der sozialen Arbeit*, **43**: 452–459

Hauser, R. 1994. Armut im Sozialstaat als Problem einer Theorie der integrierten Sozial- und Verteilungspolitik, in DFG (ed.), vol. I, pp. 291–335

1996. *Ziele und Möglichkeiten einer Sozialen Grundsicherung.* Baden-Baden: Nomos

1997a. Armut, Armutsgefährdung und Armutsbekämpfung in der Bundes-republik Deutschland. *Jahrbücher für Nationalökonomie und Statistik*, **216**, 4/5: 524–547

1997b. Vergleichende Analyse der Einkommensverteilung und der Einkom-mensarmut in den alten und neuen Bundesländern 1990 bis 1995, in Becker and Hauser (eds.), 1997, pp. 63–82

Hauser, R. and Berntsen, R. 1991. Einkommensarmut – Determinanten von Aufstiegen und Abstiegen, in Hujer, R., Schneider, H. and Zapf, W. (eds.) *Herausforderungen an den Wohlfahrtsstaat im strukturellen Wandel.* Frankfurt a.M./New York: Campus, pp. 73–97

Hauser, R., Cremer-Schäfer, H. and Nouverné, U. 1981. *Armut, Niedrigkein-kommen und Unterversorgung in der Bundesrepublik Deutschland.* Frankfurt a.M./New York: Campus (2nd edn. 1986)

Hauser, R. and Hübinger, W. 1993. *Arme unter uns. Teil 1: Ergebnisse und Konsequenzen der Caritas-Armutsuntersuchung.* Freiburg i.B.: Lambertus

Hauser, R. and Kinstler H.-J. 1995. Zuwanderer unter den Caritas-Klienten, in Hübinger, W. and Hauser, R. (eds.), *Die Caritas-Armutsuntersuchung. Eine Bilanz.* Freiburg i.B.: Lambertus, pp. 84–106

Hauser, R. and Neumann, U. 1992. Armut in der Bundesrepublik Deutschland. Die sozialwissenschaftliche Thematisierung nach dem zweiten Weltkrieg, in Leibfried and Voges (eds.) 1992a, pp. 237–271

Hauser, R. and Semrau, P. 1990. Zur Entwicklung der Einkommensarmut von 1963 bis 1986. *Sozialer Fortschritt*, **39**: 27–36

Headey, B., Habich, R. and Krause, P. 1990. *The Duration and Extent of Poverty – is Germany a Two-thirds-society?* Berlin: Social Science Centre (Working Paper P90/103)

Heclo, H. 1994. Poverty Politics, in Danziger *et al.* (eds.), pp. 396–437

Heidenheimer, A. J. 1981. Education and Social Security Entitlements in Europe and America, in Flora, P. and Heidenheimer, A. J. (eds.) *The Development of Welfare States in Europe and America.* New Brunswick, NJ: Transaction Books, pp. 269–306

Heimann, H. 1975. *Theoriediskussion in der SPD. Ergebnisse und Perspektiven.* Frankfurt a.M./Cologne: Europäische Verlagsanstalt

Heinz, W. R. (ed.) 1987. *Statuspassagen und Risikolagen im Lebensverlauf. Institutionelle Steuerung und individuelle Handlungsstrategien.* Antrag auf Einrichtung eines Sonderforschungsbereiches an der Universität Bremen, Bremen

(ed.) 1991a. *Theoretical Advances in Life Course Research.* Weinheim: Deutscher Studien Verlag

1991b. Status Passages, Social Risks and the Life Course: A Conceptual Framework, in ibid. 1991a, pp. 9–22

Heisig, M. 1994. *Armenpolitik im Nachkriegsdeutschland (1945–1964). Die Entwicklung des Fürsorgeunterstützungssätze im Kontext allgemeiner Sozial- und Fürsorgereform.* Frankfurt a.M.: Deutscher Verein für öffentliche und private Fürsorge

Held, D. 1991. Democracy, the Nation-State and the Global System, in Held, D. (ed.), *Political Theory Today.* Stanford, CA: Stanford University Press, pp. 197–235

Henkel, H.A. and Pavelka, F. 1981. Das Amt: Dein Feind und Helfer. *Sozialer Fortschritt,* **30**: 225–231

Henningsen, B. and Room, G. (eds.) 1990. *Neue Armut in der Europäischen Gemeinschaft.* Frankfurt a.M.: Campus

Hennock, E.P. 1987. *British Social Reform and German Precedents. The Case of Social Insurance 1880–1914.* Oxford: Clarendon Press

Hess, H. and Mechler, A. 1973. *Ghetto ohne Mauern. Ein Bericht aus der Unterschicht.* Frankfurt a.M.: Suhrkamp

Hilkert, B. 1998. Armut und prekärer Wohlstand. Erster Bericht zur Einkommensarmut und Sozialhilfebedürftigkeit in Groß-Gerau. Erstellt im Auftrag des Magistrats der Kreisstadt Groß-Gerau. Groß-Gerau, mimeo

Hill, M. 1992. The Panel Study of Income Dynamics. Newbury Park, London, New Dehli: Sage

Hill, M., Hill, D. and Walker, R. 1998. Intergenerational Dynamics in the USA: Poverty Processes in Young Adulthood, in Leisering and Walker (eds.) 1998a, pp. 85–107

Hockerts, H.G. 1980. *Sozialpolitische Entscheidungen im Nachkriegsdeutschland. Alliierte und deutsche Sozialversicherungspolitik 1945 bis 1957.* Stuttgart: Klett-Cotta

1986. Integration der Gesellschaft: Gründungskrise und Sozialpolitik in der frühen Bundesrepublik. *Zeitschrift für Sozialreform,* **32**: 25–41

Hohmann, K. (ed.) 1988. *Ludwig Erhard. Gedanken aus fünf Jahrzehnten, Reden und Schriften.* Düsseldorf, Wien and New York: Econ

Hollstein, W. and Meinhold, M. (eds.) 1973. *Sozialarbeit unter kapitalistischen Produktionsbedingungen.* Frankfurt a.M.: Fischer

Hoynes, H. and MaCurdy, T. 1994. Has the Decline in Benefits Shortened Welfare Spells? *American Economic Review, Papers and Proceedings*, **84**, 2: 43–48

Hübinger, W. 1989. Zur Lebenslage und Lebensqualität von Sozialhilfeempfängern. Eine theoretische und empirische Armutsuntersuchung. *Sozialer Fortschritt*, **38**: 172–180

1991. *Zur Lebenslage und Lebensqualität von Sozialhilfeempfängern. Eine theoretische und empirische Armutsuntersuchung, Diplomarbeit von 1987.* Frankfurt a.m.: Eigenverlag des Deutschen Vereins für öffentliche und private Fürsorge

1996. *Prekärer Wohlstand. Neue Befunde zu Armut und sozialer Ungleichheit.* Freiburg i. B.: Lambertus

Huff Stevens, A. 1994. The Dynamics of Poverty Spells: Updating Bane and Ellwood, in *American Economic Review, Papers and Proceedings*, **84**, 2: 34–37

Hughes, M.L. 1991. Lastenausgleich unter Sozialismusverdacht. Amerikanische Besorgnisse 1945–49. *Vierteljahreshefte für Zeitgeschichte*, **39**, 1: 37–53

Huinink, J., Mayer, K.U., Diewald, M., Solga, H., Sørensen, A. and Trappe, H. 1995. *Kollektiv und Eigensinn. Lebensverläufe in der DDR und danach.* Berlin: Akademie Verlag

Huster, E.-U. 1997. Armut in Europa – ausgewählte Ergebnisse des Armutsobservatoriums der Europäischen Union, in Becker and Hauser (eds.), pp. 199–230

Hvinden, B. 1994. En database om klientstrømmer. Noen erfaringer fra etableringsfasen. *Tidsskrift for samfunnsforskning*, No. 1, Universitetsforlaget, pp. 105–120

1995. Poverty, Exclusion, and Agency. *Research in Community Sociology*, **5**: 15–33

1999. Activation – a Nordic Perspective, in Heikkilae, M. (ed.) *Linking Welfare and Work.* Luxembourg: Office for Official Publications of the European Communities, pp. 27–42

Iben, G. 1970. *Kinder am Rande der Gesellschaft.* Munich: Juventa

Illich, I. 1976. *Medical Nemesis. The Expropriation of Health.* New York: Pantheon Books

Ireland, P. 1995. *Migration*, Free Movement, and Immigrant Integration in the EU: A Bifurcated Policy Response, in Leibfried and Pierson (eds.), pp. 231–266

Jacobs, H. 1994. Wer dramatisiert denn hier? Anmerkungen zum Forschungsprojekt 'Sozialhilfekarrieren'. *Sozialer Fortschritt*, **43**: 121–128

Jacobs, H. and Ringbeck, A. 1994. *Hilfen zur Überwindung von Sozialhilfebedürftigkeit. Eine Untersuchung zur Hilfe zum Lebensunterhalt in den alten Bundesländern. Abschlußbericht.* Stuttgart: Kohlhammer (Schriftenreihe des Bundesministeriums für Familie und Senioren, vol. 31)

Jaedicke, W., Ruhland, K., Wachendorfer, U., Wollmann, H. and Wonneberg, H. 1991. *Lokale Politik im Wohlfahrtsstaat. Zur Sozialpolitik der Gemeinden und ihrer Verbände in der Beschäftigungskrise.* Opladen: Westdeutscher Verlag

Jahoda, M., Lazarsfeld, P.F. and Zeisel, H. 1975. *Die Arbeitslosen von Marienthal. Ein soziographischer Versuch über die Wirkungen langandauernder Arbeitslosigkeit.* Frankfurt a.M.: Suhrkamp (1st edn 1933) (English 1971. *Marienthal. The Sociography of an Unemployed Community*, Chicago: Aldine, Atherton).

Janowitz, M. 1976. *Social Control of the Welfare State*. New York: Elsevier

Jarvis, S. and Jenkins, S. P. 1997. Low Income Dynamics in 1990s Britain. *Fiscal Studies*, **18**, 2: 123–142

1998. Income and Poverty Dynamics in Great Britain, in Leisering and Walker (eds.), pp. 145–160

Jenkins, S.P. 1991. Poverty Measurement and the Within-Household Distribution: Agenda for Action. *Journal of Social Policy*, **20**: 457–484

Jessop, B. 1994. Politik in der Ära Thatcher: Die defekte Wirtschaft und der schwache Staat, in Grimm, D. (with Evelyn Hagenah), (ed.) 1994 *Staatsaufgaben*. Baden-Baden: Nomos, pp. 353–389

Joas, H. and Kohli, M. (eds.) 1993a. *Der Zusammenbruch der DDR*. Frankfurt a.M.: Suhrkamp

Joas, H. and Kohli, M. 1993b. Der Zusammenbruch der DDR: Fragen und Thesen, in ibid. (eds.), pp. 7–28

Johrendt, N. and Schneider, H.R. (eds.) 1992. *Computerunterstützte Sozialberichterstattung und Sozialplanung*, Bielefeld (Schriftenreihe des Berufsverbandes Deutscher Soziologen, vol. 11)

Jordan, B. 1996. *A Theory of Poverty and Social Exclusion*. Cambridge: Polity Press

Kahler, M. 1995. *Regional Futures and Transatlantic Economic Relations*. New York: Council of Foreign Relations Press

Kappeler, B. 1994. Von allem das Beste. *Die Zeit*, No. 24, 10 June: 34f.

Kapstein, E.B. 1996. Workers and the World Economy. *Foreign Affairs*, **75**, 3: 16–37

Karstedt, S. 1975. Soziale Randgruppen und soziologische Theorie, in Brusten, M. and Hohmeier, J. (eds.), *Stigmatisierung 1. Zur Produktion gesellschaftlicher Randgruppen*. Neuwied: Luchterhand, pp. 169–196

Kaufmann, F.-X. 1973. *Sicherheit als soziologisches und sozialpolitisches Problem*. Stuttgart: Enke (rev. 2nd edn.)

1980. Kinder als Außenseiter der Gesellschaft. *Merkur, Deutsche Zeitschrift für europäisches Denken*, **34**, 387: 761–771

1982. Elemente einer soziologischen Theorie sozialpolitischer Intervention, in Kaufmann (ed.), *Staatliche Sozialpolitik und Familie*. Munich/Vienna: Oldenbourg, pp. 49–86

1988. Steuerung wohlfahrtsstaatlicher Abläufe durch Recht, in Grimm, D. and Maihofer, W. (eds.), *Gesetzgebungstheorie und Rechtspolitik (Jahrbuch für Rechtssoziologie und Rechtstheorie*, Vol XIII). Opladen: Westdeutscher Verlag, pp. 65–108

1990. *Zukunft der Familie*. Munich: Beck'sche Verlagsbuchhandlung

1992. *Der Ruf nach Verantwortung. Risiko und Ethik in einer unüberschaubaren Welt*. Freiburg i.B.: Herder

1997. *Herausforderungen des Sozialstaates*. Frankfurt a.M.: Suhrkamp

Kaufmann, F.-X. and Leisering, L. 1984. Demographic Changes as a Problem for Social Security Systems. *International Social Security Review*, **37**, 4: 388–409

Kautto, M., Heikkilä, M., Hvinden, B., Marklund, S. and Ploug, N. (eds.) 1999, *Nordic Social Policy*. London: Routledge (in print)

Kempson, E. 1996. *Life on a Low Income*. Layerthorpe: York Publishing Services for the Joseph Rowntree Foundation

Kersbergen, K. van 1995. *Social Capitalism*. London/New York: Routledge

Kitschelt, H., Lange, P., Marks, G. and Stephens, J. D. (eds.) 1999, *Continuity and Change in Contemporary Capitalism*. Cambridge: Cambridge University Press

Klanberg, F. 1977. Armutsstandards und Einkommensstatistik. *Sozialer Fortschritt*, **26**: 126–129

1978. *Armut und ökonomische Ungleichheit in der Bundesrepublik Deutschland.* Frankfurt a.M./New York: Campus

1979. Einkommensarmut 1969 und 1973 bei Anlegung verschiedener Standards. *Sozialer Fortschritt*, **28**: 127–131

1980. Sozialhilfe: Reform oder Umfunktionierung zum Volkshonorar? *Sozialer Fortschritt*, **29**: 246–252

Klee, E. 1979. *Pennbrüder und Stadtstreicher. Nichtseßhaften-Report*. Frankfurt a.M.: Fischer

Klein, P. 1994. Regelsatzentwicklung und Wandel der Lebensformen. *Nachrichtendienst des Deutschen Vereins für öffentliche und private Fürsorge*, **74**: 88–94

Klein, T. 1987. *Sozialer Abstieg und Verarmung von Familien durch Arbeitslosigkeit: eine mikroanalytische Untersuchung für die Bundesrepublik Deutschland.* Frankfurt a.M./New York: Campus

1989. Bildungsexpansion und Geburtenrückgang. Eine kohortenbezogene Analyse zum Einfluß veränderter Bildungsbeteiligung auf die Geburt von Kindern im Lebenslauf. *Kölner Zeitschrift für Soziologie und Sozialpsychologie*, **41**: 483–503

Kleinhenz, G. (ed.) 1991. *Sozialpolitik im vereinten Deutschland I*. Berlin: Duncker & Humblot (Schriften des Vereins für Socialpolitik, New Series, vol. 208/I)

Klems, W. and Schmid, A. 1992. Langzeitarbeitslosigkeit – ein ungelöstes arbeitsmarktpolitisches Problem? *WSI Mitteilungen*, **45**: 448–458

Klocke, A. and Hurrelmann, K. (eds.) 1998. *Kinder und Jugendliche in Armut. Umfang, Auswirkungen und Konsequenzen*. Opladen: Westdeutscher Verlag

Kohl, Jürgen 1994. *Alterssicherung im internationalen Vergleich. Analysen zu Strukturen und Wirkungen der Alterssicherungssysteme in fünf europäischen Ländern.* Universität Bielefeld (mimeo)

Kohli, M. 1981. Biographische Organisation als Handlungs- und Strukturproblem. Zu Fritz Schütze: 'Prozeßstrukturen des Lebenslaufs', in Matthes, J., Pfeifenberger, A. and Stosberg, M. (eds.), *Biographie in handlungswissenschaftlicher Perspektive. Kolloquium am Sozialwissenschaftlichen Forschungszentrum der Universität Erlangen-Nürnberg*. Nürnberg: Verlag der Nürnberger Forschungsvereinigung, pp. 157–168

1986a. The World We Forgot: An Historical Review of the Life Course, in Marshall, V.W. (ed.), *Later Life: The Social Psychology of Aging*. Beverly Hills: Sage, pp. 271–303

1986b. Gesellschaftszeit und Lebenszeit: Der Lebenslauf im Strukturwandel der Moderne, in Berger, J. (ed.) 1986. *Die Moderne – Kontinuitäten und Zäsuren*. Göttingen: Schwartz, pp. 183–208 (*Soziale Welt*, special issue No. 4)

1988. Normalbiographie und Individualität: Zur institutionellen Dynamik des gegenwärtigen Lebenslaufregimes, in Brose and Hildenbrand (eds.) 1988a, pp. 33–54

1990. *Das Alter als Herausforderung für die Theorie sozialer Ungleichheit*, in Berger and Hradil (eds.) 1990a, pp. 387–406

Kopnarski, A. 1990. *Gesichter der Armut. Armut im Wandel der Zeit – Ein Beitrag zur Ortsbestimmung der aktuellen Armut anhand der Ergebnisse einer empirischen Untersuchung in Konstanz.* Konstanz: Hartung-Gorre Verlag

Kortmann, K., Krupp, H.-J. and Schmaus, G. 1975. Strukturen der Einkommensverteilung 1969 – Erste Ergebnisse und Erfahrungen mit einem integrierten Mikrodatenfile für die Bundesrepublik Deutschland. *WSI Mitteilungen*, **28**: 539–552

Krause, P. 1993. Einkommensarmut im vereinigten Deutschland. Ruhr-Universität Bochum, Fakultät für Sozialwissenschaft (Discussion Paper No. 93–09)

1994a. Zur zeitlichen Dimension von Einkommmensarmut, in Hanesch, W. *et al.* 1994, pp.189–214

1994b. *Armut im Wohlstand: Betroffenheit und Folgen.* Berlin: Deutsches Institut für Wirtschaftsforschung (Discussion Paper No. 88)

1998. Low Income Dynamics in Unified Germany, in Leisering and Walker (eds.) 1998a, pp. 161–180

1999. *Zur Messung von Einkommensarmut am Beispiel des vereinigten Deutschlands – Theoretische Ansätze und empirische Analysen auf der Grundlage der Daten des Sozio-ökonomischen Panels (SOEP).* Munich and Vienna: Oldenbourg

Kreckel, R. 1992. *Politische Soziologie der sozialen Ungleichheit.* Frankfurt a.M./New York: Campus

1993. Geteilte Ungleichheit im vereinten Deutschland, in Geißler (ed.), pp. 41–62

Kronauer, M. 1997. 'Soziale Ausgrenzung' und 'Underclass': über neue Formen der gesellschaftlichen Spaltung. *Leviathan*, **25**, 1: 28–49

1998. 'Social Exclusion' and 'Underclass' – New Concepts for the Analysis of Poverty, in Andreß, H.-J. (ed.), pp. 51–75

Kronauer, M., Vogel, B. and Gerlach, F. 1993. *Im Schatten der Arbeitsgesellschaft: Arbeitslose und die Dynamik sozialer Ausgrenzung.* Frankfurt a.M./New York: Campus

Lampert, H. 1995. Voraussetzungen einer Sozialstaatsreform – kritische Anmerkungen zur aktuellen Debatte über den Umbau des Sozialstaates, *Jahrbuch für Nationalökonomie und Statistik* **214**, 5: 513–531

1998. *Lehrbuch der Sozialpolitik.* Springer: Berlin (rev. 5th edn)

Landessozialamt Hamburg 1997. *Der Sozialhilfereport No. 8.* Hamburg: Behörde für Arbeit, Gesundheit und Soziales

Landua, D. 1990. Verläufe von Arbeitslosigkeit und ihre Folgen für die Wohlfahrt von Haushalten und Individuen. *Zeitschrift für Soziologie*, **19**: 203–211

Landua, D. and Habich, R. 1994. Problemgruppen der Sozialpolitik im vereinten Deutschland. *Aus Politik und Zeitgeschichte, Beilage zur Wochenzeitung Das Parlament*, B3/94, 21 January 1994, pp. 3–14

Landua, D., Habich, R., Noll, H.-H., Zapf, W. and Spellerberg, A. 1993. '. . . im Westen noch beständig, im Osten etwas freundlicher'. Lebensbedingungen und subjektives Wohlbefinden drei Jahre nach der Vereinigung. Berlin: Social Science Centre, Working Group on Social Reporting (Working paper P 93–108)

Law Gazette 1989: Gesetzblatt der Deutschen Demokratischen Republik, I, 19, 24 October 1989, Berlin

Leenen, W.R. 1985. Sozialpolitik, in Bundesministerium für innerdeutsche Beziehungen (ed.), Vol. 2, pp. 1212–1218

Lehmbruch, G. 1991. Die improvisierte Vereinigung: Die dritte deutsche Republik, Unentwegter Versuch, einem japanischen Publikum die Geheimnisse der deutschen Transformation zu erklären. *Leviathan*, **19**: 462–486

Leibfried, S. 1977. Vorwort, in Piven, F.F. and Cloward, R.A. 1977 (English version 1971). *Regulierung der Armut. Politik der öffentlichen Wohlfahrt*. Frankfurt a.M.: Suhrkamp, pp. 9–67

1987. Projektantrag 'Sozialhilfekarrieren – Wege aus der und durch die Sozialhilfe und ihre sozialstaatliche Rahmung', in Heinz (ed.), pp. 801–861

1990. Soziale Grundsicherung – Das Bedarfsprinzip in der Sozial- und Gesellschaftspolitik der Bundesrepublik, in Vobruba (ed.), pp. 182–225

1992. Towards An European Welfare State? On Integrating Poverty Regimes into the European Community, in Ferge, Z. and Kolberg, J.E. (eds.), *Social Policy in a Changing Europe*. Frankfurt a.M./Boulder, CO: Campus and Westview, pp. 245–279

1993. Towards a European Welfare State? On Integrating Poverty Regimes into the European Community, in Jones, C. (ed.), *New Perspectives on the Welfare State*. London: Routledge, pp. 133–156

1994a. Wohlfahrtsstaatliche Perspektiven der Europäischen Union. Auf dem Wege zu positiver Souveränitätsverflechtung? *Kritische Justiz*, **27**, 3: 263–283

1994b. The Social Dimension of the European Union: En Route to Positively Joint Sovereignty? *Journal of European Social Policy*, **4**: 239–262

1997. Der Wohlfahrtsstaat zwischen 'Integration' und 'Desintegration': Europäische Union, nationale Sozialpolitiken und 'Globalisierung', Bremen University, Centre for Social Policy Research (CeS-Working Papers 15/97)

1998. Sozialstaat am Scheideweg. Innere und äußere Gründe des Veraltens wohlfahrtsstaatlicher Arrangements, *Soziologische Revue*, **21**: 427–438

Leibfried, S., Leisering, L., Buhr, P., Ludwig, M., Mädje, E., Olk, T., Voges, W. and Zwick, M. 1995. *Zeit der Armut. Lebensläufe im Sozialstaat*. Frankfurt a.M.: Suhrkamp.

Leibfried, S., Müller, R., Schmähl, W. and Schmidt, M. G. 1998. Thesen zur Sozialpolitik in Deutschland, *Zeitschrift für Sozialreform*, **44**, 8: 525–569

Leibfried, S. and Pierson, P. (eds.) 1995. *European Social Policy: Between Fragmentation and Integration*. Washington, DC: The Brookings Institution

Leibfried, S. and Rieger, E. 1995. The Welfare State and Globalization. Conflict over Germany's Competitiveness ('Standort Deutschland'): Exiting from the Global Economy? Berkeley, CA: Center for German and European Studies, University of California at Berkeley (Occasional Paper)

Leibfried, S. and Tennstedt, F. 1985a. *Politik der Armut und Die Spaltung des Sozialstaats.* Frankfurt a.M.: Suhrkamp

1985b. Einleitung, in Leibfried and Tennstedt (eds.) 1985a, pp. 13–37

Leibfried, S. and Tennstedt, F. 1985c: Armenpolitik und Arbeiterpolitik. Zur Entwicklung und Krise der traditionellen Sozialpolitik der Verteilungsformen, in Leibfried and Tennstedt (eds.) 1985a, pp. 64–93

Leibfried, S. and Voges, W. (eds.) 1992a. *Armut im modernen Wohlfahrtsstaat.* Opladen: Westdeutscher Verlag (*Kölner Zeitschrift für Soziologie und Sozialpsychologie*, special issue 32)

Leibfried, S. and Voges, W. (in Zusammenarbeit mit Lutz Leisering) 1992b. Vom Ende der Ausgrenzung? – Armut und Soziologie, in Leibfried and Voges (eds.) 1992a, pp. 9–33

Leisering, L. 1989. Origins of the Dynamics of the Welfare State. Societal Differentiation and the Formation of Statutory Welfare in England, 1795–1847. A Sociological Study. London: University of London, London School of Economics and Political Science, Ph.D. Thesis

1992. *Sozialstaat und demographischer Wandel. Wechselwirkungen, Generationenverhältnisse, politische-institutionelle Steuerung.* Frankfurt a.M./New York: Campus

1993. Zwischen Verdrängung und Dramatisierung. Zur Wissenssoziologie der Armut in der bundesrepublikanischen Gesellschaft. *Soziale Welt*, **44**: 486–511

1995a. Zweidrittelgesellschaft oder Risikogesellschaft? Zur gesellschaftlichen Verortung der 'Neuen Armut' in der Bundesrepublik, in Bieback, K.-J. and Milz, H. (eds.) 1995, *Neue Armut.* Frankfurt a.M./New York: Campus, pp. 58–92

1995b. Grenzen des Sozialversicherungsstaates? Sozialer Wandel als Herausforderung staatlicher Einkommenssicherung. *Zeitschrift für Sozialreform*, **41**, 11/12: 860–880

1997a. Individualisierung und 'sekundäre Institutionen' – der Sozialstaat als Voraussetzung des modernen Individuums, in Beck and Sopp (eds.), pp. 143–159

1997b. Wohlfahrtsstaatliche Dynamik als Wertproblem, in Gabriel, K., Herlth, A. and Strohmeier, K. P. (eds.), *Modernität und Solidarität, Festschrift für Franz-Xaver Kaufmann.* Herder: Freiburg, pp. 251–273

1997c. Soziale Ausgrenzung – Zur handlungstheoretische Fundierung eines aktuellen sozialpolitischen Diskurses, in Hradil, S. (ed.), *Differenz und Integration. Die Zukunft moderner Gesellschaften. Verhandlungen des 28. Kongresses der Deutschen Gesellschaft für Soziologie in Dresden 1996.* Frankfurt a.M./New York: Campus, pp. 1038–1053

Leisering, L., Buhr, P. and Gangl, M. 1997. Kleine Revolution. *Die Mitbestimmung, Magazin der Hans Böckler Stiftung*, **42**, 10: 39–42

Leisering, L., Geissler, B., Mergner, U. and Rabe-Kleeberg, U. (eds.) 1993. *Moderne Lebensläufe im Wandel. Beruf – Familie – Soziale Hilfen – Krankheit.* Weinheim: Deutscher Studien Verlag

Leisering, L. and Leibfried, S. 1996. Nützliche Ungleichheit – nützlicher Sozialstaat. Verteilungspolitik jenseits der Arbeitsgesellschaft, in Schulte, D. (ed.), *Erneuerung des Sozialstaates.* Cologne: Bund-Verlag, pp. 70–90

Leisering, L. and Mädje, E. 1996. *Armut im vereinigten Deutschland – Umbruch und Kontinuität*, in Clausen, (ed.), pp. 903–915

Leisering, L. and Motel, A. 1997. Voraussetzungen eines neuen Generationenvertrags. *Blätter für deutsche und internationale Politik,* **42**: 1213–1224

Leisering, L. and Voges, W. 1992. Erzeugt der Wohlfahrtstaat seine eigene Klientel? Eine theoretische und empirische Analyse von Armutsprozessen, in Leibfried and Voges (eds.) 1992a, pp. 446–472

    1997. Secondary Poverty in the Welfare State. Do Social Security Institutions Create Their Own Clients? An Application of Longitudinal Analysis, in Keilman, N., Lyngstad, J., Bojer, H. and Thomsen, I. (eds.), *Poverty and Economic Inequality in Industrialized Western Countries.* Oslo: Scandinavian University Press, pp. 205–232

Leisering, L. and Walker, R. (eds.) 1998a. *The Dynamics of Modern Society: Policy, Poverty, and Welfare.* Bristol: Policy Press

    1998b. New Realities. The Dynamics of Modernity, in Leisering and Walker (eds.) 1998a, pp. 3–16

    1998c. Making the Future: From Dynamics to Policy Agendas, in Leisering and Walker (eds.) 1998a, pp. 265–285

    1998d. Social Assistance Dynamics: Anglo-German Similarities and Disparities, mimeo

Leisering, L. and Zwick, M. 1990. Heterogenisierung der Armut? Alte und neue Perspektiven zum Strukturwandel der Armutsbevölkerung der Sozialhilfeklientel in der Bundesrepublik Deutschland. *Zeitschrift für Sozialreform,* **36**: 715–745

Lemert, E. M. 1951. *Social Pathology.* New York: McGraw-Hill

Lepsius, M.R. 1990. *Interessen, Ideen und Institutionen.* Opladen: Westdeutscher Verlag

Lessenich, S. and Ostner, I. 1998. *Welten des Wohlfahrtskapitalismus. Der Sozialstaat in vergleichender Perspektive.* Frankfurt a.M./New York: Campus

Leviathan 1997. No. 1, special issue on social exclusion and underclass

Levy, R. 1977. *Der Lebenslauf als Statusbiographie. Die weibliche Normalbiographie in makrosoziologischer Perspektive.* Stuttgart: Enke

    1996. Zur Institutionalisierung von Lebensläufen, in Behrens and Voges (eds.), pp. 73–113

Lewis, O. 1959. *Five Families. Mexican Case Studies in the Culture of Poverty.* New York: Science Editions

Lohmann, U. 1987. *Das Arbeitsrecht der DDR. Analyse und Texte.* Berlin: Spitz

Lompe, K. (ed.) 1987. *Die Realität der neuen Armut. Analysen der Beziehungen zwischen Arbeitslosigkeit und Armut in einer Problemregion.* Regensburg: Transfer

LPK, 1994. *Bundessozialhilfegesetz. Lehr- und Praxiskommentar.* 4th edn. Baden-Baden: Nomos

Luckenbill, D.F. and Best, J. 1981. Careers in Deviance and Respectability: The Analogy's Limitation. *Social Problems,* **29**: 197–206

Ludwig, M. 1996. *Armutskarrieren. Zwischen Abstieg und Aufstieg im Sozialstaat.* Opladen: Westdeutscher Verlag

Ludwig-Mayerhofer, W. 1990. Arbeitslosigkeit und Erwerbsverlauf. *Zeitschrift für Soziologie*, **19**: 345–359

1992. Arbeitslosigkeit, Erwerbsarbeit und Armut. Längerfristige Armutsrisiken im Kontext von Haushalt und Sozialstruktur, in Leibfried and Voges (eds.) 1992a, pp. 380–402

Luhmann, N. 1970. Wirtschaft als soziales System, in ibid., *Soziologische Aufklärung*. Opladen: Westdeutscher Verlag, pp. 204–231

1982. The Differentiation of Society. Translated by Stephen Holmes and Charles Larmore. New York: Columbia University Press

1990. *Political Theory in the Welfare State*. Berlin/New York: de Gruyter (German 1981. *Politische Theorie im Wohlfahrtsstaat*. Munich/Vienna: Olzog)

1994. Inklusion und Exklusion, in Berding, H. (ed.), *Nationales Bewußtsein und kollektive Identität. Studien zur Entwicklung des kollektiven Bewußtseins in der Neuzeit 2*. Frankfurt a.M.: Suhrkamp, pp. 15–45

Lynn, L. E. 1997. Welfare Reform: Once More into the Breach: A Review Essay. *Social Service Review* **71** (June): 305–317

Mädje, E. and Neusüß, C. 1996. *Frauen im Sozialstaat. Zur Lebenssituation alleinerziehender Sozialhilfeempfängerinnen*. Frankfurt a.M./New York: Campus

Majone, G. 1993. The European Community between Social Policy and Social Regulation. *Journal of Common Market Studies*, **31**: 153–170

1994a. The European Community: An 'Independent Fourth Branch of Government', in Brüggemeier, G. (ed.), *Verfassungen für ein ziviles Europa*, Baden-Baden: Nomos, pp. 23–43

1994b. The Rise of the Regulatory State in Europe. *West European Politics*, **17**, 3: 77–101

1994c. Controlling Regulatory Bureaucracies: Lessons from the American Experience, in Derlien, H.-U., Gerhardt, U. and Scharpf, F. W. (eds.), *Systemrationalität und Partialinteresse. Festschrift für Renate Mayntz*. Baden-Baden: Nomos, pp. 291–314

Mannheim, K. 1940. *Man and Society in an Age of Reconstruction. Studies in Modern Social Structure*. London: Kegan Paul, Trench, Trubner & Co.

Manow-Borgwardt, P. 1994. Die Sozialversicherung in der DDR und der BRD, 1945–1990: Über die Fortschrittlichkeit rückschrittlicher Institutionen. *Politische Vierteljahresschrift*, **35**: 40–61

Manow, P. and Seils, E. 2000, 'Adjusting badly': The German welfare state, structural change and the open economy, in Scharpf and V. A. Schmidt (eds.) (in preparation)

Mansel, J. and Neubauer, G. (eds.) 1998. *Armut und soziale Ungleichheit bei Kindern. Über die veränderten Bedingungen des Aufwachsens*. Opladen: Leske und Budrich

Manski, C.F. and Garfinkel, I. (eds.) 1992. *Evaluating Welfare and Training Programs*. Cambridge, MA: Harvard University Press

Manz, G. 1992. *Armut in der 'DDR'-Bevölkerung, Lebensstandard und Konsumtionsniveau vor und nach der Wende*. Augsburg: Maro

Marks, G., Scharpf, F. W., Schmitter, Ph. C. and Streeck, W. 1996. *Governance in the European Union*. London: Sage

Marmor, T.R., Mashaw, J.L. and Harvey, P.L. 1990. *America's Misunderstood Welfare State. Persistent Myths, Enduring Realities.* New York: Basic Books

Marshall, T. H. 1950. Citizenship and Social Class, in Marshall, T. H. 1964. *Class, Citizenship and Social Development.* Garden City, NJ: Doubleday, pp. 65–122

1981. Changing Ideas about Poverty, in ibid. 1981. *The Right to Welfare and Other Essays.* London: Heinemann, pp. 29–52

Massey, D. S. 1996. Age of Extremes: Concentrated Affluence and Poverty in the Twenty-first century. *Demography*, **33**, 4: 395–412

Matthes, J. 1964. *Gesellschaftspolitische Konzeptionen im Sozialhilferecht. Zur soziologischen Kritik der neuen deutschen Sozialhilfegesetzgebung 1961*, Stuttgart: Enke

Mayer, K. U. 1986. Structural Constraints in the Life Course. *Human Development*, **29**: 163–170

1987. Lebenslaufforschung, in Voges (ed.), pp. 51–74

(ed.) 1990. *Lebensverläufe und sozialer Wandel.* Opladen: Westdeutscher Verlag (*Kölner Zeitschrift für Soziologie und Sozialpsychologie*, special issue 32)

1991a. *Life Courses in the Welfare State*, in Heinz, W. R. (ed.) 1991a, pp. 171–186

1991b. Soziale Ungleichheit und die Differenzierung von Lebensverläufen, in Zapf, W. (ed.) 1991. *Die Modernisierung moderner Gesellschaften. Verhandlungen des Deutschen Soziologentages in Frankfurt am Main 1990.* Frankfurt a.M./New York: Campus, pp. 667–687

1994. Vereinigung soziologisch: Die soziale Ordnung der DDR und ihre Folgen. *Berliner Journal für Soziologie,* **4**: 307–322

1996. Notes on a Comparative Political Economy of Life Courses, in Institute for Social Research and the Dept. of Sociology, University of Oslo (eds.), *Comparative Social Research. Yearbook.* Greenwich, CT: JAI Press, pp. 203–226

Mayer, K. U. and Blossfeld, H.-P. 1990. Die gesellschaftliche Konstruktion sozialer Ungleichheit im Lebensverlauf, in Berger and Hradil (eds.) 1990a, pp. 297–318

Mayer, K. U. and Müller, W. 1986. The State and the Structure of the Life Course, in Sørensen, A.B., Weinert, F.E. and Sherrod, L.R. (eds.). *Human Development: Interdisciplinary Perspectives*, Hillsdale, NJ: Erlbaum, pp. 217–245

1989. Individualisierung und Standardisierung im Strukturwandel der Moderne: Lebensverläufe im Wohlfahrtsstaat, in Weymann, A. (ed.) *Handlungsspielräume.* Stuttgart: Enke, pp. 41–60

Mayer, K. U. and Schöpflin, U. 1989. The State and the Life Course. *Annual Review of Sociology*, **15**: 187–209

Mayer, K. U. and Solga, H. 1994. Mobilität und Legitimität. Zum Vergleich der Chancenstrukturen in der alten DDR und in der alten BRD. *Kölner Zeitschrift für Soziologie und Sozialpsychologie*, **46**: 193–208

Mayntz, R. 1983. Implementation von regulativer Politik, in Mayntz, R. (ed.), *Implementation politischer Programme II – Ansätze zur Theoriebildung.* Opladen: Westdeutscher Verlag, pp. 50–74

McFate, K. 1995. Trampolines, Safety Nets, or Free Fall? Labor Market Policies and Social Assistance in the 1980s, in McFate *et al.* (eds.), pp. 631–663

McFate, K., Lawson, R. and Wilson, W. J. (eds.) 1995. *Poverty, Inequality and the Future of Social Policy. Western States in the New World Order.* New York: Russell Sage Foundation

Mead, L.M. 1986. *Beyond Entitlement. The Social Obligations of Citizenship.* New York: The Free Press

1992. *The New Politics of Poverty.* New York: Basic Books

Meehan, E. 1993. *Citizenship and the European Community.* London: Sage

Mény, Y. and Rhodes, M. (eds.) 1998. *The Future of European Welfare. A New Social Contract?* London: Macmillan; New York: St. Martins Press

Merten, R. 1994. Junge Familien in den neuen Bundesländern: die vergessenen Verlierer im Prozeß der deutschen Vereinigung (II). *Sozialer Fortschritt,* **43**: 18–19

Meyer, J.W. 1986. The Self and the Life Course: Institutionalization and Its Effects, in Sørensen, A.B., Weinert, F.F. and Sherrod, L.R. (eds.), *Human Development and the Life Course.* Hillsdale, NJ: Erlbaum, pp. 199–216

Meyer, S. and Schulze, E. 1992. *Familie im Umbruch. Zur Lage der Familien in der ehemaligen DDR.* Stuttgart: Kohlhammer (Schriftenreihe des Bundesministeriums für Familie und Senioren, Vol. 7)

Moffit, R. 1985. Evaluating the Effect of Changes in AFDC: Methodological Issues and Challenges. *Journal of Policy Analysis and Management,* **4**, 4: 537–553

1987. Work and the U.S. welfare system: A review. Waltham, MA: Brandeis University (Center for Human Ressources)

Müller, K., Frick, J. and Hauser, R. 1996. Die hohe Arbeitslosigkeit in den neuen Bundesländern und ihre Verteilungswirkungen, in Andreß (ed.), pp. 197–223

Müller-Armack, A. 1948. Die Wirtschaftsordnung sozial gesehen, in Müller-Armack 1966, pp. 171–199

1960. Die zweite Phase der Sozialen Marktwirtschaft. Ihre Ergänzung durch das Leitbild einer neuen Gesellschaftspolitik, in Müller-Armack 1966, pp. 267–291

1966. *Wirtschaftsordnung und Wirtschaftspolitik. Studien und Konzepte zur sozialen Marktwirtschaft und zur europäischen Integration.* Freiburg i.Br.: Rombach

Münke, S. 1956. *Die Armut in der heutigen Gesellschaft. Ergebnisse einer Untersuchung in Westberlin.* Berlin: Duncker & Humblot

Münz, R., Seifert, W. and Ulrich, R. 1997. *Zuwanderung nach Deutschland: Strukturen, Wirkungen, Perspektiven.* Frankfurt a.M./New York: Campus

Murray, C. 1984. *Losing Ground. American Social Policy 1950–1980.* New York: Basic Books

Mutz, G., Ludwig-Mayerhofer, W., Koenen, E. J., Eder, E. and Bonß, W. 1995. *Diskontinuierliche Erwerbsverläufe. Analysen zur postindustriellen Arbeitslosigkeit.* Opladen: Leske und Budrich

Myles, J. and Pierson, P. 1997. Friedman's Revenge: The Reform of 'Liberal' Welfare States in Canada and the United States, *Politics and Society,* **25**, 4: 443–472

Nagel, U. 1993. Hilfe als Profession, in Leisering, Lutz *et al.* (eds.), pp. 149–162

Nahnsen, I. 1975. Bemerkungen zum Begriff und zur Geschichte des Arbeitsschutzes, in Osterland, M. (ed.), *Arbeitssituation, Lebenslage und Konfliktpotential.* Cologne: EVA, pp. 145–166

Natter, E. and Riedlsperger, A. 1988. Einführung. Wirksam beteiligen statt lautlos ausgrenzen, in ibid. (eds.), *Zweidrittelgesellschaft. Spalten, splittern – oder solidarisieren?* Vienna and Zurich: Europaverlag, pp. 7–21

Neckel, S. 1997. Zwischen Robert E. Park und Pierre Bourdieu: Eine dritte 'Chicago School'? Soziologische Perspektiven einer amerikanischen Forschungstradition, *Soziale Welt,* **48**, 1: 71–83

Nervik, J. A. 1997. *Offentlig politikk og klientløpebaner. Sosialhjelp og arbeidsmarkedstiltak – bidrag til selvforsørging eller ringdans i velferdsbyråkratiet.* Universitetet i Oslo: Institutt for statsvitenskap

Neumann, L. F. and Schaper, K. 1998. *Die Sozialordnung der Bundesrepublik Deutschland.* Frankfurt a.M./New York: Campus (rev. 4th edn.)

Noble, M., Cheung, S. Y. and Smith, G. 1998. Origins and Destinations – Social Security Claimant Dynamics. *Journal of Social Policy,* **27**, 3: 351–370

Offe, C. 1972. Politische Herrschaft und Klassenstrukturen. Zur Analyse spätkapitalistischer Gesellschaftssysteme, in Kress, G. and Senghaas, D. (eds.) 1972. *Politikwissenschaft. Eine Einführung in ihre Probleme.* Frankfurt a.M.: Fischer, pp. 135–164 (1st edn. 1969, EVA)

　1984. *Contradictions of the Welfare State.* London etc.: Hutchinson

　1990. Akzeptanz und Legitimität strategischer Optionen in der Sozialpolitik, in Sachße, C. and Engelhardt, H.T. (eds.), *Sicherheit und Freiheit, Zur Ethik des Wohlfahrtsstaates.* Frankfurt a.M.: Suhrkamp, pp.179–202

　1994. Wohlfahrtsstaatliche Politik in nachkommunistischen Gesellschaften. Ausgangsbedingungen, Akteure und Agenda der Reform, in Offe, C., *Der Tunnel am Ende des Lichtes. Erkundungen der politischen Transformation im Neuen Osten.* Frankfurt a.M./New York: Campus, pp. 95–134 [English edn. 1996. *Varieties of Transition.* Cambridge: Polity Press]

Oorschot, W. van 1995. *Realizing Rights: a Multi-level Approach to Non-take-up of Means-tested Benefits.* London: Avebury

　1998. Failing Selectivity: On the Extent and Causes of Non-take-up of Social Security Benefits, in Andreß, H.-J. (ed.) 1998, pp. 101–132

Osterland, M. 1990. *'Normalbiographie' und 'Normalarbeitsverhältnis'.* in Berger and Hradil (eds.) 1990a, pp. 351–362

Oswald von Nell-Breuning-Institut (ed.) 1994. *Solidarität am Standort Deutschland.* Frankfurt a.M.: Oswald von Nell-Breuning-Institut

Otto, U. (ed.) 1997. *Aufwachsen in Armut. Erfahrungswelten und soziale Lagen von Kindern armer Familien.* Opladen: Leske und Budrich

Øyen, E. 1992. Some Basic Issues in Comparative Poverty Research. *International Social Science Journal,* **44**: 615–626

Øyen, E., Miller, S.M. and Samad, S. A. 1996. *Poverty: A Global Review. Handbook on International Poverty Research.* Oslo: Scandinavian University Press

Palmer, J. L., Smeeding, T. and Torrey, B. B. (eds.) 1988. *The Vulnerable. America's*

Young and Old in the Industrial World. Washington, DC: The Urban Institute

Parijs, P. van 1995. *Real Freedom for All.* Cambridge: Cambridge University Press

1992. *Arguing for a Basic Income. Ethical Foundations for a Radical Reform.* London: Verso

Paritätischer Wohlfahrtsverband (ed.) 1989. '. . . wessen wir uns schämen müssen in einem reichen Land. . .'. Armutsbericht des Paritätischen Wohlfahrtsverbandes für die Bundesrepublik Deutschland. *Blätter der Wohlfahrtspflege,* **136**, 11/12

Park, R. E. 1928. Human Migration and the Marginal Man. *American Journal of Sociology,* **33**: 881–893

Paugam, S. 1998. Poverty and Social Exclusion: A Sociological View, in Meny and Rhodes (eds.), pp. 41–62

(ed.) 1996. *L'Exclusion. L'État des Savoirs.* Paris: La Découverte

Peters, B. 1996. Das öffentliche Bild von Armut. Aktuelle Armutsbilder im Spiegel der Presse. *Zeitschrift für Sozialreform,* **42**, 8: 518–548

Peters, H. 1968. *Moderne Fürsorge und ihre Legitimation. Eine soziologische Analyse der Sozialarbeit.* Opladen: Westdeutscher Verlag

Peters, H. and Cremer-Schäfer, H. 1975. *Die sanften Kontrolleure. Wie Sozialarbeiter mit Devianten umgehen.* Stuttgart: Enke

Piachaud, D. 1997. Social Security and Dependence. *International Social Security Review,* **50**, 1: 41–55

Pierson, P. 1994. *Dismantling the Welfare State? Reagan, Thatcher and the Politics of Retrenchment.* Cambridge: Cambridge University Press

1995. New Politics of the Welfare State. University of Bremen, Centre for Social Policy Research, Working paper 3/95

1996: The New Politics of the Welfare State. *World Politics,* **48**, 2: 147–179

1998: Irresistible forces, immovable objects: post-industrial welfare states confront permanent austerity, *Journal of European Public Policy,* **5**, 4: 539–560

Pinker, R. 1979. *The Idea of Welfare.* London: Heinemann

1992. Armut, Sozialpolitik, Soziologie. Der englische Weg von der industriellen Revolution zum modernen Wohlfahrtsstaat (1830 bis 1950), in Leibfried and Voges (eds.) 1992a, pp. 124–148

Piven, F.F. and Clowerd, R. A. 1993. *Regulating the Poor. The Functions of Public Welfare.* 2nd edn, New York: Vintage Books (1st edn 1971)

1998. *Breaking the New American Social Compact.* New York: The New Press

Polanyi, K. 1945. *Origins of Our Time. The Great Transformation.* London: Gollancz (1st edn 1944)

Preuß, U. 1997. Problems of a Concept of European Citizenship. *European Law Journal,* **1**, 3: 267–281

Rains, P. 1975. Imputations of Deviance: A Retrospective Essay on the Labelling Perspective. *Social Problems,* **23**: 1–10

Rainwater, L., Rein, M. and Schwartz, J. 1986. *Income Packaging in the Welfare State. A Comparative Study of Family Income.* Oxford: Clarendon Press

Rank, M.R. 1994. *Living on the Edge: The Realities of Welfare in America.* New York: Columbia University Press

Rendtel, U. and Wagner, G. (eds.) 1991. *Lebenslagen im Wandel: Zur Einkommensdynamik in Deutschland seit 1984.* Frankfurt a.M./New York: Campus

Rhein-Kress, G. v. 1993. Coping with Economic Crisis: Labour Supply as a Policy Instrument, in Castles, F.G. (ed.), *Families of Nations. Patterns of Public Policy in Western Democracies.* Aldershot: Dartmouth, pp. 131–178

Rhodes, M. 1996. Globalization and the West European Welfare States: A Critical Review of Recent Debates. *Journal of European Social Policy,* 6: 305–327

Riedmüller, B. and Olk, T. (eds.) 1994. *Grenzen des Sozialversicherungsstaats.* Opladen: Westdeutscher Verlag (*Leviathan,* special issue No. 14)

Rieger, E. 1992. *Die Institutionalisierung des Wohlfahrtsstaates.* Opladen: Westdeutscher Verlag

　　1995. Protective Shelter or Straightjacket: An Institutional Analysis of the Common Agricultural Policy of the European Union, in Leibfried and Pierson (eds.), pp. 194–230

Rieger, E. and Leibfried, S. 1997. Die sozialpolitischen Grenzen der Globalisierung. *Politische Vierteljahresschrift,* **38**, 4: 771–796 (English 1998: Welfare State Limits to Globalization. *Politics and Society,* **26**, 3: 361–388)

　　1999. Wohlfahrtsstaat und Sozialpolitik in Ostasien. Der Einfluß von Religion im Kulturvergleich, in Schmidt, G. (ed.), *Globalisierung.* Baden-Baden: Nomos, pp. 407–493 (special issue of *Soziale Welt*)

Ritter, G. A. 1991. *Der Sozialstaat. Entstehung und Entwicklung im internationalen Vergleich.* Munich: Oldenbourg (rev. 2nd edn.)

Rodrik, D. 1997. *Has Globalization Gone too Far?* Washington, DC: Institute for International Economics

Rohrmann, E. 1987. *Ohne Arbeit – ohne Wohnung. Wie Arme zu 'Nichtseßhaften' werden.* Heidelberg: Ed. Schindele

Rohwer, G. 1992. Einkommensmobilität und soziale Mindestsicherung. Einige Überlegungen zum Armutsrisiko, in Leibfried and Voges (eds.) 1992a, pp. 367–379

Rolf, G. and Wagner, G. 1994. Das Voll Eigenständige System der Altersvorsorge, in DFG (ed.) 1994, vol. I, pp. 336–350

Room, G. 1990. *'New Poverty' in the European Community.* Houndmills: Macmillan (ed.) 1995. *Beyond the Threshold. The Measurement and Analysis of Social Exclusion.* Bristol: The Policy Press

Rose, R. 1984. *Understanding Big Government.* Beverly Hills, CA.: Sage

Rosenow, J. 1992. Die Altersgrenzenpolitik in den neuen Bundesländern: Trends und Regulationsmechanismen im Transformationsprozeß – Differenzen zur Entwicklung in den alten Bundesländern. *Zeitschrift für Sozialreform,* **38**: 682–697

Roth, J. 1971. *Armut in der Bundesrepublik.* Darmstadt: Melzer (rev. edns. with Fischer and Rowohlt in 1974 and 1979)

Rothgang, H. 1994. *Die Einführung der Pflegeversicherung: Ist das Sozialversicherungsprinzip am Ende?* in Riedmüller and Olk (eds.) 1994, pp. 164–187

1997. *Ziele und Wirkungen der Pflegeversicherung. Eine ökonomische Analyse.* Frankfurt a.M./New York: Campus

Rowntree, B.S. 1901. *Poverty. A Study of Town Life.* 2nd edn, London: Thomas Nelson & Sons

Runciman, W.G. 1966. *Relative Deprivation and Social Justice.* London: Routledge & Kegan Paul

Rutter, M. and Madge, N. 1976. *Cycles of Disadvantage. A Review of Research.* London: Heinemann

Rydell, C.P., Palmerio, T., Blais, G. and Brown, D. 1974. *Welfare Caseload Dynamics in New York City.* New York: The New York City Rand Institute

Sachße, C. and Tennstedt, F. 1980. *Geschichte der Armenfürsorge in Deutschland: vom Spätmittelalter bis zum 1. Weltkrieg.* Stuttgart: Kohlhammer

Sackmann, R. and Leibfried, S. 1992. Soziale Dienste für alte Menschen. Kommunale Sozialpolitik im Transformationsprozeß, in Schmähl (ed.), pp. 133–165

Salonen, T. 1993. *Margins of Welfare. A Study of Modern Functions of Social Assistance.* Torna Hällestad: Hällestad Press

Salzgeber, R. and Suter, C. 1997. *Beginn und Ende des Sozialhilfebezuges. NeubezügerInnen und SozialhilfeabgängerInnen des Fürsorgeamtes der Stadt Zürich 1993–1995.* Edited by the Department of Social Affairs of the city of Zurich. Zurich: Edition Sozialstatistik No. 1

Samson, R. 1992. Analyse der Bezugsdauer von Hilfe zum Lebensunterhalt anhand der Abrechnungsdaten der Stadt Bielefeld, in Johrendt and Schneider (eds.) 1992, pp. 109–119

Sassen, S. 1991. *The Global City.* New York, London, Tokyo: Princeton University Press

Schäfer, C. 1997. Empirische Überraschung und politische Herausforderung: Niedriglöhne in Deutschland, in Becker and Hauser (eds.), pp. 83–111

Schäfers, B. 1992. Zum öffentlichen Stellenwert von Armut im sozialen Wandel der Bundesrepublik Deutschland, in Leibfried and Voges (eds.) 1992a, pp. 104–123

Scharpf, F. W. 1987. *Sozialdemokratische Krisenpolitik in Europa. Das 'Modell Deutschland' im Vergleich.* Frankfurt a.M./New York: Campus [English edn. 1991. *Crisis and Choice in European Social Democracy.* Ithaca, NY: Cornell University Press]

1993. Von der Finanzierung der Erwerbslosigkeit zur Subventionierung niedriger Erwerbseinkommen. *Gewerkschaftliche Monatshefte,* **44**: 433–443

1997. Combating Unemployment in Continental Europe. Policy Options under Internationalization. Florence: European University Institute (The Robert Schumann Centre, Policy Paper 97/3) [appeared 1999 as: National Solutions without Boundary Control, in ibid., *Governing in Europe. Effective and Democratic?* Oxford: Oxford University Press, pp. 121–155 (chap. 4)]

2000. The Institutional Capacity for Effective Policy Responses, in: Scharpf and V. A. Schmidt (eds.) (in preparation).

Scharpf, F. W. and Schmidt, V. A. (eds.) 2000. *From Vulnerability to*

Competitiveness: Welfare and Work in the Open Economy. Oxford: Oxford University Press (in preparation)

Scheiwe, K. 1994. German Pension Insurance, Gendered Times and Stratification, in Sainsbury, D. (ed.), *Gendering Welfare States.* London: Sage, pp.132–149

Schellhorn, W., Jirasek, H. and Seipp, P. 1993. *Das Bundessozialhilfegesetz. Ein Kommentar für Ausbildung, Praxis und Wissenschaft,* 14th completely rev. edn. Neuwied/Darmstadt: Luchterhand

Scherl, H. 1976. Zum Problem der materiellen Armut in unserem Land. *Sozialer Fortschritt,* **25**: 222–225

Schimank, U. 1988. *Biographie als Autopoiesis – Eine systemtheoretische Rekonstruktion von Individualität,* in Brose and Hildenbrand (eds.), pp. 55–72

Schlegelmilch, C. 1987. *Taxifahrer, Dr. phil. Akademiker in der Grauzone des Arbeitsmarktes.* Opladen: Leske und Budrich

Schmähl, W. 1991. Alterssicherung in der DDR und ihre Umgestaltung im Zuge des deutschen Einigungsprozesses – Einige verteilungspolitische Aspekte, in Kleinhenz (ed.), pp. 49–95

(ed.) 1992. *Sozialpolitik im Prozeß der deutschen Vereinigung.* Frankfurt a.M./New York: Campus

(ed.) 1993. *Mindestsicherung im Alter. Erfahrungen, Herausforderungen, Strategien.* Frankfurt a.M./New York: Campus

1998a. Insights from Social Security Reform Abroad, in Arnold, R. D., Graetz, M. J. and Munnel, A. H. (eds.), *Framing the Social Security Debate: Values, Politics, and Economics.* Washington, DC: Brookings Institution Press, pp. 248–271, 280–286

1998b. Perpektiven der Sozialpolitik nach dem Regierungswechsel. *Wirtschaftsdienst,* **12**: 713–722.

Schmähl, W. and Rothgang, H. 1996. The long term costs of public long-term care insurance in Germany. Some guesstimates, in Eisen, R. and Sloan, F. A. (eds.) *Long-Term Care: Economic Issues and Policy Solutions.* Norwell, MA: Kluwer, pp. 181–222

Schmidt, M.G. 1978. Die 'Politik der inneren Reformen' in der Bundesrepublik Deutschland 1969–1976. *Politische Vierteljahresschrift,* **19**: 201–253

1998. *Sozialpolitik in Deutschland – Historische Entwicklung und internationaler Vergleich* (2nd rev. edn). Opladen: Leske und Budrich

Schmidt, V. A. 1996. Industrial Policies and Policy of Industries in Advanced Industrial Nations: A Review Article. *Comparative Politics,* **28** (January): 225–248

1997. Discourse and (Dis)Integration in Europe: The Cases of France, Germany and Great Britain. *Daedalus,* **126**, 3: 167–197

Schmidt-Räntsch, R. 1994. *Insolvenzordnung. Einführung – Gesetz – Erläuterte Materialien.* Bonn: Bundesanzeiger

Schnapper, Dominique 1997. The European Debate on Citizenship, *Daedalus,* **126**, 3: 199–222

Schneider, L. and Lysgaard, S. 1953. The Deferred Gratification Pattern: A Preliminary Study. *American Sociological Review,* **18**: 142–149

Schneider, U. 1989. Armut in der Bundesrepublik Deutschland, in Paritätischer Wohlfahrtsverband (ed.), pp. 271–275

Schulte, B. 1991. Das Recht auf ein Mindesteinkommen in der Europäischen Gemeinschaft – Nationaler Status quo und supranationale Initiativen. *Sozialer Fortschritt*, **40**: 7–21

1993. Armutsbekämpfung im Wohlfahrtsstaat – Die Rolle der Mindestsicherungssysteme der Mitgliedsstaaten für Entwicklung und Fortbestand der Wohlfahrtsstaatlichkeit in der Europäischen Gemeinschaft. *Zeitschrift für Sozialreform*, **38**: 593–628

Schulte, B. and Trenk-Hinterberger, P. 1986. *Sozialhilfe. Eine Einführung*. Heidelberg: C.F. Müller (rev. 2nd edn.)

Schultheis, F. 1987. Fatale Strategien und ungeplante Konsequenzen beim Aushandeln 'familialer Risiken' zwischen Mutter, Kind und 'Vater Staat', *Soziale Welt*, **38**: 40–56

1992. Familienpolitik in Grenzen: Aspekte eines interkulturellen Vergleichs sozialpolitischer Leistungen für Familien im Drei-Länder-Eck, in Hoffmann-Nowotny, H.-J., Höhn, C. and Fux, B. (eds.), *Kinderzahl und Familienpolitik im Drei-Länder-Vergleich*. Wiesbaden: Boldt, pp. 42–63 (Schriftenreihe des Bundesinstituts für Bevölkerungsforschung, vol. 19)

Schulz, J. (ed.) 1994. *Sozialhilfe. Eine systematische Einführung. Ausgewählte Texte*. Weinheim/Basel: Beltz

Schütze, F. 1981. Prozeßstrukturen des Lebensablaufs, in Matthes, J., Pfeifenberger, A. and Stosberg, M. (eds.), *Biographie in handlungswissenschaftlicher Pespektive*. Nürnberg: Verlag der Nürnberger Forschungsvereinigung, pp. 67–156

Schwarze, U. 1994. Sozialhilfeverwaltung und Klientel – eine empirische Analyse anhand von Experteninterviews. Universität Bremen, Sonderforschungsbereich 186, mimeo

Sears, E. 1986. *The Ages of Men. Medieval Interpretations of the Life Cycle*. Princeton, NJ: Princeton University Press

Seeleib-Kaiser, M. 1993. *Amerikanische Sozialpolitik. Politische Diskussion und Entscheidungen der Reagan-Ära*. Opladen: Leske und Budrich

Seligman, M.E.P. 1975. *Helplessness: On Depression Development and Death*. San Francisco: Freeman

Semrau, P. 1990. Entwicklung der Einkommensarmut, in Döring *et al.* 1990a, pp. 111–128

Sen, A. 1983. Poor, Relatively Speaking. *Oxford Economic Papers*, **35**: 153–169

1992. *Inequality Reexamined*. Oxford: Clarendon Press

1997. Inequality, Unemployment and Contemporary Europe. *International Labour Review*, **136**, 2: 155–172

SFZ (Sozialwissenschaftliches Forschungszentrum Berlin-Brandenburg) (ed.) 1992. *Sozialreport, Daten und Fakten zur sozialen Lage in den neuen Bundesländern, No.III*. Berlin: Morgenbuch

Shaw, A., Walker, R., Ashworth, K., Jenkins, S. and Middleton, S. 1996. Moving Off Income Support: Barriers and Bridges. Department of Social Security Research Report no. 53. London: HMSO

Sieveking, K. (ed.) 1998. *Soziale Sicherung bei Pflegebedürftigkeit in der Europäischen Union*. Baden-Baden: Nomos

Simmel, G. 1908. *Soziologie*. Berlin: Duncker & Humblot (5th edn 1968)

1965. The Poor. *Social Problems*, **13**: 118–140 (German, see Simmel 1908, chapter 7)

Skocpol, T. 1997. *Boomerang: Health Care Reform and the Turn against Government*. New York: W.W. Norton

Smeeding, T.M., Torrey, B.B. and Rein, M. 1988. Patterns of Income and Poverty: The Economic Status of Children and the Elderly in Eight Countries, in Palmer *et al.*, pp. 89–119

Smeeding, T.S., O'Higgins, M. and Rainwater, L. (eds.) 1990. *Poverty, Inequality and Income Distribution in Comparative Perspective: The Luxembourg Income Study*. London, Washington, DC: Wheatsheaf Press, Urban Institute Press

Sørensen, A. and Trappe, H. 1994. Life Course Convergence and Gender Inequality in the German Democratic Republic. Berlin: Max-Planck-Institute for Human Development and Education, Section Education, Work and Social Change, Project 'Life Courses and Historical Change in the Former GDR', Report No.6

Soskice, D. 1990. Reinterpreting Corporatism and Explaining Unemployment: Co-ordinated and Non-co-ordinated Market Economies, in Brunetta, R. and Dell'Aringa, C. (eds.) *Labour Relations and Economic Performance*. London: Macmillan in association with the International Economic Association, pp. 170–211

1991. The Institutional Infrastructure for International Competitiveness: A Comparative Analysis of the U.K. and Germany, in Atkinson, A. B. and Bruneta, R. (eds.), *The Economics of the New Europe*, London: Macmillan, pp. 45–66

Sozialenquête 1966 [Commission of Enquiry into Social Policy]. *Soziale Sicherung in der Bundesrepublik Deutschland. Bericht der Sozialenquête-Kommission.* Stuttgart: Kohlhammer

Specht, T., Albrecht, G. and Großkopf, H. 1979. Grundlagen einer Theorie und empirische Analysen zur Nichtseßhaftigkeit. Zentrale Strukturmerkmale biographischer Verläufe vor Beginn der Nichtseßhaftigkeit (Kurzfassung der wichtigsten Ergebnisse des Forschungsberichts zur 'Grundlagenstudie Erscheinungsweisen, Verlaufsformen und Ursachen der Nichtseßhaftigkeit') Bielefeld: BAG, mimeo

Spicker, P. 1992. *Poverty and Social Security. Concepts and Principles*. London: Routledge

SPIEGEL, Der 1973. *Unterprivilegiert*. Neuwied: Luchterhand

Standfest, E. 1979. *Sozialpolitik als Reformpolitik. Aspekte der sozialpolitischen Entwicklung in der Bundesrepublik Deutschland*. Cologne: Bund

Statistisches Bundesamt [Federal Bureau of Statistics] 1962. Fachserie K, *Öffentliche Sozialleistungen*, Reihe 1, *Öffentliche Fürsorge 1961*. Stuttgart: Kohlhammer

1974a. Fachserie K, *Öffentliche Sozialleistungen*, Reihe 1, *Sozialhilfe, Kriegsopfer-fürsorge, Sonderbeitrag Laufende Leistungen der Hilfe zum Lebensunterhalt, Juni 1972*. Stuttgart: Kohlhammer

1974b. Laufende Hilfe zum Lebensunterhalt. Ergebnis einer Zusatzstatistik zur Sozialhilfestatistik im Juni 1972. *Wirtschaft und Statistik*, **26**: 518–524

1982a-1997a. *Statistisches Jahrbuch für die Bundesrepublik Deutschland*. Wiesbaden: Metzler-Poeschel (until 1988: Stuttgart: Kohlhammer).

1983b. Fachserie 13, Reihe S. 6, *Sondererhebung Laufende Leistungen der Hilfe zum Lebensunterhalt, September 1981*. Stuttgart: Kohlhammer

1983c. Laufende Hilfe zum Lebensunterhalt. Ergebnis einer Zusatzstatistik zur Statistik der Sozialhilfe im September 1981. *Wirtschaft und Statistik*, **35**: 254–264, 430–432

1992b-1998b. Fachserie 13, Reihe 2, *'Sozialhilfe'*, Stuttgart: Metzler-Poeschel

1998c. Statistik der Sozialhilfe. Empfänger/-innen von laufender Hilfe zum Lebensunterhalt am 31.12.1996 – Arbeitsunterlage. Wiesbaden: Statistisches Bundesamt, mimeo

Stelzer-Orthofer, C. 1997. *Armut und Zeit. Eine sozialwissenschaftliche Analyse zur Sozialhilfe*. Opladen: Leske und Budrich

Stichweh, R. 1997. Inklusion/Exklusion, funktionale Differenzierung und die Theorie der Weltgesellschaft. *Soziale Systeme*, **3**, 1: 123–136

Strang, H. 1970. *Erscheinungsformen der Sozialhilfebedürftigkeit. Beitrag zur Geschichte, Theorie und empirischen Analyse der Armut*. Stuttgart: Enke

1985. *Sozialhilfebedürftigkeit. Struktur – Ursachen – Wirkung, unter besonderer Berücksichtigung der Effektivität der Sozialhilfe*. Hochschule Hildesheim, mimeo

Strengmann-Kuhn, W. 1997. Erwerbs- und Arbeitsbeteiligung der Armutspopulation in der Bundesrepublik Deutschland, in Becker and Hauser (eds.), pp. 113–133

Tennstedt, F. 1976a. Sozialgeschichte der Sozialversicherung, in Blohmke, M. *et al.* (eds.), *Handbuch der Sozialmedizin*. Stuttgart, vol. III, pp. 385–492

1976b. Zur Ökonomisierung und Verrechtlichung in der Sozialpolitik, in Murswieck, A.M. (ed.), *Staatliche Politik im Sozialsektor*. Munich: Piper, pp. 139–165

Tobias, G. and Boettner, J. (eds.) 1992. *Von der Hand in den Mund: Armut und Armutsbewältigung in einer westdeutschen Großstadt*. Essen: Klartext

Townsend, P. 1979. *Poverty in the United Kingdom*. Harmondsworth: Penguin

1985. A Sociological Approach to the Measurement of Poverty: A Rejoinder to Prof. Amartya Sen. *Oxford Economic Papers*, **37**: 659–668

Transfer-Enquête-Kommission. 1981. *Das Transfersystem in der Bundesrepublik Deutschland*. Stuttgart: Kohlhammer

Trappe, H. 1994. Handlungsstrategien von Frauen unterschiedlicher Generationen zur Verbindung von Familie und Beruf und deren Beeinflussung durch sozial-politische Rahmenbedingungen. Berlin: Max-Planck-Institute for Human Development and Education, Section Education, Work and Social Change, Project 'Life Courses and Historical Change in the Former GDR', Report No. 8

Ungaretti, Giuseppe. 1975. *The Buried Harbour*, translated by Allen Mandelbaum. Ithaca: Cornell University Press

Vaskovics, L.A. 1976. *Segregierte Armut. Randgruppenbildung in Notunterkünften.* Frankfurt a.M./New York: Campus

Veit-Wilson, J. H. 1986. Paradigms of Poverty: A Rehabilitation of B.S. Rowntree. *Journal of Social Policy*, **15**: 69–99

1998. *Setting Adequacy Standards. How Governments Define Minimum Incomes.* Bristol: Policy Press

Vincent, J., Ashworth, K. and Walker, R. 1991. Taking Account of Time in the Targeting and Administration of Benefits. Centre for Research in Social Policy, Loughborough University of Technology (Working Paper no. 141)

Visser, J. and Hemerijck, A. 1997. *A Dutch Miracle. Growth, Welfare Reform and Corporatism in the Netherlands.* Amsterdam: Amsterdam University Press

Vobruba, G. (ed.) 1989. *Der wirtschaftliche Wert der Sozialpolitik.* Berlin: Duncker & Humblot

(ed.) 1990a. *Strukturwandel der Sozialpolitik.* Frankfurt a.M.: Suhrkamp

1990b. Lohnarbeitszentrierte Sozialpolitik in der Krise der Lohnarbeit, in ibid. (ed.) 1990a, pp. 11–80

1991. *Jenseits der sozialen Fragen, Modernisierung und Transformation von Gesellschaftssystemen.* Frankfurt a.M.: Suhrkamp

1995. Arbeit und Einkommen nach der Vollbeschäftigung. *Leviathan,* **23**, 2: 154–164

1996. Die Faktizität der Geltung. Gerechtigkeit im sozialpolitischen Umbau-Diskurs, in Clausen (ed.), pp. 963–975

Voges, W. (ed.) 1987. *Methoden der Biographie- und Lebenslaufforschung.* Opladen: Leske und Budrich

1992. *Zur Thematisierung von Armut in Deutschland.* Vorwort, in Manz, pp. VII-XII

Voges, W. and Leibfried, S. 1990. Keine Sonne für die Armut. Vom Sozialhilfebezug als Verlauf ('Karriere') – Ohne umfassendere Information keine wirksame Armutsbekämpfung. *Nachrichtendienst des Deutschen Vereins für öffentliche und private Fürsorge,* **70**: 135–141

Voges, W. and Rohwer, G. 1991. Zur Dynamik des Sozialhilfebezugs, in Rendtel and Wagner (eds.), pp. 510–531

1992. Receiving Social Assistance in Germany: Risk and Duration. *Journal of European Social Policy,* **2**: 175–191

Vranken, J., Geldof, D. and Van Menxel, G. 1997. *Armoede en sociale uitsluiting. Jaarboek 1997.* Leuven: Acco

Wagner, W. 1982. *Die nützliche Armut. Eine Einführung in Sozialpolitik.* Berlin: Wagenbach

Walker, R. (with Ashworth, K.) 1994. *Poverty Dynamics: Issues and Examples.* Aldershot: Avebury

Walker, R. 1998. *Rethinking Poverty in a Dynamic Perspective*, in Andreß (ed.), pp. 29–49

Walker, R. and Leisering, L. 1998. New Tools: Towards a Dynamic Science of Modern Society, in Leisering and Walker (eds.) 1998a, pp. 17–33

Walker, R. and Shaw, A. 1998. Escaping from Social Assistance in Great Britain, in Leisering and Walker (eds.) 1998a, pp. 221–242

Walker, R. and Wiseman, M. 1997. The Possibilities of a British Earned Income Tax Credit, *Fiscal Studies*, **18**, 4: 401–425

Wallace, H. and Wallace, W. (eds.) 1996. *Policy-Making in the European Union*. 3rd ed. Oxford: Oxford University Press

Wallerstein, J. and Blakeslee, S. 1989. *Second Chances*. London: Bantam

Weber, A. 1996. Sozialhilfe im sozialstrukturellem Wandel. Sozialhilfeempfänger in den 80er Jahren. Bremen University, Centre for Social Policy Research, Ph. D. Thesis, mimeo

Weidenfeld, W. and Korte, K.-R. 1996. *Handbuch zur deutschen Einheit*. Bonn: Bundeszentrale für politische Bildung

Wenzel, G. 1995. Sozialhilfereform aus der Sicht der Bundesländer, in Forschungsinstitut der Friedrich-Ebert-Stiftung (ed.), *Sozialreform und Zukunft der Sozialhilfe*. Gesprächskreis Arbeit und Soziales No. 58, Bonn: Friedrich-Ebert-Stiftung, pp. 85–102

Wenzel, G. and Leibfried, S. 1986. *Armut und Sozialhilferecht. Eine sozialwissenschaftlich orientierte Einführung für die Sozialhilfepraxis*. Weinheim/Basel: Beltz

Wilson, W. J. 1987. *The Truly Disadvantaged. The Inner City, the Underclass, and Public Policy*. Chicago, IL/London: The University of Chicago Press

Wingen, M. 1993. *Vierzig Jahre Familienpolitik in Deutschland – Momentaufnahmen und Entwicklungslinien. Zugleich ein Beitrag zu 40 Jahren Familienministerium*. Grafschaft: Vektor Verlag

1994. *Zur Theorie und Praxis der Familienpolitik*. Frankfurt a.M.: Deutscher Verein für öffentliche und private Fürsorge

Wiseman, M. (ed.) 1991a. Research and Policy: A Symposium on the Family Support Act of 1988. *Journal of Policy Analysis And Management*, **10**: 588–666

1991b. What did the American Work-Welfare Demonstrations Do? Why Should Germans Care? University of Bremen, Centre for Social Policy Research, Working paper No. 9/91

Wohlrab-Sahr, M. 1992. Institutionalisierung oder Individualisierung des Lebenslaufs? Anmerkungen zu einer festgefahrenen Debatte, *BIOS (Zeitschrift für Biographieforschung und Oral History)*, **5**: 1–20

Wohlrab-Sahr, M. 1993. *Biographische Unsicherheit. Formen weiblicher Identität in der 'reflexiven Moderne': Das Beispiel der Zeitarbeiterinnen*. Opladen: Leske und Budrich

Wolf, J. 1991. Die Vergesellschaftungslücke. Der Vorruhestand in den neuen Bundesländern. *Zeitschrift für Sozialreform*, **37**: 723–735

Wolff, K. and Beck, M. 1993. Defizite der amtlichen Sozialhilfestatistik, Armutsdiskussion und Statistikreform. *Zeitschrift für Sozialreform*, **38**: 417–443

Wright, E. O. 1997. *Class Counts. Comparative Studies in Class Analysis*. Cambridge: Cambridge University Press

Zander, H. 1973. Sozialarbeit und Armut – Der Begriff der Armut in seiner

Bedeutung für eine marxistische Theorie der Sozialarbeit, in Otto, H.-U. and Schneider, S. (eds.), *Gesellschaftliche Perspektiven der Sozialarbeit*, Vol. I, Neuwied/Darmstadt: Luchterhand, pp. 233–266

Zapf, W. (ed.) 1974. *Soziale Indikatoren. Konzepte und Forschungsansätze.* Frankfurt a.M./New York: Campus

1976. *Sozialberichterstattung: Möglichkeiten und Probleme.* Göttingen: Schwartz

1994. *Modernisierung, Wohlfahrtsentwicklung und Transformation. Soziologische Aufsätze 1987 bis 1994.* Berlin: edition Sigma

Zapf, W. *et al.* 1987. *Individualisierung und Sicherheit. Untersuchungen zur Lebensqualität in der Bundesrepublik Deutschland.* Munich: Beck

Zürn, Michael. 1998. *Regieren jenseits des Nationalstaats. Globalisierung und Denationalisierung als Chance.* Frankfurt a.M.: Suhrkamp

Zukunftskommission der Friedrich-Ebert-Stiftung 1998. *Wirtschaftliche Leistungsfähigkeit, sozialer Zusammenhalt, ökologische Nachhaltigkeit. Drei Ziele - ein Weg.* Bonn: Dietz Verlag

Zumpe, P. 1951. Die Sozialfürsorge im Fünfjahresplan. *Arbeit und Sozialfürsorge,* **6**: 327–328

Zwick, M. (ed.) 1994. *Einmal arm, immer arm? Neue Befunde zur Armut in Deutschland.* Frankfurt a.M./New York: Campus

Subject index

abuse of benefits *see* Social Assistance
  (claiming), abuse
Accident Insurance of 1884ff. (*Gesetzliche
  Unfallversicherung*) 45, 300f.
administration of poverty *see* Social
  Assistance (law and administration)
Advance Alimony Law of 1980ff. (*Unter-
  haltsvorschußgesetz*) 46, 271, 301
agency *see* careers in poverty; coping;
  enabling state/policies; poverty, active vs. passive poor and deliberate
  poverty; rationality
  active clients – active policies 264
  endurance vs. action (*Erleiden* vs.
    Handeln) 123f., 124 n. 6, 132–5
  'free agent' 20, 37
  and the life course 36, 281
  the poor as agents 39f., 257f.
  and social change 291
  structure and action (Gerhardt) 283f.
Ages of Men, The (plate) 1
anti-poverty policy *see* Social Assistance
  (law and administration); social
  policy; welfare state
  active policies 264
  changes 1949–1999 193–5, 194 (table 7.1)
  compared to USA (new perspectives)
    277f.
  'dynamic policies' 258, **264**
  economic policy as 175f., 193
  German 267–73
  integrated social policy 266–73, 322
    vertical (upward and downward inte-
      gration; harmonisation) 268–70;
      horizontal 270; integration with tax
      policy and family policy 270–2
  modernisation lag 266
  municipal reform 266f.
  new perspectives **258**, **316f**
    enabling approach 258, 263–6; inte-

grated social policy (upward and
  downward integration; harmonisation) 258, 266–73; life-course policy
  258–63; reflexive policy 273–6
vs. politics of functional poverty *see*
  functional poverty
'poverty proof' welfare state 271f.
problem groups [*see also* problem groups]
  vs. 'time groups' 258f.
reflexive policy
  social reporting 273f.; monitoring
    274–6
separation from social insurance policy
  see welfare state, Germany
and types of poverty careers 262f.
'welfare to work' 264–6, 315f.
asylum seekers, Asylum Seekers Benefit Act
  of 1993ff. (*Asylbewerberleistungsgesetz*) *see also* immigration, asylum
  seekers
Aussiedler see immigration, settlers
Australia 28

Basic Income 172, 185, 189, 257, 269f.,
  312
  demogrant (*Bürgergeld*) 270, 315
  problems (fiscal, economic, political)
    312–16
Beschäftigungsobservatorium
  Ostdeutschland 1990ff. 205 n. 2,
  206–8
biographical approach 111
  bias of research 30
  'biography' vs. 'life course' 36
biographical interviews [*see also* qualitative
  study] 22
'biographisation' 37, 125, 262
  of poverty 239, **240–2**, 262
  as reflexivity of modern self 36f.
  by Social Assistance claimants 125, **159**

Bremen Longitudinal Study of Social
  Assistance (LSA) *see also* cohorts;
  Halle/Saale; poverty, new picture of
  approach 22, 58, 239
  criticism 58 n. 2, 79, 227, 254, 281 n. 1
  impact on policy-making 257, 266
  methods 22, **56f.**, 64–7, 64 n. 3, 114 n. 3,
    151, 152 n. 10, 172 n. 3, 283f.
  sample **56f.**, 70, 70 n. 9, 90, 90 n. 3, 114 n.
    3, 155 n. 13
  sources 20f.
  similar studies 57, 75, 152 n. 11, 228
*Bundesanstalt für vereinigungsbedingte Son-
  deraufgaben* (BVS) 1995ff., 208 n. 5
Bureau Maatwerk 265, 317

Canada 48 n. 27
capability (Sen) 21
Care Insurance of 1994ff. (Gesetzliche
  Pflegeversicherung) 32, 45f., 87, 172,
    190, 314, 318
career (issue cycle) of 'poverty' 175, 190 n.
    11, 192–6, 194 (table 7.1)
careers in poverty [*see also* life course] 8, 241
  and anti-poverty policies 262f.
  central hypotheses 113f.
  concepts, old and new 109–13
  concepts, sociological (class mobility,
    deviance, social coping) 111f., 137–8
    (table 5.2)
  decline vs. ascent 109f., 113–6
  methodology of career analysis 113, 114
    n. 3, 283
  models of careers (deterministic – 'one-
    way street'; probabilistic – 'corridor';
    contingent – 'cross-roads') 110–**13**,
    136–8 (table 5.2), 140f.
  perspectives of social integration 136–40
    vs. social inequality 140–3
  related socio-cultural models 139f.
  types of careers (entrenched, welfare-
    state normalised, optimised poverty
    management) 132–40, **132f.** (table
    5.1), 247, 262f.
Caritasverband 198
'Change' (*Wende* = German unification in
    1990) **200**, 207
Child Benefit of 1954ff. (*Kindergeld*) 46, 271
children 94ff., 296
  child care 155, 234
  child poverty 46, 184, 190, 243, 301f.
Christian-Democratic Party (*Christlich-
  Demokratische Union*, CDU) 148,
    186, 195, 197f., 266
citizenship 3
  European 320

social citizenship 294–6, 312
  three stages (T.H. Marshall) 23f.
class *see* inequality
cohorts
  Bremen cohorts of first claims of Social
    Assistance
    of 1983 to 1989, 56, 64, 75f., 90 n. 3,
      114, 224, 225–30; of 1989 to 1994,
      56, 63–88, 90 n. 3, 224, 225–30
  cohort approach 67, 113
  Halle cohorts of 1990ff. 231
  comparisons
    West German, 1983–89 vs. 1989–94
      cohort, 225–30; West vs. East
      German 231–5
Compensation Act of 1952ff. (*Lastenausgleichsgesetz*) 177, 180, 303f.
constitution *see* Federal Constitution
control, social 123f., 199
coping 21, 40, **124f.** (figure 5.2)
  biographical concept of 124f.
  managing consequences vs. managing
    consequences and causes **137**–9, 138
    (table 5.2)
  and models of poverty careers 112f.,
    137
  modes of dealing with Social Assistance
    124f., 131, 159
    (passive) enduring 125–7; (active)
      coping 125, 127–30; strategic use
      125, 130f., 160f., 163–5
  psychological vs. socio-economic c. 125
  types of dealing with Social Assistance
    125
    biographical copers (128–30),
      pragmatic copers (127f.), strategic
      users (130, 160f., 163–5), mere
      survivors (126f.), victims (125f.)
  women cope better 142
cross-sectional accounts 66 n. 5, 86, 254,
    272f.
  accounting perspective 67, 273
  overestimate long-term claims **67**
  point in time sample 67 n. 6
cultures (images) of poverty/social policy
    see poverty, images (cultures) of
cycle of deprivation (disadvantage) *see*
  dynamics of poverty, careers in
  poverty

debt 46, 270, 295, **299–301**
  definition 299 n. 4
  bank liability 300
  bankruptcy of individuals 299
  national 307
deferred gratification 242

'democratisation' of poverty ('transcendance', *Entgrenzung*) 9, 239, **240, 242f.**, 258, 279, 295
demogrant *see* Basic Income
dependency (on Social Assistance) [*see also* poverty, state-induced] 11, 57f., 90, 101f., 133f., **144–68**, 226
(dependent) class 41f.
compared
USA and Germany (Duncan/Voges) **154–7**; in Western societies 145 n. 3
or heterogeneity of claimants? 151f.
influenced by behaviour or mechanistic occurance 147
models of potential dependency 159–65
marginalised claimants 160, 161; subjects of unanticipated outcomes 160, 162f.; strategic users 160f., 163–5
and political choice/values 154, 157, 167, 265
qualitative tests 157–65
quantitative tests 150–7
subjective criteria for probability of long-term effects 157–65
types of long-term effects (Ellwood: rational choice, psycho-social, cultural)
defined 149f.; tested 152f., 160–5, 165f.
deprivation 5, 246–8, 251
multiple 76
discourse *see* poverty, debates
disparities, horizontal (Offe) 185f.
distribution according to
need 177, 273
merit 177, 260f.
division, social 250f., 253
divorce 302f.
dramatisation *see* poverty, images (cultures) of
dynamic approach to poverty [*see also* Bremen Longitudinal Study; dynamics of poverty; life-cycle perspective] 6, 14–21, 239
ambivalence 239
dynamic elements in conventional research 17f.
founding father of dynamic research (Rowntree) 15
impact on policy-making (Germany, USA) 12, 257, 266
sources of 20f.
static conventional research 18–20
studies (national and comparative) 14f., 57

dynamics of poverty [*see also* careers in poverty; dynamic approach to poverty; measurement of poverty, duration; Social Assistance (claiming), duration ...] 14–22
'cumulative social decline' 109, 116f., 125f., 134, 137
static vs. dynamic 9, 16
static perspective misleading 16; fluid part vs. hard core 253f.
transitory 289f.
USA 224

economic miracle (1950s) 175
economic policy as poverty policy 175f., 193
East Germany 1990ff. [for 1949–1990 *see* German Democratic Republic; *see also* 'Change'; immigration; life course; pension system; poverty; Social Assistance (claiming and law and administration); Unemployment Insurance] 189–92, 215–23, 228f., 288, 303f., 309f.
attitudes 232, 235
attribution of poverty 303f.
collective poverty 191
expectations 200f., 221, 235
feeling of relative disadvantage 221
few immigrants in Social Assistance 232
migration to the West 229f.
improved living conditions 221
increase in net income inequality 222
integrative function of welfare state 234f.
as *mezzogiorno*? 222
minimum pension *see* pension system, in East Germany
patterns of development 231f.
polarisation between winners and losers 235
as 'poor house' of Germany? 221f., 230–5
poverty 215–8 (table 8.3)
prospects 221–3
retrenchment 223
shifting unification's costs to all insured 33
Social Assistance [*see* Social Assistance (claiming, law and administration), in East Germany]
Solidarity Surcharge (Tax) of 1991ff. (*Solidaritätszuschlag*) 223, 288
transfer payments from the West 223
transformation
process 231f.; transitional policies only 43, 208, 220
'welfare state gigantism' 207, 223

East Germany 1990ff. (*cont.*)
  wholsesale extension of West German in-
    stitutions 170
  women, stronger work orientation of 209,
    234
education 7, 129, **142f.**
  certification vs. training on the job 51
  German Democratic Republic 202
  expansion of education since the 1960s in
    Germany 25
  Hauptschule 163
  hidden curriculum 34f.
  loss of value 27
  opportunities vs. outcomes 26
  as part of social policy (Anglo-Saxon
    concept) 26 n. 2, 319
Education Benefit Act of 1986ff.
  (*Erziehungsgeld*) 187, 225
employment *see* unemployment
  employment-related life courses: conti-
    nuous vs. dis-continuous
    employment careers 115–20
Employment Promotion Act of 1969ff.
  (*Arbeitsförderungsgesetz*) [*see also*
  Unemployment Insurance;
  unemployment; labour market; working poor] 61, 185, 188, 266
Employers Liability Insurance Associations
  of 1884ff. (*Berufsgenossenschaften*)
  300
enabling state/policies 263–6, 311
European Community of 1957ff. (Union of
  1992ff.) [*see also* globalisation] 296,
  304, **317–22**, 320f.
  Economic and Monetary Union (EMU)
    321
  European citizenship 320
  European Court of Justice (ECJ) 320
  Maastricht Treaty 320
  Poverty Programmes 8, 196, 321, 321 nn.
    23 and 24
  as 'reinsurer' of national welfare states
    321
  and 'social exclusion' (replacing 'poverty')
    8, 249
  TSER 8
exclusion, social [*see also* inclusion] x, 114,
  224, **246f.**, **249–51**, 254, 292, 321
  debate 5, 8, 196, 249f., 280
  and poverty careers 138 (table 5.2),
    140

family [*see also* lone parents] 243
  allowances for civil servants 167
  changes 225
  male-breadwinner model 261
  marriage as basis of entitlement 267
  family reasons for Social Assistance
    claiming 72; leaving 79
  policy 267, 270, 278, 302, 307
  new risks 46f.
  as structuring family-related types of life
    courses 116, **118f.**, **121f.**
Federal Administrative Court (*Bundesver-
  waltungsgericht*) 30
Federal Constitution (*Grundgesetz*) 25, 264,
  298
Federal Constitutional Court
  (*Bundesverfassungsgericht*) 46, 167,
  187, 190f., 271f.
Federal Educational Support Act of 1971ff.
  139, 185
Federal Labour Agency (*Bundesanstalt für
  Arbeit*) 206–9
Federal Maintenance Act of 1950ff.
  (*Bundesversorgungsgesetz*) 177
Federal Minister of Finance (*Der
  Bundesminister der Finanzen*) 223 n.
  13, 272
Federal Minister of Labour and Social
  Affairs (*Der Bundesminister für
  Arbeit und Sozialordnung*) 171, 208,
  220, 277, 288, 307, 318
Federal Parliament (*Deutscher Bundestag*),
  Papers (*Bundestagsdrucksachen*) 60 n. 1,
  184
  Proceedings (*Stenographische Berichte*)
    61, 257
Federal Social Assistance Act of 1962
  (*Bundessozialhilfegesetz*) [*see mainly*
  Social Assistance] **180f.**, 211, 264,
  295
  social assistance East vs. West
    before 1990 214; from 1990 218–21
  effective in East Germany 1991,
    218–21
  reforms
    federal Social Assistance reforms
      1962–96, 183, 184, 187, 189–91;
      Federal Social Assistance Reform
      Act of 1996, 7, 165 n. 19, 167, 191,
      266; Social Assistance Act in East
      Germany (1 July-31 December 1990)
      218
  withering away of Basic Income Support?
    expected in 1961, 31, 43, 60; but not
    realized 86f., 148
Federal Social Budget (*Sozialbudget,
  statistical annex of Sozialbericht*)
  171, 272
Federal Social Report of 1968ff. (*Sozialbericht*) 171, 272

federal statistics [*see* Federal Statistical Office]
Federal Statistical Office (*Statistisches Bundesamt*) 19, 19 n. 16, 22 n.19, 31 n. 10, 66 n. 5, 70, 171, 179, 219, 221, 226, 227 n. 1, 228, 229, 230, 257, 272
  Data Report (*Datenreport*) 273
  reformed statistics on Social Assistance 66, 69, 228
foreigners (resident*)* [*see also* immigration] 31, 68f., 243–5
  guest workers (*Gastarbeiter*) 249, 288
  Turkish 68f.
France 43, 312, 321
  RMI (*Revenue Minimum d'Insertion*) 275
social exclusion 8
Fürsorge or *Sozialfürsorge* (Social Welfare) [*see* also GDR; Social Welfare] 180
Fürsorgewissenschaft (Science of Social Welfare) 198
functional poverty 285–92, 310
  concept 286f.
  in Germany 282–9
  politics of functional poverty 287, 289
  'productive poverty' 287, 290

GATT 1947ff./1995ff. 320
gender [*see also* men, women] 50f., 262, 294
  gendered concept of life course 34 n. 12
  coping 142
  family-related vs. employment-related life courses 116–22
  gendered institutionalisation of life course in German pension scheme 34
  gendered poverty careers **141f.**
  German welfare state 34, 50f.
generational contract 243
generations 17f., 26, 184, 218, 290
German Association for Public and Private Welfare 1880ff. (*Deutscher Verein für öffentliche und private Fürsorge*) 180
German Democratic Republic, GDR (1949–1990) [from 3 October 1990 *see* East Germany] 36, 170
  as authoritarian 'provider state' 170, 202
  'Change' (*Wende*) 200, 297
  collapse 170, 207
  company social policy 203
  Constitution of 1968 204
  education 26, 202
  general collective poverty 48
  in-kind strategy in social policy 212
  life-course regime 49, 51f., 201–5

migration to West Germany 68f., 189, 229f.
poverty [*see also* poverty; Social Welfare Regulation] 210–4
  among the elderly 211 (table 8.1), 212; collective poverty by general supply shortage 212f.; income poverty in East Germany 210–13, 222 (table 8.1); as a non-issue 192, 210; redefined as health problem 192; socialist image of poverty 192
  retirement delayed 202
  right to work 203
  Social Assistance Act (from 1 July 1990) 218
  as welfare state 207
German Life-Course Study (K.U. Mayer) 282
German National Science Foundation or Research Council (*Deutsche Forschungsgemeinschaft*, DFG) xvf., 15
German Trade Union Congress 1949ff. (*Deutscher Gewerkschaftsbund*, DGB) 315
Germany *see* German Democratic Republic (1949–1990), East Germany (1990ff.), unification, ...
globalisation 3f., 287, 305
  global cities 280
  welfare state as barrier to adjustment? 319
  'social policy nationalism' 320
  social clauses 320
  world-wide welfare state? 320
Graduate Support Act of 1971ff. (*Graduiertenförderungsgesetz*) 185
Green Party (*Bündnis 90/Die Grünen*, Alliance 90/The Greens) 172, 189, 197, 241, 257, 269, 305, 312, 317
GSOEP *see* Socio-Economic Panel (Germany)

Halle/Saale, location of East German twin study 56, 231
Health Insurance of 1883ff. (sickness funds) (*Gesetzliche Krankenversicherung*) 29, 42, 45, 59, 146, 166
  Sickness Benefits 42, 59
Housing
  Agency 128
  Allowances in Social Assistance 313
  and rent arrears 191
  policy 193
Housing Benefit Act, Second, of 1970ff. (2. *Wohngeldgesetz*) 93, 185, 271

ILO 1906/1919ff. 320
Immediate Aid Act of 1948ff. (*So-forthilfegesetz*) 177, 180
immigration (immigrants) 46, 226, 229
    (figure 9.1), 243, 249, 288f., 296, 318
  asylum seekers 68 (figure 3.3), **69**, 87, 189,
    226, 228–9 (figure 9.1), 244, 288
  Asylum seekers Benefit Act of 1993ff.
    (*Asylbewerberleistungsgesetz*) 30, 32,
    46, 190, 219, 244, 227f.; civil war
    refugees 228; tolerated refugees 69
  impact on Social Assistance 31f., 68
    (figure 3.3.), 70, 72, 226–30, 244f.
  definition of 'immigrant' **68**, 226
  foreigners (resident) *see* ibid.
  from German Democratic Republic (until
    3 October 1990) (*Übersiedler*) 68
    (figure 3.3), **69**, 189, 229 (figure 9.1),
    230
  integration by Social Assistance 70
  limiting access (1990s) 59, 228
  and multi-cultural society 243, 289
  new immigrants claiming Social
    Assistance
    in Bremen 1989 68–70; East vs. West
    Germany 232
  and poverty 243–6
  refugees *see* immigration, asylum seekers
  'settlers' from Eastern Europe and the
    former Soviet Union (*Aussiedler* of
    ethnic German origin) 68 (figure
    3.3), **69,** 189, 226, 228–9 (figure 9.1),
    244f.
  as 'state-induced' poverty [*see* poverty,
    state induced] 72, 228
inclusion, social [*see also* citizenship] 246,
    249, 312
  and poverty careers 138 (table 5.2), 139
  secondary inclusion 138 (table 5.2), 139f.
  through Social Assistance 70, 139f., 235
indebtedness *see* debt
indexing of welfare state benefits 179, 185
individualisation [*see also* self] 20, 279
  defined (U. Beck) 38
  individualism (sociological concepts)
    37f.
  of inequality 20, 279f., 284
  also among the poor **39f.**
  of poverty 9, 9 n. 7, 20
  rise of the modern individual 6f., 23
  and 'secondary institutions' 20
  social change in postwar Germany 284
  and the welfare state 23f., 38f.
Income and Expenditure Sample Survey
    (*Einkommens- und Verbrauchs-stichprobe*, EVS) 22 n. 19

inequality, social [*see also* social mobility]
    175, 245
  based on equality of opportunity 17
  biographical concept (Kohli) 284f.
  changes **250f.**
  class (analysis) x, 185, 279–84, 290
  fluidity vs. rigidity 279–83, 289f.
  functional [*see also* functional poverty]
    288, 291
  horizontal vs. vertical 279–92
  individualisation of (Beck) 20, **279f.**, 284
  vs. 'life course' x, **280f.**–5
  'normal' and 'deviant' 13
  vs. 'poverty' 175, 288, 291
  vs. 'poverty careers' 140–3
  qualitative methodology (Gerhardt) 283f.
  research ix, 12f., 17, 21
  structural inequality buffered by
    individual dynamics 17
  impact of welfare state 42 n. 20
infantilisation of poverty (Hauser) 44
insecurity [*see also* risk] 3, 242, 251, 292,
    309f.
Insolvency Law, reform of 1994ff. (effective
    from 1999) (*Gesetz zur Reform des
    Insolvenzrechts*) [*see also* debt] 299
Ireland 48 n. 27

Japan 311, 319
Joint Constitutional Commission of both
    Chambers of Parliament
    (*Gemeinsame Verfassungskommission
    von Bundestag und Bundesrat*) 288
justice xii
  productivist concept 286, 289, 310

labelling approach [*see also* marginal
    groups] 18f., 19 n. 17, 110, 199
Labour Law Code of 1961ff. (*Ar-
    beitsgesetzbuch*) [*see also* GDR] 204
labour market [*see also* unemployment, Un-
    employment Insurance; working
    poor] 271
  actively vs. passively institutionalised
    policies 205, 207, 219f.
  deregulation 289
  low-pay sector 289f., 310
  short-time work 206 n. 3
  transitional jobs 289f.
Lebenslage (life situation) 21, 62, 111
Left and Right [*see also* poverty, images
    (cultures) of] 162
  and 'dependency' 167f.
  and dynamic approach 10
less eligibility [*see also* working poor] 152,
    165, 190, 272

Liberals, Liberal Party (*Freie Demokratische Partei*, FDP) 183, 187, 315
life-course approach x, **6**, 9
life course(s) (*Lebenslauf*) [*see also* life cycle perspective, life-course policy] ix, 6f., 279
  vs. 'biography' 36
  changes 52f., 308f.
  continuous vs. discontinuous 116
  de-institutionalisation, de-standardisation 52, 308–10
  East Germany 201–5
    women 201f., 207f.; rupture in life course regime 222
  as 'endogenous causal nexus' 37, 41
  fluidity vs. rigidity in the life course 280–5, 308
  gendered (divided) institutionalisation 34
  institutionalisation 24, 36
  vs. phases of claiming 109
  plurality of the 279
  in poverty, varied 113ff.
  regimes compared
    East Germany 47–53; Sweden 47–53; UK 47f.; USA 47–53; West Germany 47–53
  in relation to social structure 115f.
    employment-related 116–21; family-related 118f., 121f.; benefit-related 122f.
  and research 14–22
  and the Self (J. W. Meyer) 7, 24, 41
  and the state *see* life-course policy
  status passages in the 240f.
  types of **115** (figure 5.1), 131–3 (table 5.1)
    critical 116–19; normalised 119–23
life-course policy/politics
  active life-course policies 183, 185, 310
  as new anti-poverty policy **258–63**
  dimensions (structuration/differentiation, integration, formation) **25f.** (figure 2.1)
  individual 'life-course politics' 36, 308f.
  model of 24–6, 41
  state as custodian vs. moulder of life course 154f.
  tacit (vs. explicit) 33–5
  types of 24–6
    education 26f.; provision for old age 27f.; social risk management 29–33, 255, 309
  and the welfare state 7, **23–35**
life-cycle perspective
  on poverty 16–18
  vs. life-course perspective 16
  on impact of welfare state 23, 23 n. 1

lone parents 8, 47, 92, 94f., 163, 163 n. 17, 226, 230, 234, 243, 261, 265, 317
  and dependency 5, 145 n. 3
  duration of claiming social assistance Germany vs. USA 154–7; West and East Germany 84, 234
  as subjective bridgers 94–6
  German income experiment (Schultheis) 163
  stronger work orientation in East Germany 234
  use of Social Assistance as a biographical resource 244
  limited work requirement 61
longitudinal approach [*see also* dynamic approach to poverty; dynamics of poverty, duration measurement; Bremen Longitudinal Study of Social Assistance] 86
longitudinal studies [*see also* PSID, SOEP] 14f., 57, 252, 254
Low Income Panel Study (1998ff.) 253 n. 9
LSA 1988ff. [*see also* Bremen Longitudinal Study of ...] 56

machine tax (*Maschinensteuer*) *see* Product Levy
maintenance principle (*Versorgungsprinzip*) 177
marginal groups (*Randgruppen*) [*see also* labelling approach] 322
  as candidates for dependency 160f.
  discovery in the political debate 182–7
  dynamic character of research 18
  German research (biased towards downward careers) 13, 16f., 184, 249
  German vs. US discourse 249
  homeless families (*Obdachlose*) 110–12, 182, 185, 263
  and poverty careers 110–2
  social problems approach 13, 16f., 175, 199
  street people (*Nichtseßhafte*) 110–12, 182, 185
measurement of poverty
  duration of Social Assistance claims concepts: spell, gross and net duration 65f. (figure 3.2); sampling: 'point in-time' and 'ever begun' cohort 67, 254
  cross-section vs. longitudinal 67, 254, 274
  intra-household (children, women) 301f.
  poverty line 19, 183, 186, 281
  poverty standards in United Germany 216f.

men [*see also* gender; women] 117, 136, **141f.**
male bias 302
young 164f.
merit *see* distribution according to
methods *see* Bremen Longitudinal Study ...
middle classes 267, 295
minimum benefits [*see* Basic Income;
    pension system; Social Assistance;
    tax policies; Unemployment Insur-
    ance] 312–7
minimum standards 190, 314
Minister for Labour and Social Affairs *see*
    Federal Minister ...
moral economy 312, 322
moral hazard 164

need (*Bedarf*) *see* distribution according to
New Federal Territories 1990ff. (*Neue
    Bundesländer*) *see* East Germany
New Poverty
    in Germany (*Neue Armut*) 11, 78, 111,
        148, **188f.**, 234
    critical assessment **225, 229f.**
    in Europe 8
new service proletariat 290
New Social Question 1975ff. (*Neue Soziale
    Frage*) 148, 185f.
Nichtseßhafte, single street people *see*
    marginal groups
non-governmental welfare organisations
    (*Wohlfahrtsverbände*) 198
non-state welfare production 310–12

Obdachlose, homeless *see* marginal groups
OECD 3f., 317
Old-Age Pensions *see* pension system;
    Pension Reform Act of
Oswald von Nell-Breuning Institut 250

Panel Study of Income Dynamics,
    Michigan *see* PSID
Paritätische Wohlfahrtsverband, Der
    (DPWV) 198
Partei des Demokratischen Sozialismus
    1990ff. (PDS) 215
patient careers (Gerhardt) 21, 30 n. 7,
    112
pension adjustment laws until 1953 178
Pension Adjustment Act of 1990 (*Rentenan-
    passungsgesetz*) 220
Pension Reform Act of (*Rentenre-
    formgesetz*)
    1957 (Great Pension Reform) 25, 60, 148,
        179f., 295, 311, 314
    1972, 309

1989/1992, 45, 225, 267, 307, 309
1997 (partially suspended 1998 until the
    end of the year 2000) 45, 275 n. 7,
    308, 314
pension system, originally Invalidity and
    Old-Age Pension Insurance of
    1891ff. (*Gesetzliche Rentenversiche-
    rung*) 45 n. 24
    benefits 92, 112
    contribution credits for child-raising 187
    delayed retirement in the German
        Democratic Republic 202
    disability pensions (*Erwerbs- und Berufs-
        unfähigkeitsrenten*) 44f.
    dynamic pension (*dynamische Rente*) 179
    early retirement (*Frühverrentung*) 45, 309
    in East Germany 32
        the elderly as winners of unification 32,
            234; minimum pension 211f., 318;
            poverty of pensioners in East
            Germany 211f.; Pre-Retirement-
            Benefit of February 1990
            (*Vorruhestandsgeld*) 206; retrench-
            ment in East Germany 223; success
            of transition policy for the aged 218,
            234; transformation of social insur-
            ance 202 n. 1; Top-Up Supplement
            (1990 until 1993/96) (*Sozialzuschlag*)
            32, 191, 220; Transitional Benefit for
            the Elderly of October 1990 (*Alters-
            übergangsgeld*) 206
    and divided (gendered) institutionalisa-
        tion of the life course 34, 256
    financing
        contribution-based 28; pay-as-you-go
        32
    Low Earner's Top-Up (*Rente nach
        Mindesteinkommen*) 185
    minimum pension 269
        absent by design 32, 179, 185, 267; de-
            manded 271; rejected by Federal
            Minister (Blüm) 318
    Partial Pensions of 1992ff. (*Altersteilzeit*)
        45, 309
    increase in pension entitlement-age 45
    and poverty/Social Assistance *see*
        poverty, elderly
        aged inadequate incomes and basic
            pension benefits 87; dominance of
            elderly poor subsided 228; longer
            claims by the elderly 83; pension
            benefits prior to Social Assistance
            226; Social Assistance to top up 73,
            122
    'social pensioners' (*Sozialrentner*) 179, 181
    typical pensioner (*Eckrentner*) 27
    viability at risk 28

People's Welfare Organisation
 (*Volksfürsorge*) 192
Petrarca-Master (woodcuts) 169, 237
pluralisation of social divisions 251
poverty *see also* anti-poverty policies;
 careers in poverty; dynamic
 approach to poverty; dynamics of
 poverty; functional poverty; marginal groups; measurement of poverty; New Poverty; Social Assistance
 (claiming and law and administration); social reporting; types of
 poverty
 absolute vs. relative 197 n. 15
 active vs. passive poor 10, 21, 36, 39f.,
 114, **123f.**, 125–31, **134f.**, 153,
 159–65
 asset-poor 82
 causes 70–82, 297–306
 changes in
 risk characteristics (incidence,
 duration, clustering, new risks) 43–7;
 numbers **216** (table 8.3); social
 structure of poverty 250f.
 of children 46, 184, 190f., 243, 301f.
 and class 240, 243
 classes
 welfare or foster class 262; benefit class
 262; transition class 263
 collective
 generalised **176–81**, 193; East-Germany
 191f., 195f., 303; GDR 212f.
 debates [*see* also poverty, images; career
 (issue cycle) of 'poverty'; Left and
 Right; 'Two-Thirds-Society'; exclusion, debate] 8f., 251, 273, 280
 deliberate 241
 the deprived vs. the excluded 246
 and disadvantage 182
 and diswelfares
 policy of 'productive' diswelfares 289;
 transitional vs. permanent diswelfares 289–92
 in East Germany (from 1990)
 compared to GDR 216; change
 1990–97, 216 (table 8.3), 217; duration 217f.; compared to West 216
 (**table 8.3**)–218
 elderly
 focus on the 'aged poor' in the 50s,
 177–81; old women: the poor of the
 1960s, 243; receding dominance of
 the aged poor 228
 many faces ix, 9, 239
 in the GDR 210–14
 groups of poor *see* problem groups
 as indicator of the state of society 5

individualisation of 9, 9 n. 7
images (cultures) of *see also* poverty, debates
 denial **10–14**, 176, 193f., **196–9**;
 dramatisation **10–14**, **196–9**, 232,
 292; neutral ground 11–14
 as income deficiency 186
 vs. inequality 175, 288, 291
 intergenerational transmission 17f.,
 184
'latent' poor *see* Social Assistance
 (claiming), non take-up
new risks 45f., 298
and non-material want 182
and the middle class 240, 245, 247, 251
new picture of poverty 9, **239**–43
 'biographisation' 239, **240**–2, 262;
 'democratisation' ('transcendance',
 Entgrenzung) 9, 239, **240**, **242f.**, 258,
 279, 295; temporalisation (*Verzeitlichung*) 9, 239, **240**, 258, 262, 279
old and new perspectives 8–10, 18
political ignorance of poverty 242
the poor as a 'residual category' 11
the poor as a socio-economic class vs. as
 recipients of relief 42f.
the poor as victims 39, 124, 125f.
Of Poverty (plate) 159
and 'precarious welfare' 247, 296
rediscovery 194
reference units 193
reports *see* social reporting
rising? 43, 43 n. 23, 217, 225, 229
secondary (vs. primary) poverty [*see*
 poverty, state-induced] 147
 according to Rowntree 147 n. 6
 as a 'settling tank' 5
short vs. long term 43, 196
and social change 225ff.
and social movements 242f.
sociology of poverty (German) 12, 17
spatial concentration, less ghettoisation
 156, 253
as a stage in the life course 9, 239
state-induced 32f., 145–9, 164
 through claims of immigrants 228;
 causes 275; pension reform 267;
 waiting cases 71f., 79–82, 92; concept
 146; in different countries 148f.; political perception 147f., 186; types
 (frictional, transfer and status poor)
 148f.
stigma lessening 172f.
as a structural issue 12
traditional cycle of 15f., 242
transitory [*see also* dynamics of poverty]
 289f.

poverty (*cont*)
and unemployment [*see also* New Poverty; unemployment; Unemployment Insurance] 187–9, 195
dominance of the unemployed poor 228
urban 253, 280
the visible poor 196, 248
'precarious welfare' (Hübinger) 247, 296
private insurance 311
problem groups of poverty (*Problemgruppen*) 9, 17f., 83, 168
and anti-poverty policies 259f.
and duration types 84f.
in social policy debate 243, 251
within-group differences 88
Product Levy (*Wertschöpfungsabgabe*) 304f.
PSID (US Panel Study of Income Dynamics) 15, 155 n. 13, 224, 282

qualitative study 90–108, **114–43**, **157–65**
sample and method 21, 56f., 90 n. 3, 114 n. 3, 283f.
translation of interviews 92 n. 8

rationality 38, 145, 149, 160, 165
redistribution 7, 28, 177, 298, 303f., 307
refugees *see* immigration, asylum seekers
regimes of ... *see* worlds of ...
regulation 310–12, 321 n. 22
definition 297 n. 2
retrenchment 5ff., 225, 293, 307f.
Right vs. Left *see* Left vs. Right; poverty, images (cultures) of
risks, social
causal attribution (primary, secondary) 297–306, **305**
defined by law 42
indicators of changes in risks 43
new risks 45f., 297f.
not confined to marginal groups [*see also* democratisation] 46
poverty as a risk 42f.
vs. problem career and welfare class 41f.
social risk management 29–33, 255, 309
time dimension 262
welfare state as risk [*see also* poverty, state-induced] 145–7, 171
Risk Society (*Risikogesellschaft*, Beck) x, 240, 242, 243f., 250 n. 7, 279–85, 293
rule of law 310

sample *see* Bremen Longitudinal Study ...
secondary institutions 38
self (Giddens, J.W. Meyer) 7, 24, 37f., 41
settlers *see* immigration, settlers
'Seventy-Twenty-Ten Society' 252f.

Social Assistance (*Sozialhilfe*) (**claiming**) *see also* Federal Social Assistance Act of 1962ff.; Social Assistance (law and administration); poverty
abuse of Social Assistance 158, 161, 167, 226, 263, 265
awareness by claimants 98f.; qualified 130, 158, 161, **164f.**, 167
biographical balance sheets **108**
biographical evaluation of 102–8
'biographisation' of Social Assistance 125, **159**
change in number of claims 1990–1997, 31, **219** (table 8.4)
claimants by type in the mid-1960s (Strang) 181
comparative studies of [*see also* cohorts, comparisons; dependency, compared; dynamics of poverty, compared] 4, 30, 48 n. 27
degenerated into pension-like benefits? 9, 86
discontinuous claims 64
duration of Social Assistance claims (gross duration) **63f.** (figure 3.1)
explained 82–4; by reasons for claiming 74–9; reasons of short claims 79f. (figure 3.9); short claims and 'waiting' 79–82; short claims by immigrants and the unemployed 74–6; of social groups 74–9, 83f.
duration of Social Assistance claims (intra-nationally compared)
change in historical time, Germany 76, 172f., 227f.; USA 224; West Germany 1980s vs. 1990s, 225–30; East vs. West Germany 230–5
duration types 77, 77 n. 14, 84f.
dynamic policies required 264
in East Germany
attitudes towards 232; seen as dependency 191; dominance of short-term receipt 228f., 233
East vs. West Germany
escape routes from Social Assistance different 233f.; proportion of new immigrants in Social Assistance 232
as education support 72
as enabler **114ff.**, 123f.
evaluation of Social Assistance by claimants (four patterns) [*see also* Social Assistance (law and administration), evaluation] 102–8
exit from Social Assistance as end of poverty? 58 n. 2, 86, 138f.
and experts 183, 192
as a form of poverty 22, 57, 58, 58 n. 2

foreigners 31, 68f.
'German income experiment' 316 n. 16
and the labour market [*see* Social
Assistance, types of . . ., Employment Schemes . . . and and work op-
portunities] 165 n. 19
paradox of Social Assistance (Ludwig)
161, 262
positive role of Social Assistance 255
reasons for claiming 70–82
chief 70–3 (figure 3.4); combinations of
76–9 (figure 3.7); reasons for short
claims 79–82 (figure 3.9)
reasons for leaving 73f. (figure 3.5)
residential status, not nationality
determines duration 83
routes onto Social Assistance 70–3,
115–19 (figure 5.1)
routes off Social Assistance 21, 73f., 115f.
(figure 5.1), 119–23, 138f., 233
as social control 123f., 123 n. 5
spells
definition 65; single vs. multiple 63ff.;
multiple spells 233; 'recidivism' 156
subjective time conceptions, types **91**
(figure 4.1)
subjective bridgers 90–6; unsuccessful
bridgers 90, 96–8; subjective long-
term claimants 90, 98–101;
calculated vs. non-calculated
claiming 96, 98f.; subjective vs.
objective time 91f., **101f.**, 259
the unemployed as the dominant group of
the 1980s 228
waiting cases 71f., 80f., 92f.
concealing structural problems 81;
ideal type of w. c. 81; and short
duration 79–82
Social Assistance (*Sozialhilfe*) **(law and
administration)** see *also* Federal Social Assistance Act ...; Social
Assistance (claiming); anti-poverty
policy
administration of poverty
inferior and discriminatory 268; New
Control Models 265; passive institutionalisation 256, 265, 276
benefit levels 87, 302
benefit scales (*Regelsätze*) 181, 313, 271,
272
budget standard system
1962 (*Warenkorb*) 181, 190; 1990
(*Statistikmodell*) 190; the 1993ff.
'muddle' of de-standardisation 190f.
characteristics of, some
categorical vs. comprehensive 30;
constitutional right to benefits 30,

40, 181, 267; exhaustive range of
services 30; functioning as basic income 62f.; as indicator of social
problems 5, 30; paradigm shift:
income transfers to services 182; as
social risk management 29–34; as a
welfare state threshold 22
cycles of
expansion in the 1960s and early 1970s,
182; retrenchment in the second half
of the 1970s, 182; retrenchment in
the 1980s and 1990s, 187f., 190f.
in East Germany
installed 1990 as provisional system
231, 231 n. 3; as integrative
mechanism 235; lack of administrative capacity 32; changing
number of claims 218f. (table 8.4),
228f.
evaluation of effectiveness 58, 64, 86, **255f.**
family liability 267f.
and health services 313f.
Housing Allowance in Social Assistance
(*Aufwendungsersatz für Wohnung und
Heizung*) 191, 313
as a legal right **30**, 40, **181**, 267
and local governments [*see also* social reporting, local] 197, 266f.
as a loan 61, 93, 298
non take-up (*Dunkelziffer*) 30f. n.8, 166f.,
186f., 239, 268, 276f.
delayed entry 93
and Nordic welfare state 48 n. 27
one-time payments (*einmalige Beihilfen*)
313 n. 14
principles
Individuality (*Individualisierung,
Einzelfallhilfe*) 60; Help towards Self-
help (*Hilfe zur Selbsthilfe*) 60f.;
Residuality (*Subsidiarität*) 60
no longer side issue 315
Social Agency (*Sozialamt*) 97, 99, 101,
104, 151f.
as social integration 70, 139f., 235
'time' in Social Assistance Law 59–63
no time limit of claiming 43, 61; ambi-
guity/dualism 43, 60, 62
types of benefits/services see *also*
immigration, asylum seekers
Basic Income Support (*Hilfe zum
Lebensunterhalt*) 30f., 56, 60, 167,
189, 181, 314; Special Needs Support
(*Hilfe in besonderen Lebenslagen*) 30,
60, 167, 181, 183f., 190, 314; Employment Schemes (*Hilfe zur Arbeit*)
74, 152
as welfare state in reserve 5

Social Assistance (*cont.*)
  and work opportunities
    regular employment contracts 268; and
      wage subsidies 315; workfare 268
  work requirement and job offers 61f.,
    164
social citizenship *see* citizenship
social contract [*see also* generational
    contract] 304, 322
Social-Democratic Party (*Sozialdemokrati-
    sche Partei Deutschlands*, SPD) 183f.,
    197f., 307, 315, 321
social exclusion *see* exclusion
social indicators *see* social reporting
Social Market Economy 178, 288, 310
social mobility [*see also* careers in poverty;
    dynamics of poverty] 6f., 17, 281
social policy (*Sozialpolitik*) see *also* anti-
    poverty policy; Basic Income; life-
    course policy; welfare state
  descriptive research tradition 13, 17f., 26
    n. 2
  vs. educational policy 26 n. 2, 51, 319 n. 20
  explicit vs. implicit/tacit 33 n. 11
  new perspectives
    flexible risk management **308–10**;
      regulatory control of non-state
      welfare production **310–12**; social
      policy in a welfare society **316f.**
  security vs. equality *see* welfare state,
    security vs. equality
  situational vs. biographical programmes
    256
  unintended consequences of social policy
    [*see also* dependency] 144f.
social problems approach *see* marginal
  groups
'Social Question' (*Soziale Frage*) [*see also*
    New Social Question] 11, 148
social reporting 258
  institutionalisation 273f.
  poverty reports (*Armutsberichterstattung*)
    (local, *Länder* and national) 171,
    186, 257, 272, 321
  social indicators 21, 186, 199
social risks *see* risks
Social Science Research Centre Berlin
    (*Wissenschaftszentrum Berlin*) 21
Socio-Economic Panel (German) 14, **21**, 57,
    57 n. 1, 64 n. 4, 70 n. 8, 86, 215, 226,
    235, 252f., 254
Social Welfare (GDR) (*Fürsorge* – based on
    Social Welfare Regulation – *Verord-
    nung* – of 1947ff., then 1956ff.) 213f.,
    230f.
  recipients 214 (table 8.2)
SOEP *see* Socio-Economic Panel (German)

Solidarity Surcharge (Tax) of 1991ff.
    (*Solidaritätszuschlag*) 223, 288
Sozialenquàte of 1966 (Commission of
    Enquiry into Social Policy) 62
Sozialpädagogik (social education, social
    work) 198
*Sozialwissenschaftliches Forschungszentrum
    Berlin-Brandenburg* (SFZ) 221
Sozialstaat (German concept of welfare
    state) 25, 181
Special Research Programme 186 of 1988ff.
  on Status Passages and Risks in the
    Life Course (*Sonderforschungsbe-
    reich 186: 'Statuspassagen und
    Risikolagen im Lebensverlauf'*) xv, 29
    n. 4
SPES project of 1971ff. 186
Spiegel, Der 181f., 182, 184f., 188
state [*see also* welfare state] 6f., 23, 41
  as 'creator' of the individual 23
  as regulator (no monopoly)] 297f.,
    311
status, master 89, 108,124f.
Sweden 4,28, 277
  duration of claims 77 n. 14
  moderate retrenchment 50
  fewer status poor 149
  residual social assistance 48 n. 27
  welfare/life course regime compared
    47–53
  as 'worker's state' 50

tax policies [*see also* Federal Constitutional
    Court] 46, 270, 304f.
temporalisation of poverty (*Verzeitlichung*)
    9, 239, **240**, 258, 262, 279
time *see also* temporalisation; biographisa-
    tion; Social Assistance (law and ad-
    ministration), 'time'; life course;
    life-course policy; transitions; dyna-
    mic approach to poverty; dynamics
    of poverty; careers in poverty
  biographical time 259, 262
  as dimension of social analysis iv
  historical time 224, 286
  institutional (administrative) time 57,
    144–68, 260
  living time 57, 109–43, 261
  objective (chronological) time 57, 63–88,
    150–3, 259
    dimensions (duration of claiming, con-
      tinuity of claiming) 63f.; vs. subjec-
      tive 91f., 101f., 259
  political time 260f.
  and social risks 262
  subjective time 57, 89–101, 157–9, 240,
    259

trade unions 186
Transition Benefit of 1993ff. for settlers
    (*Übergangsgeld*) 226
transitions
    societal and individual 70, 79–82, 91–6,
        194 (table 7.1), 235, 285–92
    welfare state as support 223, 289–91
Tree of Estates, The (plate) 237
Treuhandanstalt 1990–1995 (Public Trustee
    Agency) 208 n. 5
Turkey 68f., 291
'Two-thirds Society' 8, 17, 21, 33, 110, 188,
    194 (table 7.1), 195, 243, **251–4**, 280
    Seventy-Twenty-Ten Society 252 (figure
        10.1)
types of poverty *see also* poverty; Social
    Assistance, claiming and law and
    administration
    by duration (short, medium, long, very
        long) 77, 84
    by social type (inclusion–exclusion
        continuum) (insecure middle, long-
        term deprived, long-term excluded,
        new immigrants, unsettled existence,
        people on low income) 245f., 246–9
    by subjective time orientation (subjective
        bridgers, unsuccessful bridgers,
        subjective long-term claimant) 91
        (figure 4.1), 247f., 291
    by type of career *see* careers in poverty,
        types

Übersiedler see immigration, from GDR
UK 4, 11, 31, 151 n. 9, 179, 264, 277, 312f.,
    316
    dependency 145 n. 3, 152 n. 11, 265
        as dominant form of state-induced
        poverty 147; no 'culture of
        dependency' (Dean and Taylor-
        Gooby) 150
    dynamic research 9 n. 8, 15, 16 n. 14
    categorical approach (earners vs. non-
        earners) in social assistance 30
    compared
        with Germany 30, 48 n. 27, 53;
        German Social Assistance 5, 149,
        312; duration of assistance spells 47,
        77 n. 14
    coping 112 n. 2
    Income Support reforms 7
    Job Seeker's Allowance of 1996 7, 264
    and lone mothers (child care) 47, 155, 317
    National Health Service 149
    poverty research, escape careers 113
    pronounced 'transfer poverty' 148f.
    relatively undeveloped higher benefit tiers
        147

stages of development of citzenship 23f.
tax credit 316
welfare state with integrated safety net 48
    n. 27
working poor compared 73
UN Declaration of the Rights of the Child
    1989 302
underclass [*see also* careers in poverty;
    dependency; exclusion; dynamics of
    poverty; poverty; Social Assistance
    (claiming)] 8, 66, 145 n. 3, 249, 250
    n. 6, 280, 286
unemployment/unemployed 43, 111, 144f.,
    296
    acceptance/ignorance of 242, 317
    blurring of concept 254
    combined with other social problems 77
        (figure 3.7)
    democratisation 240, 242, 250f.
    dynamic research 57
    in East Germany 205ff., 223
        poverty among unemployed less likely
        and shorter than in West 219f.
    fight against 264–6, 304
    fluctuation vs. hard core 250, 253f.
    heterogeneity 244, 250
    incentives 315–17
    long- (vs. short-) term 76, 76 n. 13, 126f.,
        225, 244, 248, 250
    and poverty 219f., 228, 243f.
    and Social Assistance 71f., 75–8, 126f.,
        220
    trade-off with inequality 4
    in West Germany, for the 1980s see *also*
        New Poverty
        in the 50s, 177; the 1980s vs. the 1990s,
        225–30; late 1990s 4, 223
Unemployment Insurance of 1927ff.
    (*Arbeitslosenversicherung*) [*see also*
    Employment Promotion Act; New
    Poverty; unemployment] 29, 42, 45,
    111, 121–3, 178, 188
    Unemployment Assistance (*Arbeitslosen-
    hilfe*) 59, 42, 104, 122, 135, 140, 269,
    272, 315
    Unemployment Benefit (*Arbeitslosengeld*)
    59, 71f., 92, 98, 104, 122, 164
        as prior benefit 226; speedy delivery
        266
    in East Germany 205–10, 219–21
        ABM (*Arbeitsbeschaffungsmaßnahmen*)
        206; Top-Up Supplement of
        1990–1991/95 (*Sozialzuschlag*) 191,
        220; Unemployment Benefit and So-
        cial Assistance 220; vocational train-
        ing 207f.; Wage Subsidies of 1993ff.
        (*Lohnkostenzuschüsse*) 206f.

Unemployment Insurance of 1927ff. (*cont.*)
    minimum benefits 272f.
    pension-like 9
    retrenchment 223, 225
unification [*see* East Germany; 'Change']
    189–92, 205–10, 307
USA 4, 11, 74, 171, 224, 249, 274, 307,
    313f., 319, 322
    Department of Health and Human
        Services 12
    dependency
        cultural denial 154; as dominant form
            of state-induced poverty 147; social
            science debate 144–6, 149f., 151 n. 9,
            162
    duration
        of claims 77 n. 14; historical change of
            d. of welfare claims 224
    Earned Income Tax Credit of 1974ff.
        (EITC) 315
    education
        education system 51; education
            emphasis in welfare state 7
    experience rating of Unemployment
        Insurance 300 n. 5
    and Germany compared 30, 147
        dependency (time of lone mothers on
            social assistance) 154–7; discourses
            on marginality 249; life-course/
            welfare state regime 47–52; reform
            perspectives of social assistance
            277f.; working poor 73
    health insurance (health reform) 4, 153f.,
        157, 278
    Income Maintenance Experiments 275
    life course
        loose coupling: life course/welfare state
            48f.; life-course research 6
    poverty
        'normal', not a particular risk 48;
            poverty research, escape careers 113;
    Welfare
        defined 144 n. 1; AFDC 155; (Clinton)
            Reform of 1996 (TANF) 7, 12, 47f.,
            59, 154f., 162, 257, 260, 264
    welfare state characteristics
        the dominance of the transfer poor
            148f.; lone parent focus 30, 39f., 47,
            317; residual welfare state 48f.; unde-
            veloped higher benefit tiers 147; not
            a welfare state 154; but a 'workfare
            state' (Jessop) 50; a 'public assistance
            state' 28 n. 27

voluntary welfare associations (*Wohlfahrts-
    verbände*) 198

War Victims Benefits of 1950ff. (*Kriegs-
    opferversorgung: Bundesver-
    sorgungsgesetz*) (war victims) 167,
    177, 178
War Compensation of 1949/1952ff. (*Lasten-
    ausgleich*) [*see* Compensation Act of
    1952ff.] 178
war damages, people affected by (*Vertriebe-
    ne* and other affected groups) 177
Welfare
    Germany *see* Social Assistance
    USA *see* USA, Welfare and welfare state
        characteristics; dependency,
        compared
welfare classes (*Versorgungsklassen*;
    Lepsius) 24, 146
'welfare mothers' 5, 8, 154
welfare society (*Wohlfahrtsgesellschaft*) **294**,
    297f., **308–12**, 316f.
welfare state (*Wohlfahrtsstaat*) *see also*
    Sozialstaat; poverty, state-induced;
    redistribution; welfare (state) re-
    gimes; life-course policy; life course,
    regimes compared; state
    all-party 171
    challenges 293f., 320
    concepts of welfare state as
        social state (*Sozialstaat*, German
            concept) 25, 181; state as reinsurer
            301; enabling state (Gilbert) 264,
            311; regulatory state 297, 310; work-
            fare state (Jessop) 50; productive
            welfare state 290; welfare state in a
            welfare society 308, 316f.; structurer
            of life course 25f., 285; monopolist
            of accountability 297
    as 'creator' of the individual 23
    critique 145, 166–8
    and decommodification 166
    directive vs. facilitative impact 35–40,
        297f.
    effects/functions 25f., 53, 290, 293
    elite support for 308
    and federalism 5, 33
    and gender 50f., 294
    Germany
        a Bismarckian welfare state? 3, 11, 180,
            204; dual structure/two tiers 147,
            267f.; laggard? 3; policy for workers
            (*Arbeiterpolitik*) vs. policy for the
            poor (*Armenpolitik*) 179, 197, 272;
            social insurance state 28, 49 (table
            2.1), 51; welfare state with integrated
            safety net 48 n. 27
    and graduation of transfer payments
        34

high expectations in East Germany 235
impact on life course (structur-
ation/differentiation, integration,
formation) 25f. (figure 2.1)-35, 41
indexing *see* indexing welfare state
benefits
new and flexible institutions vs.
dismantling 308–10, 316
legitimisation 315
and life course
challenges to welfare state management
of the life course 42; as structuring
benefit-related types of life courses
116, 122f.; USA vs. Europe 6
limits 7, 53, 223, 317
and the middle classes 267, 315
monopoly
of accountability 297; but no social
monopoly for action 297
and poverty *see also* dependence; poverty,
state-induced; Social Assistance
cause of or response to poverty? 9; and
the production of poverty [*see*
dependency; poverty, state-induced]
145–9
productive 290
shifts rationality ('substantive' to
'functional') 38, 145, 160
reconstruction (*Umbau*) 306f.
reform *see* social policy, new perspectives;
anti-poverty policy, new
perspectives; welfare society 294
induces second order risks 171 n. 2
security vs. equality 7, 28
and Social Assistance ('welfare state in reserve', Leibfried) 4f.
three tiers of welfare production 271
types of welfare states
authoritarian provider state 170, 203;
citizenship provision 49; social insurance state 51; residual welfare state
48, 269f., 322; workfare state 50; *cf.*
typology in table 2.1, 49; public

assistance state, state with residual
social assistance and state with
integrated safety net (Eardly et al.),
48 n. 27; conservative, liberal and
social-democratic welfare state
(Esping-Andersen) 4.
welfare (state) regimes 3f., 6, 147
compared 47–52
as life course regimes 6, 48f.
in view of social assistance 48 n. 27
Welfare Survey (*Wohlfahrtssurvey*) 22 n. 19
welfarisation [*see also* dependency] 144, 147,
152
Wheel of Fortune, The (plate) 55
women [*see also* gender; men; lone parents]
117ff., **141f.**, 154ff., 163ff., 278, 284
and disability pensions 45
duration of claiming Social Assistance
74f., **84** (figure 3.11)
EITC (Earned Income Tax Credit, USA,
1974ff.) 47
and the German pension scheme 34, 185,
269
separation, consequences of 164f., 166
work programmes *see* Social Assistance
(law and administration), and work
opportunities, work requirements
...; anti-poverty policy, 'welfare to
work'
free riding 316
working poor 48, 73, 165 n. 19, 230, 245f.,
278, 295f., 316, 290
worlds (regimes) of (capitalism, employment, life course, stratification and
welfare state) [*see also* welfare (state)
regimes; life course, regimes
compared] 3f., 6, 48, 147
WTO 195ff. 320

York 15, 16 n. 13
young 142, 164, 233
longer claiming duration 83
men 164f.

Index of names

Abelshauser, Werner 177
Achinger, Hans 171
Adam, Hans 186 n. 8
Adams, Ursula 182
Adamy, Wilhelm 183, 188
Adenauer, Konrad 176, 177, 179
Alba, Richard D. 32
Alber, Jens 3 n. 1, 24, 307
Albrecht, Günther 111, 184 n. 7
Alcock, Pete 8, 16 n. 14, 239 n. 1
Allmendinger, Jutta 3, 6, 23 n. 1, 26 n. 2,
    27, 28, 33, 34, 34 n. 12, n. 13, 48 n. 26, n.
    28, 51 n. 29, 162 n. 16, 203, 255, 282, 319
Anderson, Jeffrey J. 320
Andorka, Rudolf 14 n. 11
Andreß, Hans-Jürgen 3, 9 n. 7, 57, 76, 205
    n. 2, 225
Anweiler, Oskar 202
Ashworth, Karl 14 n. 11, 77 n. 14
Atkinson, Anthony B. 16 n. 13, 18, 210 n.
    6, 321 n. 23

Bach, Abraham 1
Backhaus-Maul, Holger 204
Bäcker, Gerhard 270, 272
Balsen, Werner 188
Bane, Mary Jo 6, 12, 14 n. 10, 67 n. 6, 77
    n. 14, 149, 153, 154, 162, 257, 260, 277,
    278
Beam, Charles R. 304
Beck, Martin 19, 257, 273
Beck, Ulrich 16, 20, 20 n. 18, 37, 37 n. 16,
    38, 38 n. 17, 240, 242, 244, 250 n. 7, 279,
    280, 284, 293, 297, 300 n. 300, 309
Beck-Gernsheim, Elisabeth 37, 38
Becker, Howard S. 89 n. 1, 110
Becker, Irene 8 n. 5, 22 n. 19
Becker, Ulrich 318
Beisheim, Marianne 317 n. 17
Bellebaum, Alfred 123 n. 5

Bentham, Jeremy 35, 311, 311 n. 11
Berger, Peter A. 9 n. 7, 13, 14 n. 11, 15,
    16, 37 n. 16, 40 n. 18, 57 n. 1, 240, 250 n.
    7
Berghahn, Sabine 203
Berntsen, Roland 57 n. 1, 64 n. 4
Best, Joel 112
Beyme, Klaus von 183
Bieback, Karl-Jürgen 188
Biedenkopf, Kurt 269
Bismarck, Otto von 3, 27, 300
Blair, Tony 4, 7, 264, 265
Blakeslee, Sandra 283
Blank, Rebecca M. 151 n. 9, 275
Blossfeld, Hans-Peter 37, 281
Blüm, Norbert 318, 320
Blum, Rudolf 123 n. 5
Blume, Otto 16
Boettner, Johannes 21
Bolte, Karl Martin 13 n. 9
Bonß, Wolfgang 14 n. 11, 15, 57 n. 1
Borchert, Jens 307
Borjas, George 70 n. 8
Bourdieu, Pierre 36, 176
Brandt, Willy 184
Breier, Bernd 167
Breuer, Wilhelm 165, 272
Brose, Hans-Georg 36, 37
Brück, Gerhard W. 62
Brückner, Erika 34 n. 13
Brückner, Hannah 34 n. 13
Büchel, Felix 70 n. 8
Brügge, Peter 181
Buhr, Petra 14, 18, 42 n. 21, 59, 67, 70 n.
    9, 71, 83 n. 16, 89, 103, 151 n. 9, 152 n.
    10, 175, 176 n. 1, 224, 257, 265 n. 5, 273
Bujard, Otker 112
Burkart, Günter 39
Burkhauser, Richard V. 301 n. 7
Busch-Geertsema, Volker 79, 196 n. 14

Bush, George 48
Butterwegge, Christoph 281 n. 1

Castel, Robert 275
Cazes, Sandrine 321 n. 23
Christiansen, Ursula 184 n. 7
Clinton, William J. 4, 7, 12, 154, 157, 257, 260, 277
Cloward, Richard A. 30
Coffield, Frank 113
Colla, Herbert-Ernst 176, 199
Conrad, Christoph 27
Cornia, G. Andrea 301 n. 7
Cremer-Shäfer, Helga 123 n. 5

Dahrendorf, Ralf ix–xi, 26, 53
Daly, Mary 58 n. 2
Dangschat, Jens 8 n. 5, 253 n. 9, n. 10, 280, 281 n. 1
Danziger, Sheldon S. 30, 50, 301 n. 7
Day, Beryl 89
Dean, Hartley 145 n. 3, 150, 154 n. 12
Delsen, Lei 309
DeParle, Jason 12
De Swaan, Abram 145 n. 2, 320
DiPrete, Thomas A. 48 n. 26, 282
Ditch, John 4
Döring, Dieter 11–1, 176, 188 n. 10, 189, 251
Drauschke, Petra 107, 209
Duncan, Greg J. 6, 14, 14 n. 10, 47, 64 n. 4, 66, 155, 155 n. 13, 156, 282, 301 n. 7

Eardly, Tony 4, 48 n. 27
Ebert, Friedrich 315
Eden, Frederick 287
Eichhorst, Werner 318
Elias, Norbert 145, 145 n. 2
Ellwood, David T. 6, 12, 14 n. 10, 67 n. 6, 77 n. 14, 149, 149 n. 7, n. 8, 150, 153, 154, 159, 160, 162, 257, 260, 277, 278
Elsner, Ilse 179
Engels, Dietrich 165, 272
Erhard, Ludwig 11, 176, 178, 180
Erikson, Robert 17 n. 15, 282, 284 n. 2
Esping-Andersen, Gøsta 4, 6, 42 n. 20, 48, 166, 282, 289, 290, 310, 315
Ewald, François 297, 300 n. 6

Falkingham, Jane 23 n. 1, 298
Farwick, Andreas 253 n. 10
Ferrera, Maurizio 48
Field, Frank 265
Fink, Ulf 266
Fischer, Andrea 257
Foucault, Michel 40

Frerich, Johannes 203, 204, 212, 214
Frey, Martin 203, 204, 212, 214
Freyberg, Thomas von 244
Fridberg, Torben 14 n. 11
Friedrich, Hannes 111, 184 n. 7
Friedrichs, Jürgen 37 n. 16, 253 n. 10
Fritzsche, Andrea 203
Fürstenberg, Friedrich 249
Furstenberg, Frank, F. 113, 283

Galbraith, John Kenneth 286, 286 n. 3, 287
Gangl, Markus 152, 265 n. 5
Gans, Herbert J. 34 n. 14, 286, 287
Garfinkel, Irwin 275
Gebhardt, Thomas 257
Geisel, Eike 177
Geißler, Heiner 148, 186
Geißler, Rainer 215
Geldof, Dirk 8
Gerhardt, Uta 21, 30 n. 7, 40, 40 n. 19, 112, 113, 114 n. 3, 124 n. 6, 125, 141 n. 12, 283, 284, 285
Gerstenberger, Heide 281 n. 1
Giddens, Anthony 6, 36, 37, 38, 38 n. 17, 40, 145 n. 2, 281, 283, 309
Giesbrecht, Arno 111
Giese, Dieter 183
Gilbert, Barbara 311
Gilbert, Neil 311
Girvetz, Harry 146 n. 5, 298
Glaser, Barney G. 124 n. 6, 240
Glatzer, Wolfgang 16, 21, 186 n. 8, 199, 205 n. 2, 273
Glotz, Peter 188, 243 n. 2, 251, 252, 280
Göckenjan, Gerd 27
Goldthorpe, John H. 17 n. 15, 282, 284 n. 2
Gorbachov, Michail 69
Groenemeyer, Axel 112, 141
Großmann, Heidrun 209
Grünert, Hans 207
Gusfield, Joseph R. 146 n. 5
Gustafsson, Björn 14
Gysi, Jutta 203

Habich, Roland 14n. 11, 15, 21, 22 n. 19, 57 n. 1, 69, 216, 250, 259 n. 1
Hacker, Jacob 278
Häußermann, Hartmut 280
Haferkamp, Hans 110
Hagen, Christine 57, 225
Hagenaars, Aldi J. M. 89 n. 2
Handler, Joel F. 48
Hanesch, Walter 32, 57 n. 1, 205, 206 n. 3, 218, 272, 273
Hartmann, Heinz 21, 31 n. 8, 149

Hartmann, Helmut   186
Hasenfeld, Yeheskel   48
Hauser, Richard   8 n. 5, 12, 13, 19, 20, 22
    n. 19, 44, 51, 57 n. 1, 69, 69 n. 7, 185, 186,
    198, 216 n. 9, 217, 221, 222, 246 n. 3, 268,
    270, 271, 276, 277, 312 n. 12, 321
Headey, Bruce   14 n. 11, 15, 21, 57 n. 1, 252
    n. 8
Heclo, Hugh   50, 322
Heidenheimer, Arnold J.   26 n. 2, 319
Heimann, Horst   183
Heinz, Walter R.   14, 29 n. 4, 240
Heisig, Michael   180
Held, David   318
Henkel, Heinrich A.   123
Hennigsen, Bernd   321 n. 23
Hennock, E. Peter   53
Hess, Henner   19, 184 n. 7, 199
Hildenbrand, Bruno   36, 37
Hilkerft, Bernhard   57
Hill, Daniel   282
Hill, Martha   15, 282
Hills, John   14 n. 11, 23 n. 1, 298
Hilton, Lynette   70 n. 8
Hinz, Thomas   3, 6, 48 n. 26, 51 n. 29, 255,
    282
Hock, Beate   57, 225
Hockerts, Hans Günter   148, 179
Hoffman, Saul D.   67
Hohmann, Karl   176 n. 2
Hollstein, Walter   123 n. 5
Hoynes, Hilary   224
Hradil, Stefan   13
Hübinger, Werner   20, 21, 107, 221, 247,
    251, 268, 270, 271, 276, 277, 296
Huff Stevens, Ann   224
Hughes, Everett C.   89 n. 1
Hughes, Michael L.   177
Huinink, Johannes   36
Hurrelmann, Klaus   301 n. 7
Huster, Ernst-Ulrich   8, 47
Huth, Sabine   209
Hvinden, Björn   14 n. 11, 263 n. 4, 265 n. 5

Iben, Gert   184 n. 7, 199
Illich, Ivan   35, 145, 166, 171
Ireland, Patrick R.   318

Jacobs, Herbert   22, 103, 107, 257
Jaedicke,Wolfgang   196
Jahoda, Marie   18
Janowitz, Morris   7, 171
Jarvis, Sarah   14 n. 11
Jenkins, Stephen P.   14 n. 11, 301 n. 8
Jessop, Bob   50
Joas, Hans   215

Johnson, Lyndon B.   183
Jordan, Bill   8

Kahler, Miles   319
Kappeler, Beat   52
Kapstein, Ethan B.   320
Karstedt, Susanne   18, 199
Kaufmann, Franz-Xaver   3 n. 1, 28, 33 n.
    11, 35 n. 15, 46, 53, 154, 293, 296 n. 2,
    298, 302 n. 9, 309
Kempson, Elaine   112 n. 2
Kersbergen, Kees van   3 n. 1
Kinstler, Hans-Joachim   69 n. 7
Kitzchelt Herbert   3
Klanberg, Frank   186 n. 8
Klee, Ernst   184
Klein, Peter   190
Klein, Thomas   27, 244
Klems, Wolfgang   76, 76 n. 13
Klocke, Andreas   301 n. 7
Kohl, Helmut   187, 208, 221, 242, 288, 307
Kohl, Jürgen   47, 321 n. 23
Kohli, Martin   7, 14, 16, 24, 34 n. 12, 36,
    40, 40 n. 19, 41, 52, 124 n. 6, 141 n. 10,
    215, 280, 284, 285, 309 n. 10
Kopnarski, Aribert   22
Korte, Karl-Rudolf   223 n. 13
Kortmann, Klaus   186 n. 8
Krause, Peter   14 n. 11, 15, 18, 21, 43 n. 23,
    57 n. 1, 64 n. 4, 69, 216, 217, 218 n. 11,
    226, 253, 281
Kreckel, Reinhard   13, 207
Kronauer, Martin   8, 248, 280
Krupp, Hans-Jürgen   16, 186 n. 8, 273

Lae, Jean-François   275
Lampert, Heinz   3 n. 1, 293 n. 1
Landau, Detlef   57, 201, 215, 221, 250, 259
    n. 1
Lange, Ulrich   112
Lash, Scott   38 n. 17
Leenen, Wolf Rainer   203
Lehmbruch, Gerhard   208
Leibfried, Stephan   4 n. 2, 5, 10 n. 8, 13,
    14, 20, 46, 48 n. 28, 53, 62, 149, 179, 188
    n. 10, 192 n. 12, n. 13, 202 n. 1, 251, 256,
    259, 265, 270 n. 6, 275 n. 8, 276, 277, 290,
    293 n. 1, 317, 317 n. 17, 318, 318 n. 18,
    319, 320, 321, 321 n. 22, n. 23
Leisering, Lutz   6, 8, 14, 20, 23 n. 1, 24, 28,
    38, 44, 46, 47, 51, 53, 67 n. 6, 77 n. 14, 85,
    124 n. 6, 145 n. 4, 149 n. 7, 152 n. 10, 171
    n. 2, 176 n. 1, 188 n. 10, 192, 196, 216 n.
    8, 246 n. 4, 263 n. 4, 264, 265 n. 5, 274,
    275 n. 7, 280, 282, 287, 288, 290, 305, 308,
    309, 311 n. 11, 313, 314 n. 15

Lemert, Edwin M.   147 n. 6
Lepsius, Mario Rainer   24, 207
Lessenich, Stephan   4 n. 2
Levy, René   29 n. 6, 34 n. 12, 53 n. 30
Lewis, Oscar   110
Lødemel, Ivar   265 n. 5
Lohmann, Ulrich   204
Lompe, Klaus   19, 21, 103, 111, 112
Luckenbill, David F.   112
Ludwig, Monika   56, 109, 110 n. 1, 114,
    161, 175, 241, 257, 262 n. 3
Ludwig-Mayerhofer, Wolfgang   57
Luhmann, Niklas   45, 197, 280, 287
Lynn, Lawrence E.   154
Lysgaard, Sverre   241

McCurdy, Thomas   224
Madge, Nicola   18, 113
Mädje, Eva   57, 107, 142, 200, 203, 216 n.
    8, 244, 288
Majone, Giandomenico   297 n. 3, 320 n.
    21
Malthus, Thomas   287
Mannheim, Karl   38, 110
Manow[-Borgwardt], Philipp   204, 307
Mansel, Jürgen   301 n. 7
Manski, Charles F.   275
Manz, Günter   210, 211, 212, 213, 214,
    215
Marks, Gary   320 n. 21
Marmor, Theodore R.   300 n. 5
Marshall, Thomas Humphrey   23, 175
Marx, Karl   284
Massey, Douglas   8 n. 5
Matthes, Joachim   198
Mayer, Karl Ulrich   14, 23 n. 1, 26, 29, 29
    n. 5, 33 n. 11, 37, 38, 41, 48 n. 26, 52, 145,
    160, 207 n. 4, 209, 210, 280, 281, 282, 290
Mayntz, Renate   297, n. 3
McFate, Katherine   3, 290
Mead, George Herbert   141 n. 10
Mead, Lawrence M.   296 n. 2, 297
Mechler, Achim   19, 184 n. 7, 199
Meehan, Elisabeth   320
Meinhold, Marianne   123 n. 5
Menxel, Gerard van   8
Mény, Yves   320, 21
Merten, Roland   209
Meyer, Dagmar   203
Meyer, John W.   7, 24, 37, 41
Meyer, Sibylle   209
Micklewright, John   210 n. 6
Miller, S. M.   321 n. 23
Moffit, Robert   224
Motel, Andreas   308, 314 n. 15
Müller, Klaus   244

Müller, Walter   32 n. 1, 29 n. 5, 38, 52, 145,
    160
Müller-Armack, Alfred   176 n. 2, 178, 181
Münke, Stephanie   21, 198
Münz, Rainer   249 n. 5
Mutz, Gerd   57
Myles, John   47

Naegele, Gerhard   183, 188
Nagel, Ulrike   240
Nahnsen, Ingeborg   111
Natter, Ehrenfried   188 n. 10, 252
Neckel, Sighard   250 n. 6
Nervik, Jon Arve   14 n. 11
Neubauer, Georg   301 n. 7
Neumann, Lothar F.   3 n. 1
Neumann, Udo   13, 51, 198
Neusüß, Claudia   57, 107, 142, 203, 244
Niggemeyer, Maria   61
Noble, Michael   14 n. 11
Noll, Heinz-Herbert   22 n. 19, 205 n. 2

Offe, Claus   166, 185, 186, 204, 210 n. 6,
    246
Olk, Thomas   200, 204
Oorschot, Wim van   149
Osteland, Martin   254
Ostner, Illona   4 n. 2
Otto, Ulrich   301 n. 7
Øyen, Else   196, 248, 321 n. 23

Parijs, Philippe van   270 n. 6
Park, Robert Ezra   249
Parsons, Talcott   37, 38 n. 17
Paugam, Serge   8
Pavelka, Franz   123
Pencz, Georg   55
Peters, Bärbel   190 n. 11
Peters, Helge   123 n. 5
Petrarca, Francesco   169, 237
Petrarca-Master, The   169, 237
Piachaud, David   145 n. 3, 149 n. 7
Pierson, Paul   4 n. 2, 47, 48, 52, 307, 308,
    318 n. 18, 321, 321 n. 22
Pinker, Robert   13, 294
Piven, Frances Fox   30
Plum, Wolfgang   14 n. 11, 15, 57 n. 1
Polanyi, Karl   287
Preuß, Ulrich   320
Proske, Rüdiger   179

Rains, Prudence   19 n. 17
Rainwater, Lee   14 n. 10, 33 n. 11, 39, 91 n.
    4
Rank, Mark Robert   39
Reagan, Ronald   48

Reday-Mulvey, Geneviève 309
Rein, Martin 14 n. 10
Rendtel, Ulrich 15, 57 n. 64 n. 4
Rentzsch, Doris 224
Rhein-Kress, Gaby von 45
Rhodes, Martin 317 n. 17, 318 n. 18, 320
   n. 21
Ricardo, David 287
Riedlsperger, Alois 188 n. 10, 252
Rieger, Elmar 53, 171 n. 1, 317, 317 n. 17,
   319, 320
Ringbeck, Anna 22, 103, 107
Ritter, Gerhard A. 3 n. 1
Rodrik, Dani 317, 319
Rohrmann, Eckhard 111
Rohwer, Götz 14 n. 12, 17, 57 n. 1
Rolf, Gabriele 269
Room, Graham 8, 18, 321 n. 23
Rose, Richard 171 n. 1
Rosenow, Joachim 45, 206
Roth, Jürgen 184
Rothgang, Heinz 32, 308, 314
Rowntree, Benjamin Seebohm 15, 16, 147
   n. 6, 242
Ruhstrat Ekke-Ulf 79, 196 n. 14
Runciman, Walter Garrison 105
Rutter, Michael 18, 113
Rydell, C. Peter 14 n. 10

Sachs, Hans 55
Sachße, Christoph 24
Sackmann, Reinhold 192 n. 13, 202 n. 1
Salonen, Tapio 14 n. 11, 18, 77 n. 14
Salzgeber, Renate 14 n. 11
Samad, Syed Abdus 321 n. 23
Samson, Reinhard 57, 225
Saraceno, Chiara 14 n. 12
Sassen, Saskia 280
Schäfer, Claus 296
Schäfers, Bernhard 176 n. 1, 189
Schaper, Klaus 3 n. 1
Scharpf, Fritz W. 28, 75, 270 n. 6, 315, 317
   n. 17, 318 n. 18
Schaufelberger, Hans-Jürg 184 n. 7
Scheiwe, Kirsten 34 n. 13
Schellhorn, Walter 61
Scherl, Hermann 186 n. 8
Schimank, Uwe 29 n. 6
Schlegelmilch, Cornelia 27
Schmähl, Winfried 202 n. 1, 210 n. 6, 270
   n. 6, 308
Schmid, Alfons 76, 76 n. 13
Schmidt, Manfred G. 3 n. 1, 183, 293 n. 1,
   308
Schmidt, Vivien Ann 317 n. 17, 318 n. 18
Schmidt-Räntsch, Ruth 299

Schnapper, Dominique 320
Schneider, Louis 241
Schneider, Ulrich 75
Schöpflin, Urs 23 n. 1
Schütze, Fritz 40 n. 19, 124, 124 n. 6
Schulte, Bernd 61, 275, 321
Schulte, Dieter 315
Schulte, Katja 9 n. 7
Schultheis, Franz 145, 163, 163 n. 17, 272,
   316 n. 16
Schulz, Joachim 176 n. 1
Schulze, Eva 209
Schwartz, Karl 14 n. 10
Schwarze, Uwe 172 n. 3, 256
Sears, Elizabeth 55
Seeleib-Kaiser, Martin 48
Seewald, Hermann 19, 257
Seifert, Wolfgang 249 n. 5
Seils, Erik 307
Seligman, Martin E. P. 150
Semrau, Peter 22 n. 19, 44, 211
Sen, Amartya Kumar 4, 21, 197 n. 15, 317
Shaw, Andrew 14 n. 11, 152 n. 11, 157 n.
   14
Sieveking, Klaus 318
Simmel, Georg 5, 40, 89, 191 192, 246 n.
   4, 263 n. 4, 272
Skocpol, Theda 278
Smeeding, Timothy S. 301 n. 7, 321 n. 23
Sørensen, Annemette 201
Solga, Heike 26, 207 n. 4, 209
Sopp, Peter 37 n. 16
Soskice, David 3, 307
Specht, Thomas 184 n. 7
Spéder, Zsolt 14 n. 11
Spicker, Paul 30
Standfest, Erich 183
Stelzer-Orthofer, Christine 14 n. 11
Stichweh, Rudolf 280
Strang, Heinz 18, 21, 22, 181, 197 n. 15,
   198
Strauss, Anselm L. 124 n. 6, 240
Strengmann-Kuhn, Wolfgang 296
Suter, Christian 14 n. 11

Taylor-Gooby, Peter 145 n. 3, 150, 154 n.
   12
Tennstedt, Florian 5, 24, 179, 188 n. 10,
   192 n. 13, 203, 212, 251
Tobias, Gertrud 21
Townsend, Peter 197 n, 15
Trappe, Heike 201
Trenk-Hinterberger, Peter 61

Ulrich, Dieter 249, 5
Ungaretti, Giuseppe xii

Vaskovics, Laszlo A. 184 n. 7
Veit-Wilson, John 16 n. 13, 313 n. 13
Vincent, Jill 274, 277
Vobruba, Georg 30, 242, 250 n. 7, 286, 290
Voges, Wolfgang 10 n. 8, 13, 14, 51, 57 n. 1, 71, 145 n. 4, 149 n. 7, 152 n. 10, 155, 155 n. 13, 192 n. 12
Vranken, Jan 8

Wagner, Gert 15, 57 n. 1, 269
Wagner, Wolf 34
Walker, Robert 6, 9 n. 14, 14 n. 11, 47, 67 n. 6, 77 n. 14, 152 n. 11, 157 n. 14, 259, 264, 274, 282, 313, 316
Wallace, Hellen 320 n. 21
Wallace, William 320 n. 21
Wallerstein, Judith 283
Webb, Beatrice 311
Webb, Sidney 311

Weber, Andreas 152 n. 10, 224
Weber, Max 21, 59, 113, 114 n. 3, 124 n. 6, 283, 284
Weidenfeld, Werner 223 n. 13
Weisser, Gerhard 111
Wenzel, Gerd 62, 313 n. 14
Wilson, W. Julius 39
Wingen, Mathias 187
Wiseman, Michael 275, 316
Wohlrab-Sahr, Monika 30 n. 7, 309 n. 10
Wolf, Jürgen 45, 206
Wolff, Klaus G. 273
Wolski-Prenger, Friedhelm 209
Wright, Erik Olin 281

Zander, Hartwig 199
Zapf, Wolfgang 38, 186, 231, 235, 309
Zürn, Michael 317 n. 17, 320
Zumpe, Paul 214
Zwick, Michael 14 n. 11, 77 n. 14, 85